Mrs Frances Jordan,
With the kind regards & remembrance
of — Thomas C. Upham

Brunswick, Maine,
March 7th, 1860.

John. Ch. 17. vs. 20. 21. 22. 23.

Engraved by J C Buttre from a Daguerreotype.

Thomas C. Upham.

THOMAS C. UPHAM, D.D.

PROFESSOR OF MENTAL PHILOSOPHY &c. IN BOWDOIN COLLEGE.

LETTERS

ÆSTHETIC, SOCIAL, AND MORAL,

WRITTEN FROM

EUROPE, EGYPT, AND PALESTINE.

BY

THOMAS C. UPHAM,

PROFESSOR OF MENTAL AND MORAL PHILOSOPHY IN BOWDOIN COLLEGE.

PHILADELPHIA:
HENRY LONGSTRETH, 915 MARKET ST.
1857.

STEREOTYPED BY L. JOHNSON & CO.
PHILADELPHIA.

PREFACE

TO A PRIVATE EDITION.

I HAVE assented to the wishes of a few friends, and allowed this small edition of four hundred copies of these letters to be published. I have no personal preferences to gratify, either in publishing or withholding. But I cannot at present persuade myself, that they would be likely to possess any special interest beyond a very limited circle.

The letters will, for the most part, explain their own history. It will not be necessary, therefore, to go into details here. I should do injustice, however, to my feelings, if I did not refer in a few words to my fellow-travellers, Rev. Mr. Thompson, and Mr. and Mrs. Walcott. Mr. Thompson is the pastor of the Tabernacle Church in New York. I had previously known him in America; and it was with pleasure I met him in London. Mr. Thompson is the editor of the popular and able religious paper, the Independent; and is the author of a number of valuable works. Since his return from his travels, he has published an interesting and well-written volume on Egypt. Without saying anything of its high literary merits, I can venture, from having been with him in all the places which he visited in that country, to bear testimony to the strict accuracy of its details. It was chiefly through his encouragement and aid that I was enabled to pursue my journey.

Mr. Walcott, whom I also met in London, is the founder and owner of a large manufacturing-establishment near Utica, N. Y., known as the "New York Mills." Around this establishment there has grown up a large and beautiful village. The operatives, many of whom are from foreign countries, experience from Mr. W. a friendly and judicious interest in their welfare, which more than satisfies all their reasonable expectations; and he has thus laid the foundation of a sincere and permanent friendship. The public and joyous reception which his operatives and others gave him on his return from his long travels was an evidence both of their strong attachment, and of the personal virtues which have given rise to it. In these feelings Mrs. Walcott, who was also the much-respected and valued companion of our travels, is a full sharer. I could say much of the kindness which I received from these highly-esteemed friends, but am restrained from feelings of delicacy; and will only add my earnest desire, that they may long experience in their own persons the happiness which they have been the means of communicating to others.

Nearly all the letters were first published, as they were written, in the Congregationalist, a well-known and able religious newspaper issued at Boston. And I wish here to express my obligations to its editors and publishers for the kindness I have received from them. As to the letters themselves, it will be enough perhaps to say here that they were written for the most part in ill health and under unfavorable circumstances. If they have any merits, (which must be left to others to decide,) they are certainly not free from imperfections. And this will be some excuse for limiting their circulation. With these few words I leave them in the hands of those whose kindness, I am confident, will go far in disarming criticism.

THOMAS C. UPHAM.

BRUNSWICK, MAINE, March 24, 1855.

CONTENTS.

LETTERS

ÆSTHETIC, SOCIAL, AND MORAL.

(I.)

New York Bay—The steamship—Remarks on the character of the passengers—The merchant from Buenos Ayres—The lady from Missouri—Relation of woman to home—Lines to my wife.

AT SEA,—STEAMSHIP ARCTIC, SEPT. 25, 1852.

WE sailed from New York for Liverpool on Saturday, the 18th of September, in the steamship Arctic, Captain Luce commander. The day was bright and beautiful. As the majestic steamer sailed down the broad and noble Hudson, a magnificent scene presented itself. The wide expanse of water which opened to view, the hills and woods of Hoboken, the shipping and the spires of Jersey City, the Battery and Castle Garden, the mighty throng of masts in the East River, the splendid residences and churches of Brooklyn, the frowning fortifications, the boats passing and repassing amid the shipping that floated lazily in the river and in the New York Bay, formed a group of unsurpassed beauty and magnificence. In a few hours we crossed the Bay of New York, passed through the Narrows, and were moving swiftly over the broad ocean.

The introduction of the steamship, in itself and in its relations, constitutes an event of no small moment in the history of man. It is not only an indication of the progress of the arts and of the extension of commerce, but of the advancement of civilization. Those who first discovered the uses and applications of steam, and those who by their expanded thought and generous efforts have secured its highest practical results, have deserved and won the gratitude of men. Why should not the names of Collins and of Cunard, in their appropriate place and degree, be associated on the pages of history with the memorable name of Fulton?

Every thing which exists or takes place not only has its history but its teachings, but the lesson which it reveals will be differently read and interpreted by different minds. The steamship carries not merely merchandise, but MEN; a congregation, or if you prefer it, a *cargo* of human hearts, each of which has strong and often tender ties, reaching in every direction. Other persons will read different lessons on board the steamship, as it thus carries forth its precious load of immortal beings; but that which I read first and with very deep interest was the great lesson on *social humanity*. The great problems of SOCIALITY—its foundation, its infinitely varied ties, its mighty strength—were forcibly illustrated by the occurrences which presented themselves.

On the very afternoon of our departure, as I was walking alone on the deck, I encountered a gentleman, whose manners and intelligent countenance arrested my attention. We entered into conversation. Asking me of what country I was, I told him I was an American; and in reply to the same interrogation put to himself, he said he was a Dane. Pleased to find one who was ready to converse and to yield him his confidence, he sat down with me and told me his history. He left his native country at an early period, and for more than twenty years had been a merchant in Buenos Ayres. He gave me the history of Rosas, whose remarkable but bloody administration of that country is so well known. He knew him well, and expected to meet him in England. "But," said he, "I am going home; back to my native land, back to the enjoyment of early ties and early associations. My mother still lives. I have closed my commercial relations in Buenos Ayres. Having business in the United States, and wishing to see the people of a nation so remarkable, I came this way; but I have sent my wife and children to the place of our future residence, by another and more direct route. After a life of toil and exposure, I wish to spend the remainder of my days in peace, in the bosom of my family." He then took from his pocket a beautiful daguerreotype of his wife, and another of his three children, two beautiful daughters and his little boy, whom the artist had placed between them, and showed them to me; and we gazed upon them together. And I could not help saying to myself, as I saw the strong emotions working in his countenance, "How sacred are the relations of family! How strong and wonderful are those ties which God has implanted in our nature!"

But this was only one of many similar instances

which came under my notice. Strangers on board an Atlantic steamer, and standing in need of each other's aid and sympathy, soon get acquainted. A lady was pointed out to my notice, who had come from the State of Missouri. Her story, as I understood it, partly from her own lips, was this. Her husband was a military man, and some years since, in some of the revolutionary movements in Germany, held the rank of captain. Experiencing reverses, they had fled to America, and established themselves on a farm in Missouri. Even now it would be dangerous for her husband to return; and hence she was travelling with her three little children, unattended and unprotected by their father, on this long journey of four thousand miles, that she might see once more in her native land the faces of her parents and brothers.

The mighty principle of family love, stronger perhaps than any other in our nature, operates in a great variety of directions. Sometimes, in consequence of the variety of its objects, it becomes antagonistical to itself, and has the effect to separate very near friends, and to lead the objects of it into distant lands. On board of our vessel was an American lady, estimable for every virtue, who was leaving her native land and its many pleasant associations and joys, in order to take up a permanent residence in Scotland. I had known her in our own country; had been well acquainted with her parents while they lived, and her brothers and sisters, who are still living; and could not therefore be ignorant, how much she suffered, and how much she sacrificed in fulfilling her purpose. I asked her one day why she did not take a different course, and permit her husband to go abroad, and transact his business without her. Her answer, disinterested as it was beautiful, was, that undoubtedly her husband would consent to such a course, but that she could not bear to see him spend his life in labor without the consolations of a *home*. In this generous answer I recognized the expression of a great truth, which seems to me to have a close connection with man's happiness. It is, that man without woman has not, and cannot have, a HOME. He may have a place, a locality, a country perhaps; but a *home*, the resting-place of hopes and desires, the locality of the heart's sacred affections, he has not and cannot have, without woman.

And on such a subject could I not speak from my own experience? Could I be insensible, as I thus left my native land, to the ties which bound me to home and kindred? Without professing to be more or less susceptible of affections than others, I am obliged to say, that my heart involuntarily turned to a beloved object in a distant place. Faithful in its homage to its unchanging attachments, it thought of one who thought of me. I gave expression to my feelings; but how inadequate is language to embody and give substance to cherished remembrances and affections!

> The wind has heaved the billow's breast;
>   The ship is rocking on the sea;
> And time and tide, that never rest,
>   Have brought the destined hour to me.

I leave thee, Mary! Oh, how dear,—
None but thyself can ever know.
Hide from my heart that scalding tear,
Unfold thine arms, and let me go.

Oft on the dark and raging sea,
Or when in distant lands I roam,
My aching heart shall think of thee,
Think of our dear and cherished home.

Oceans may roll between; but never
Can rend our mutual souls apart.
Mountains may rise; but cannot sever
The bond that binds us, heart to heart.

For lands and oceans have a place,
And lines and limits gird them round;
But LOVE is conqueror of space,
And lives a life that knows no bound.

(II.)

Captain of the Arctic—Man an æsthetic as well as social being—On the sublimity of the ocean—Remarks on the subject of beauty and sublimity—The moral effect of the ocean—Poetry.

LIVERPOOL, ENGLAND, SEPT. 30, 1852.

WHEN I went on board the steamship, a friend pointed out the commander, Captain L. As the commander necessarily embodies in himself, to a considerable extent, the destiny of the ship and of those who sail in it, my attention was at once fastened upon the man who held, as it were, the bond of my life. My judgment of him at that time was of course based upon slight premises; but I think it will be found correct. He passed silently through the crowd, bowing slightly but gracefully to those whom he knew. His firm step indicated habits of command; but without any display. It was obvious to me, that he possesses a mind which is conscious of no inconsiderable resources, but which generally concentrates its action within itself; so that he develops what he really is, not so much by words, as by *occasions*. Moderate in stature, and quiet and unassuming in his general deportment, still, there is something in his keen black eye and in his weatherbeaten and sunburnt countenance, which indicates that he is abundantly equal both to duty and danger. He may be relied upon as a man who, in those emergencies which test men's characters, will boldly and skilfully fulfil all that he promises.

As we were about to start, I saw him move to an elevated position above the wheel; and it was interesting to see how quickly and completely the inward thought or purpose alters the outward man. He stood a few moments silent and thoughtful. He gave a quick glance to every part of the ship. He cast his eye over the multitude coming on board the ship, among whom was the American ambassador to England, who, if the captain may be said to embody the ship, may be said with equal truth to embody in his official person a nation's rights and a nation's honor. He saw the husbands and the wives, the mothers and the children, entrusted to his care; and his slender form, as he gave the orders for our departure, seemed at once to grow more erect and firm; the muscles of his face swelled; his dark eye glowed with a new fire; and his whole person expanded and beautified itself by the power of inward emotion.

I have often noticed this interesting phenomenon; and have come to the conclusion, if man or woman wishes to realize the full power of personal beauty, it must be by cherishing noble hopes and purposes; by having something to do and something to live for, which is worthy of humanity; and which, by expanding the capacities of the soul, gives expansion and symmetry to the body which contains it.

In my last letter I gave the lesson which a voyage on the ocean furnishes on the subject of our *social* nature. But man is an *æsthetic*, as well as a social being. That is to say, he is not only the subject of those desires and sympathies which are the foundation of his social nature and which bind him in various ways to his fellow-man, but is also the subject of *emotions*,—those emotions which we experience in witnessing the great objects and works of art and nature, the emotions of beauty and sublimity. The ocean is spoken of by æsthetic writers as a sublime object. And it must be conceded, if sublimity can properly be ascribed to any object whatever, it would be difficult to find one which has higher claims. I acknowledge, that, in relation to this subject, I was desirous to test my own feelings. I remarked to you that we sailed on the eighteenth, which was Saturday; and, experiencing the common fate of those who are making their first voyage, I was confined to my room by sickness for some days. On the next Tuesday morning, when we were already far off on the broad Atlantic, I went on deck; and taking a position where I should not be likely to be disturbed, I watched for a long time the vast and wonderful scene before me. There was nothing in sight as far as the eye could reach, but the boundless waters, which were agitated and tossed in every direction by a strong head-wind. My soul dilated and swelled with emotion.

The conception itself was vast—as if there opened before me a window of eternity, in the reflection and imaging of which I could behold the infinite of the future; or as if the mighty and boundless Divinity himself had condescended to assume a form, which corresponded in some degree to the infinite of his existence. And this enlarged and mighty conception was followed by a correspondent intensity of feeling in the emotional nature.

On only two occasions before, have I had the same expansion and intensity of thought and feeling. Many years ago I visited the celebrated mountain region in the northern part of New Hampshire. I succeeded in reaching the top of Mount Washington, more than six thousand feet above the level of the sea. It was a clear, bright day of July. Not a cloud was upon the sky. And standing on the small rocky platform, which formed the summit of the mountain, I had before me, distinctly visible in every direction, a sixty miles' circuit of thickly wooded and dark forest, not on a plain, but thrown into every variety of mountainous position, — a vast, boundless sea of mighty wooded summits, standing side by side, and varying in height from two thousand to four thousand feet. The whole scene was on such a vast scale, that the soul, laboring with thought and emotion, could scarcely endure it. The other occasion to which I refer was more recent and different in character. It was a visit to the Falls of Niagara. The contemplation of that immense cataract, that world of waters, apparently broken loose and poured out from some higher and unseen world,—a scene in nature so often described, and yet never fully realized and understood except by those who have witnessed it,—constitutes an era in a man's life. He can never forget it; and in natural scenery he can never again see anything equal to it or like it. The emotions which I experienced on these two occasions, were similar in character, and at least as intense in degree, as those which I now experienced on viewing the vast and agitated ocean.

The development of mind, in connection with situation and action, and in all the various forms in which it takes place, has been a somewhat favorite subject with me. And as I write not merely for the purpose of giving a momentary amusement, but also in the hopes either of imparting some instruction to others or of settling more fully some opinions of my own, I will briefly express my views on some controverted doctrines which have relation to the Sublime and Beautiful.

And one obvious principle on this interesting subject is this:—that the beautiful will be found, in all cases, to be the basis of the grand and the sublime. Take the sublime scenes, to which we have referred. The tossing wave of the ocean, for instance, thrown into every variety of position and flashing out in many varieties of color as it rolls in the shade or the sunshine, is a beautiful object, and nothing more than beautiful. But when the wave is expanded and raised to a great height by the wind, and when wave is added to wave in the multiplications of infinity, it then exhibits an aspect of grandeur or of sublimity. And so in other cases. In a multitude of instances I have endeavored to analyze the foundation of these emotions. And I cannot doubt, that there must be law, order, symmetry, beauty at the bottom; otherwise there can be nothing which is truly grand or sublime. There is order and truth, there is harmony, although it may perhaps be the *violence* of harmony, even in the movements of an angry ocean.

A second remark, which I have to make in relation to some of the controverted topics of æsthetics, is this. The emotions which we are considering, have their foundation in the immutable condition of things, in the constitution and permanencies of nature, and therefore may be spoken of as *intrinsic* and *original;* and are not as some valuable writers seem to suppose, the result of mere *association.* This opinion, which in my own case is a very decided one, is founded on personal experience. Previously to the occasions which I have mentioned, I had never ascended the summit of Mount Washington, nor stood at the foot of the cataract of Niagara. And in the experience of those strong emotions, which then agitated my breast, what did I, or could I owe to any previous association? I agree with Alison and Jeffries and other writers, to whom I have alluded, that in many cases much may be ascribed to the associating principle. But association does not and cannot explain all. It was far, very far, from explaining the mighty revelations of thought and feeling which then crowded upon me. A voice, which

I had never heard or known before, came out from the depths of nature,—an utterance which I was confident was not fabricated out of any previous experience by means of some associating process; but deep, mighty, as if God himself were speaking, it seemed to rush from the immensity of its original hiding-place, and to sound from eternity to eternity.

A third remark, which I wish to make, is this. I cannot agree with Mr. Burke and other writers who think with him, that the true emotion of the sublime is really heightened by conceptions of danger and by feelings of dread. Upon this point also I have taken every favorable opportunity to test my own feelings. But I will mention only one here, which occurred upon this voyage, and which, therefore, is appropriate in this letter. On Tuesday morning, the 28th of September, we came in sight of the coast of Ireland, which arose in a clear sky and dazzling sunlight, fresh and beautiful from the morning wave. Absorbed in the historic associations which are connected with this celebrated "Isle of the ocean," the hours flew rapidly by, as we passed in succession Cape Clear, the light of Kinsale, the cove of Cork, the city of Waterford, and other places on the coast. In the afternoon we entered the mouth of the Irish or St. George's Channel, and were rapidly approaching the well-known point of land called Holyhead, which is situated on the English side of the channel. We were about sixty-five miles distant from this place, and in a position which is considered a dangerous one without the aid of a pilot, when suddenly a very violent storm commenced. The rain fell in torrents. The wind blew from the north-east, a full gale, and directly ahead. The sea rolled in terrible fury, in one vast sheet of foam. The vast ship, with all the steam she could bear, made but slow way, as the infuriated waves, rent asunder as they came in terrible contact with the struggling Arctic, rushed by on each side, foaming and roaring like a two-fold cataract of Niagara. The storm continued ten hours; and so violently agitated was the sea that no pilot was able to approach the vessel the next morning until ten o'clock.

At this time, it may well be supposed, we had around us and before us, above and beneath, all the mingling elements which are understood to furnish occasion for the highest emotions of the sublime. But the result was not such, (and I think it will never be found to be such,) as the æsthetical theories on the subject would lead us to anticipate. That the soul was deeply agitated, is true. But the agitation was not caused exclusively, nor chiefly, by the exercise of a pure and unmixed emotion of sublimity. The simultaneous discharge of an hundred pieces of cannon in itself considered, is sublime; but it ceases to be sublime in the view of a person who is standing within range of the balls, because the emotion of sublimity, instead of being increased, is perplexed, and would be likely to be entirely annulled, by the sentiment of danger. And it will be so, in a greater or less degree, in every similar case. It was so in the magnificent but terrific scene which I have attempted to describe. If we had felt perfectly secure, the scene would have been one of unparalleled sublimity; but the sense of danger transferred the action of the mind from the contemplation of the sublime object to the consideration of our personal exposure.

The mistake of writers on the subject is, that they confound things together which are very unlike. The emotion or rather the passion of fear, if carefully analyzed, will be found to be very different from an emotion of grandeur or sublimity. Both, it is true, may agitate the soul. But one does it in view of the beauty and greatness of its object; the other on account of its deformity and hatefulness, or because it causes dread. In order to experience the highest possible emotion of sublimity, there may be an enlargement or intensity of the object to any extent whatever, but the object thus expanded and intense must merely occupy the soul with the corresponding expansion and intensity of feeling, without causing personal alarm or anything else which might perplex the mind's attention.

I will only add one remark more. There is a voice in the ocean, which addresses the moral as well as the emotional and æsthetic nature. In its vastness and its agitations, it has a subduing and devotional effect upon the mind, like that which one experiences who dwells in the midst of the forests, and pointed rocks, and solitary echoes of lofty mountains. It is impossible to look upon it, especially when it is greatly agitated, without receiving the impression, that there is somewhere in the universe of things, a strength, a substantial greatness, which can have its foundation and be fully realized only in God. And this suggestion of strength in the Infinite is connected with the idea—never brought home so closely before—of our own feebleness.

Oh God! When tost upon the wave,
My heart instinctive turns to Thee;
Thou hast the power to smite or save,
The arbiter of destiny.

Though wide and wild this vast expanse,
It brings this solace of the soul,—
That 'tis not accident or chance,
Which makes these mighty billows roll.

'Tis God, who gives the high behest,
Which makes them fall or makes them rise:
Which sinks the caverns in their breast,
Or sends them foaming to the skies.

He guards the sparrow on the shore;
He rocks the sea-bird on the sea;
And here, amid the billows' roar,
Will not my Father think of me?

(III.)

Arrival at Liverpool—Appearance of the city—American ambassador—Death of the Duke of Wellington—Emigration to Australia—American books and authors.

LIVERPOOL, ENGLAND, OCT. 4, 1852.

WE reached Liverpool, Wednesday, the 29th of September, early in the afternoon. The city ascends gradually from the water, and displays itself advantageously; although the first view gives but an imperfect idea of its great extent and wealth. The crowded sails in the river Mersey and in the artificial docks on the borders of the river, with the passing and repassing of numerous boats in every direction, confirmed the reputation which this city has long enjoyed for commercial enterprise. In a short time we went on shore. I felt, on stepping for the first time on the soil of England, like the man who returns, after many years' absence, to his father's home. The unity of origin more than counterbalanced the difference of nationality. I had come to my own people,—to the land of my ancestors.

The growth of Liverpool has been very rapid. The number of its inhabitants in the year 1700 was five thousand. Its population is estimated at the present time at 350,000. As I walked along its wharves and among its crowded streets, everything indicated intelligence, boldness of enterprise, and successful activity. Liverpool is a place of commerce rather than of the arts; and has greater attractions for the merchant and the man of business than for the scholar and the man of artistic taste. It has, however, its valuable philanthropic and literary institutions; and a number of well constructed and even elegant public buildings. Among these St. George's Hall and the Exchange are likely to attract the particular attention of strangers. The latter is a building of great size and beauty, well adapted to the purposes of business and of the interchanges of commerce for which it was erected;—and may justly be regarded as one of the great centres of the commercial intercourse of the world. In the area of this building is an imposing naval monument, erected in honor of Lord Nelson.

But I must recur a moment to some other topics, which may be better noticed here than elsewhere. Perhaps I ought to say, that in my contemplated and yet uncertain wanderings from place to place, I shall endeavor to keep some record, so far as my health will permit, not only of places and things and of the outward man, but of the associations, emotions, and other facts and operations of the human mind. And in saying this, I do not mean to exclude my own mind. I have already referred to the powerful effect upon my feelings produced by a view of the ocean soon after leaving America. And I spoke of this experience as throwing some light, as it seemed to me, on those emotions of the sublime and beautiful, which in works of art and taste are often denominated *æsthetic* emotions. At another time, in the course of our voyage across the Atlantic, I was personally the subject of some mental experiences, which illustrated in a remarkable manner the operations of the human mind in another respect, namely, the workings of the associating principle. To detail them distinctly would require a letter of some length; but you shall have them at some future time. I omit to give an account of them now, through fear of forgetting or omitting some incidents which have given variety and interest to our voyage.

I have already referred to the fact, that we had on board, the American ambassador to England, Mr. Ingersoll of Philadelphia. I had formed a slight acquaintance with this truly excellent and distinguished man many years ago; and was happy to renew it at this time. Every one found him easy of access, when his health permitted him to be about the ship; and the day before our arrival in Liverpool, being called upon for that purpose, in an appropriate manner he made a chaste and graceful address in the presence of the passengers and others, which was characterized by kind and patriotic sentiments.

There is great significancy in the intercourse of nations at the present time. It not only indicates the progress of social and international humanity, but is also an index of the intellectual character, and of the political morality and honor of particular nations. And I do not doubt that the American government, in assigning this important embassy to Mr. Ingersoll, has consulted its reputation and honor, as well as its interests. The new American ambassador to the Court of St. James is not a mere political or party man; but a scholar in a high and commendable sense of that term,—a man of wide information and cultivated literary taste. Nothing will be likely to come from his pen which will discredit the high place which is already assigned to the diplomatic papers of America.

Mr. Ingersoll was well received in Liverpool, but being met there, even before leaving the Arctic, by letters from Mr. Lawrence, his predecessor in the important office to which he had been appointed, he proceeded almost immediately to London.

Mr. Lawrence leaves this country with the respect of Englishmen, and with the respect and gratitude of American citizens. Nothing can be more unlike than these two ambassadors. The personal appearance of Mr. Ingersoll, though entirely good, is not of such a marked kind as to attract attention, by distinguishing him, either physically or in dress, from the common mass of men. He is modest and rather retiring in his manners; and everything about him indicates the plainest republican citizen; so much so that I am inclined to think his great merit must be sought before it is known. He certainly will never proclaim it himself.

Mr. Lawrence is differently constituted in all respects. He is not a man of public or liberal education; and in matters of literature, of taste, and in the knowledge of civil and political history, must probably yield in place to his accomplished successor. Mr. Lawrence, however, is a man of great natural intellect, and of thorough practical knowledge on a wide variety of subjects. He is a man noble and graceful in his person; but his easy eloquence and generous heart relieve it from the dignity of distance. Mr. Lawrence has sometimes been characterized as aristocratic;—an epithet which is sometimes applied hastily and improperly. If, however, by aristocracy be merely meant *wealth*, it must be admitted that he belongs to the class of those who possess great riches. But it is equally well known that his wealth has always been accessible for the poor man's benefit: and no man, whether rich or poor, ever goes from his presence without feeling that he has a sympathetic and republican heart.

On our arrival at Liverpool three topics seemed at that moment to be uppermost in the public mind, (in addition to the anomalous and amazing movements in France, which are laying the foundations of a new dynasty and empire,) namely, the death and funeral obsequies, not yet determined upon, of the Duke of Wellington, the emigration to Australia, and the disclosures contained in that remarkable advent in American literature, entitled Uncle Tom's Cabin. Expecting to be present at the opening of

Parliament, and to witness the funeral solemnities which a grateful nation proposes to enact in honor of a name which stands prominent and perhaps first in British military history, I shall defer what I have to say upon this remarkable man to some future occasion. The vast emigration to Australia, which seems to be chiefly of Englishmen, at first strikes one as merely a commercial incident, a new development of the courses of trade and of the intercourse of men and nations; but to the eye of the reflecting and philosophical observer it carries with it the seeds of empires, and new and important destinies of the human race. The vast countries in that part of the world are destined to be occupied by the Anglo-Saxon race; carrying with them intelligence and the arts, the Protestant religion, and the indomitable spirit of independence. At such a distance they cannot remain long dependent upon a predominant power, but will set up for themselves, and fulfil the destiny which Providence has allotted them.

You will perhaps be surprised to hear me intimate that the work of Mrs. Stowe, interesting and valuable as it undoubtedly is, is one of the things which at the present time occupies to a considerable extent the attention of the British nation. It is not often that a literary work, whatever its merits, produces what may be called a national sensation. But such is the fact in the present case. Partly owing to the nature of the subject, and partly to the intrinsic merits of the work, it is universally read; and it has been asserted, on what seemed to be good authority, that the popular writings of Walter Scott and of Dickens have had at no time a circulation so general and rapid as Uncle Tom's Cabin. It is published by a multitude of booksellers in all forms, and with all sorts and degrees of decorations and prices, and is found in all bookstalls and booksellers' shops.

The effect of this work upon the English mind seems to be favorable. I do not know that it increases the Englishman's hostility to slavery, which was sufficiently decided and emphatic before. But it reveals to him the multiplied alliances and intricacies of the system; the impossibility of removing or re-adjusting it without great wisdom and kindness; and the real benevolence of many slaveholders, who are ready as Christians and as patriots to do what they ought to do as soon as they can ascertain what it is. It also opens to the English reader, by means of intimations and statements in the latter part of the work, some new light in another direction. The allusions to the Liberian Republic disclose very clearly the tendencies and anticipations which exist at the present time in the mind of the talented and benevolent authoress. And they are not only understood, but they have their effect here. The inquiry arises in thinking minds, Are there not some designs of Providence, connected with the history of the African race in America, which have been as yet imperfectly appreciated among us? Is it not possible that the Supreme Being, in permitting this race to be carried to America, has done it with the design of giving them a knowledge of the English language, of modern arts and civilization, of free political institutions, and especially of the Christian religion,—in order that, in due time and under the providence of God, they may carry back the arts, and freedom, and Christianity, to benighted and suffering Africa? And if such is the design of Providence, may we not soon expect, by consultation and proper co-operation of effort, to see Christian States and republics arising on the coast of Africa which shall vie in all that is great and good with the Christian States of Europe and America?

If the effect of the work is to suggest such considerations, and to subdue in some degree the bitterness of feeling which unhappily has existed towards the Southern States of our Republic, we must certainly regard it as favorable. But Mrs. Stowe's is not the only American book which is read in England. In many bookstores I have found works by American authors; and it was pleasant, in reading advertisements and lists of publications at so great a distance from my native land, to meet very frequently the familiar and popular names of Irving, Cooper, Webster, Story, Longfellow, Abbott, Bryant, Hawthorne, and others.

There are other evidences of a public sentiment increasingly favorable. The newspapers of England, which seem to me to be conducted in general with greater ability than our own, indicate the estimation in which America is held. A larger space is given in these papers to the commercial, political, and local news from the American States, than is given to the events occurring in other foreign countries, unless there is something very peculiar in their situation, which is the case in France at the present time. On the whole, it seems to me very obvious, even from the limited opportunities of observation which I have already enjoyed, that England, laying aside the jealousies which might naturally be expected, is preparing with increased cordiality to open her heart and arms to young America.

Before I left America, letters had reached me in my retired and almost obscure residence, from a gentleman of Liverpool, who had become acquainted with some imperfect works which bear my name. He received me at his house with the utmost cordiality and kindness; which confirmed the impression to which I have already alluded, that, in going to England, I did not go among an unknown and foreign people. His marked and unexpected kindness to one who had never seen him before, left impressions upon my mind which can never be effaced. I shall have occasion in another place to refer again to this excellent and much-esteemed friend.

I have visited and spent a day at Manchester, which is but a short distance from Liverpool by the railroad conveyance. Of this busy and great city, so often mentioned and so well known in the United States, I could have wished to say something;—though it would have been only the statement of an imperfect and passing impression. But as I am just starting for Oxford, it is possible that I may find something of more interest for you there.

(IV.)

Arrival at Oxford—Story of the martyrs, Cranmer, Ridley and Latimer—Place of their martyrdom—The martyr's memorial—Inscription—Poetry.

OXFORD, ENGLAND, OCT. 7, 1852.

As I intimated in my last, I have found my way to Oxford. I left Liverpool, after remaining there and at Manchester a week, and arrived here yesterday: a distance, I should judge of at least an hundred and fifty miles, through a well cultivated country, but not so beautiful to my eye as New England. I must say, however, that England, in all the attributes of comfort, general prosperity, education, and morals, exceeds my expectations. I have seen as yet but little evidence of want and suffering; not so much as I have witnessed in New York, with the exception perhaps of the city of Manchester, where there is a large manufacturing population, many of whom undoubtedly suffer much.

In the religious department of my mind, if I may so express it, Jerusalem, of all earthly localities, stands first, and beyond all comparison. In the merely intellectual or literary department, there are other distinguished names and places which attract much of thought and memory; and among them Oxford stands side by side with Rome and Athens. And here I am in Oxford,—amidst walls and towers and colleges that carry me back a thousand years;—and on the banks of that Isis, flowing as beautiful as ever, which was associated in my early reading and recollections with the Tiber and the Illissus. I will endeavor, in a few days, to give you some account of what is before me.

Before proceeding to do this, I must do homage to my own feelings, my sacred attachments to the doctrines and the cross of Christ, which remind me that in Oxford, and near the place where I now am, the celebrated martyrs, Cranmer, Ridley and Latimer, were burnt at the stake. Their deeply interesting story had been familiar to me from childhood; but it naturally assumed in my mind a new clearness and strength of reality, when I found myself near the place where they were tried and imprisoned and at last put to death. I had been in the city but a few hours when I employed a person, who is acquainted with its interesting localities, to guide me to the place. The precise spot where those justly renowned men and Christians perished in defence of the Protestant faith, is in the northern part of the city, in Broad street, and directly opposite to Baliol College, and is marked by a stone cross of moderate dimensions laid horizontally in the ground. At a little distance is a large memorial cross or monument, nearly eighty feet in height, in which sculpture has combined its aid with architecture to do honor to their memory. Repeatedly, since I have been here, have I visited this sacred place, and gazed with deep emotion upon the horizontal cross which indicates, after the lapse of centuries, where the flames were kindled, and where the martyrs died.

And I can assure you it has required but little effort of the imagination, to see those venerable men chained to the stake, to hear their last prayers, and to witness the agonies of their fiery dissolution.

When a man is willing to die for his principles, I feel that human nature is honored; or rather that God is honored, who inspires within him the inflexible faith, the indomitable will, without which he would not be enabled to endure such suffering. It is true, that persons of different forms of faith have died as martyrs. But what does that indicate but that there is a principle beneath the form; and that religion, or that principle which recognizes the God of the Bible and has confidence in him, is essentially the same under a variety of forms. These noble martyrs belonged to a form of faith different in some respects from that in which I have been brought up; but I do not cherish and honor their memory the less on that account. And I cannot doubt, (saying nothing of multitudes who sympathized fully in their personal religious relations and in the peculiar form of their belief,) that their willingness to die that cruel death has strengthened the faith, and given new impulse to the piety, and encouraged the hopes of multitudes in other communions.

On the lofty monument to which I have referred, called the MARTYRS' MEMORIAL, a sketch of which I send you, on the north face of the basement story, is the following inscription :—

TO THE GLORY OF GOD,
AND IN GRATEFUL COMMEMORATION OF HIS SERVANTS,
THOMAS CRANMER,
NICHOLAS RIDLEY,
HUGH LATIMER,
PRELATES OF THE CHURCH OF ENGLAND,
WHO, NEAR THIS SPOT,
YIELDED THEIR BODIES TO BE BURNED;
BEARING WITNESS
TO THE SACRED TRUTHS
WHICH THEY HAD AFFIRMED AND MAINTAINED
AGAINST THE ERRORS OF THE CHURCH OF ROME;
AND REJOICING
THAT TO THEM IT WAS GIVEN
NOT ONLY TO BELIEVE IN CHRIST,
BUT ALSO TO SUFFER FOR HIS SAKE;
THIS MONUMENT
WAS ERECTED BY PUBLIC SUBSCRIPTION,
IN THE YEAR OF OUR LORD
MDCCCXLI.

And now you will allow me to add a little testimonial of my own, which, without claiming any other merit, certainly has that of being written upon the spot, in deep sympathy with the events which occurred there, and by a stranger from a foreign land.

My feet have press'd the place of fire,
Where Oxford's holy martyrs died;
Led by a just and high desire
Not to deny the Crucified.

It was no strife for earthly fame,
No selfish contest for the wrong;
But homage to a Saviour's name,
Which made them true and made them strong.

'Twas here they stood beside the stake;
In chains, but still in faith and love;
Willing the cup of flame to take,
And find their recompense above.

And standing round their fiery cross,
They still had power to pray and praise;
And while their bodies burned like dross,
Their souls grew brighter in the blaze.

Oh, life of love that cannot die!
From earth by fire and fagot driven,
Angels shall welcome thee on high,
And thou shalt bless thy native heaven.

(V.)

General view of the city of Oxford—Visit to Magdalen College—Its eminent men—Addison's walk—Character of his writings—Botanic Gardens—University College—Christ Church College.

OXFORD, ENGLAND, OCT. 9, 1852.

THE city of Oxford, renowned for its historical and literary associations, is situated near the junction of the beautiful rivers, the Isis and the Cherwell. These two rivers, which have their place in history and in English song, particularly the classic Isis, unite together, after nearly insulating the city; and flowing on through Abingdon as far as Dorchester, mingle their waters with the still more celebrated Thames. Ascending one of the eminences to the east of the city, I had, in one sudden and wide view, before me, a scene of remarkable beauty; the fields and gardens, limited and shut in with green hedges, and bearing everywhere the marks of high cultivation; the humble but comfortable home of the laboring cottager; the more splendid residence of the wealthy; hills, valleys, rivers, forests, intermingled, especially in the direction and in the vicinity of the city, with spires, domes, and towers,—the vast and venerable representatives of different ages and of different degrees of civilization. Afterwards, going up to the outer balustrade of the celebrated edifice known as the Radcliffe Library, I obtained another and nearer panoramic view of the city,—its streets, squares, churches, monuments, halls, bridges, colleges,—which, although the scene will change continually in itself, will remain a picture in my own mind, distinct as life and lasting as memory.

I have no hesitation in saying, limited as my acquaintance in these things is, that Oxford may justly be regarded as one of the most remarkable and most interesting cities in Europe. With more than twenty thousand inhabitants, and carrying back its history a thousand years, it is not without interest in its civil, political, and historical relations. But to us, on the other side of the Atlantic, it is known chiefly by its University, and by the relations which it thus sustains, through its justly-celebrated schools of learning, to English literature and intellectual culture generally. It was her University which interested me most.

As you enter the city in the eastern direction, over a bridge of beautiful architecture which crosses the Cherwell, you first come in sight of Magdalen College; one of the noblest in the sisterhood of colleges which constitutes the University of Oxford. Its large and magnificent tower, an hundred and fifty feet in height, and which dates back in its origin as far as 1492, attracts particular notice. At this point commences the street called the High Street, which is distinguished by the number and remarkable character of its public buildings. On the right of this street the stranger enters the college, through a gateway in the Gothic style, which is quite recent in its construction, and was erected from a design by Pugin. Over the gate is a Latin inscription, indicating that the founders and administrators of the college are willing to recognize their dependence on a higher power, which may be translated into English as follows: "He, whose name is holy, hath done great things for me." On entering the court and passing on to the interior, the various parts of the Gothic gateway and of the college building, including the chapel, present points and objects which arrest the attention and please the eye of persons who are capable of appreciating the beauties of architecture and sculpture;—figures of the Virgin and Child;—figures in niches over the west windows of the chapel, representing St. John the Baptist, Edward IV., and others;—stained windows, on one of which is a representation of the last judgment;—Corinthian pillars of great beauty, canopied statues, and monuments of no small elegance. One of these monuments enlists the notice of the visitor from the circumstance that it is erected to the memory of two brothers, members of the college, who were drowned in the Cherwell, one in endeavoring to save the other.

The library is ornamented with portraits and busts, among which are the busts of Locke and Bacon—and what is of more consequence, contains a large and valuable collection of books. There is obviously no want of the opportunities and means of mental improvement. I entered a number of the rooms of the inmates and members of this college fraternity, and found them, though dating far back in their origin, sufficiently convenient and well adapted to purposes of study. Among the men who pursued their studies here, and whose names are familiar on both sides of the Atlantic, were Cardinal Wolsey, Fox the martyrologist, Collins the poet, Gibbon the historian, and Addison.

The mention of Addison reminds me of the picturesque grove, with its large old elms, which forms a part of the college grounds, and particularly of the beautiful walk near the banks of the Cherwell, known as Addison's walk. This walk, which has been elevated with much labor above the low and green meadows around, is of considerable length, and is shaded with lofty trees. And the tradition is, that Addison, while connected with Magdalen College, spent much of his time here; and that it was here that he either completed or planned many of his admirable writings. Addison has always been a favorite with me. To his writings I was early directed as models of style; and these soon became interesting to me for other reasons. His merits were not always understood at first; but they become more and more obvious on a close acquaintance. So perfect is his mastery of the English language, that it is difficult to alter his sentences, even in a slight degree, without taking something from their simplicity or beauty. Everything which he says is true to nature and in excellent taste; and is often heightened in its effect upon the mind by its high moral tone or its sweet quiet humor. Many have been the pleasant and profitable hours which I have spent over his writings; and I can assure you it was with no small emotion that I found myself treading on the place which aided the contemplations, and contributed to the happiness, of this great and good man.

Opposite Magdalen College, are the Botanic Gardens; occupying the place which, at some former period, is said to have been used as a burying-ground by the Jews, many of whom dwelt here anciently. These beautiful gardens, auxiliary to study and improvement in a very important department of knowledge, are worthy of the especial attention of travellers. They may be visited without expense; and the courteous curator, who has the reputation of being a learned and skilful botanist, is ready to give any information which may be desired. It may not be out of place to add, that they are entered through a handsome gateway, which, independently of its own beauty, naturally attracted notice from the circumstance of its being built from a design by the celebrated architect, Inigo Jones.

On the opposite side of High Street, and very near where I have found a quiet and comfortable residence in the Angel Hotel, is another of the old and distinguished members of the great Oxford University; the college, founded in 1249, and which is known as the University College. This college presents a front on the street of two hundred and sixty feet. It is divided in its interior into two courts, and is entered by two towered gateways. The chapel, which constitutes a part of the college edifice, is an object of much attraction. Like the other chapels, it is ornamented with many monuments, which are more or less chaste and beautiful in their design. There is one, made by Flaxman, which is erected to the memory of Sir William Jones. This is particularly interesting, not only for its own beauty, but also on account of the great name which it honors, the author of the "Digest of the Hindoo Laws," distinguished as a Judge, and still more for his knowledge of Oriental literature.

The window in what is denominated the Ante-Chapel, representing "Christ driving the buyers and sellers out of the temple," was painted by Henry Giles, an English artist. The paintings on the windows in the Inner Chapel, which are more rich and beautiful in their execution and coloring, are by an artist more generally known, Van Linge. Jacob's Vision of the Ladder, Elijah's Ascent to Heaven in a chariot of fire, Abraham preparing to offer up Isaac, and other Scripture scenes and events, are represented on them. They were painted in 1641.

The HALL of the college, small in size but remarkable for its beauty, is adorned with a number of portraits of distinguished men. Among the eminent men who have been members of this college, it may be proper to mention Dr. Radcliffe, the founder of the Radcliffe Library; Archbishop Potter, the author of the "Archæologia Græca," a work so well known to Greek scholars; Earl Eldon, late Lord Chancellor of England; Lord Stowell, Judge of the Court of Admiralty, whose clear and able admiralty decisions cannot have escaped the notice of American lawyers, and Sir William Jones.

This college is of great antiquity. Some writers carry the date of its origin further back than I have mentioned, the year 1249. And portions of the building, discolored and crumbling with age, show that the works of man, however skilfully and laboriously made, have not that inward principle of renovation and life which characterizes the works of God. This is the source of one of the unpleasant and unfavorable impressions which all persons, especially those from the New World, are liable to receive here. The Isis flows as beautiful as ever; the gardens put off their splendor only to remodel and restore it with original freshness; and in the lofty and magnificent trees, which stand as guards to walls and towers and monuments, there is a principle of reproduction, which gives a lease of perpetuity; but upon everything which man has made, though wrought out of the solid rock, and with ages of labour, there are marks of decay and dissolution. The very marble, struck with the sickness of centuries, crumbled in my hand, and I felt that there is no true and permanent life but in the great SOURCE OF LIFE.

Oxford is a city of colleges and public institutions; and they are found not in a particular locality, as one would be likely to suppose, but scattered over its whole extent. Christ Church College, for instance, is situated at some distance from those which I have mentioned, on St. Aldgates' Street. This college was founded in 1524 by Cardinal Wolsey. It displays a front of four hundred feet in length; and as it is viewed in certain positions, with its turrets and battlements, has something of the appearance of a castle. In the centre is a large octagonal Gothic tower, which is truly a magnificent object. It is here, through the large gateway called *Tom Gate*, that the visitor enters, and finds himself at once in the quadrangle of the college, which is said to be the most spacious and beautiful in the city. The gateway has its name from the large bell which is suspended in the cupola above; which is seventeen thousand pounds in weight, being double the weight of the large bell of St. Paul's Church in London, and is known by the name of the "Great Tom of Oxford." This bell is a great favorite of the Oxford students, particularly those of Christ Church College, who insist upon it that it is the best bell in England, which, however, is said to be a matter of considerable discussion. This bell has an important part to perform in the discipline of the college, especially in the night. It is tolled every night at five minutes past nine; at which time, under penalty of being reported as delinquent to the college authorities, every undergraduate is expected to be at his room. The students insist, however, that it shall be struck one hundred and one times, and this has become the fixed and invariable custom in the matter.

In speaking of these colleges, I have had occasion to refer to paintings and sculpture. I do not pretend to any technical knowledge in these matters; and yet I have an æsthetical system of my own, founded in some degree upon an analysis of my own emotions, which enables me to give some opinion or judgment upon works of art, which is tolerably satisfactory to myself. It has seemed to me, however, that the highest results of art are not generally secured in that class of works, whether of painting, architecture, or sculpture, which are constructed on the principle of a hieroglyphical or allegorical significancy. The full effect upon the mind is disturbed and diminished by the thoughts being divided between the consideration of the object in itself, and its relation to the moral or other meaning which it is intended to convey.

Perhaps the best illustration of this topic will be found at Magdalen College. In the great quadrangle of the college, southwest corner, are two figures, the Lion and the Pelican. And they are placed here, the Lion, to indicate emblematically the attributes of courage and vigilance;—the Pelican as an emblem of parental tenderness and affection. And by combination they are intended to shadow forth the character of a good governor of a college. And accordingly we find them, in connection with these important intimations, appropriately placed under the windows of the head or president of the college. At a little distance is the figure of a Hippopotamus or river-horse, carrying his young one upon his shoulders. This, we are told, is the emblematic representation of a good Tutor or Fellow of a college, who is more intimately related to particular pupils in the college, and through whose prudence and labors they are to be guarded and kept amid the dangers to which they are exposed on first entering into the world.

All this would have done in the days of the Egyptian or Assyrian empires, when it found its justification in the imperfection of language, but does not harmonize with the nineteenth century. I did not notice anything precisely of this kind at Christ Church College.

The Refectory or Dining Hall of this college, although it may be thought to have a closer connection with the material than the mental wants of its members, is worthy of notice on account of its great extent, being an hundred and fifteen feet in length, forty in width, and fifty high; and also on account of its various and rich decorations. The roof is of richly-carved oak, and is ornamented with the numerous armorial bearings of Henry VIII. and Cardinal Wolsey. The walls are adorned with an hundred and twenty original portraits of persons who had been at various times members of the college. Some of these pictures are by the hands of the most distinguished artists. In this capacious and richly-ornamented hall a grand entertainment was given in 1814 to the allied sovereigns of Europe and to Metternich and Blucher, and other renowned statesmen and warriors, at the time of their visit to England after the defeat and fall of Napoleon.

Of the Chapel of Christ Church College, which possesses great historical and antiquarian interest, and of the noble library, adorned with busts and paintings from the most celebrated masters, I cannot stop to speak. Tired with looking at these interesting objects, without being able to stop and examine them as they deserve to be examined, I walked out, and gave rest and refreshment to my mind, in the beautiful meadow in the immediate vicinity. This meadow, which I understand to be the property of the college, is bounded on two sides by the Cherwell and Isis, which here meet and mingle their waters; and, adorned as it is with spacious walks and noble avenues of trees, it is justly regarded as one of its valuable acccessories and ornaments.

Among the distinguished men, who have been at different periods members of this college, were Atterbury, Bishop of Rochester, Dr. Robert South, the Earl of Mansfield, Bolingbroke, Boyle, Philip Sidney, the author of the Arcadia, the poets Ben Jonson and Otway, George Canning, and Sir Robert Peel. At Oxford, as everywhere else since I have been in England, I have been reminded of America. Numberless are the remembrances and ties which bind us together. And here, in reading over the list of those, whose powers were developed and disciplined in Christ Church College, these sympathetic and fraternal remembrances flowed up within me as I stopped at the name of William Penn, the founder of Pennsylvania. Most persons have an idea of William Penn as a man of portly form, wearing a plain coat with large buttons, with an amplified hat and a cane in his hand; adding perhaps the accessory conception, which they have imbibed traditionally, that he made some amicable treaties with the Indians. But this, although it is well as far as it goes, is not all. Penn was a man not only of deep religious sensibility, but of vast grasp of intellect. If he wore a coat which indicated his relationship to a particular party or sect, he nevertheless had a soul of great dimensions, which took in the past, the present and the future; and which, moved as it were by a divine inspiration, foresaw, anticipated, and in part regulated, the destinies of humanity. And his numerous writings, when examined on the principles which decide literary merit, showed that he was an accomplished scholar. In his remarkable Treatise entitled "No Cross, no Crown," which was written at an early period of his life, there are many passages characterized by chasteness of taste and beauty of expression, as well as truth and sublimity of thought; and which, as it seems to me, cannot well be explained, except in connection with the fact, which perhaps is not well known even to his own people, that his mind, in its intellectual department, was trained and disciplined in this seat of learning.

This is the college of Locke also, who took an interest in, and whose name is associated historically with, the affairs of America. But Locke, the author of the Essay on the Human Understanding, like Plato and Fenelon, does not belong to any one age or country; but transmits himself, by means of his great qualities, into all ages and lands. Undoubtedly those who have succeeded him in some of the departments of mental philosophy have seen further and understood better in some things; but this is the necessary result of human progress, and suggestions and criticisms of this nature will apply to the great names of all periods. What is imperfect is completed by time. And it still remains true, that, owing to the clearness and originality of his perceptions, the variety and extent of his learning, the excellence of his character, and the vast and favorable influence he has exerted, that his name may be said to have transcended the limits of nationality, and to have taken its place in the catalogue and in the brotherhood of those great men who belong not so much to a nation as to the human race.

I ought to add, that there is, at this college, a whole-length statue of Locke, in marble, by Roubillac.

(VI.)

Trinity College—Its library—Distinguished members—Bodleian Library—Chantrey Gallery—Statue of Cicero—Copies of the Cartoons of Raphael.

OXFORD, ENGLAND, OCT. 11, 1852.

THERE is necessarily a similarity in institutions founded for the same object. However they may differ in extent and decorations, there must be in all, rooms for the students, libraries, places of worship, rooms and galleries for the arts, and whatever else may be necessary for convenience, or for developing intellectual and moral culture. When you have a knowledge of one, you have essentially a knowledge of the elements of all. Of the other colleges which contribute to constitute the great Oxford University, Oriel, Baliol, Trinity, Pembroke, Worcester, Merton, Queen's College and others, each has its advantages and attractions; and each its distinct and honorable history. Trinity College, founded in 1554, is later in origin than some of the others to which I have directed your attention, but it has a high reputation.

The library of this college, not deficient in other respects, is particularly valuable for the many ancient works it contains. Among others there is a Latin manuscript of Euclid, which is said to be six hundred years old. And it is stated further in relation to it, that it was translated into Latin from the Arabic, before the original Greek was discovered.

In the list of the distinguished members of Trinity College are found the names of Archbishop Sheldon, Selden the Antiquarian, Chillingworth, so celebrated for his controversial writings, and the poets Denham, Warton, and Bowles. It was a matter of interest to me, as it would naturally be to an American, to notice also among its celebrated members the names of Ireton and Ludlow, who held a rank so distinguished among the generals of the time of the English Commonwealth. On the catalogue of this college, also, is the name of the elder Pitt, the Earl of Chatham, so renowned in the annals of the British Senate, the friend of revolted America, because, in allowing to Americans the principles and rights which he claimed for Englishmen, he deemed the cause of America to be just;—a great and memorable orator, whose reasonings had the aspect of intuitions, and whose declamations were a flame of fire.

I must confess to you that I was solicitous to know what sort of men these colleges had produced. You are aware that much has been said in relation to the position of Oxford and the practical value of its system of education. The attacks which are made upon it both in and out of England, the statements and intimations unfavorable to the idea of its usefulness, are very frequent. Perhaps there is some foundation for this. It is quite probable that this great University—vast in its relations and interests, and restricted by ancient charters, which it is bound not to violate—has found it difficult to adjust itself at once and in all respects to the real improvements and the true spirit of the age. It may not be suitable for me, the citizen of another country and educated under different influences, to give an opinion on the subject-matter of this controversy; but one thing is certain, that Oxford, like every other college or university, has the right to point to the sons she has educated, and to require that they shall be taken into account in forming a judgment. Others may explain it and modify it as they think proper; but the fact still remains imperishable as history, that in this university, in different periods of its progress, minds have been trained and have gone out into the world, that have explored and successfully expanded the departments of science,—men whose perfected literary culture has approached that of Rome and Athens;—religious and civil reformers and republicans, who have defended and illustrated liberty by reason and eloquence, and who have fought at the head of armies, or shed their blood at the stake.

Her monuments may decay, her busts and statues may be broken, the massy walls of her colleges may crumble into dust; but her imperishable minds, brought out into strength and symmetry by her cherishing culture, will testify in all coming ages, whatever may be true of her imperfections or her faults, that she is, nevertheless, a child of Providence and an heir of immortality.

Among the places which no person should leave Oxford without seeing, are the Bodleian Library and the University Galleries. In noticing the books contained in the Bodleian Library, the attention of the visitor is called to the fact, that the valuable library of the learned Selden, consisting of more than 8000 volumes of printed books and manuscripts, makes a part of it. There is also deposited in the same library a celebrated collection of Greek manuscripts, more than 200 in number, formed by Giacomo Barocci, a Venetian nobleman. This library, beside its ancient manuscripts and its immense collection of books, is the depository of numerous valuable manuscripts, containing the researches of learned men in more recent times, which have been deposited at different periods. Entering the painting-galleries in an upper story of the building, which is occupied in part by some beautiful models of ancient and modern buildings, my attention was arrested by the portraits of distinguished men which grace its walls; particularly of Sir Kenelm Digby and the unfortunate Earl of Strafford, by Vandyck; —and of Handel, the great musical composer, a portrait taken by Hudson, *and the only one for which he ever sat.* Among the curiosities to be found in this room, some of them calculated to suggest painful recollections, I saw in a window-place near the entrance of the gallery a fac-simile of the death-warrant of Charles First. I had nearly forgotten to say, that, on entering this gallery, I complied, like other visitors, with an invitation to seat myself in a venerable chair, made of part of the ship in which Admiral Drake sailed round the world. To this chair is appended an inscription in verse, in his peculiar style of writing, by the old English poet, Abraham Cowley, as follows:—

To this great ship, which round the globe has run,
And match'd in race the chariot of the sun,
This Pythagorean ship, (for it may claim,
Without presumption, so deserved a name,)
By knowledge once, and transformation now,
In her new shape this sacred port allow.
Drake and his ship could not have wish'd from Fate
A happier station or more blest estate;
For, lo! a seat of endless rest is given,
To her in Oxford, and to him in heaven.

(Abraham Cowley, 1662.)

Not less interesting to the stranger than this celebrated library, is the recent but important establishment called the University Galleries, designed expressly and almost exclusively for the reception of statues, paintings, engravings and other curiosities, belonging to or which may be left to the Oxford University. In the building of the University Galleries, is the gallery called the "Chantrey Gallery;" a large apartment, an hundred and eighty feet in length, by twenty-eight in width, containing the original models of the greatest works of the late Sir Francis Chantrey. Among them are the busts and statues of Bishop Heber;—of the second Pitt, whose majestic form and ample brow harmonize with the idea which we naturally attach to this great master of the destiny of nations;—of James Watt the engineer, Roscoe of Liverpool, and Sir Joseph Banks;—of General Rollo Gillespie, of Grattan, Canning, and Washington. Another apartment, the principal Sculpture Gallery, contains numerous casts of antique statues and busts, the greater part of which were taken at Rome, from moulds made for the Emperor Napoleon. Among them are casts of the Laocoon and his sons, of the Torso of Belvidere, and of the Venus de Medici. These, as also the models in the Chantrey Gallery, have been recently presented to the University by the widow of Chantrey.

In another part of the building, amid a multiplicity of works of ancient art, I was struck with an ancient statue of Cicero, of marble, about seven feet high. I know nothing of the history of this statue, but I felt that it was, or might be, the true representation of the mighty orator himself, of the real Cicero of the Senate of Rome. The drapery in which he is clothed is of remarkable propriety and beauty. He stands as if preparing to speak;—a scroll in his left hand, the SUDARIUM in his right; —every line of his countenance full of intelligence, made alive and intense by flashes of indignation; —in a word, such as I can imagine him to have been and to have appeared, when preparing to utter his orations against Catiline or Mark Antony.

In the Picture Gallery, which is a room ninety-six feet long, by twenty-eight wide, are admirable copies, by an English painter of the name of Cooke, of the celebrated colored drawings on paper, of Raphael, called the *Cartoons*. I believe that the Cartoons are regarded, by those who are intimately acquainted with his works, as among the most striking evidences and results of the wonderful genius and skill of Raphael. To describe them fully and properly, would seem to require something of the genius of the author of them;—and at any rate I will not undertake anything of the kind now, as I am not without some hopes of seeing, and of examining more at leisure, the originals at the palace of Hampton Court. I will merely name the subjects of them :—(1) The intended sacrifice to Paul and Barnabas by the people of Lystra, Acts xiv. ;—(2) The miraculous draught of fishes, Luke v. :—(3) Christ's charge to Peter, John xxi. :—(4) Peter and John healing the lame at the gate of the temple, Acts iii. :—(5) The death of Ananias, Acts v. :—(6) Elymas the Sorcerer struck with blindness, Acts xiii. :—(7) Paul preaching at Athens, Acts xvii.

In the University Galleries are to be seen the *original* sketches and drawings, in different degrees of completeness, of many of the works of Raphael and of Michael Angelo; an hundred and sixty-two of Raphael, and seventy-nine of Angelo. One will notice here, in this remarkable collection, which probably has not its parallel in the world, how the various striking and sublime conceptions, which are discoverable in their works, gradually broke in upon their minds; and how by repeated touches and after-thoughts they were raised from the first imperfect outline to their ultimate perfection. So true it is that the greatest geniuses master their subjects by degrees; and that men, who aim to produce anything truly worthy and enduring, accept the pains of labor as the purchase of renown.

In closing this letter, you will allow me to refer to the name of one man whose influence is widely felt in America, that of John Wesley. It would be doing injustice to rank Wesley with the ordinary leaders of religious sects; at least as far as intellectual power and literary culture are concerned. Take him in the various combination of his qualities, the clearness and breadth of his perceptions, the warmth of his heart, the purity and vigor of his style of speech and writing, his moral daring, his unconquerable perseverance, and where will you look for his superior or even his equal? It was at Oxford, at first, in Christ Church College, and subsequently in Lincoln College, that the powers of this remarkable man were trained.

(VII.)

Visit to the palace of Blenheim, the residence of the Duke of Marlborough—Town of Woodstock—Triumphal arch—General appearance of the park and palace of Blenheim—Works of art—Statue of Queen Anne—Rosamond's bower—Roman villa.

OXFORD, ENGLAND, OCT. 11, 1852.

About eight miles distant from Oxford, is the palace of Blenheim, the residence of Churchill, the justly-celebrated Duke of Marlborough. This splendid pile of architecture, named the palace of Blenheim, from the village of Blenheim on the banks of the Danube, where Marlborough successfully fought the French and Bavarians, was erected under the direction of Sir John Vanbrugh, an eminent architect in the reign of Queen Anne. The numerous works of Vanbrugh are characterized by architectural skill; but the evidences of genius which they display have not exempted them from the criticism of heaviness in their appearance;—a criticism which was so frequently and in some cases so justly made, that it gave rise to the caustic couplet, which it was thought might appropriately form a part of his epitaph:—

"Lie heavy on him, earth; for he
Laid many a heavy load on thee."

It is not clear to me, that strictures of this kind, if they are meant to imply an architectural defect, are justly applicable to the palace of Blenheim, which combines beauty with strength and solidity, and is certainly a magnificent building. Blenheim palace was built, chiefly though not exclusively, at the expense of the English nation, for the Duke of Marlborough; and in acknowledgment of his great services, both in council and in many a hard-fought field of battle. Among the distinguished men of England, Marlborough stands prominent; and the remark is sometimes made, that in many of his traits of character, and especially in the incidents of his political and military history, he resembled the Duke of Wellington, whose recent death has produced so profound a sensation.

In visiting the palace of Blenheim, it was a pleasure to me to pass through the ancient town of Woodstock, which was once a flourishing place, and has some historical celebrity. I found none of the smaller towns of England, in the arrangement and appearance of their streets and buildings, carrying back my mind so distinctly to the state of things as it probably existed two centuries ago. It may be proper to remark here, that Chaucer, who may justly be regarded as the father of English poetry, and who will compare well with the poets of any age or country, resided here for some time, and has made a number of allusions in his writings to the beautiful scenery in its neighbourhood. Some of the most interesting scenes in Scott's novel of Woodstock are laid in this vicinity.

In going to the palace, I passed from Woodstock

through a quadrangular space on the right hand of which Chaucer resided, and then through a large triumphal arch, erected by the Duchess of Marlborough, the year after the decease of the Duke. This arch, which is of the Corinthian order, is an object of considerable attraction. On the side next to Woodstock is a Latin inscription, with an English translation on the opposite side, to this effect:—that it was erected by his wife as a monument of her husband's glory and a testimonial of her own affection.

I had advanced within the gateway of this arch but a few paces, when I felt myself to be in the presence of a combined scene of the works of art and nature, rarely exceeded in extent and beauty;—before me in a southern direction the vast palace, with its turrets and minarets, obscured in part, but not with any unfavorable effect on the general outline, by the luxuriant beeches and elms; in another direction a fine sheet of water spanned by a superb stone bridge; on the rising grounds beyond the bridge, a lofty column erected to the memory of the duke;—and on every side the park with its undulating grounds, its green openings, its herds of deer reposing quictly or standing gracefully erect at gaze, and its clumps and groups of trees. The column, erected in honor of the duke, stands on an elevated piece of ground; and being itself of the great height of an hundred and thirty feet, and surmounted at its summit by a lofty statue of the distinguished man to whom it is erected, with no buildings or other objects near, which might have the effect to divert one's attention from it, it has the aspect of some mighty but solitary existence, standing in the calm repose of conscious majesty and strength, and surveying at leisure the splendid domain around him.

Passing on to the MALL, which is a wide and thickly-shaded avenue, leading from another gate of the Blenheim domain, called the Kensington Gate, and turning to the right and passing through the vast iron doors of the Eastern Gateway, I found myself within the walls of this splendid palatial monument, erected by a nation's munificence in honor of the public services of one of her distinguished sons. Blenheim is not only a palace, but a great repository of the works of art; and on entering within it I almost forgot the vast extent and strength of the building and the genius displayed in its construction, in the contemplation of the sculptures, statuary, and paintings which adorn it within. I will not undertake to give an account of the various rooms which are politely opened to the visitor, any further than to say they are adorned on every side with works from the hands of the most distinguished masters;—painting on the ceiling by Thornhill; bronze statues by Benzi; busts and statues by Rysbrach;—paintings, which require no interpreter to explain their merit, by Hudson, Holbein, Reynolds, Rubens, Vandyck, Raphael, Carlo Dolce, Kneller, Teniers, Rembrandt, Titian, and others. In different places I have seen excellent paintings from some or all of these masters; but in the various attributes of invention, arrangement, coloring, and whatever else constitutes the excellence of a painting, I think some of the best of their works are to be found at Blenheim. The first and second State Drawing Rooms are hung, in part, with beautiful tapestries, representing some of the successful battles and sieges which were conducted under the lead of Marlborough;—among others the battle of Dunnewert on the Danube, in Bavaria, which was fought July 3d, 1704, the battle of Lisle, which was fought Dec. 9th, 1708, and the siege of Lisle, which took place in the same year. I was surprised to find in this palace, erected as it was without any specific view to literary or scientific objects, a very valuable library, consisting of seventeen thousand volumes. The Library Room, an hundred and eighty-three feet in length, occupies the entire south-west front of the palace, and favorably impresses the visitor by its size, proportions, and numerous and rich decorations. In this room there is a white marble statue of Queen Anne, highly finished, by Rysbrach. She is represented in her coronation robes, and on the pedestal is the following inscription:—

TO THE MEMORY OF QUEEN ANNE!
UNDER WHOSE AUSPICES
JOHN DUKE OF MARLBOROUGH
CONQUERED,
AND TO WHOSE MUNIFICENCE
HE AND HIS POSTERITY
WITH GRATITUDE
OWE THE POSSESSION OF BLENHEIM.
A.D. MDCCXXVI.

England is to me classic ground. It is not only the place of the residence of my ancestors, and thus endeared by a series of associations which are strong and peculiar, but almost every spot which a stranger visits has some close and interesting connection with history and literature. In this vicinity, for instance, was the residence of Chaucer; here is the scene of one of the popular novels of Scott; here are the memorials of a man who fills, with one or two exceptions, the most conspicuous place in English history; and here within these very domains, its site marked by two large sycamore-trees, was once an ancient palace which had its attractions in its day and was the frequent resort of royalty; of which, however, there are at present no remains. It was within the walls of this ancient royal residence, that the princess Elizabeth, afterwards Elizabeth, Queen of England, was confined as a prisoner by her sister, Queen Mary. During her imprisonment here, the room assigned her was once on fire, (whether by design or otherwise is not known,) and her life was endangered by it. With that high and impassioned spirit of which she afterwards gave evidence, she felt her imprisonment very keenly; and one day when she saw a milkmaid passing by her window and singing in the gaiety of her humble heart, the tears rolled down the cheek of the princess, and the wish escaped her lips—a wish expressed by many others in high stations—that a condition in life equally happy and equally humble had been her own. She composed, while immured here, a number of verses, written with charcoal on the window-shutter of her prison-room, which have been preserved,—beginning as follows:—

> "Oh, fortune! How thy restless wavering state
> Hath fraught with cares my troubled wit."

Here also—a place not uninteresting to those who wish to know the history and resources of guilty passion—is Rosamond's spring or well, the supposed place of Rosamond's bower, and of the secret labyrinth which connected the bower and the old palace; the "*fair* Rosamond," well known in tradition and song, who was so wrongfully loved and sought by Henry Second.

About three miles distant from the palace of Blenheim, but on the lands of the Duke of Marlborough, a small quadrangular Roman villa has lately been discovered. Like many ancient towns and cities, it had been covered up and hidden for centuries in the earth which had gathered around it, but has been brought to light within a few years. Time did not allow me to go and see it, but I learned that the foundations of an ancient building had been traced; that rooms and passages, ornamented with tesselated pavements, had been discovered,—also, baths, urns, and articles of earthenware. It is said, that numerous coins, some of them silver, have been excavated. The Romans evacuated Britain in the year 448; and the supposition, therefore, is, that the remains of this villa must be at least fourteen hundred years old.

I do not know that I have anything further to say of Oxford and its vicinity at present. What I have said is only an outline, a sketch; made partly to assist my own remembrances. My visit has been a pleasant and profitable one; though I cannot deny, that here and elsewhere I have found one drawback from that happiness which I might otherwise have experienced. It is that very many of the public works and monuments, and also many private works of art, have relation, in various ways, to a state of war, and to those sentiments of ambition and military glory which have connection with war. Bolingbroke, in speaking of Marlborough, says, "I honor his memory as the greatest general and as the greatest minister that our country, or perhaps any other, has produced." The inscription on the lofty column erected to his memory, which is said to have been written by Bolingbroke, speaks of his military achievements, "performed within a few years, as sufficient to adorn the annals of ages." Happy will be the day when it shall be understood that peace has its trophies;—that the whole system of war, which may be described as a system that arrays selfishness against selfishness, is based upon wrong principles and wrong feelings;—that the doctrines of the gospel, which have never had their full effect, contemplate the substitution of confidence for jealousy, of love for hatred, and the establishment of universal pacification and harmony.

(VIII.)

Visit to Dover in England, and to Calais in France—Remarks upon Dover—Shakspeare's Cliff—Explanations of emotions of beauty and sublimity—Historical associations connected with the English channel—Siege of Calais by Edward III.—Story of Eustace de Pierre.

LONDON, ENGLAND, NOV. 2, 1852.

After the date of my last letter, I came to London. Since then, for a practical purpose, I have made a short excursion to France, and returned here again. In this excursion I made a little stay at Dover and Calais.

The town of Dover is situated at the straits of the English channel. It derives its name from a Saxon word which means *declivity* or *steep place*, and which indicates, therefore, one of its striking natural features. Dover is interesting by its locality and its history. From this point, more frequently perhaps than from any other, the traveller to the continent starts on his tour of pleasure, of knowledge, or of mercantile speculation. From this point fleets and armies have set out on their destination of blood and conquest; and here, justified, as I suppose, by a necessity which would not exist if men were what God requires them to be, "the meteor-flag of England" still floats, but not as an emblem of pacification and confidence, amid the bayonets and cannon of her castle and numerous fortifications. The town is imbosomed in high hills, which are cultivated to the top; but which, on the side of the ocean, break down perpendicularly, and present, for many miles in length and hundreds of feet in height, their white chalky bosoms to the gaze of the mariner. One of these remarkable eminences, three hundred feet in height, is known as "Shakspeare's Cliff." Early in the morning, inspired by my recollection of what Shakspeare has said of it in the tragedy of Lear, I ascended to the summit of this cliff, and, approaching cautiously to its very edge, and looking down upon the beach and the wide-expanded ocean, I can bear testimony, in this instance at least, to the remarkable truth and power of his description.

The morning was dark and lowering, and heavy mists hung over the distant coasts of France. The ocean's wave broke angrily upon the shore, but I could scarcely hear its sound so high. Large ships were in sight, though diminished to the eye in the distance; the fishermen's boats, of which a number could be seen, were but small, moving specks upon the ocean. The sea-birds, small as I looked down upon them, floated lazily by; and I experienced at this great height the very sensation to which the great poet has alluded in the first lines of his description :—

> "How fearful
> And dizzy 'tis, to cast one's eye so low!
> The crows and choughs, that wing the midway air,
> Show scarce so gross as beetles. Half-way down
> Hangs one that gathers samphire,—dreadful trade!
> Methinks he seems no bigger than his head.
> The fishermen, that walk upon the beach,
> Appear like mice.
> I'll look no more,
> Lest my brain turn, and the deficient sight
> Topple down headlong,"

There was one feature in this scene as it was presented to my eyes, which Shakspeare has not described, and which I am at a loss to conjecture how he would have disposed of. While I was standing upon this giddy eminence, the railroad-cars for London came suddenly in sight; and with lightning speed, as if they had the power of sundering mountains, dashed through the tunnelled base of the vast cliff which bears his name. When will a moving rail-car with its iron steed take its place in the imagination and be embodied in the language of a Shakspeare?

The incidents which I have related naturally lead to another topic. When the feelings are excited in any considerable degree, it is difficult to analyze them, and to ascertain the laws by which they arise and by which they are regulated. What I experienced on this occasion, however, as it appeared both at the time and in my subsequent reflections, tended to confirm the opinions I had entertained, and to which I have referred in a former letter, in relation to the principles of the sublime and beautiful. Undoubtedly one of the elements of sublimity is great height; but it is also true, I think, (and this is the view which is taken in Burke's treatise on the subject,) that great depth, opened distinctly before us, is likewise calculated to excite sublime emotions. But to my mind it is clear also, that these emotions are not heightened by our being in a position where we suppose that there is some personal danger, and where the feeling of dread arises. It is true there is generally greater mental agitation, there is really at the moment more development and exercise of the mental susceptibilities; but it is a mixed state, and not exclusively and purely the experience of sublime emotions. Fear is a painful feeling; it is always based either upon a sense of wrong-doing or a conviction of comparative littleness and feebleness; and although it agitates the mind, and has great power, it is a power rather to convulse and to detract, than to harmonize and to add. But the experience of sublimity, when that experience exists in the highest degree, is always attended with tranquillity: the soul gives itself fully and peaceably to the influence of the sublime object; it discovers there truth and beauty, as well as power and magnitude; and receiving, therefore, the influence of the sublime object into itself without the mental diversions and hinderances occasioned by personal danger and fear, it becomes conscious of new elements of beauty and sublimity, hidden in its own nature, and expands and ascends—I think it may be said in something more than a metaphorical sense—into a higher sphere of existence. And therefore I think that angels (and all pure and holy beings, whatever may be their name) have a truer and deeper sense of the sublimity of things, than impure and wicked beings can possibly have; although the latter may probably have as clear a perception of height and depth, and other natural elements of greatness, as the former.

When standing upon the Dover Cliffs, and casting my eye abroad upon the English channel, I could not but remember how often these seas, destined under better auspices to float the navies of a peaceful commerce, have borne hostile fleets and armies, and have been red with blood. Upon these very waters have passed and repassed, again and again, the kingly invaders of France and England,—flushed with victory, or trembling with defeat. It was here, in part at least, and in combats disgraceful to humanity, and especially disgraceful to those who bear the Christian and Protestant name, that Van Tromp and De Ruyter, names baptized in English blood, gained their terrible celebrity. It was here at an earlier period that the Spanish Armada, vainly styled the Invincible, floated in strength and in terror, till, awakening the displeasure of a higher power, it was touched by the breath of the Almighty, and scattered by the ordinance of God.

The reminiscences of those sanguinary times and

wars, and of the jealousies and hatreds which characterized them, are to be found on both sides of the channel. Dover and other accessible places on the English coast are bristling with fortifications, and with the various appurtenances and implements of war; but not more so than the towns on the other side, both on the coast and in the near vicinity. If it would be folly for France to attempt the invasion of England, it would be equal folly for England to attempt to invade France, which, if my eye has not deceived me, has placed herself in a state of formidable preparation at every assailable point. As a general thing, I took but little pleasure in examining the numerous and massive fortifications to which I have referred, and which are in poor keeping with modern civilization and hopes; but I must confess my curiosity led me to make an exception in favor of the old walls of Calais, which are still in a great measure standing as they stood centuries ago. Walls and fortifications are added, but the old one, in its great strength, still exists; —Calais being an exposed point of France, and having been the theatre of many sieges and battles.

There is one incident in the history of this ancient city which was recalled to my mind during the short visit which I was enabled to make to it. The student of English history will perhaps recollect that the city of Calais was besieged in 1346 by Edward III. of England. It was for a long time obstinately defended by its inhabitants, until, having exhausted all their provisions, and being in the extremities of famine, their governor, John de Vienne, appeared upon the walls of the city, and offered to capitulate.

The King of England, incensed at their obstinate resistance, which had kept him eleven months before the city, sent one of his distinguished officers, Sir Walter Manny, to acquaint the governor that the only terms he would either propose or accept would be a surrender at discretion. The patriotic governor remonstrated, and, at the suggestion and advice of many, Edward at last consented to grant their lives to all the soldiers and citizens, on the condition that six of the principal inhabitants should come to him with the keys of the city, and with ropes about their necks. And there was no doubt on the minds of any, that their immediate death was to be made the expiation of the obstinate bravery which had been manifested in the siege.

As would naturally be expected, the proposition thus to give up six of their principal citizens to certain death in order to save their own lives plunged the people of Calais in the greatest distress, and they knew not what to do. In the agony of silence and tears which followed, a citizen of distinction and wealth, Eustace de Pierre, came forth before the multitude, and offered himself as one of the six who should thus devote their lives for the people. Animated by his example, another patriotic and distinguished citizen soon came forward, and then another and another, till the number was completed. With a generosity of which we have hardly an equal example in all history, these noble-minded men passed through the opened gates of Calais; and bare-headed and bare-footed, with ropes about their necks, came into the presence of the incensed and revengeful Edward. Everything indicated that they were soon to die. Tears, remonstrances, advice, had no effect upon the king; till at last his queen, whose virtuous and noble character is the theme of historians, seeing him about to commit an act disgraceful to himself and dishonorable to humanity, appeared before him in their behalf, and did not hesitate, with earnestness and on her knees, to supplicate their lives. It was thus that woman occupied the sphere of beneficence which Providence has assigned her. Love conquered vengeance. The king, yielding to affection what he had designed as the victim of his hatred, granted her request. And this noble princess, not satisfied with this, conducted the excellent citizens whom she had saved to her apartments, treated them with marks of kindness and distinction, and dismissed them with presents.

In connection with this subject I will mention one or two incidents further, which have some relation to it. I was walking alone in the streets of Calais, amusing and instructing myself with notices of its ancient streets and buildings, and also with the groups of men, women and children, with countenances, costumes and habits quite different in many respects from those to which I had been accustomed; and as I looked upon them, conversing, chattering, laughing, buying, selling, singing, weeping, each acting out his own dispositions in his own way, I found my own identity, if I may so express it, enlarging itself and mysteriously entering into a partnership with the common feeling. "It is good," I said to myself, "to see men and nations, if for no other reason, because it teaches us the lesson of a community of hearts, and that the distinctions of nationality do not and cannot destroy the wider bond of universal brotherhood." And as I stood thus talking with my own heart, a French gentleman came near me, obviously a man of intelligence, who understood English better than I did French, and who told me, in answer to my inquiries, that the public square of Calais, on one side of which I was then standing, was the place in which the people assembled, with grief and dismay, when the terrible *ultimatum* of Edward was announced to them. And, with the kindness and grace which I found everywhere in Frenchmen, he invited me, perceiving me to be a stranger, into the ancient town-hall of Calais, and showed me a large painting, (the name of the painter has escaped my memory, but the painting seemed to me to be a work of very considerable merit,) which had for its subject the touching transactions which I have mentioned. And I must confess it made a strong appeal to my feelings, when I saw before me, in figures as large as life, and on the very spot of their proffered martyrdom, the noble and self-sacrificing men who offered their lives for their country, bearing to the English tents the keys of the city, and with ropes about their necks, and followed by their distracted wives and children and the agitated multitude of the people. The memory of these transactions lives indelibly in the hearts of the people of Calais,—both a monument and a stimulant to great virtue.

This is one of those affecting incidents which give interest to history, and which show, amid the degradation and crimes of our race, that there is still something which imparts dignity to man.

In passing the channel from Dover, my eye rested for a long time upon the long line of chalky cliffs which terminate the coast of England; but the similarity of geological appearance in some places on the Calais side suggested the idea that France and England at some former period may have been united at this point, and subsequently rent asunder by the action of the ocean. Worthy of notice, and in the vicinity of Calais, (at least in its vicinity since the establishment of railroads,) are the cities of St.Omer and Lille;—St. Omer known for its seminaries, and Lille for its manufactories;—both strongly fortified, and both of them, especially Lille, memorable by their historical associations. In Lille, which has been in a remarkable degree the theatre of sieges and battles, is one of the strongest citadels in Europe, erected under the direction of the celebrated Vauban. The country in this part of France is low, level, and marshy. It appeared to me to be neither fertile nor well cultivated; at least as compared with the fertility and the cultivation which are often seen in England and in many parts of America. But I was told that I should find it different in the south of France.

(IX.)

ILLUSTRATIONS OF MENTAL ACTION.

LONDON, ENGLAND, NOV. 5, 1852.

In one of my former letters I referred to some mental experiences of which I was the subject during my passage across the Atlantic, which seemed to me to illustrate and confirm some general principles of mind. One of the questions of interest in mental philosophy is the inquiry,—Whether the mind is so constituted, that it is susceptible, by its own laws of action, of reviving entirely its past history,—however distant that history may be in time, or however indistinct its outline.

Lord Bacon has somewhere expressed the opinion very distinctly, that such is the fact; and that whatever has been a portion of man's mental history can never be absolutely lost, but remains forever in allegiance to and in connection with the mind, although it is not always a subject of immediate consciousness. And this, as is well known, was a favorite opinion of Coleridge; and I infer, from some passages in his writings, that it was an opinion also of President Edwards, as it has been undoubtedly, and is, of many others. My own mental history confirms this view, of which I will now give an illustration,—with which, however, I am obliged to connect a few prefatory details.

Many years since, in the earlier period of my life, news came to the village in which I resided, that one of our esteemed citizens, the captain of a merchant-vessel, was lost at sea. When the sad and unexpected news reached his wife, who loved him tenderly, she was entirely overcome, and died in a short time of a broken heart. Seeing in the street one day a little boy, who seemed lonely and sad, I learned that he was the child of the parents who had thus been taken away; and, feeling pity for him, I took him home, gave him my own name, and adopted him as a son. I allowed my affections to twine around him; and endeavored, with God's assistance, to be not only a friend but a father. When he became of fourteen or fifteen years of age, that instinct of the ocean which had led his father to be a sailor began to exhibit itself, and he expressed to me a wish to follow the same course of life. My recollection of the sorrowful fate of his parents, and (I may add) my desire to do my whole duty to him and for him, led me to refuse at the time my assent to his wishes,—qualified by the remark, however, that when he should reach his nineteenth year, if these views and wishes continued, I should probably feel it my duty to let him decide for himself. In the mean while I taught him daily, both in human knowledge, and in the principles of religion; and for some time he was a member of a college. Continually he grew in my affections; and had become, I may perhaps say, a part of my existence. When he reached the period of life which I have specified, I found that the same strong desire of a seafaring life existed; and the commander of a merchant-vessel from our own place, a man to whom he was related and of great excellence of character, offering to take a special interest in him, I consented, not without sorrow and misgiving, to his departure.

The vessel sailed from a port in Massachusetts. It was the unfavorable month of December. And on the fourth day of its departure it was overtaken by a most violent storm. Some of the vessels that sailed about the same time returned to port dismasted or otherwise injured; but, after some weeks of suspense, the news came that this vessel was lost. When I heard the intelligence, I was greatly affected; and, retiring to my private room, I re mained for some time alone, without being able to communicate it to others. My imagination placed before me those sufferings and that last cry of agony which I could neither share nor control. But while I was thus mourning alone, that sympathetic instinct which interprets the signs of calamity almost without knowing them spread a gloom over the family; and in a little time a knock was heard at my door, and the only sister of my shipwrecked son came in, whom I had also taken and adopted as a daughter. There were only two of them, and they loved each other with great affection. With a lip tremulous with emotion, she asked me if her brother was lost. I was obliged to answer, such was the nature of the intelligence, that I had no hope of seeing him again. We sat together, and wept bitterly.

Under those impulses of our nature which those understand who have lost beloved friends, I visited the place from which the vessel sailed. It was a melancholy satisfaction to me to tread the place which was marked by his last footsteps when he left the shore. I learned the course of the winds, the direction of the vessel, the probable distance at sea; and, ascertaining afterwards that a portion of the cargo had been found in a particular latitude, my own mind at last located, with some degree of precision, the scene of this heavy calamity. And there, in that definite spot of the ocean, which had become settled in my thoughts and imagination, I buried the orphan boy whom I had adopted and loved. Always afterwards when I thought of him, it was in that particular locality. Imagination, acting upon a few facts and probabilities, had selected a burial-place and erected a tomb in the depths of the sea, and had even adorned it with flowers, and affection accepted and sanctified the memorial; and after that there was no change. So painful was this event that I seldom alluded to it in conversation. Perhaps I may say that I never told my sorrow, because language has no expression for it. And yet I nourished it in my memory. Often, very often, has my heart alone gone down into the depths of the ocean, and held communion with that solitary and sea-beaten tomb.

When recently I sailed from New York in the Arctic, about to trust myself to the same uncertain ocean, it is strange to me that I did not think of this poor boy. But so it was. It was perhaps owing to the many trying thoughts and feelings which then crowded upon me. We had sailed more than a thousand miles, when he first recurred to my memory; and when the ship was passing in that region, and perhaps I may say over the very spot, where I had located his tomb. And in a moment, under these peculiar circumstances, my awakened memory placed him before me; distinct as life; not a trace in his form or features altered. There he stood, like one coming up from the midst of the waves. And to my quickened imagination, and to my agitated heart which converted a vision into reality, he threw his arms around my neck and said, "Father, you are come." Men may call such things an illusion, but they have a truth, a basis of reality, in them; and my heart felt its power. My emotions became uncontrollable. I was obliged to go to the little room assigned me in the ship; and there I shut myself up all the day; and this sad and dear image was with me all the time. It was not an ordinary form of remembrance, but a combined action of imagination and memory, and so vivid as to make the image it presented a virtual reality. My lost boy was before me. And all his early life was recalled, our walks and our conversations, and the home which he loved so much, and our happy hours, and his sister, and the other orphans I had taken and brought up with him. I wept continually, but I had no power and no disposition to remove him from my side.

But I find I cannot go on with this subject. The very recollection overcomes me. I will only add, in relation to the topic with which I began this letter,—the power of restoration which exists in the mind,—I am quite certain of one thing, that my own soul has not, in any proper and absolute sense of the term, lost anything which it ever knew; at least it has lost nothing *which it ever loved.* There are depths and lodging-places in it which may be hidden for a while; but which decay can never reach, which time can never alter, which seem to me to be beyond the explanations of atheism and materialism; and which—I would say it with humility but with confidence—are written over with the marks and signatures of a divine power, and are held in the keeping of immortality.

Unable, at the time to which I refer, to see or converse with any one, my feelings took the turn which they sometimes do when they are strongly moved, and embodied themselves in the following stanzas:—

LINES FROM THE OCEAN, ON A SON LOST AT SEA.

Boy of my earlier days and hopes! Once more,
Dear child of memory, of love, of tears!
I see thee, as I saw in days of yore,
As in thy young and in thy lovely years.

The same in youthful look, the same in form,
The same the gentle voice I used to hear,
Though many a year hath pass'd, and many a storm
Hath dash'd its foam around the cruel bier.

Deep in the stormy ocean's hidden cave,
Buried and lost to human care and sight,
What power hath interposed to rend thy grave?
What arm hath brought thee thus to light and life?

I weep:—the tears my aged cheek that stain,
The throbs once more that swell my aching breast,
Embody years of anxious thought and pain,
That wept and watch'd around that place of rest.

Oh, leave me not, my child! Or, if it be
That, coming thus, thou canst not longer stay,
Yet shall this kindly visit's mystery
Give rise to hopes that never can decay.

Dear, cherish'd image from thy stormy bed!
Child of my early woe and early joy!
'Tis thus at last the sea shall yield its dead,
And give again my loved, my buried boy.

(X.)

The river Thames—Bridges—The Thames Tunnel—The Tower and its curiosities—Algernon Sidney—Houses of Parliament—Churches—St. Paul's and its monuments—British Museum—Remarks.

LONDON, ENGLAND, NOV. 6, 1852.

THE week which closes to-day has been characterized by events which have great significancy,—the election of a President of the United States, upon which will be likely to turn the movements of a great nation; the assembling of the British Parliament, a body of men who hold in their hands the political control of a large portion of the human race; and the meeting of the Senate of France, assembled for the purpose of taking the initiative in the re-establishment of the French empire. These events take hold of the future, and have a connection with results which no human eye can foresee; but which may be left without misgiving or fear in the hands of that Great Being who forgets neither men nor nations.

I have not as yet attended the meetings of Parliament, because they have necessarily been occupied almost exclusively with the verification of the claims of the members, and the taking of the customary oaths. This I intend to do at an early opportunity. In the mean while I will take a little survey of London, which, although it does not stand alone and without competitors, yet seems to me to be *first* among the great centres of modern thought, enterprise, and civilization. And in speaking of London it is not well to forget that which is in reality its origin, and the source of its long-continued greatness and wealth; I mean the river Thames, whose history, like that of the Nile and the Euphrates, has become a part of the history of the human race. England is the great mother of free states and kingdoms; and at some future time, when her palaces and towers shall have crumbled, her children from distant parts of the world will stand upon the banks of the Thames, and exclaim, with filial homage, "It was here that a nation was born."

The Thames, if we regard the Isis as its principal

source, arises in the county of Gloucestershire; and, flowing through some of the best portions of England, is increased by various tributaries. Easy of access and central in its position in relation to the great channels of commerce, it becomes at London Bridge, and thence onward in its progress of sixty miles to the ocean, wide enough and deep enough to float the mercantile navies of nations. The immense amount of shipping collected together in the Thames is an indication, in addition to that furnished by its population of two millions, of the greatness and wealth of London; and that it is the centre of communications which extend to all parts of the world. The city presses the crowded banks of the river on both sides; and the Thames, which a century ago was crossed by one bridge only, is now spanned by seven; and most of them exhibit a high degree of architectural beauty. Southwark Bridge is of cast iron, laid upon stone piers. It has three arches; the centre arch having a span of two hundred and forty feet, and said to be the largest span of *curve* in the world. Near Hungerford Market is the Suspension Bridge, for foot-passengers only. The chains supporting it are carried over two large brick piers, erected on the bed of the river and nearly eighty feet in height; making, besides two smaller ones, a central span of nearly six hundred and eighty feet.

In connection with the bridges of London, it is very natural for one to speak of the Thames Tunnel, which is certainly one of the most extraordinary and stupendous works which have resulted from the invention and power of man. It was projected and carried through by Isambert Brunnel, a distinguished architect no longer living. The Thames Tunnel is a subterraneous road, twelve hundred feet in length, carried under the river Thames, and thus forming a communication in this remarkable manner between important parts of the city. As I passed through it, it was quite a new form of experience and association, when I called to mind that a vast river with its collected shipping was floating over my head.

The tunnel consists of a square mass of brick-work, thirty-seven feet in width by twenty-two in height, which contains within it two arched passages, each of them a little more than sixteen feet wide. The passage through which I went was well lighted with gas, and is approached at both ends by means of great circular shafts, into which there is a descent over convenient and handsome staircases. The effect, as one looks through the tunnel at either end, brilliantly lighted up in its whole length and so unique in its position and structure, is exceedingly impressive.

I employed a waterman of the Thames to take me in his boat from the London Bridge to the tunnel; and in going down the river, as we wound our way amid its various shipping, I passed in sight of and very near to that celebrated mass of buildings known as the Tower of London. The tower, which I had visited and examined a little before, is situated in the eastern part of the city, and was originally the fortified residence of the English monarchs.

I will say a few words here of this remarkable place. The Tower, in its whole extent, covers a surface of twelve acres, enclosed within a strong wall. Within the wall there is a lofty square building, called the White Tower. It is built upon rising ground, and is ninety-two feet in height, with walls seventeen feet in thickness. It was erected by William the Conqueror, and is the most ancient part of the Tower buildings; and for a long time it formed, of itself, the "Tower of London." Our boatman, as he rowed us by the side of these celebrated buildings, pointed out the water-gate, called the "Traitor's Gate," through which persons guilty or supposed to be guilty of high political offences are brought to the Tower. There is a square tower near the water-gate, called the "BLOODY TOWER," from the circumstance that it was the place of the murder of two infant princes by their uncle, Richard III. It was through the gateway of the Bloody Tower that I had previously passed, in order to examine what it is permitted visitors to see. One of the objects of special interest, because it throws light upon history and social progress, is the "Horse Armory." The principal apartment in its interior, a room of an hundred and fifty feet in length, is occupied by an imposing line of equestrian figures, representing distinguished persons of different periods, clothed in the iron armor of the ages in which they lived, from the period of Edward First to that of James Second. The view on entering this room is exceedingly imposing, and enables us to realize at once what we had often read before in history, but of which it was difficult to form an adequate conception. In reading the military history of nations a few centuries back, we are almost as much at a loss in understanding it, as we oftentimes are in reading that of the Greeks and Romans. But in the various armories of the Tower of London we have an explanation far better than we can obtain in books, in their general forms and in all their varieties, of the numerous instruments which the ingenuity of men has formed for purposes of defence or of mutual destruction; the bill and spear, the glaive, the battle-axe, the halberd, the pike, the helmet, the "twisted mail."

I was here shown the executioner's axe, and the block upon which the victims were struck, which still bears the marks of the sharp blows which fell alike, at different periods, upon the innocent and the guilty. This axe is said to be the one with which the unhappy Anne Boleyn and the Earl of Essex were executed. And if so, it was probably the axe which severed the head of Algernon Sidney,—a celebrated name, which is cherished with respect and sympathy in America. In that part of the White Tower called Elizabeth's Armory, is the apartment where Sir Walter Raleigh suffered his twelve years' imprisonment. Like Sidney, though perhaps less pure and inflexible in principle, he was one of the distinguished men of England; and, in consequence of the naval enterprises he projected, his name has become associated with American history. In this prison Raleigh wrote many of his works; particularly his History of the World. His wife, at her own earnest suggestion and entreaty, was permitted to share his imprisonment with him, and his youngest son was born in the Tower. But neither the affection of his wife, nor his great talents and distinguished public services, nor his learning, nor his advanced age, saved him from a violent death. When his final hour came, the executioner asked him which way he chose to place himself on the block. He replied, "If the heart be right, it is no matter which way the head lies."

I observed here the cloak on which General Wolfe died in the bloody but victorious battle which gave Quebec and the Canadas to England.

In the Tower are kept the REGALIA or crown jewels, which may be examined with pleasure, not only on account of their richness, but because they are reconcilable with ideas of kindness and peace; but as a general thing the Tower can only be regarded, both in what it has been and in what it now is, as a great historical monument of the art of war and of human bloodshed.

Higher up the Thames (for every thing seems to spring from this river as if it were a permanent source of life) are the new Houses of Parliament,—a magnificent pile of buildings, presenting a front on the river of nine hundred feet, enriched, perhaps too much so, with every thing which architectural art can furnish, in the shape of mouldings, tracery, carvings, and heraldic devices. The most striking external feature in this mighty range of buildings is the Victoria Tower, which, when completed, will be three hundred and forty feet in height.

Among the royal palaces in London, the first which naturally claims attention is that of St. James. It is its historical associations, however, and not its architecture, which seem to give it that place. It was built for the most part by Henry VIII.; and, for more than a century previous to the year 1837, was the city-residence of the royal family. Since that time the present Queen of England, who spends the greater part of her time at Windsor Castle, has occupied, when in London, the Buckingham Palace. Those who have visited the interior of St. James Palace speak of its numerous and well-arranged apartments as convenient and richly furnished; but the casual visitor who sees nothing but the outside will find but little to excite his admiration. Buckingham Palace is not far distant. It occupies a large space of ground, forming a quadrangle, with a front facing St. James Park, and another towards the private grounds. As compared with St. James, it not only occupies a position far better, but is really a beautiful and imposing edifice. The royal standard is now floating over it, which indicates that Victoria is here.

The toleration of religious opinion which exists in England has been favorable to the growth of the religious sentiment; at least we should naturally infer so, from the fact that there are said to be more than five hundred places of worship, of different denominations of Christians, in the city of London;—many of them small, it is true, and making no pretensions to magnificence, but still not inconsistent with true and high developments of religious feeling. There are some things worthy of a traveller's notice in St. Margaret's church; and not the least circumstance of interest about it is, that here Sir Walter Raleigh was buried on the day that he was executed. The church of St. Martin, in Trafalgar Square, is an imposing and beautiful building; and the same might be said of many other churches both in London and in other places; but by universal consent there is but one St. Paul's.

The length of St. Paul's church from east to west, within the walls, is five hundred feet; its total height from the ground four hundred and four feet. It was built under the direction of Sir Christopher Wren; and seems to have been designed not merely as a place of worship, for which one of very different dimensions might have answered; but, like Westminster Abbey, as a grand national monument to the illustrious dead of England. At least, if such were not Wren's original design, such has been the practical result; for if it became impossible to fill this vast space with living auditors brought within hearing-distance, the next best thing which could be done was to occupy large portions of it with the dead and their monuments. On entering the church, it is the monuments of the dead, the works of eminent artists, which first arrest the visitor's attention; and I was here painfully reminded, in this great temple of the Prince of peace, of the continued struggles and violences of war, as I read the names and saw the sad but proud memorials of Ponsonby, Riou, Duncan, Cornwallis, Nelson, Collingwood, Brock, Pakenham, and many others. I paused with different feelings at the name of Johnson, who has illustrated morals and literature in his writings; of Heber, a name dear to religion as well as to literature; and of Howard, the philanthropist. Howard is represented as wearing the Roman costume, and as trampling on fetters;—with a scroll in his left hand, inscribed with the words, "Plan for the improvement of Prisons and Hospitals."

There is a basso-relievo on the face of the pedestal of his statue, which represents the interior of a prison, where he appears in the act of distributing food and clothing.

I think there was no one of the public institutions which on the whole gave me more satisfaction, than the great national institution, the British Museum;—an institution which stands out to the notice of the world, not only on account of its valuable library of 300,000 volumes, its zoological collections and fossil remains, but for the remains of works of art,—some of them recently collected,—Roman, Grecian, Egyptian, Assyrian, which throw light upon the history of nations;—and some of which will probably be found important in illustrating the earlier parts of the scriptural records.

As we look upon these wonderful remains of antiquity, as they are thus collected together and arranged and preserved with great care in the British Museum, we obtain impressions of departed empires, distinct, vivid, mournful;—such as conform exceedingly well to the abstract statements of history, but which history alone could never give. Egypt, like life from the dead, starts up before us, bearing in her hands her tombs;—and we know her at once in her superstitions, in her domestic life, in her conceptive power, in her artistic skill, in the length and breadth of her rude but massive grandeur. And when it is said, in the Scriptures, that Moses was "learned in all the *wisdom* of the Egyptians," it is a satisfaction to know, from these varied and wonderful remains, that the sacred historian, in describing these Egyptians as a wise people, which implies the development, in various ways, of thought, feeling and skill, has uttered a precise historic truth, which scepticism will in vain attempt to discredit. And if the monuments themselves are a memorial of a truth, there may be something, and perhaps much more, remaining in the inscriptions which they bear. Who knows what further and various light may be disclosed from these sources, when the interpretation of the hieroglyphics so happily begun by Champollion shall become a completed and undoubted system?

I never doubted the Scriptures. I received my faith from the lips of my mother; but it was confirmed afterwards by thought and inquiry. To me, therefore, the Bible has been and now is a living reality. And still it has often seemed to me surprising, although it has never disturbed my belief, that the Bible so frequently indicates the existence of cities and nations (of the Assyrian empire, for instance) which could hardly be exceeded in wealth and numbers, in civilization and power; and yet that these cities and nations should have entirely passed away, with no memorials left behind. I have nevertheless had full confidence, that Providence in its mysterious methods of operation would ultimately settle all such suggestions and difficulties. And now on the banks of the Nile, the Tigris, and the Euphrates, the evidences of their greatness and splendor, long buried in the dust, have been brought to light,—evidences so transcending all our conceptions as to furnish another great miracle, if other miracles were wanting, in order to sustain man's faltering faith.

I feel bound to say, that some of the remains of Assyrian art—remains which are unlike those of Egypt, or any other people—exhibit a spirit of conception and a power of execution, which is unsurpassed, and in some respects, as it seems to me, unequalled, by those of any other nation. I have reference in this remark particularly to their massive grandeur, and that true spirit of the object, whatever the object is, which seems to increase and dilate itself, without losing its distinctive nature, in conformity with the vastness of the masses in which the artist has embodied it.

These works, as well as those of Egypt, throw light upon the Scriptures. It will be likely to occur to the reader of the Scriptures, for instance, that the *horn*, as an emblem of power, is often mentioned in the Old Testament. And one of the first things which attracts the notice of a stranger, on entering the Nineveh Gallery in the British Museum, is the sight of horns, issuing, upon a number of the Assyrian sculptures, from a human head, and twining around it so gracefully as to be an ornament as well as an emblem. The symbolic existences so often occurring in the books of Daniel and Ezekiel, and so different from any thing which is found in other writings,—lions with human heads and with wings, and the like,—are found among these remains; and it is quite possible, as it seems to me, that some of the very sculptures which are now seen in the British Museum and in the Louvre of Paris had been seen by, and had received the admiration of, these prophets themselves.

It is true we do not as yet understand to any

great extent the precise import of these remarkable symbols; but still the impression is left distinct and deep upon the mind of one who beholds them, that they really had a meaning, whatever it was, which was well understood by the people of those early times, and that their presence in the minds and in the writings of the prophets was wholly in harmony with the national mental culture and associations. And a remark similar to that which has been made in respect to the Egyptian remains will apply here. Perhaps it will be found that the numerous inscriptions on these remains, which are very distinct and some of which have been translated, will throw more light upon the scriptural narrative than the monuments themselves.

I began this letter with the intention of giving some idea of the city of London; but I find I must end, when I have hardly made a beginning; and I should probably be obliged to say much the same thing, if I had written much more. To speak of its streets and squares, its parks, its numerous monuments, its charitable institutions, its courts of justice, its commerce, and other things which would naturally present themselves, would require much more time and strength than I am able to claim at present.

(XI.)

The opening of Parliament—The Queen of England—Respect in which she is held—Queen's speech—Distinguished members of Parliament—Brougham, Macaulay, and Cobden—Rooms of the Peers and Commons.

LONDON, ENGLAND, NOV. 11, 1852.

THIS day the Queen of England went in state to the House of Lords, to open the session of Parliament with a speech from the throne. The procession was formed at Buckingham Palace, which is distant about three-fourths of a mile from the Houses of Parliament, and consisted in part of six carriages, all with one exception drawn by six horses, conveying the various members of the royal household; some of them persons of distinguished name and character. These were followed by the queen's marshal-men, footmen, and a party of the yeomen of the guard. Then came the state carriage, distinguished not only by its richness and peculiarity of form, but by its being drawn by eight cream-colored horses; conveying the queen and her husband, Prince Albert, and some other distinguished persons.

This is one of those occasions on which the people of England obtain a glimpse of their sovereign. It was interesting to me to witness their earnest and respectful curiosity; nor do I profess to have been personally exempt from this feeling; although it is mingled with other feelings of gratitude, homage, and affection in the heart of an Englishman, which a stranger from another land cannot be supposed to realize.

The present Queen of England is beloved by the people, it seemed to me, as the sovereign of no other people is loved. There have been female sovereigns who have been despised or hated; but it is not so with Queen Victoria. The affection for her is not merely a tribute to sovereignty, not merely official, but may properly be described as *personal;* and is general and sincere. And the explanation of it—at least the explanation in part, and in a considerable degree—is still more interesting than the fact itself. The people of England recognize in her the great truth, that there is nothing among men higher than humanity, when humanity is true to God and itself; and that the woman is greater than the queen. They honor their sovereign, therefore, not merely and not chiefly on account of the fact of her sovereignty, but because, in being a good wife and a good mother, and in thus setting a good example before the wives and mothers of England, she is true to virtue and to womanhood. It is no tinge of shame for vices published to the world, but the expression of just gratitude and pride for domestic and womanly excellencies universally known, which stands upon the face of an Englishman as he utters the name of his queen. This sentiment of veneration and love, existing so deeply, and so universally expressed, and having its foundation in a great degree in the reason I have given, is in my view one of the most affecting and striking testimonies to the value and power of moral goodness.

Standing in the multitude through which the queen proceeded to meet the assembled Parliament, I felt it truly a privilege to look upon this excellent woman, who, in being faithful to herself, has been true and faithful to her crown, and has established her sovereignty in a nation's heart.

It is hardly necessary to remark that the speech delivered to-day before the Commons and Lords was not prepared by the queen herself, but by the ministers of the crown, who are her constitutional advisers; and, as the ministers are supposed to be sustained by a majority of the Commons, the speech, in the theory of the Government, is the voice of the people itself, uttering its own wants in the ear of its own administrators. And the theory is practically carried out to a considerable extent; so that England, though moving slowly, on account of the great multiplicity of her interests, gradually adjusts herself, by a succession of reforms, to the altered circumstances of ignorance and knowledge, of want and supply, of time and providence; and thus, by keeping policy and humanity in alliance, escapes the terrible shock of revolutions. The speech of to-day confirms this remark, which is conciliatory and national in its spirit, and suggests a number of practical reforms.

Since writing the above, and since the date of this letter, I have attended the meetings of both Lords and Commons; and although I heard no debates of great interest, yet I had the opportunity of seeing a few of the men, Brougham, Sugden, Walpole, Lyndhurst, Hume, Palmerston, Lord John Russell, Disraeli, Gladstone, and some others who are understood to hold a high parliamentary position, and to hear some remarks from nearly all of them, uttered in a good spirit and with good sense. The presence of the British ministers, and the practice of putting questions to them, gives to the discussions here a more familiar and less formal aspect than might otherwise exist. Set and formal speeches, although there is no absolute exemption from them, are not very likely to be uttered, except on occasions which require and justify them.

In the course of the remarks which I have heard in the House of Commons, reference has been made to the United States; the "great Republic," as the queen was pleased to call us in her speech. The topic was the existing relations of England and America in the matter of the fisheries; and it was of course gratifying to an American to observe that everything which was said in relation to his own country was respectful and conciliatory.

Some reference having been made in the House of Lords to the various Law Reforms which are in progress, I was pleased to notice that they arrested the attention of Brougham, and called from him a few remarks. It was pleasing to hear the voice of this celebrated man, whose name has been so long associated with literature, with social and educational reforms, and with the great political movements of England; a justly great and celebrated name, although it was painfully obvious that age, which respects no name and no greatness, had subtracted something from his power.

In thus referring to the distinguished members of the English Parliament, I ought not to forget that among them, inferior to none and an ornament to the whole body, is Mr. Macaulay, the historian, who is returned from the city of Edinburgh. I have had no opportunity of hearing him speak; and therefore can express no opinion, except what I have been enabled to form from his published writings and speeches. It is obvious, however, from what he has written, and from his speeches on various occasions, that he is not only a man of great historical and political learning, but, what is essential in a leading member of Parliament, possesses a thorough command and mastery of that noble language which among the languages of modern times may justly be styled the language of liberty. He not only knows what it is proper and wise to say, but in what manner to say it, so that the most refined scholar, seeing the thought giving birth to the expression, and the expression fitting the thought, cannot read his speeches, even on ordinary political topics, without finding something which pleases a truly literary taste. Nor is he deficient, when occasion calls for it, in subtle logic and in keen sarcasm; and he knows also in what manner and at what times to inflict those ponderous blows of eloquent and impassioned declamation, of which we have illustrations in Edmund Burke.

Another prominent member of the present Parliament is Richard Cobden. I had the pleasure of spending an evening in the company of this truly excellent and distinguished man, and can thus aid my general impressions by means of a personal acquaintance, although a slight one. Mr. Cobden, without the advantages of what is termed a liberal education, has risen to his present position of eminence by his strength of intellect, high moral purpose, and untiring perseverance and labor. It is thought by some, that he does not at the present time exercise that influence to which he is entitled; but the principal reason of this seems to me to be one which is very creditable to him. And I mean, in saying this, that, being a man of a reflective turn of mind, he sees far and clearly into the spirit of a true and Christianized humanity, and, being true to himself, he is willing, even at the cost of personal popularity, to act up to the light which he has. And among other things implied in this general remark, he is decidedly opposed to a state of war, as being the great hinderance to increased and perfected civilization, and as the great source of the wrongs which grind the poor and suffering, and of the power which sustains the oppressor. And in accordance with these views and principles, he made a motion in the English Parliament on the 24th of June, 1851, and supported it by an able speech; a motion which is required by the spirit of Christianity, but which, unhappily, is without an example; as follows,—That an address be presented to her Majesty, praying that she will direct her Secretary of State for Foreign Affairs to enter into communication with the Government of France, *and endeavor to prevent in future that rivalry of warlike preparation in time of peace which has hitherto been the policy of the two governments, and to promote, if possible, a mutual reduction of armaments.*

This important motion he sustained in a speech, simple in its style, but replete with argument, sound sense, and enlightened philanthropy. It is true that he was not able at that time to accomplish his object, and the two great nations on the opposite sides of the English channel not only maintain but are increasing their armaments at important points. His remarks, however, were heard with attention; and every day's experience shows their wisdom. And it is to be hoped, availing himself of the high position in which Providence has placed him, that he will continue to press this great subject upon the attention of the English Government. His past history shows that he is not a man who is likely to be discouraged by the vast difficulties arising from national prejudices, and still less to be diverted from a purpose which he has honestly formed by the sneers or threats of interested individuals who cannot comprehend him.

The room or chamber in which the Peers assemble is large and well proportioned; ninety-seven feet in length, forty-five in height, and the same in width. At the south end of the chamber is the royal throne, rich with the emblazonry of the royal arms around, and surmounted by a superb Gothic canopy. The walls, the windows, the ceiling, are enriched by the devices of art, and almost gorgeous in their combined splendor. The room of the Commons is smaller in size, and less decorated; but seemed to me to be equally convenient, and perhaps more so, for the purposes of discussion and debate.

But it is the great voice of truth and liberty, which I doubt not will from time to time resound through these halls, carrying dismay to despotism, and hope and encouragement to the suffering and oppressed, which will give a lustre to them, in the eyes of all thinking and just men, greater than that which painting or sculpture can bestow.

(XII.)

Windsor Castle and its vicinity—Visit to some of its apartments—The Waterloo chamber and its portraits—The guard-chamber—Parks and the Long Walk—Windsor Forest—Runny Mede—Eton College—Gray's Ode.

LONDON, ENGLAND, NOV. 16, 1852.

I HAVE recently availed myself of a pleasant day to visit Windsor Castle, the residence of royalty, and, on many accounts, one of the most interesting places in the kingdom.

On the spot where the Castle of Windsor now stands, about twenty miles southwest from London, a fortress of considerable size was erected by William the Conqueror; which was subsequently enlarged by Henry the First. From the time of Henry, the fortress or castle, thus enlarged and improved by him, may be regarded, as it was in fact, one of the royal residences. And successive monarchs, Edward Third, Henry Eighth, Queen Elizabeth and Queen Anne, contributed much, with a view to render it the more suitable for this purpose, in erecting additional buildings and in adorning the grounds. George the Third made it his principal residence; as did also George the Fourth, who in the course of a few years expended more than a million sterling upon it. It is at the present time the principal and favorite residence of Queen Victoria.

I spent a day, and might easily and pleasantly have spent a longer time, in visiting this palace and its beautiful grounds. Entering by the Gothic porch adjoining King John's Tower, I was conducted, in company with a number of other persons, through the apartments, in the order in which they are usually shown to strangers:—the Queen's Audience Chamber, adorned with tapestry, representing Scripture subjects, and also with a few portraits—the Vandyck Room, so called from its containing twenty-two paintings by Vandyck, chiefly portraits of distinguished persons; among which the equestrian portrait of Charles First is regarded as possessing special value as a work of art—the Queen's State Drawing Room, also called the Zuccarelli Room, from the circumstance of its being adorned with nine paintings by Zuccarelli, an Italian painter, who once enjoyed a celebrity which does not appear to be awarded to him now—the State Ante-Room, chiefly remarkable for some exquisite specimens of carving by Gibbons, and historically for having been occupied by Charles First a short time previous to his execution.

The next room to which we were introduced is called the Waterloo Chamber; so named from the circumstance that it is hung almost exclusively with the portraits of the distinguished men who were connected, either in war or diplomatically, with the trying series of events which had their termination at Waterloo. This apartment, which is equally chaste and beautiful in its decorations, is quite large; being nearly an hundred feet in length. There are portraits in it, the most of them painted by Sir Thomas Lawrence, of Castlereagh, Humboldt, Canning, Hardenberg, Alexander of Russia, Capo d'Istrias, Nesselrode, Schwartzenberg, Picton, Platoff the leader of the Cossacks, Anglesea, Czernistcheff, Metternich, Wellington, and Blucher. I mention these names in particular and without hesitation, because no person can pretend to a knowledge of modern history without having some acquaintance with their political relations and acts or their military achievements.

We are apt, as every one knows, to form opinions from countenances, either from the outline or the expression, or from a combination of the two; and it is but justice to say, that the looks of these distinguished men, as they are given in these fine portraits, do not belie their personal history; and that in general they appear like men who are capable of great deeds. As he is represented in the portrait suspended in the Waterloo chamber, even Metternich, who has had an influence in European affairs second only to that of Talleyrand, has a countenance intellectual, open, frank, generous; so much so as to perplex very much my previous unfavorable impressions, and to lead me to suppose, that his anti-republican policy was dictated more by the exigencies of his situation than by his heart; and that under other circumstances he might have applied his great powers to the furtherance of liberty.

I will not detain you with this part of my visit here any further than to say, that the Guard-Chamber, which is also shown to visitors, seemed to be the special place of curiosities. Here are whole-length figures, in armor;—a bust of Nelson with a pedestal made from a mast of the Victory;—suspended banners, an elaborate shield made by Benvenuto Cellini, and among other things two small pieces of ordnance, captured by Lord Cornwallis. Perhaps it is unnecessary to add, that they were taken by him at Seringapatam, and not in his campaigns in America. And near the bust of Nelson, in singular juxtaposition, are two relics,—one allied to war, the other to poetry. One is a chair made from an elm-tree which grew on the field of Waterloo;—the other is a chair made from an oak-beam taken from the old haunted church of Alloway, which Burns has made so famous in his wonderful Tam O'Shanter.

After visiting these and other apartments, we ascended the great Round Tower;—a most remarkable stone structure, varying but little in its size from three hundred feet in circumference and the same in height. It answers the double purpose, or rather such were the objects to which it was formerly applied, of a fortress and a prison. The Earl of Surrey, who is favorably known among the early poetical writers of England, was at one time confined here as a prisoner; as also was John, King of France, and David Bruce, King of Scotland, who were defeated and taken prisoners by Edward Third. The prospect from the summit of this tower is extensive and beautiful in the highest degree. It is said that on a clear day no less than twelve counties of England can be seen from it. In the distance was pointed out to me the residence, still standing, of our own William Penn, and his descendants; and hardly any object could have brought up more interesting associations to my mind; and also the church whose churchyard with its sleeping inhabitants gave rise to the inimitable Elegy of the poet Gray. Nearer, and almost directly below us, amid groves and lawns, the Thames flowed by in majestic beauty; crowned with villages and country-seats, and Eton College with its spires and "antique towers," which Gray also, who was the poet of these regions, has given to a lasting fame.

After visiting St. George's Chapel, where sleep the remains of Henry VIII., and which is adorned by a painting of the Lord's Supper by West, I spent some hours, in the closing part of a bright and delightful day, in excursions through the walks and parks in the vicinity of the palace. I have seen nothing which exceeds the noble avenue, three miles in length, called the Long Walk. It is perfectly straight; and has a road in the centre for carriages, with footpaths on each side, and is shaded by a double row of aged elms of great size. This splendid walk may be said to terminate at a place called Snow Hill, an abrupt pile of woods and granite, surmounted by an equestrian statue of George Third. As I paused here and looked back upon the vast expanse around and beneath me, magnificent with forests or rich with cultivation, with the walls and towers of Windsor Castle in the centre and the floating banner of England bright with the setting sun, I felt a new sentiment of beauty and grandeur opening at my heart, with gratitude to that great Being who hath made all things beautiful in their season, and with feelings of respect and affection for the land of my ancestors.

Somewhere in one of these parks—the Home Park, I believe—there is an old withered oak, surrounded with palings, which is said to be the identical oak to which Shakspeare has alluded in a striking passage in the Merry Wives of Windsor.

> "There is an old tale goes, that Herne the hunter,
> Sometime a keeper here in *Windsor Forest*
> Doth all the winter time, at still midnight,
> Walk round about an oak, with great ragged horns,
> And there he blasts the tree, and takes the cattle,
> And makes milch-kine yield blood, and shakes a chain
> In a most hideous and dreadful manner."

A few miles beyond Snow Hill, but within the royal grounds and on the borders of the beautiful expanse of water called the Virginia Water, are large masses of granite, marble, and porphyry collected together, and so arranged as to give the appearance of the ruins of an ancient temple. These large masses, upon which I came suddenly and unexpectedly, were brought from Greece, and arranged so entirely in harmony with my previous conceptions of ancient ruins that the illusion was complete. It was difficult to believe that they were not the ruins of an edifice which had been erected in early times and had gone to decay on this very spot.

There is one place in this vicinity which I did not visit; but which, although there may be nothing in the form of paintings or architecture to recommend it, is so associated with the protection of human rights and liberty, that it has a permanent and memorable name. On the banks of the Thames, and within four miles of Windsor, is that Runny Mede which holds so conspicuous a place in the civil and political history of England; where the Barons and people of England compelled King John to assent to the principles of Magna Charta. And it was on an island near by in the river, that the Great Charter, which stands as the basis of English liberty, was actually signed by that unhappy monarch. I know that England had a charter and liberties before; but it was at that time and at that place, and under the memorable circumstances of that occasion, that they received an enlargement, a definiteness, and a sanction which had never previously existed; so that in all succeeding times, both in England and America, what was signed at Runny Mede has been referred to as one of the true voices of humanity, one of the great proclamations of freedom.

There was another place, which I saw from the Round Tower but did not visit,—Eton College, which for scores of years has been associated in my heart and memory with the beautiful poetry of Gray. Until I came to England I did not know, or rather did not distinctly appreciate, the wide and powerful influence which the literature of England had exerted in my mental training. And the reason perhaps in part was, because in America I knew it in its effects only; but here I see it in its source. I ever felt that Gray was a true poet. He possesses an element of power, which embodies itself from time to time in gorgeous conceptions and in forms of language that dilate and agitate the mind; but his most striking characteristic is his perfection of taste, formed upon the Roman models, and which frequently reminds one of the exquisite terms of expression and combinations of expression which are found in the Augustan writers. And as I stood in sight of the groves where he had walked, of the college where he was educated, of his "silver-winding" Thames, and of the distant churchyard which inspired his unequalled Elegy, I felt anew, how the genius of literature has the power to consecrate nature and to perpetuate existence.

As I have thus diverted your attention from the objects around me to the subject of English poetry, I must make my defence, and at the same time close my letter, by a few lines from the Ode on Eton College:—

"Ye distant spires, ye antique towers,
  That crown the watery glade
Where grateful Science still adores
  Her Henry's holy shade;
And ye that from the stately brow
Of Windsor's heights the expanse below
Of grove, of lawn, of mead survey;—
  Whose turf, whose shade, whose flowers among
  Wanders the hoary Thames along
His silver-winding way!

"Ah, happy hills! ah, pleasing shade!
  Ah, fields beloved in vain!
Where once my careless childhood stray'd,
  A stranger yet to pain:
I feel the gales that from ye blow
A momentary bliss bestow
As, waving fresh their gladsome wing,
  My weary soul they seem to soothe,
  And, redolent of joy and youth,
To breathe a second spring."

(XIII.)

Funeral of the Duke of Wellington—His early military career—Remarks on war—His personal character—Funeral procession—Stanzas composed on this occasion.

LONDON, ENGLAND, NOV. 18, 1852.

TO-DAY I saw the Duke of Wellington carried to his tomb. My position was in the Strand, fronting the termination of a wide street opposite, in full view of the procession and of assembled thousands of the people. Amid the marching of troops, with the sound of cannon and of martial instruments, and with the attendance of the distinguished personages of England and of other countries, the remains of this great man, the pride and boast of England, were borne to their final resting-place. On all the streets through which the procession was to pass on its way to St. Paul's church, vast masses were collected, influenced by the mixed motive of witnessing the pageantry of the procession, and of manifesting their real interest in the memory of the dead.

Wellington began his military career at an early period of life in the East Indies; and at Ahmednugger, Assaye, Argaum, and other places in those distant regions, the scenes of sad and equivocal bloodshed even in the view of his own countrymen, he established a reputation for bravery and skill which caused him to be selected as a leader in those fierce European wars which originated in the ambitious purposes and attempts of Napoleon. Taking in the year 1809 his position in Portugal, which then seemed to be the last foothold of liberty, he drew that sword which flashed in so many battlefields from Vimiera and Talavera to Waterloo. His heart and his arm grew stronger in these later contests; and he showed himself a greater man than he had done in India, because he felt he had more truth and justice in his cause, and because his position more fully harmonized with the innate elements of his character.

He fought; but not without understanding and lamenting the miseries of war. After the battle of Waterloo he shed bitter tears, and made the remark, that even such a victory was no compensation to him personally for the death of his friends, whatever relations it might have in other respects. In regard to civil wars in particular, he once made the decisive declaration, which shows that in his case the spirit of war had not quelled or overruled the spirit of humanity, that such was his sense of the horrors of civil war, if he could be the means of preventing even one month of civil contest in his own country, he would sacrifice his life in order to do it.

I have no sympathy with wars. Indeed, I might express myself more strongly. I believe them to be opposed to the spirit and the letter of the gospel. Wars have thrown back civilization, humanity, religion. It is a great doctrine of the Scriptures, that they "who take the sword shall perish by the sword;" and it is a great truth of history, written in fire and blood, that, though liberty has sometimes been won by the sword, the same sword has destroyed it. And still my feelings on this subject do not, I trust, deprive me of the power of estimating men who think and act differently, and of making the proper and just distinctions among them. I should think unworthily of myself, and discredit the idea of all true mental guidance, if I were left, for instance, to the folly of confounding such a man as Washington with other military men, who have fought as bravely, but without principle and without humanity. I am willing, therefore, in view of the vast pageant which has just passed before me, to give my opinion of the man whom it was designed to honor, without ceasing to regret the necessity, or rather the supposed necessity, which organizes armies, and which associates fame with blood.

There are men who have combined greatness of intellect with restriction and narrowness of the heart;—there are men who are historically great without being morally great; but the Duke of Wellington was a great man in no limited sense of the term. In the first place, he possessed great intellectual powers. And I mean, in saying so, that he was quick in perception, and also in comparison and combination, together with that capacity of taking a large and comprehensive view of things which renders the other qualities available on great occasions. I am aware the remark is often made, that great generalship does not necessarily imply great talents; and I am willing to admit that generals of subordinate rank, by means of the fiery courage and devotedness with which they executed the duties assigned them, have sometimes become famous with but little originative or administrative power. But it seems to me very clear that no man can hold, as Wellington did, the position of chief of an army, and successfully plan and carry on a series of campaigns on a large scale, without possessing consummate ability. And the general impression in relation to eminent military commanders, the Alexanders and Hannibals, the Cæsars and Marlboroughs, of history, seems to be, that they were men of great intellectual power, whatever may be thought or said of the justice of their wars, or of the rectitude of their morals.

But there are various kinds of greatness. And I am willing to admit, that a man may be a great general who is not possessed of great virtues; as might be inferred from the history of some of those to whom reference has just been made. War itself is felt by most persons, even by those who do not condemn it in all cases, to partake of the nature of an immorality. Humanity practises it, without responding to it as the right and benevolent adjustment of things. It is out of harmony with the order of the universe; at least with that order which the universe is struggling to realize; and hence it is, that a bad man, a very bad man, will fight well, and in that sense will make a good soldier; and many men, placed in the highest military position, have skilfully conducted great campaigns, who have had but little of the sentiment of justice, and still less of benevolence.

But Wellington was not only a great captain, in the sense of possessing great military capacity: he was also a just and benevolent man. I can favorably appreciate his energy of character and his great capacities of thought; but I am far more affected by what I believe to have been his quick and high sense of justice and his real benevolence. When he laid down his sword at Waterloo,—a sword which he had wielded not without perplexity and sorrow,—he allowed the sympathetic and benevolent element of his character to take its true position, and to retain it during the remainder of his life. And being placed, either by office or by his great personal influence, at the head of the civil and political administration of England, and holding as it were for more than thirty years both war and peace in his hand, he took, in every instance of rising passion and of threatening discord, the side of forbearance, of adjustment, and of peace. Perhaps he felt that one who had been connected with wars so long, and had known so much of their horrors, owed more than other men to the principles and claims of pacification. As a republican, therefore, and as one sincerely attached to pacific sentiments, I feel it no discredit to say that my heart was deeply affected, in common with the multitudes of Englishmen around me, when I saw the lifeless body of Wellington carried to its grave.

I am confident that the great tribute paid to his memory (and it was really great,—perhaps more so in some of its aspects than history has ever recorded) was not more a tribute to his capacities and victories in war than to his acknowledged virtues. One of his marked traits of character was his simplicity; and I mean, by that, his forgetfulness of self and his singleness of purpose. It was so natural and easy for him to do what he considered it his duty to do, that his thoughts did not revert to himself, as if he had done something worthy of notice and applause, even if he had done it more thoroughly and better than other men. There is nothing which so much commands the admiration of men as this trait of character, when it is combined with great capacity. If Wellington had not been such a man as I have described him to be,—if he had been an immoral man, if he had been a mere fighting-man, a man of blood without the sentiments of justice and benevolence,—in a word, had his history recorded his achievements without the noble record of his character,—the honors which have been paid to his memory to-day could not have been awarded him. It marks the progress of civilization and of religious sentiment, that success in war alone, without acts and attributes that appeal to other and higher parts of our nature, can no longer give permanent fame. So much as this, if I have viewed things aright, is gained to humanity and truth. And, if the progress of opinion continues to advance as it has done, the question will be asked at a time not far distant,—not who is first in war and in the conquests of nations, but who is first in peace and in the establishment of national fraternity.

The funeral-car which bore the body of Wellington to its destined resting-place by the side of Nelson was preceded by large detachments of infantry, artillery, and cavalry,—by carriages containing deputations from public bodies,—by the dignitaries of England, barons, earls, viscounts, and bishops,—by the ministers of England and members of the Houses of Parliament,—and by distinguished men, who came as the representatives of foreign countries to pay their homage to his memory. The eyes of the multitude, attracted for a moment by the splendor of the troops, rested fixedly and with tears upon the car and the coffin which it bore. The history of a long generation, filled with bloody or with mighty acts, seemed to be resting there; and the body which had moved among them and given them form and life was passing to its final home. The funeral-car, itself a magnificent object, was drawn by twelve large black horses, three abreast, adorned with velvet housings, on which the arms of the deceased were richly embroidered; and, waving with each movement of their proud necks their lofty black plumes, they seemed to be conscious, as they struck their hoofs slowly and in harmony to the earth, of the grandeur and solemnity of the hour. The horse of Wellington occupied a place alone in the procession; but the rider was not there.

The movement of the immense cortège, as if borne down and repressed by the weight of memory and of sorrow, was slow and measured. Arms were reversed; drums were muffled; and the tolling of bells and the sound of distant cannon mingled with the wailing voice of countless instruments. And all sadly harmonized not only with the voice of sorrow in the million of mourning hearts, but with that voice of mysterious destiny which says, "Dust thou art; to dust thou shalt return."

I can give you no further particulars at present. The stanzas which are added originated on this occasion, and may help to convey to you some of the thoughts and emotions which filled my mind:—

With grief and tears, unknown before,
  And slow and melancholy tread,
And trumpet's wail and cannon's roar,
The vast and mourning people bore
  The dust of England's dead.

And ah, what memories mark that day!
  What thoughts of battles fought and won!
As thus they came, in long array,
At Nelson's earlier tomb to lay
  The lifeless Wellington.

They sleep. To them the battle's cry
  Has hush'd its voice on land and wave;
And thus, in silence as they lie,
They teach us that the great shall die,
  The victor has his grave.

And Thou, to whom our thoughts arise
  As round their kindred tombs we bend,
Oh, grant, great Ruler of the skies,
At whose command the warrior dies,
  That war itself may end.

(XIV.)

Palace of Hampton Court—Built by Cardinal Wolsey, and presented by him to Henry VIII.—Paintings—The gigantic porter of Kenilworth—The original Cartoons of Raphael—Remarks upon these paintings—Visit to Richmond Hill—Grave of Thomson.

LONDON, ENGLAND, NOV. 22, 1852.

THERE is an old poem, the authorship of which is unknown to me, which reads in a certain place as follows :—

" Let any wight—if such a wight there be—
To whom thy lofty towers unknown remain,
Direct his steps, *fair Hampton Court,* to thee,
And view thy splendid halls."

In accordance with the advice thus given, and desirous of seeing objects of interest which I shall never have another opportunity to see, I recently went in company with others to this celebrated place,—celebrated for what it is in itself, celebrated for what it contains, and perhaps not less so for being closely associated with the names of Wolsey, Henry VIII., Charles II., Oliver Cromwell; and I know not how many others.

The royal palace of Hampton Court, beautifully located on the north bank of the Thames, about twelve miles from London, was built originally by Cardinal Wolsey, who possessed great power and influence in the time of Henry VIII., and whose name the poetry of Shakspeare, still more than his personal achievements or merits, has made familiar to all. It was originally of great extent and magnificence; so much so that it caused considerable dissatisfaction and even envy in the mind of Henry VIII., who saw himself excelled in splendor by one who held the place of a subject. Wolsey, rather than encounter the effects of this dissatisfaction, and making a virtue of necessity, gave this magnificent palace to the king. Large and splendid under the expense and labors of the cardinal, it was further greatly enlarged and enriched by the king himself. Since that time parts of the old palace have been taken down and replaced by later structures. But it is still an imposing pile of buildings, well worthy the attention of visitors.

The clear, silvery Thames flows by in beauty; the walks and gardens are laid out with taste and elegance; there are flowers and fountains and green terraces and shady trees, all attracting and delightful in their place and season: for nature, having life in herself, changes, but never dies. But when I entered the palace itself, and passed through the long succession of rooms the names of which indicated that it had been the residence of monarchs, I felt a sense of loneliness and desolation, as if I were treading among the memorials of buried ages and of departed greatness. Indeed, were it not for the numerous paintings and tapestries which have been collected together here as in one vast repository, it might be said that nothing remained but the walls themselves. There are no banquetings now, such as are described by Cavendish. No lord-cardinal, "booted and spurred," comes suddenly in among the revelling guests. Henry and Cromwell, at whose voice the mighty fabric trembled, have become dust and ashes;—and the tread of royalty has departed, to return no more.

I gazed, nevertheless, upon the paintings on the

walls; and, passing rapidly by many works which failed to attract me, either from a want of genius and skill in the authors, or from the want of a proper light to see them in, I paused at others with the feelings of admiration to which they are entitled. And when I say that among them are to be found the works of Giulio Romano, Kneller, West, Rembrandt, Rubens, Titian, Vandyck, Holbein, and other artists of great merit, I feel justified in adding, that, if the living are not here to inspire admiration by their personal presence, the feeling is at least inspired by the dead who live upon canvas,—either by the character of the subject or by the skill of the artist.

I will mention here an incident, which was unexpected, but not without some interest. In the historical romance of Kenilworth, which holds, if not the first, at least no second place among the writings of Walter Scott, the author has introduced with great effect the gigantic porter of Queen Elizabeth, and with such gifts of size and proportions as to seem almost an exaggeration. But I have no doubt that he sketched his picture from a prototype which actually existed. On entering the Guard Chamber of Hampton Court, one of the objects which first attracted my notice was a full-length portrait of this porter. The painting is by Frederick Zuccaro; and is dated 1580. It is from life, and is seven feet six inches in height.

There was one object at the palace of Hampton Court, which took so much of my attention and interest as to leave but a small share for objects which, under other circumstances, would have well deserved them. I mean the original Cartoons of Raphael. It is true I had seen well-executed copies of them at Oxford; but this did not take away my desire to see the originals. The Cartoons are said to have been executed in the year 1515 or '16. These paintings, which were designed in the first instance as merely the original sketches or patterns from which the weavers of Arras were to prepare a series of tapestries for Leo X., are upon a thick paper, sometimes called a card or pasteboard paper; and hence the name of *Cartoons* which has been given them. Before the tapestries were completed, Leo was assassinated, and the weavers, being unpaid, retained in their possession the cartoon-patterns,—which actually remained neglected and almost forgotten in a cellar in Arras one hundred years. Three of them were by some means lost. The others were finally obtained by Rubens for Charles I., whose object was, like that of Leo, to have tapestries woven from them; and thus, after various vicissitudes, in which they were once saved by Oliver Cromwell, they have at last found a resting-place in Hampton Court.

The Cartoons were originally ten in number. The subjects of those which are lost were the stoning of St. Stephen, the conversion of St. Paul, and St. Paul in his dungeon at Philippi. The seven which remain are all of them to be seen here. The first, as they are arranged in the gallery which is called the Cartoon gallery, is the death of Ananias, Acts v. In size this painting is a little more than seventeen feet by eleven. In the midst of nine apostles, standing upon a raised platform, is seen St. Peter with his hand uplifted as if in the act of speaking. On the left, in the background, is Sapphira, the wife of Ananias, who is ignorant of what is taking place, paying some money with one hand, but withholding money in the other;—and St. John and another apostle occupy a position to the right of Peter, and are in the act of distributing alms. The position of Peter is a prominent one, because it is through him that the mighty power of God, which is manifested in opposition to cupidity and deception, may be said to be revealed. Nevertheless, the figure which chiefly arrests the attention of the beholder is the prostrate and lifeless Ananias. Such a picture of life struck into death, of vitality retaining its *form* but extinct in its *essence*, is nowhere else to be found. Every man's consciousness, who beholds this terrible scene, corresponds to the conception of the great painter; and he says instinctively, and without any hesitation,—so distinct is the mingled expression of astonishment and hopeless agony, and such the sudden and obvious helplessness of every prostrate limb,—that it was thus he fell and died; and a man struck in a moment, and by a secret and divine power, could not have fallen and died in any other way.

The next painting, as they are arranged in the Hampton Court gallery, is that of Elymas the Sorcerer, struck with blindness. In this painting there are seventeen figures. The Proconsul Sergius, who occupies a central position, is seen seated on a throne, with two lictors on his right hand,—his countenance filled with a mixed curiosity and astonishment at the effect which is produced by the words of the apostle.

On his right hand is St. Paul, his countenance and action full of that conscious rectitude and dignity which may properly characterize the prophet and messenger of God. But in this painting, as in that of Ananias and Sapphira, the figure which exercised and called into action in the highest degree the imaginative power of the painter, and which is central to the feelings of the spectator, is that of the wretched Elymas, with his hands extended, and groping about in his blindness and horror. So far as the conception of this sad and terrible figure is concerned, there can be no doubt that it should be ranked among the truest and greatest results of creative imagination.

There is a story told of Garrick in relation to this painting. Being in company with Benjamin West and some other persons, the conversation turned upon Elymas, as he is represented crouching and holding out his hands. Garrick, not having noticed, or not recollecting at the moment, any thing of the kind in real life, remarked that the attitude of Elymas seemed to him unnatural. West thought differently, and, desirous of vindicating a great painter, requested Garrick to shut his eyes and walk across the room. Garrick, who had no objection to experiments of that kind, closed his eyes; but he had no sooner begun to walk about, than he instinctively put out his hands, and assumed that crouching, cautious, and groping position which he had before criticized as unnatural.

The third of the Cartoons, as they are here arranged, is the healing of the lame man at the gate of the Temple called the "Beautiful;" which exhibits a high degree of inventive power, though it did not interest me so much as the others. The next is the Miraculous Draught of Fishes, of which we have an account in the fifth of Luke. The size of this painting is thirteen and a half feet in length by ten and a half in height. In looking at it, the attention is at once occupied with the two fishermen's boats, and the waters of the Lake of Galilee, under a clear bright sky, rippling gently around them. In one of these boats, in a central position, is the Saviour; finely conceived and represented, with a countenance full of benevolence and dignity. He is seated, and in the act of speaking to Peter, who is on his knees before him and is represented with a countenance expressive of humility and awe. Behind Peter, in the same boat, is a young man. On his left is the other boat, in which is one man steering it, and two other men, finely drawn, in the act of taking up the net laden with fishes. The net is heavy, and the drawing is such as to indicate the muscular effort of the men in taking it up. The fishes are very natural. But one of the most striking features in this painting is the three tall black cranes, standing in the edge of the water, with their short wings, long necks, and open bills. They have a singularly strange and wild appearance, but perfectly natural, and giving to the whole scene an aspect of reality which it might not otherwise have had. I think there is no one of Raphael's paintings which has left upon my mind a deeper impression than this.

The subject of the fifth Cartoon is Paul and Barnabas at Lystra, as recorded in the fourth of Acts. The part of this painting in which Raphael puts forth the strength of that conceptive power which enabled him to place nature upon canvas, and to enchant the belief of the spectator into the midst of a reality actually passing before him, is the uplifted arm and axe of the sacrificer, and the upturned head of the helpless ox, held in its position to receive the terrible blow. The sad and abhorrent feeling of the spectator is almost equal to that of St. Paul, although it may be in part from a different cause.

The subject of the next painting is Paul preaching at Athens. There is in this painting, as there is in the others, a centre of interest to the spectator; as there was a central thought or idea in the mind of the painter.

All these paintings illustrate what seems to me to be one of the happiest expressions of the theory of beauty, namely, *unity in variety*. It is true, that a complete analysis of the beautiful cannot be supposed to be involved in these few expressions; but they enunciate a great truth, and probably furnish the best basis of speculation on this difficult subject. The idea of unity, considered in relation to any work of art, or in relation to any other work, is that of a *central thought*;—central, when the term is used in the highest sense, both in its motive and its results;—embracing both the beginning and the end, and thus having a oneness in itself. The true name of such a comprehensive yet centralized conception is UNITY. And when this is accompanied by variety,—that is to say, by subordinate objects or acts, different from each other and from the main object or act in form or place or in other numerously varied ways, and yet harmonizing with such unity, namely, the unity of the main purpose and the main result,—we have then the leading and indispensable elements of the sublime and beautiful.

Unity is necessary to the mind's repose,—to its true satisfaction with itself and its works. Variety is necessary to meet the wants of its active nature. The instincts of a great mind feel this and act accordingly. To act without a central view, and to fail to harmonize variety with centralization, would be to act in discordance with its own nature and to nullify itself. No great work of art, no painting, no sculpture, no great work of science, no great oration in the senate, no great forensic argument, no related and consecutive series of moral acts, ever did or ever can fulfil the true conditions of the sublime and beautiful (without which such work or such series of acts cannot be called *great* in the highest sense of that term) unless it is found to conform to this view.

Such are the Cartoons. Such are the works of Raphael.

The leading or central object in the Cartoon of Paul preaching at Athens is St. Paul himself,—announcing for the first time in Athens the great truths of religion, standing elevated above the multitude around him, with arms extended, in the attitude of addressing them,—and with his countenance and whole person inspired by the greatness and solemnity of the occasion. Behind him and around him are wise men and the pretenders to wisdom, the Sophists and philosophers, the Platonist, the Cynic, the Epicurean;—some disputing among themselves, and others listening with expressions of doubt and of inward inquiry and reflection to the new and strange doctrine which the great orator of Christianity is propounding to them.

The auditors, taught in the schools of Athens, are men of thought, and are finely drawn. Among them is one who appears to be wholly occupied in deep reflection. His eyes are closed; and the drapery is drawn closely around him. It is of this figure that Sir Joshua Reynolds made the remark that he appeared to think from head to foot.

The subject of the seventh of these paintings is the charge to St. Peter:—"Feed my sheep." The most striking figure in this Cartoon is that of Christ; but, though noble in its conception and execution, there is less which corresponds to our ideas of the Saviour, less of divinity in it, than is found in the countenance of the Saviour as he is represented in the painting of the Miraculous Draught of Fishes.

I am free to confess that paintings—even those which come from the hands of great masters—are in many respects so far short of nature, or are so far short of what a creative imagination might be supposed to originate in harmony with nature, that in general they do not fully satisfy me. But there are exceptions. I have no drawbacks of this kind in viewing the paintings of Raphael. They produce upon the mind the same effect which we feel in reading the sublimest poems of Milton and Shakspeare; dilating and occupying it to its utmost capacity;—so that we seem to feel ourselves in the presence of some superior and mighty intelligence, who makes to us a new revelation, and thus extends the boundaries of our own existence.

I returned from Hampton Court by the way of Richmond,—a pleasant town, about four miles from Hampton. The town is partly built on the side of a ridge, the summit of which overlooks the valley of the Thames for a long distance. This is the "Richmond Hill," which Thomson has celebrated in his delightful poem of The Seasons, and which, in allusion to the beautiful scenery of Italy, travellers have denominated the "Tivoli of England." It is a place of great resort; and certainly it presents a view which in extent and beauty can scarcely be surpassed. The old Saxon name of Richmond was *Shene*, which signifies brightness or splendor, in allusion probably to the great beauty of the place; and this is the name which Thomson employs in the beginning of the passage to which I have referred:—

"Say, shall we wind
Along the stream? or walk the sounding mead?
Or court the forest glade? or wander wild
Among the waving harvest? or ascend,
While radiant summer opens all its pride,
Thy hill, delightful Shene?"

The remains of Thomson are buried at Richmond. I sought his grave. With a melancholy satisfaction I stood beside the ashes of one whose writings in distant America had been the delight of my father's fireside, and had left the impress of their beauty on our young hearts. I called to mind that touching stanza of Collins, which I had read and repeated many times without supposing I should ever realize its solemn beauty on the very spot to which he refers:—

"In yonder grave a Druid lies,
  Where slowly winds the stealing wave;
The year's best sweets shall duteous rise
  To deck its poet's sylvan grave."

And I will venture to add another exquisite stanza from the same ode, in which one great poet has paid his homage to another :—

"Remembrance oft shall haunt the shore
  When Thames in summer wreaths is dress'd,
And oft suspend the dashing oar
  To bid his gentle spirit rest."

(XV.)

Visit to Bunhill Fields and Westminster Abbey—Character of the men buried in the Fields—Dr. Thomas Goodwin—Dr. John Owen—Watts and Bunyan—Westminster Abbey—Its tombs and monuments—The tablet of Milton—Reflections—Poetry.

LONDON, ENGLAND, NOV. 1852.

THERE is a place in London called Bunhill Fields. It is the burying-place of the Dissenters. I went one day to this place in company with the excellent friend who had accompanied me to Windsor and to Hampton Court, Rev. Mr. Thompson, of New York, whom I had known in America but had unexpectedly met in London. Much of the interest which I experienced at this time, and at other times and places, is due to him.

Bunhill Fields is a large open space some five or six acres in extent, and surrounded with a brick wall. In this old burying-ground are interred a large number of the leading Congregationalists, Baptists, Presbyterians, and other Dissenters, of England. It is not a place which one would be likely to visit on account of any remarkable displays of monumental art. It has its attractions, however, for men of puritanic beliefs and associations; and many Americans go to Bunhill Fields.

We went from tomb to tomb. The inscriptions which they bear indicate the general character of the men. They were men of strong religious faith; —believers in the Bible and in Jesus Christ; who understood and felt the nothingness of man, and therefore sought help from God; and, though differing from each other in some speculative opinions, yet all agreeing in this,—that religion, while it manifests itself in outward forms, is essentially an inward life, which is born of God's Holy Spirit. It was from the life which once shone in this now mouldering dust that much of that American and Puritan spirit sprang up which crossed oceans, defied stormy winters, levelled forests, planted school-houses and churches, and laid the strong foundations of religious and republican liberty. It may well be supposed, therefore, that the place was not wanting in great interest for me, however it might be deficient in the attractions of art.

There was something in the names which I read upon the stones that reminded me of home. Here are buried the Allens, Andersons, Bradfords, Browns, Abbots, Clarks, Haywards, Lawrences, Parkers, Palmers, Goodwins, Robinsons, and others; whose names, borne by descendants or relatives, are so well known and so often met with in the northern parts of America.

Many eminent men of the Dissenters are buried

here. This is the last earthly resting-place of Dr. Thomas Goodwin,—a learned preacher and writer of the Dissenters in the time of Cromwell. He was educated at the University of Cambridge; and such was the estimation in which he was held for his learning and other qualities, that he was selected by the Parliament of England, in the time of the English Commonwealth, to be President of Magdalen College in Oxford. Here also are deposited the remains of Dr. John Owen, another distinguished man of the same class of religionists and living nearly at the same period. He was educated at Oxford,—a man of great learning, of eminent capacity, and who has always been regarded as one of the most distinguished of the illustrators and defenders of the Independent or Congregational views. This class of men are entitled to great credit for the position they took and for their labors and trials in support of the great principles of religious toleration and freedom. Here is the tomb of Dr. Isaac Watts,—a name that is much respected among all denominations of Christians. He was for fifty years the minister of a Dissenting congregation in London. Bunyan, the justly-celebrated author of Pilgrim's Progress, lies here.

In recalling this visit to Bunhill Fields, I am reminded of Westminster Abbey. I will briefly speak, therefore, as I may have no better opportunity, of Westminster Abbey now.

While in London, I went repeatedly to this memorable pile of buildings. It is near the banks of the Thames,—at a little distance from the Parliament-House of England. It arises in great majesty and beauty, adorned with pinnacles and towers, and with the power to arrest and control the attention of the beholder, notwithstanding the defacements it has suffered from the lapse of successive centuries.

I went through its chapels, cloisters, arches; I trod upon the places where the ashes of the dead repose, and beheld the sculpture of their tombs and monuments; and here, too, as well as in the burying-ground of the Puritans, catching something of the inspiration of the place and its histories, I left it with the impression that there are but few spots in the world which can originate sentiments at once so varied and profound.

Here are monuments and tombs which contain the dust and perpetuate the memory of kings and queens;—of the old Saxon king Sebert and of his queen Athelgoda, who died more than a thousand years ago;—of Edward First and Queen Eleanor his wife; of Edward the Confessor; of Edward Third and his Queen Philippa; of Henry Third; and of Richard Second and his queen.

Celebrated statesmen have been buried here, or are commemorated by monuments. Here is the dust of Hunsdon and Cecil,—names which are associated with the reign of Elizabeth. All that was mortal of William Pitt, of Canning, Grattan, and Wilberforce, lies within these walls. Here are monuments which commemorate the learning or statesmanship of Fox, Chatham, and Mansfield.

Nor does this great repository of the dead withhold the homage which is due to scientific genius and to literary attainment. Monumental tablets commemorate the genius and labor of Watt, the distinguished improver of the steam-engine; of Telford, the architect of the Menai bridge, and of Newton, whose name needs no specification.

Beneath this gorgeous roof is the dust of Samuel Johnson. The earthly remains of Denham, Cumberland, and Sheridan are here. Monuments and tablets are erected in commemoration of Goldsmith, Thomson, Gray, Mason, and Shakspeare. In that portion of this great architectural sepulchre which bears the name of the chapel of Henry Seventh, sleep the ashes of Addison. These great literary and moral teachers—these guides and suggesters, to some extent, of my own early thought—seemed to be restored to life and to be standing near me, as if I had seen the forms or heard the mysterious voices of another world.

I stopped at the tablet of Milton. It was not the result of the attraction arising from the memory of his poetical merit alone. A light often shines upon memory from the region of principles and beliefs. He stood before me not only as a poet, but as a teacher and leader in the justly-memorable period of the English Commonwealth. Standing as I did in this great monumental abode of kings and nobles, and impressed with all that respect for their history which the place cannot fail to suggest, I felt, nevertheless, that it would not be necessary for me to make any apology for Milton, because he was a republican, and because he became blind in his laborious defence of republican principles. Nor shall I stop to take any exception to what has been said of him and against him by the able men who differed from him in opinion. The world is made wiser by conflicts of thought. All words, all acts, all things, have their place and purpose in the arrangements and decrees of Providence; the true evolve themselves from the false; and all are destined to stand or fall in accordance with the changeless tests of immortality.

Some things belong to the past; some to the present; some to the future. The acts and words of Milton are prophetic,—the signs and intimations and precursors of the things which are to be hereafter; gathering strength as they approach the period of their fulfilment; thundering and flashing along the great abyss of ages; carrying terror to the heart of despotism; but full of hope to the men of the new order of things, to the generations of the humanitarian dynasty.

As I beheld these tombs and monuments, adorned by art and venerable by age, I stood overwhelmed and confounded. In the multitude of thoughts I was reminded of the difference between the thoughts and purposes of man and those of God. Man rears monuments to perpetuate man's fame; but God perpetuates man himself. The monument of man, wrought in stone and marble, is the continuance, the perpetuity, of a name. The monument of God is the continued life of the soul itself, with the development and increase of all its virtues; truth added to truth, purity added to purity, goodness added to goodness; the immortality of a spiritual existence crowned and blooming with the buds and flowers of holiness.

LINES WRITTEN ON VISITING WESTMINSTER ABBEY, NOV. 1852.

Pierced in its citadel of life,
The body, beautiful at first,
But conquer'd in the final strife,
Goes down and crumbles into dust;
And o'er that dust, with many tears,
Its monument Affection rears.

That monument itself, where art
Hath wrought with all its power and pride,
Grows sick with time, and loses heart,
And seeks the dust it sought to hide;
And that which gave the dust to fame
Is scatter'd, and bequeaths no name.

Though ruin thus smites where it can,
Its dart hath not the power to fly
Within the centre of the man,
And smite his immortality:
The victor in the outward strife,
It falls before the inner life.

The soul, triumphant in the war
Which smites both man and monument,
Smiling ascends,—to be the star
Which looks down from the firmament;—
Its own inscription there to write
In letters of eternal light.

(XVI.)

Visit to the Pantheon—Form an acquaintance with the old soldier Paulin—Visit to the seminary of St. Sulpitius—The Champ de Mars and the events connected with it—The Hotel of the Invalids—The tomb of Napoleon—Reflections in the Elysian Fields.

CITY OF PARIS, FRANCE, DEC. 2, 1852.

I MADE a short excursion from London to Paris in October, and have again visited it. I shall combine the impressions received then with those made since, and give them in one view. Paris, the great centre of wealth and population, is the London of France;

but it differs in this circumstance, that it is not London enveloped in smoke. On the contrary, it is something which can be easily seen, and of which some estimate can be formed at a single glance.

It was a clear, bright day in October when I ascended the lofty dome of the Pantheon, or rather of what was once the Pantheon, but now, by a very proper restoration of its ancient name, the church of St. Genevieve. The ascent is more than two hundred feet. There were others who went up with me; but I did not know them; and I stood and meditated alone. It was a new position; new to the eye and new to the heart.

As I cast my eye around and below me, to the objects near at hand and those in the distance,—on the island of the early Parisii which they beautifully called "the dwelling of the waters,"—on the winding Seine, the Seine more beautiful though less magnificent and mercantile than the Thames,—on the twin-towers of Nôtre-Dame, which have lifted their lofty heads for centuries,—on the colossal pile of the Hotel of the Invalids, where sleep the ashes of Napoleon,—on the Louvre, the Luxembourg, and the Tuileries, those ancient residences of kings,—on the "Champ de Mars," the place of military assemblages and of popular enthusiasm,—beholding everywhere, as far as the eye could reach, streets, squares, places of business, public gardens, ancient walls, hospitals, prisons, churches, schools of learning, monumental pillars, triumphal arches, in all varieties of architecture, in all degrees of newness and decay, bounded in one direction by the imposing summit of Montmartre, and in another by that wonderful city of the dead, the cemetery of Père La Chaise,—I felt, with these vast and multiplied objects before me, that I was looking down, not only upon one of the great combined works of art and nature, not only upon a mighty panorama of living and present existence, but upon a vast map of the past, inscribed and legible everywhere, with a thousand years of human history.

I came down thoughtfully. Such a scene addresses itself to the eyes of the inward mind still more strongly than to the sight of the outward senses. I crossed the bridge De la Concorde, and, passing near the great Egyptian obelisk, went to the Hôtel de la Terrasse, in the street Rivoli. Meurice's Hotel, which is a great resort of American travellers, was full.

Day after day I walked abroad. I had no letters of introduction, not being willing to occasion any unnecessary trouble to any one; and I knew not an individual in Paris,—not one in all the wide sea of existence that was floating around me. But there was no want of instruction,—no want of interest. The history of Paris was engraven on my memory; and at every step I found the records and evidences of its correctness. And besides, he who has the living eyes of the *heart*, even if he is without personal acquaintances and cannot even speak the language of the people, will still be able to recognize the features of humanity, and to find a brother in a strange land.

One day I was walking near the Bridge of Austerlitz. This bridge is a beautiful piece of architecture; but it is a memorial of bloodshed. Wishing to make some inquiries, I addressed in broken French an old man who happened to be near. He perceived that I was a stranger, and politely answered me in English, which gave me pleasure. I took the liberty to ask him who he was. He said his name was Paulin; that he lived in a narrow street not far from the Hôtel de Ville, and had been a soldier in the wars of the Emperor. He was poor; his wife worked out daily for her bread; and as for himself he did what he could, and, having learnt some English during the Emperor's wars, he was happy in being able sometimes to earn a little, no matter how small a sum, by acting as a servant or guide to gentlemen from England or America. He showed me a paper, speaking very highly of him, and signed by his commander when he left the army. The old man's looks, aided by his gray hairs and tottering step, plead earnestly in his favor; and we were not long in making a bargain. And I could not help thinking it was a singular coincidence, that a "peace man" from America (as those are called there whose convictions lead them to distrust and discredit the right and expediency of war) should be walking through the streets of Paris arm-in-arm with an old soldier of Napoleon.

The old man asked me where I wished to go. I told him I wished to find the church of St. Sulpitius and the seminary connected with it. He looked doubtfully, and said it was a place somewhat out of his knowledge; and wished to know if there was anything there which particularly attracted my attention. I replied I believed it was an interesting spot on some other accounts; but that I was particularly desirous of seeing it, because St. Sulpitius was associated with the early life and education of the good Fenelon. The old soldier's recollections and mine were a little out of harmony. He knew the Emperor; the names and persons of Ney, Soult, and Macdonald, were familiar to him; but, like too many of his countrymen, he either had not known or had forgotten Fenelon.

After a long walk, however, which was diversified with some interesting conversations, we were able to reach the place. I told my companion that I felt at home here; and that for half an hour or more I could excuse him from the trouble of attendance, and that he might employ himself in any manner he thought proper. I went into the church, and found people assembled there in the act of religious worship. I sat down, and allowed my feelings, in harmony with the place and its associations, to take the channel of religious recollection and sentiment. The seminary of St. Sulpitius, which seemed to have been rebuilt at a recent period, is near the church. At a little distance, in a circular niche of a square column ascending from the fountain of St. Sulpitius, there is an imposing statue of Fenelon. It was enough for me to know, in order to induce feelings of great interest, that it was here, in this interesting locality and among these walls dedicated to religion and science, that Fenelon had dwelt; that here the powers of his mind were unfolded and strengthened; and that it was a place which he ever held dear in his grateful recollections;—Fenelon, admired for his learning and eloquence, but who is still more dear to men and to nations for the inspirations of his expansive and benevolent love. Before leaving the spot I stood for some moments in contemplation of the noble statue which is erected to his memory, and felt my heart strengthened in those principles of union with God and man, and of universal philanthropy, which characterize his writings. Then, giving a signal to the old soldier, to whom my feelings seemed an entire mystery, and once more putting myself under his direction, I asked him to guide me to any objects of special interest in that part of the city. His countenance kindled up, and he proposed, obviously with a feeling of conscious pleasure, a visit to the Champ de Mars and the tomb of Napoleon.

The Champ de Mars, otherwise called the "Champ de Mai," is a large oblong space on the south side of the Seine, about one hundred rods in length by half that distance in width, surrounded by a ditch faced with stone. It is entered through gates at five different places, and is adorned by four rows of trees on each side, which give it a shady and pleasant appearance. The sloping embankments still remain which were erected by the population of Paris on the occasion of the grand assembly which was held here, under the auspices of La Fayette, on the fourteenth of July, 1790. On this occasion Louis XVI., in the presence, it is said, of more than a million of people, took an oath to observe the Constitution which had been recently adopted. It was here also that Napoleon, a short time previous to the battle of Waterloo, held an immense assembly, with a view to restore the confidence of France, and to gain strength for the new wars which were before him. The military school established by Louis XV. fronts the Champ de Mars at the southern extremity; and, with its dome, projecting portico, and sculptured pediment, constitutes a striking feature in the scene which is here presented to view.

Following the guidance of my old soldier, who, with a sort of professional instinct and with obvious high spirits, had put me upon the track of military associations, I next went to the Hotel of the Invalids, a vast establishment, founded by Louis XIV., but greatly enlarged from time to time, and at the present time covering with its numerous courts sixteen acres of ground. I do not know that the Christian and the philanthropist, who regard wars as among the greatest of wrongs and evils, ought to look upon such an institution as this with disapprobation,—the principal object of which, although it is true that war furnishes the occasion, is to relieve and not to increase human suffering. It ought to be no subject of regret that war has its humanities. As we went on, soldiers in military armor glittered around us. We passed a number of pieces of heavy artillery as we approached the gate of entrance; and everywhere, at the gate, and in the court and galleries, some seated on chairs and some walking, some with one arm remaining and others with one leg, with diversities of uniform but all apparently in good spirits and chattering excessively, were the old associates of my guide, the broken but indomitable remnants of the wars of the Emperor.—Too old to fight and too much mutilated to labor, they felt themselves happy in not being obliged to beg.

The Hotel of the Invalids, constructed with a view to the accommodation of a large number of soldiers, displays a front of six hundred and twelve feet: there are four refectories or dining-rooms for the occupants, each an hundred and fifty feet in length, and eight spacious dormitories, besides smaller ones, containing fifty beds each. The dome of the Invalids, which has a sort of historical celebrity, is spacious and lofty, and is seen at a great distance. Among the other accommodations pertaining to this remarkable establishment, it has a library of 1500 volumes, consisting chiefly of works of general literature, jurisprudence, and military strategy; and it is there, as might naturally be expected, that we find deposited many of the trophies which the French have taken from their enemies. In the time of Napoleon there were three thousand flags collected here, the memorials of war and of conquest, all of which were burnt by the French themselves on the evening previous to the entrance of the allied armies into Paris, March 31, 1814: so certain it is that war brings with it its own retribution.

In this building are the remains of Napoleon; the dust and ashes of the man who was for many years the idol of France and the terror of Europe. It is not surprising that visitors should constantly flock to see the splendid monument of a man of such wonderful power and of such strange vicissitudes;—at the age of twenty-eight the conqueror of Italy; at thirty the First Consul of France, and at thirty-five the Emperor of France; but in his purpose of conquering Europe driven back by the flames of Moscow, defeated at Waterloo, and finding death on the rock of St. Helena. The hoof of his war-horse trod in the blood of millions. History, estimating men by each other, will pronounce him a great warrior, without being unanimous as to his practical wisdom, his patriotism, or his morals. His glory was military, which fades in the distance, while the glory of virtue grows brighter and brighter. And the thought occurred to me as I stood beside his tomb that future and more peaceful generations might recall and cherish the name of Fenelon with greater interest than that of Napoleon.

As I returned from this place the sun was setting behind the distant hills. I passed through the majestic grove of the Elysian Fields. The autumnal leaves, gleaming in the departing radiance of day, fell around me. My heart went back to America. The sound of her rivers was in my ears. Her vast forests spread out before me. I remembered the vastness, the wildness, the repose, of nature. And I said to myself, "These works which I have seen in foreign lands, the efforts and the memorials of genius, are still the works of man. Imperfection marks their origin, decay completes their progress. Beauty and deformity, life and death, are mingled together. Man is here, but where is the Maker of man? I sigh for my native land. I wish to hear again the prayers and the hymns of her cottagers, inspired by the blessings around them. Her rivers are her lines of beauty;

her hills are her monuments; the mighty firmament is her cathedral; and God,—heard in the sighing of the winds, seen in the richness of the forests, and eternal in the reproduction of her wild and varied magnificence,—God is everywhere."

(XVII.)

Garden of the Tuileries—Of statuary and paintings as compared with living existences—Historical notices of the Tuileries—Triumphal arch and bronze horses—Hôtel de Ville and events connected with it—Margaret Porette and the Quietists—Visit to the home of Paulin.

CITY OF PARIS, FRANCE, DEC. 3, 1852.

UNDER the influence of that wandering propensity of which I gave you some of the results in my last letter, I went out early the next forenoon. You will recollect that it was in October; and it was again a beautiful day. I found Paulin waiting for me, leaning patiently against a post. The Hôtel de la Terrasse, at which I was stopping, is opposite the garden of the Tuileries. And after a little deliberation, in which it gave me pleasure to pay due deference to the suggestions of the old soldier, we concluded to take a stroll through its beautiful grounds.

The garden of the Tuileries was laid out by the celebrated Le Notre. I call him celebrated (and he undoubtedly has more claims to the title than some who have obtained it on the battle-field) because his name is so closely associated with the history of scientific gardening and with so many localities which his taste contributed to beautify.

I will not detain you in giving a description of this garden any further than to say that it is of immense size, a parallelogram of sixty-seven acres; and that there are in it abundance of beautiful flower-plats, beautiful fountains and statues, and beautiful trees and shady walks; although, if one were disposed to be critical, he might justly add, that the grounds are laid out in some places in a style of straight lines and angles which seem too artificial; and, still more decidedly, that some of the statues, although displaying artistic skill, lose their æsthetic power and value by calling into revolt the sentiments of modesty and morality. But I recollect that I sat down, with old Paulin by my side, near the brink of a beautiful fountain; and that I fed from my hand two queenly swans that floated proudly on its bosom; and, seeing over my head the nodding magnificence of the glorious lime-trees and chestnut-trees, with flowers of all varied and brilliant hues, (for there were many yet remaining,) I was disposed to enjoy the beautiful and to forget the deformed. In other words, I had no disposition for criticism. And especially because there is something to be seen here every pleasant day, far more interesting to me than anything I have mentioned; I mean happy groups of men, women, and children.

What a glorious creature is man!—at least when he stands erect in truth and simplicity of spirit. Statuary and painting can give the semblance, but not the reality. I look, for instance, upon a statue; and I admit with pleasure the truth of its likeness and the skill of the artist; but at the same time

I say, almost instinctively, that it is not a man; it is not a woman. It is something which satisfies the eye of the senses rather than the eye of the heart; —it is a thing which *is done* rather than a thing which *is;*—it has no inward history, no conceptions which reach forth into the infinite and eternal, no palpitations of beneficence, no heavenly filaments of love going out in every direction and encircling universal humanity. But a true man and a true woman is all this. It is the living, therefore, far more than their semblances in marble, which awaken the emotions of the soul. And whenever I see groups of men, women, and children, with the marks of truth and innocence sanctioning a true or a restored humanity, my heart goes out in the deepest sympathy with their innocent pleasures; and the sight of their happiness is the source of my own. These are the true ornaments of the garden of the Tuileries;—statues that have life, the works of God and not of Praxiteles;—flowers that bloom without fading because they live in perpetual succession.

At the eastern end of this garden is the Palace, —a magnificent pile of buildings, reaching from the Rue Rivoli to the Seine. It is called the Tuileries, or palace of the *tile-kiln*, from the circumstance that it is erected on the spot where a tile-kiln formerly stood. The mighty palatial edifices which are found everywhere in Europe fascinate the eye and call forth feelings of admiration; but it is necessary, and sometimes painful, to remember that they have required ages in their construction, and have taxed the wealth and labor, and perhaps the tears, of a nation. The erection of this edifice was begun by

Catherine de Medicis in 1564; the works were continued by Henry IV. and Louis XIII.; and it was not till nearly a century after its beginning that Louis XIV., in 1644; gave directions to have it finished. Built at different periods, it exhibits different styles of architecture, which elicit their just and appropriate degrees of admiration,—an evidence of what the lovers of art begin more fully to understand,—that beauty is infinite in its developments, though it may be contemplated and appreciated from different points of view in different periods of civilization.

Napoleon resided for some time in this palace; and it bears the impress of his active and inventive mind, as well as of those who preceded him. It was Napoleon who erected the triumphal arch which forms the principal entrance to the court and palace of the Tuileries on the eastern side. This beautiful arch is sixty feet wide and forty-five feet high, and is constructed after the plan of the arch of Septimius Severus at Rome. And those who claim to be judges regard it as equalling the beauty of the original. It has three passage-ways, the central one fourteen feet in width, and is adorned on both fronts with Corinthian columns, and with bas-reliefs representing the victories of the Emperor. The whole is surmounted in the centre by a triumphal car and four bronze horses, modelled after the celebrated horses of Lysippus, which ornament the Square of St. Mark in Venice. The originals were once here, but in the reverses of war have been carried back again. Repeatedly I found myself looking with deep interest at this picturesque group of horses. They are certainly executed with great skill. With their dark breasts, with their wild curving necks and uplifted hoofs, they seemed, on their lofty position, like mighty beings conscious of their strength and marching through the air.

In examining this part of the city, I called into requisition the recollections of the old soldier who accompanied me as a guide; and, besides other objects of interest, he pointed out a number of localities whose memorials had been written in blood. I do not know that it would be profitable particularly to repeat them. The Tuileries itself has been the theatre of revolutionary movements, which have affected at different times the destinies of France. And I was surprised to find, that it was at the west end of the garden of the Tuileries, at a little distance, in the place now called the Place de la Concorde, that Louis XVI. and his queen Antoinette were executed.

The story of the trial and execution of Louis XVI. and his queen, together with the trying incidents connected with their residence in the prison of the Temple, as related by Clery, forms one of the most deeply-interesting personal histories which are to be found in the records of the human race. I went through the splendid mansions of Versailles, where they had once resided amid scenes of magnificence which had never been surpassed; I visited the prison of the Temple, a part of which still remains, and saw the rooms of their humiliation and suffering, and the two trees, still standing, where the good king took his sad and solitary meals in the last days before he was led out to death; I went down into the gloomy cell of the Conciergerie prison where the queen was confined after being transferred from the Temple, the deep and dark place of her increased suffering and tears, of her prayers and religious hopes; and now stood upon the spot where both fell under the blow of the executioner. The whole world, enabled to contemplate these transactions in consequence of the high position of the sufferers,—the world in the utmost extent of its civilization sitting in judgment upon the judges,—pronounced the victims innocent and the nation criminal; and Providence, which judges all things,—that unerring Providence "which destroys with the sword those that take the sword,"—confirmed the decision.

I found my old soldier, in whom I had begun to take quite an interest, well acquainted with these localities. We wandered together through the Louvre, the Palais Royal, and along the banks of the Seine. He evidently was a man of a good deal of information and of a true heart; and, though he kept with me some eight or ten days, I never noticed any disturbance of his patience and equanimity except at this time. Happening to notice near the *Place du Carrousel* a book-stall containing many ancient books, I stopped to read. I found among them an English copy of Wesley's hymns,—those beautiful hymns which I have so often heard the good Methodists sing in America,—and read longer than usual. Meanwhile Paulin, as he was a little apt to do when he saw me take a book, wandered off a little distance. He came back, however, in due season, but very considerably excited, alleging that he had been insulted. I asked by whom and in what way. As to the person, he said he did not know and did not desire to know, but that in passing him the fellow had impertinently looked him in the face, and asked him, without preamble or reason, by what authority he wore his mustache,—a very unnecessary question, he said, to be put to an old soldier of the Empire. Such are the strange and almost ludicrous incidents which mingle in everywhere. I condoled with the old man, whose feelings were evidently hurt, and proposed to him to exchange the place of such discreditable encounters for the Hôtel de Ville.

The Hôtel de Ville, begun in 1533 and completed in 1606, is the place where the Prefect of the Department of the Seine resides, and is properly regarded, with its modern improvements, as one of the finest municipal buildings in Paris. It contains a number of large and elegant apartments, adorned with paintings and statues, besides the hundred and fifty smaller rooms occupied by the public offices which are necessary in the municipal transactions. The city library of 60,000 volumes, and occupying three large rooms, is here,—containing, among other works of interest, four thousand volumes of official American publications. The Hôtel de Ville is one of the historical places of France. It was to the Hôtel de Ville that Louis XVI., in the memorable epoch of 1789, was escorted by the agitated people, when, with a violence originating in fears and anxieties, which they at least supposed to be well founded, they compelled him to leave his beautiful Versailles. It was here, by means of committees and councils which have acquired a sanguinary celebrity, that many of the patriotic or bloody movements of the first Revolution were organized. It was here, in a room which is still shown, in the year 1794, that Robespierre fled and was wounded, previously to his trial and execution. It was here, in the year 1830, after the sanguinary encounters which resulted in the expulsion of Charles X., that Louis Philippe met and embraced Lafayette in the presence of the people, and initiated the Orleans dynasty. And here were the tumultuous scenes in the Revolution of 1848, which Lamartine has so eloquently described, and in which he personally had so large and honorable a share.

In front of the Hôtel de Ville is the place or square which is used often for festival and other public occasions, called the *Place de Greve.* In former times this was also the place of public executions; and there are few places which have been more frequently stained with human blood. And one transaction occurred here, which I am tempted particularly to recall. It was as far back as the year 1310. It was here, at that time, that a young woman of sincere piety and unblemished character was put to death as a heretic. Her name was Margaret Porette. She never thought of fame; but her name can never be forgotten. She belonged to that remarkable class of people (they will not allow themselves to be called a *sect,* because they are averse to the denominations and restrictions of party) called the Mystics and sometimes Quietists. The state of inward religious experience at which they aim, and which they profess to attain, is that of divine union, or union with God; in such a sense that the soul, having its evil passions subdued and cast out, is in the true *recipient state*, and has its thoughts, affections, and purposes from God alone. They believe also in an overruling Providence, which has the control of all things in a general sense, but which, in the case of those who are reunited to the Godhead, regulates in everything every movement and incident of their destiny. And this destiny, whether high or low, whether an allotment of tears or of joy, they accept with resignation and with smiles. Christ is their model, and the Sermon on the Mount their text-book. They hold to the doctrine of pure or perfect love—that is to say, of unselfish love—as the only true principle of life. They return good for evil; and suffer in silence. This class of persons is unknown to the world, because the world cannot comprehend it. They suffered or died in prison in the person of Molinos and Madame Guyon; they were banished in the person of Fenelon; but neither banishment, nor imprisonment, nor death, quenched the waters of life which flowed in their souls. They died, and history gave no record, because they made no resistance and gave no sign except this one:—"Father, forgive them, for they know not what they do." For holding these pure and exalted principles, Margaret Porette, in the bloom of life, was put to death. This is the place which heard her last prayer and was moistened with her virgin blood. Standing on the very spot more than five hundred years after, I found something in my heart which disposed me to cherish the memory of her piety and of her sorrowful but triumphant end.

With a heart thus filled with historical and religious recollections, I turned to Paulin. He reminded me that he resided in this part of the city. The shadows of evening began to gather around us. And he invited me urgently, and as much on his own account, he said, as mine, to take my evening meal with him. His invitation harmonized with my own feelings; and in fact I had previously given him to understand that I would not leave Paris without seeing him at his own home. He was the more urgent because he said his wife, of whom he spoke with affection and pride, would expect us. I followed the old soldier, whose tottering step seemed to acquire its ancient military precision and firmness as he led me through street after street, growing more and more winding and narrow and sunless, till I found myself in one of those places which nourish the principles of revolt and where the fires of revolution are ever burning. As we passed, one after another, the laborers and disbanded soldiers that dwelt in these gloomy precincts, they stood silent and stern. They have their mutual understandings, their watchwords and leaders; and Paulin, whom they all knew, introduced me to the man who seemed to be judge and leader among them. I shall not easily forget his slight but muscular frame, and his dark, searching eye, at first doubtful and hostile, but afterwards, when he had conversed with Paulin and understood that I was an American, softening into confidence and respect.

We passed from the narrow lane into a lofty and dark building, which must have been built centuries ago, and, after going through narrow and winding passages without light, we began to ascend. One flight of stairs succeeded another, originally strong but now worn and tremulous. The balustrades were gone; and their place was supplied by single ropes extended from the top to the bottom of each flight of stairs. Paulin went in advance and invisible; for only here and there, at considerable intervals, a little light broke through the thick walls which enclosed this old castle. But I heard the old man's voice, directing me to hold on by the rope,—a direction which was hardly necessary, as there seemed to be nothing else to which I could conveniently attach myself. When we had reached a landing-place somewhere in the fourth or fifth story, two little boys suddenly rushed out of a door, with a light, and holding a vessel in their hands with coals in it. I asked Paulin what was the meaning of this. He said there were forty families in this old building; and that the boys belonged in this part of it, and were trying to kindle a little fire to cook their supper with. I was glad to find that I was still within the precincts of human existence; when I heard again in the darkness the "memento" of the old man, not to mind the boys, but to hold on by the rope. We reached at last the final landing-place; and thrusting my head from a small open window near it, and looking down into a dark court below, where I could see no bottom, I had all my ideas confirmed of my singular and interesting position.

Paulin opened the door of his little room, and, with a grace which seems to be natural to a Frenchman, introduced me to his excellent wife. She was neatly and almost elegantly dressed. Fifty years had given her some gray hairs, but had not bowed her form nor dimmed the lustre of her eye. "This," said Paulin, "is our little room; and it is all the room we have." I was pleased to see that every thing in the room was neat and comfortable. The fire was kindled; the table was spread: we ate together; and I spent a pleasant hour in conversation with these poor and virtuous people. Poverty had not hardened their hearts; sorrow had not clouded their brow; age itself had not extinguished the truth and vivacity of humanity.

The wife of Paulin was grateful that I had come. I encouraged her to speak of her personal history. I learnt from her (what I had suspected from some remarks of her husband) that she was the daughter of a rich and titled family, and had been well educated. But, in those convulsions and reverses of which there have been such frequent exhibitions in Europe, she became an outcast from her early home and exceedingly poor. She accepted her allotment without murmuring, married a common soldier, and worked for her daily bread. She spoke of America with interest. She said she once had a sister who resided there, and, if she were young, would be disposed to go there herself. She lived now amid walls of darkness,—but without ceasing to love the open air and the blue heavens. "There are birds," she said, "in America:" and she would love to hear again the singing of birds, as in the days of her happy childhood. She had been the mother of children,—the most of whom had died. And when, in her broken English, which she aided in making intelligible by the eloquence of her countenance and manner, she spoke of her two little boys, both buds of promise bright and beautiful, and both dying nearly at the same time, the tear stood in her rich dark eye; and old Paulin, moved by this affecting remembrance, bowed down his white head.

I left these good people with feelings of respect and affection. They lighted me down through the dark passages which I had so much difficulty in ascending. I found my way towards the banks of the Seine. The clear sky was studded with stars, which threw their silver light on the trees of the garden of the Tuileries and the mirror of the beautiful water. Many reflections crowded upon my mind. And my heart ascended to that great Power, whose eye is in every place, that he would give freedom to the oppressed and comfort to the poor.

(XVIII.)

Unexpected meeting with American friends—Departure from Paris for Lyons—Voyage down the river Saone—The city of Lyons—The meeting of the Saone and the Rhone—Character of the French people.

LYONS, FRANCE, DEC. 9, 1852.

On the evening of the 7th of December I left Paris for Lyons, on my way to Sardinia. A number of incidents occurred on that day which have since been recalled to mind with much interest. In the course of the forenoon the door of my room opened, and I unexpectedly found myself in the company of one with whom I had formerly been much associated. We had lived in the same village, been members of the same church, and had labored on many occasions in the promotion of the same objects of Christian benevolence. To meet under such circumstances was to live again the life of memory. But time has its sad as well as its pleasant recollections. The hand of sorrow had been upon him. His young and beautiful wife had died. Her dust sleeps in America; but her name was recalled with sadness and affection in a foreign land.

Towards the evening of the same day I was visited by another person, a graduate of Bowdoin College, who had formerly sustained to me the relation of a pupil, but now, in the increased maturity of his powers and hopes, was pursuing his studies in the schools of Paris. With my recollections of his talents and energy of character, I was not surprised to find him here. He spoke of his Alma Mater with interest and affection, and of his country with a patriotic pride, which showed that the attractions of Europe had not perverted the spirit of liberty or weakened his attachment to his native land.

At this time my residence was at the Hotel of Meurice. It was after dark when I heard the sound of carriages in the court of the hotel. It was the signal for the departure of our little party,—consisting of Rev. Mr. Thompson, Mr. and Mrs. Walcott, and myself. The night was cloudy and dark; but the long, splendid streets of Paris were lighted up, and I gave a parting look to the illuminated expanse of the Place de la Concorde and of the Elysian Fields. We departed by the railway called the Paris and Lyons Railway, which will lead, when completed, by the most direct route, to the large and beautiful city of Lyons, in the South of France. With darkness over our heads and the thunder of our iron wheels under our feet, we passed rapidly through a portion of the heart of this great kingdom. The necessity of thus travelling by night, occasioned by some previous delays, deprived us of the pleasure of seeing Melun, Fontainebleau, Dijon, and some other interesting places. Early the next morning we reached Chalons on the Saone; called by the French *Chalons-sur-Saone,* to distinguish it, I suppose, from a town of some note on another river, Chalons-sur-Marne. Chalons, a town of twelve thousand inhabitants, is situated upon the banks of the river which gives it its distinctive name,—two hundred and fifty miles southeast from Paris. As the railroad was not completed farther than this place, we embarked on one of the steamboats of the Saone. The boat was peculiarly constructed, being long and narrow,—at least a hundred and fifty feet in length by fifteen in breadth. Five such steamers descend the Saone daily to Lyons. A heavy mist hung upon the waters. As the sun arose, which has its cheerful light for all lands, the mists gave way, and unveiled the face of nature in its aspects of beauty. The Saone reminded me of the rivers which were familiar to me in America. It is a large river,—apparently about the size of the

Connecticut above Hartford, or of the beautiful Kennebeck at Augusta, in Maine. At this time it was swollen by recent heavy rains to its utmost capacity, and rushed on with great violence. The smoke-pipe of the steamboat was lowered when we reached the numerous bridges; and even then the Saone ran so high that we passed under them with difficulty. With deep interest my eye rested upon the continually-changing scene of hills and valleys, cottages, gardens, forests, and vineyards. We passed a number of beautiful villages, besides the larger towns of Maçon, Thoissey, and Trevoux. In some low places the river had swollen over its banks and inundated the neighboring country; so that we had the appearance of sailing in the midst of a lake interspersed with islands.

The boat was filled with Frenchmen, Americans, and Englishmen. The Americans and English appeared happy. They bore the step and the look of freemen. The French, notwithstanding their natural vivacity, were sad and silent. They had just passed from the Republic to the Empire. Many of them had perhaps voted for the Empire, in consequence of what they considered the necessities of their position. They preferred the easy quiet which is secured by cannon and the bayonet, to the free thought and the forensic agitations of liberty. Undoubtedly liberty has its storms; but the storm has its health and its grandeur. In the days of the Cæsars there were no thunders in the Senate of Rome. And in France too the voice of her orators is silent,—that voice of reason and of mighty eloquence which gave inspiration to the thoughts and purposes of other nations. If the French should find that, in going back in the career of liberty, they have sullied their national honor in the eyes of the world, and especially in the eyes of those chained and bleeding communities which have looked to them for hope, they will not be likely to rest easy until they have readjusted their position.

Chalons is seventy-six miles from Lyons; and the distance was run in some five or six hours. As we approached the city, the swollen river became compressed between banks which are lofty and picturesque. Occupying a large space, and containing two hundred thousand inhabitants, the city of Lyons is beautifully situated on the point of land where the Saone and the Rhone unite, extending itself, however, over both banks of both rivers. The communication between different parts of the city is maintained by means of numerous substantial bridges, eight of which are thrown across the Rhone; and the Saone is spanned by a still greater number. Lyons is three hundred and twenty-six miles southeast from Paris.

We stopped about the middle of the day at a good hotel, which the French, with a harmless but characteristic amplification, have styled the Hotel of the Universe. It is near the large square called BELLECOUR, which the Lyonese, and apparently with a good deal of reason, assert to be one of the most beautiful squares in Europe. It is very spacious, is adorned with rows of lime-trees, and in the centre is an equestrian statue of Louis XIV. Walking out alone, and desirous of combining the aspects of nature with those of human art and labor, I went from the Square of Bellecour to the Rhone,—the Rhone memorable in history, the beautiful child of the Alps, but here swollen to a large river. Going upon one of the bridges which are thrown over this river, and looking down its channel, I saw, as I supposed, at the distance of about a mile, the place of its junction with the Saone. Feeling an interest to see the meeting of these rival waters, I walked in the direction of the place. The Rhone dashed along beautifully,—fresh from its native mountains, and curling its blue and noisy waters, as if laughing and singing in the fulness of its purity and happiness. I felt my heart grow warmer, and my step more firm and proud, as I walked by the side of this noble stream. As I reached an elevated position on the point of land where they meet, the Saone, swelled by the late inundation of rains, wheeled in from the right with mighty force, ploughing across and stopping the Rhone in a moment. After this freak of momentary power, its dark and turbid current resumed its original direction, and, taking her blue sister from the Alps by the hand, they went onward gaily to the ocean. And thus it generally happens, that beauty, though less strong and violent at first, conquers in the end. From this point onwards the two rivers are married into one; and the Saone, forgetting itself in the charms of its associate, takes the name of the free and bright daughter of the mountains.

On the very next day after reaching Lyons—the day of the date of this letter—we have already made our preparations, and are about to leave France for the Alps and Sardinia. And, in departing from this beautiful country, I am obliged to say that I have found some of my previous opinions in relation to the French modified; but modified in their favour. The French and English represent in modern times the Greeks and Romans of antiquity. If the English may be regarded as inheriting the wide intellectual grasp with the fixed and obstinate courage of the old Romans, the French seem to possess the inventive power, the refinement, the vivacity and enthusiasm, of the Greeks. In estimating the French character, it would be a mistake to set aside the women of France. It is well known that the French women have great influence in all the relations of life in France; and their influence is the natural result of the characteristics which are usually and justly ascribed to them. No one doubts the courage of a Frenchman; but it is not the quiet, calculating, indomitable courage of an Englishman. It is obvious, excitable, declamatory: he may be said to carry it upward and onward, in the sight of everybody, on the point of the bayonet. In the Frenchwoman, who is excluded by her sex and position in society from the battle-field, love takes the place of courage; and there is a similar outward development of it. It moves in her step; sparkles in her eye; is heard in the sweet intonations of her voice; lives in her unaffected but animated gesticulation. These interesting traits necessarily give the women of France power,—a power, however, which may be turned to evil as well as to good.

Under other and more favorable circumstances the French people would take a still higher stand than they have hitherto held. They need, in the first place, well-regulated liberty. I know that some persons maintain that the French are not capable of maintaining a republic. But I must confess that these well-meaning persons appear to me too easily frightened, besides doing no small injustice to the French people. Break from a poor prisoner's arms the chains which have bound them for twenty or thirty years; and it is but natural that he should leap from the ground, if he has strength to do it, and utter loud cries of joy, and in his ecstatic flourishes scandalize the sobriety or disturb the quiet position of his neighbor. But give him a little time, and it will be seen that the violent vibrations of early liberty will settle down into a just and peaceable movement. It will be the same with liberated nations.

And in order to the perfection of the Frenchman's character, it should be said, further, that he needs, in common with all men and all peoples, a deep religious sentiment,—such as would naturally spring from a more general and thorough study of the Bible and its great truths. I believe it is conceded on all hands, that there is no character more interesting, none more suited to the fulfilment of all public and private duties, than that of the Frenchman, when those interesting natural traits which he possesses are purified by the influences of religion. What nation, what people, would be likely to furnish missionaries and preachers of equal ardor and eloquence? I have heard their prayers in their little assemblies; I have listened to their burning aspirations for the good of man; and I cannot suppress the hope that this noble people will not only possess freedom and religion in their own land, but will yet have a prominent part in extending them to other nations.

(XIX.)

Savoy and its wild mountain-scenery—Rousseau—A night-scene—The limestone cliff—Hannibal and Napoleon—City of Chambery, the capital of Savoy—The Pass of Mount Cenis—Italy.

TURIN, KINGDOM OF SARDINIA, DEC. 13, 1852.

IN company with my much-valued travelling-companions, I came from France into Italy through the Savoyard Alps, and by the Pass of Mount Cenis. The day of our departure from Lyons was mild and pleasant, notwithstanding the lateness of the season. Taking the nearest route to Chambery, the principal town of Savoy, we passed through a portion of the French territory, which exhibited everywhere marks of fertility and good cultivation, besides being rich in variegated scenery. At this season of the year it would be difficult, and perhaps dangerous, to attempt to enter Italy by some of the other routes, filled as they are said to be with snows and exposed to avalanches. In journeying from Lyons to the village of Pont Beauvoisin, situated on a small river called the Guiers Vif, which separates France from Savoy, we were in full sight during a part of the day of Mont Blanc and other Alpine peaks, which reared their snow-covered and well-defined forms in the distance.

Savoy is now a part of the kingdom of Sardinia. And in the part of the village of Pont Beauvoisin which is on the Savoy or Sardinian side of the

Guiers Vif, is a custom-house, where our baggage was subjected to a slight examination.

Travellers sometimes complain of these things; but I must confess that they did not trouble me much. We found here men and women under a new and different government, speaking a language different from our own and inhabiting a soil never trodden by us before; but the instinctive interpretations of the heart, sacred as the source from which they spring, recognized the bonds of universal relationship; and I loved them without knowing them.

On leaving this village we found ourselves, in the course of a few miles, in the midst of the elevated and difficult mountain-passes called the gorge of La Chaille. The Guiers Vif, having its origin in the neighboring mountainous region of the Grand Chartreuse, dashes onward from precipice to precipice through this gorge. This region has been described in an eloquent passage of Rousseau. And certainly this is one of the sublime and eloquent places of nature. The road has been formed on the edge of the precipices which overhang the foaming stream beneath,—sometimes by blasting a passage through the solid rock, sometimes by terraces or embankments of solid masonry built up along the edge of these frightful abysses. The shades of evening closed upon us when we were passing through this remarkable region; but I saw and felt enough to enable me easily to imagine how these wild and terrific scenes must have operated upon the creative and vigorous mind of Rousseau.

We travelled the whole of that night. There was no light of the moon; but the stars shone clear and brightly. And, as we moved along with considerable rapidity and frequently changed our direction, they seemed to be dancing and playing in the green dark tops of the mountains. From time to time another light shone lower down on the mountainous declivities, and yet hundreds of feet above us. It was the light of the cottage on the rocks,—the star of the poor man's hearth, and of domestic relationships and love. On the other side of us and only a few feet distant were dark abysses. As I looked down, I could see nothing but darkness robed in mists. So near did we approach, that sometimes we seemed to be riding on the wings of a dark cloud; and from the depths invisible came up the troubled sound of foaming waters.

On the route to Chambery there is a little village called Les Echelles, which is situated also upon the mountain-river Guiers Vif. There is a valley here, through which the road leads; but the farther end of it is shut up by a vast limestone rock thrown directly across the way. It is eight hundred feet high. It reminded me of the rock which Livy describes as having stopped the passage of Hannibal for a time when entering Italy through the Alps; and which he was obliged to soften by heating it and then pouring vinegar upon it, and over which he made his way by cutting steps in difficult places when he had softened it in this manner. The road which we took winds part of the way up this massive pile of limestone, and then passes through an immense artificial tunnel in its centre, which is wide enough to admit two carriages abreast and is twenty-five feet high. It is about a thousand feet long.

The excavation of this tunnel, a gigantic conception indicative of the mind of its author, was commenced by Napoleon, but was finished by the King of Sardinia in 1817.

It was under these circumstances that I was reminded of the two great military leaders of ancient and modern times,—Hannibal and Napoleon. Hannibal passed over the rocks; Napoleon went through them. This was the difference between the two men. Hannibal ascended. He loved high places. His foot was on the top of the mountains. He was a soldier, but he had the soul of a republican. Napoleon, too proud or too powerful to go over them, shaped the mountains to his own model; and he treated men and institutions in the same way. Napoleon too was a soldier and a monarchist. The one modified and vitiated his principles by his inordinate love of his country. The other sacrificed his principles to his ambition. Both took the sword; and both fell by the sword. Hannibal, showing to his soldiers, from the peaks of the Alps, the plains of Italy, and overthrowing mighty armies at Thrasymene and Cannæ, carried his standards to the gates of Rome. But the tide of aggressive war, in its terrible revulsion, and by a law of reaction which never fails, rolled back again, and swept away his city and nation. Napoleon too, the conqueror not only of Italy but of Europe, carried the eagles of his legions to the gates of Moscow; but they had no power to go beyond that barrier of fire. The sea of proud and oppressive violence, rolling back, not only overwhelmed his nation, but dashed their ruined leader on the rocks of St. Helena. And this is the great lesson which history teaches. What is gained by the violence of the sword is lost again; but what is gained by truth and love *is gained forever*.

The night is favorable to reflection; and such thoughts passed through my mind as I travelled through the mountains of Savoy under the light of the stars. At midnight we arrived at Chambery. Through the region of that city and its neighborhood, I believe it is conceded on all sides, that Hannibal made his way into Italy. This is an old city of ten thousand inhabitants, and is the capital of Savoy. It is the birthplace of Xavier Le Maistre, the author of the Leper of Aost and other popular writings; and Rousseau, whose genius took its hue in part from the wild scenes of nature, resided for a long time in its vicinity. It is situated in the midst of mountains which rear their heads around it. It has its manufactures, its public library and college; but its objects of interest are not such as to detain the stranger in it for a long time.

After resting a short time, we continued our journey during the remainder of the night. The dawning light of the next day found us again in the midst of mountain-scenery and rapidly advancing towards the pass of Mount Cenis,—through which, as if through the gates of some great and lofty fortress, we were to descend into the plains of Italy. In reaching this mountain we passed through the town of Montmeillan, situated on the right bank of the river Isere. From the bridge which is thrown over the Isere there is a good view of Mont Blanc. At this place there was formerly a strong castle, which was taken and demolished by Louis XIV. Not far from Montmeillan the Isere is entered by a beautiful tributary, called the Arc. After reaching this tributary stream, which now offered itself as our guide, we continued our journey on its banks, and travelled for a long time through the extended valley which is formed by it. On each side the mountains rose to a great height,—their heads being covered with snow. In some places they presented an irregular and naked surface of rocks, in others were covered with earth and cultivated to a great height. Small cottages were seen on their sides, and sometimes on their summits:—a terrible position; but woman is there; the family is there; the gray hairs of the father and the beauty of the daughter. Frequently torrents, white with foam, were seen, dashing around these mountain-cottages, and rushing from precipice to precipice in channels which they had worn for ages. This is a place of tempests, as well as of grandeur and sublimity. Sometimes the storms which collect in these rocky caverns and gorges are terrible,—black with clouds, and marching with thunder and lightning through these gateways of nature and nations, and detaching with vast power large fragments of rock, which lie at frequent intervals along the path of the traveller.

We were thus hemmed in, among these extraordinary manifestations of the works of nature, for some thirty or forty miles; our journey all the way being close upon the banks of the swift and noisy Arc, which seemed sometimes to be angry and sometimes to sing and rejoice as it ran along. The whole distance was a gradual ascent. So that, having passed the villages of St. Jean Maurienne, St. Michel, Modane, and some others of less importance, we were thousands of feet above the level of the sea, at the village of Lanslebourg, which is at the foot of Mount Cenis. The mountain was covered with snow; but we were able to ascend it with the aid of extra horses in about four hours. The day had again closed; but we went on. The culminating point of the pass, through which the road goes, is a short distance below the summit, which has been ascertained to be 6780 feet above the sea-level. I got out of the carriage, and, leaving the road for a short time, ascended still farther on the sides of the summit, and gave myself up to the reflections inspired by the place. Some scattered clouds rested heavily over the mountain's summit. The light of the stars was reflected from the snows and icy rocks. And thus, after ascending hill after hill and mountain after mountain, we had Italy at our feet;—Italy, dear to the scholar and the Christian;—Italy, once honored by a Senate which was described as an assembly of kings;—Italy, the mistress of the world by its arms, and again and still more truly the mistress of the world by its arts, civilization, and literature.

Every people has its position, its character, its history. In the strong emotions excited by our approach to Italy, I am not willing to forget the people whom I have just left behind. The humble Savoyard, though far from the seats of literature and the glare of power, has a heart which beats true to the snow-crowned hills and cliffs of his birthplace. He is "part and parcel" of our common humanity. But man is to be estimated by his place, as well as his nature. It is place which gives character to nature. The Savoyard is what he is by being *where* he is. No other people has or can have his thoughts and feelings. His position has drawn out and nurtured his soul, because his soul is wedded to his position. He knows the history of each rock, of each rude fortification on the mountain's side, of each rivulet and noisy torrent, of the den of the wolf and the nest of the eagle. He has heard the story of the falling avalanche which destroyed the cottage and its dwellers, and has wept for their fate. He has the sorrows and the joys which are common to our nature. I saw him at work in his field. I beheld him seated at the door of his humble cottage. I knew not his name nor his history. But I felt an interest in him, because he was a man.

(XX.)

City of Turin—Parliament of Sardinia—Visit to the Waldenses—Character of the people—Ascent of one of the mountains—The cottager and his family—Religious services on the Sabbath—Prayer-meeting in the evening—Persecutions of the Waldenses—Milton's sonnet.

GENOA, KINGDOM OF SARDINIA, DEC. 15, 1852.

I AM writing this letter in the city of Genoa, and in sight of the Mediterranean. Genoa, including some small territory around it, was once a republic, celebrated for its wealth, power, and wisdom. I had hardly reached the city, before I went abroad into its narrow streets. I beheld its marble palaces, now defaced by time and sorrow. I trod with a melancholy satisfaction the halls where its celebrated councils had assembled. There are many things which remind one of its departed greatness. No longer a distinct state, it is now a part of the kingdom of Sardinia. But some incidents, to which I wish now to refer, will not allow me, at the present time, to enter into details in relation to this interesting place.

My last letter left our little party at the Pass of Mount Cenis, and at our entrance into Italy. Passing through Susa and some other places of small importance, we reached Turin,—a city of more than an hundred thousand inhabitants, and situated on the left bank of the Po, near its confluence with the Dora Riparia. It is the capital of the Sardinian kingdom. The government of this kingdom, which includes within its limits a large portion of Northern Italy, is a constitutional monarchy. The Sardinians feel, as compared with many other States of Europe, that they enjoy a high degree of liberty. The king is popular. At the time of our visit the Parliament of Sardinia was in session. Through the kindness of an Italian gentleman who had formerly resided in America, I was able to visit the House of Deputies. I was much pleased with the appearance of the members. They seemed to be men of intelligence,—calm and deliberate in their manner, and yet with some sparks, not yet extinguished, of the old Roman fire. They were discussing the subject of modifications and improvements of the criminal code, which indicated that they had begun to appreciate human rights, and were desirous of consolidating liberty by the establishment of justice. The same day I went to the hall of the Senate; but its meeting had just closed. Witnessing as I did with painful emotions the extinction of the republic in France, I was pleased to find that the voice of liberty had found an utterance—imperfect, perhaps, but still real and emphatic—in the beautiful region of Northern Italy. Religion in the Protestant form is tolerated; and a large Protestant church has recently been built. In consequence of the troubles and oppressions in other parts of Italy, particularly in Milan, many Italian exiles, estimated by some as high as thirty thousand, have taken up their residence in Turin and other parts of the Sardinian territory.

Finding at Turin that we were not far distant from a people who, though few in number, occupy an interesting position in religious history, we thought it desirable to visit them. I refer to the Vaudois of Piedmont,—better known as the *Waldenses.* They are scattered on the heights and in the valleys of the Piedmont side of a number of mountains sometimes distinguished as the Cottian Alps, which separate a part of France from Piedmont. Not being able to visit all of the Waldensian settlements, we selected the valley and the village of La Tour, as being the principal settlement and in some respects the most interesting place among them.

Mr. and Mrs. Walcott, not being able to make this excursion, proceeded on their way to Genoa. This diminished our pleasure. But I was accompanied by Mr. Thompson, to whose religious sympathies and personal attention I owe much of the pleasure and beneficial results of my long journeys.

Impelled by kindred recollections and interests, we went together to the valleys and mountains which the Waldenses inhabit. And there we found a people whose character corresponded with what history had led us to expect,—simple in their manners, sincere in their religion, firm in their purposes, and giving no small evidence of intelligence. It is difficult to conceive of scenery more picturesque and sublime than is here presented,—a fit residence, as it seemed to me, for those who had learned the two great lessons of God and liberty. The inhabitants generally spoke the French language; and we found a few persons (owing perhaps to the circumstance of their being frequently visited by Protestants) who had command of a broken and imperfect English. As soon as they learned that we were Americans, they recognized at once, and as if by an instinctive impulse, the bond of union and sympathy which led us to their secluded homes. We learned from them that they had not only the church and the school-house, but also, what I had not expected to find, the college. This college was founded in 1837, and is now in a flourishing condition. They had the Bible in their hands; their humble and rough pathway in life had been illuminated by the light of divine truth; and the influences of an evil world, kept at a distance by labor and poverty, had not corrupted them.

It was a natural impulse which led us to climb their mountain-heights. We ascended cliff after cliff; and at every practicable point we found the cottage. In this rude ascent everything interested us,—not only the wild aspects of nature, but, still more, the cottage and its people. Among a number of little incidents I will mention one. We met a little boy about ten years of age. We talked with him; and his frank and manly answers pleased us. His countenance was fresh with the mountain-breeze, and his dark eye sparkled with the fire of mountain-liberty. He seemed like a child of the rocks and a companion of eagles. In a few moments a little girl of nearly the same age came along, with the same open and intelligent countenance,—with the same free step and look. She was his cousin. At once, strangers as we were, a thousand thoughts and gentle aspirations gathered around these flowers that bloomed upon the cliffs, —these young but immortal products of the mountains. They showed us the cottage where they resided; and we went there. The mother of the boy stood at the door; not the less pleased with us that we were pleased with the children. In a few moments the father made his appearance and invited us in. And I must be permitted to say, though I have been in the palaces of kings, my heart beat with a higher and more sacred emotion when I found myself seated at the hearth of a Waldensian cottage.

I looked around the room with deep interest. It was obvious that its inmates were poor. The man wore a dress of coarse and cheap cloth; but, on entering into conversation with him, I could perceive that it covered a heart which was true to its immortal origin,—one which tyranny could not break, which superstition could not bend. A fire, kept alive by small billets of wood, blazed feebly upon the hearth. A sick daughter lay upon a bed; but a smile passed across her pale and meek countenance, as she turned her dark eye from the father to the strangers, and from the strangers to the father. It was a novel scene to her; but she seemed to know, by a sort of Waldensian instinct, that the deep and common sympathies of religious and political feeling were at the bottom of it. The walls of the cottage were rude; but they were not unpleasant to me. I had seen such in America, and known personally that great excellence of character often dwells beneath them. The father pointed us to a small shelf filled with books, which he called his library; and, taking down a large Bible in the French language, he showed it to us, and also a beautiful copy of the New Testament in the Vaudois dialect, which did not differ much from the French, and which I could read without difficulty. And he showed us also a number of other religious books,—some of them in the English language, of which he had some knowledge. He knew the history of the struggles of religion and liberty. He was himself a man of prayer. The name of Jesus was dear to him as it was to us. And we found, though separated by nations and oceans, that our hearts, like the mountain-torrents which met and mingled in the valley below us, flowed together in the unity of a common love of freedom and a common Christian hope.

The period of our visit to the Waldenses included the Sabbath. Supposing that this excellent people might have something corresponding to our Sabbath-schools and Bible-classes, we went at an early hour of the Sabbath-day to their church, which was not far distant. It is a neat and substantial edifice, painted white, and capable of holding nearly a thousand persons. We were glad to see that a considerable number of people, assembled together in this early part of the day, were engaged in the study of the Bible; and that they appeared to listen with attention and interest to the explanations and exhortations of their pastor. At a later hour, at the time which is usually appropriated to the forenoon religious worship in America, the people of all classes, the young and old, were seen coming up from the banks of the rivulets which flow through the valleys of La Tour and down the sides of the mountains. They were neat in their appearance and dress,—the women, with but few exceptions, wearing caps of snowy whiteness without bonnets,—and they assembled together and entered the house of worship with the aspect of persons who venerated and loved the place. The women occupied exclusively one side of the house; the men the other. The forenoon service was in French, which is the language spoken by the greater number; in the afternoon it was in Italian, and was conducted by one of the professors in the college to which allusion has already been made.

The interest of the religious services which took place in the course of the day was repeated and heightened by the social prayer-meeting in the evening. A large room, with smaller rooms adjoining, was closely filled at an early hour. Many of those who came together had their Bibles and hymn-books. One of the number read a portion from the Bible,—the first chapter of the second epistle of Peter,—and accompanied it with remarks. Others followed; adding such remarks as were naturally suggested by the chapter which had been read, but making in every instance an earnest and experimental application of them. These remarks were interspersed with repeated and earnest prayers and with singing. There was something exceedingly touching, as their full, sweet voices united in their hymns. Near the close of the meeting, Mr. Thompson arose, and made a short address to them in the French language. They listened with great attention, and in their parting prayer commended us affectionately to our common Father. They closed the meeting by singing a Doxology; and, as they went out, many of them, and among others the cottager and his wife whom we had visited on the mountain, took us kindly by the hand. Such is the power of religion; renovating the heart, strengthening the intellect, and restoring the broken bonds of human brotherhood.

Not far from this delightful place of prayer, and in sight of the church where we had worshipped during the day, there is a vast naked cliff, projecting from the side, and in fact forming a part of the side, of one of the mountain-heights. Rising almost perpendicularly, and apparently to the height of a thousand feet from its base, it throws its dark and ragged shadow over the valley below. I was told that this was one of the rugged cliffs to which the Waldensians fled in the days of their bitter persecutions. Followed by the soldiers with their sharp weapons of death, they climbed to the summit and went out to the projecting points and last footholds of this terrible mountain-rock. There they stood, the man with gray locks, the husband and the wife, the mother and the infant on her bosom; rejecting all compromise, holding the truth above life, and leaving it to their powerful enemies either to concede to them the rights of Christians and freemen, or to destroy them. These poor people, who had learned Christ from the Bible and at their humble firesides, without power, without wealth, and with but little education, may be said nevertheless, in some important sense at least, to have held in their hands the destinies of Christianity. God gave them strength to meet this terrible crisis. They offered themselves a sacrifice for the truth.

Long, and with deep emotion, did I look upon this great altar of the blood of these humble but truly heroic martyrs. I had read their history, but it was something more to stand upon the place and let the mountains tell me. Memory would not rest. Imagination, prompted by a bleeding heart, placed the scene before me. I seemed to see it all, as if it were now present. But among that band of believing sufferers there was one that most of all fixed my attention. Upon those sharp and lofty cliffs stood the Waldensian *mother*. In her poverty she wrapped her coarse garments around her, and pressed her naked feet upon the rocks. With one hand she clasped her infant to her bosom; and, with the other lifted in earnest prayer, in which the strong faith of Christianity enabled her to remember and to forgive her persecutors, she awaited the fatal moment. Cruelty triumphed over love and mercy. And it is not surprising that nations were filled with sorrow and shame, and that the heart of humanity wept, when it was told that the mother and her infant were hurled down the rocks.

It was these events, so sad and yet illustrating so wonderfully the power of religion, which gave occasion for the touching and sublime sonnet of Milton:—

> "Avenge, O Lord, thy slaughter'd saints, whose bones
> Lie scatter'd on the Alpine mountains cold:
> E'en them who kept thy truth so pure of old,—
> When all our fathers worshipp'd stocks and stones,—
> Forget not. In thy book record their groans
> Who were thy sheep, and in their ancient fold
> Slain by the bloody Piedmontese, that roll'd
> Mother with infant down the rocks. Their moans
> The vales redoubled to the hills, and they
> To heaven. Their martyr'd blood and ashes sow
> O'er all the Italian fields, where still doth sway
> The triple tyrant; that from these may grow
> A hundred-fold, who, having learned thy way,
> Early may fly the Babylonian woe."

The story of the Waldenses, which constitutes at the same time the brightest and the darkest page of history, illustrates one great truth, namely, that one of the great forces of Christianity, perhaps its greatest in its contest with the evils of the world, is its ability of patient and forgiving endurance and suffering. The women and children of these celebrated mountains, in consenting to be immolated on the rocks, fought a greater and more effective battle for truth and freedom than the battles of Marathon and Yorktown. They taught the world how to conquer. No marble column marks their grave; but the mountains are their monument, and their memorial is in the bosom of God.

(XXI.)

Journey from Turin to Genoa, Pisa, and Florence—Towns of Moncalieri and Alessandria—Plain and battle of Marengo—Death of Desaix—Arrival at Genoa, and some account of it—Protestantism in Genoa—Gulf of Spezia—Napoleon—The Æneid—Passing of the river Magra—Mountains of Carrara—Pisa—Cathedral, Baptistery, and Leaning Tower—Leghorn—The Baptism.

FLORENCE, DUCHY OF TUSCANY, DEC. 21, 1852.

IN prosecuting our journey towards Rome from Turin, we took the route of Genoa and Florence,—a route which has this advantage: that the traveller can be conveyed from Turin to the town of Arquata, a distance of seventy-eight miles, by railroad. The railroad-station at Turin is within the limits of the city, and at the end of the street called the Strada Nuova. The road runs along the banks of the river Po, till it reaches the pleasant town of Moncalieri, which is distinguished by being the site of one of the royal palaces. The palace is on the summit of a hill which overlooks the town, and is the favorite residence of the present royal family of Sardinia. At Moncalieri the railroad crosses the Po, and, taking the direction of the city of Asti, which is a considerable place of twenty thousand inhabitants, it there follows the valley of the river Tanaro. The next important town on this route is Alessandria, situated near the confluence of the Tanaro and the Bormida. The road, on leaving Alessandria, runs along the western side of the plain on which was fought the great battle of Marengo, on the 13th of June, 1800. In this bloody battle twenty thousand French, under the command of Napoleon, tried their strength against forty thousand Austrians, under the command of the old General Melas, who was then eighty-four years of age. Few battles have been more furiously contested. The French were driven from their positions, and in full retreat, when the celebrated Desaix, one of those remarkable men whom the first French republic brought into notice, appeared upon the field with an additional force. Meeting Napoleon as he was retreating, he said to him, "I think this is a battle lost." With characteristic pertinacity, but with a foresight which justified the reply, Napoleon answered, "I think it is a battle won." Desaix led his fresh forces into the contest. The First Consul formed his broken troops behind him. The tide of battle turned. The Austrians were defeated. Desaix was killed.

The railroad stops at Arquata, but will be ultimately completed to Genoa. Its completion is delayed for the present, in consequence of the necessity of cutting a tunnel through the Apennines, which cross the line of its path. From Arquata, therefore, we reached Genoa by the ordinary line of conveyances. We took our lodgings at a place well known to travellers, the Hotel Feder; which I mention the more particularly because, in the days of the Genoese republic, and of its maritime ascendency, it was the palace of the Admiralty, and is thus intimately associated with Genoese naval history. It is near the water, and the room which I occupied gave a beautiful view of the harbor, shipping, light-house, and a portion of the surrounding heights. Genoa was anciently styled "SUPERBA," and her commerce, arts, wealth, her marble palaces, her spirit of liberty, seemed to justify the appellation. But, though seated on rocks, and girded by mountains, and with her feet washed by the waters of the Mediterranean, she has not escaped the common destiny of states and nations, which brings, in their appointed time, the marks of weakness and decay. With mingled feelings of admiration and sorrow I walked through the streets. The beauty has faded from her palaces; much of her commerce has passed to other cities; her republican independence is merged in the constitutional monarchy of Sardinia; sorrow sits upon the brow of her people; but the king and parliament of Sardinia, in the spirit either of sympathy or of patriotism, have respected the character and historical reminiscences of the Genoese, by endeavoring to give them the second place in the kingdom; and it was pleasant to see, if much of their ancient glory had departed, that a degree of courage and hope still remained.

I could say something of the churches and other public buildings of Genoa, and of the paintings and statuary with which they are ornamented; but as Italy may be said to be filled with them, and as Florence and Rome and Naples yet remain to be visited, I will leave it to others. I ought to say, however, as a matter of religious interest at the present time, that the Protestant religion, as might naturally be expected from the incorporation of Genoa with Sardinia, is tolerated here. There is a place where the English Episcopal service is regularly performed. The French Protestants also sustain their method of worship. It came to our knowledge, also, that a considerable number of republican exiles from other parts of Italy had found a residence and protection in Genoa. With one of these—a man of intelligence, and whose principles had been tested by sacrifices and sufferings—we formed some acquaintance.

Our route from Genoa to Florence, which for some time was near the Mediterranean, was diversified by alternations of valleys and reaches of rocky and mountainous heights, from which many picturesque and sometimes wild and romantic views were presented. The vine, the olive, the mulberry, and fields of wheat, were everywhere seen. We passed a number of pleasant villages, and the more considerable towns of Sestri, Spezia, and Sarzana. Spezia, a town of seven thousand inhabitants, is situated upon the gulf of the same name,—a spacious body of water susceptible of being easily fortified, and sufficiently extensive to contain the largest navies. This beautiful and justly-celebrated gulf was known to the ancients under the name of the Gulf of Luna.

It was the intention of Napoleon, after his conquest of Italy, to make this gulf the great naval station of his empire. He wished to incorporate his name with the ocean as well as with mountains. Everywhere, from the Seine to the Nile, the traveller is reminded of the magnificent conceptions, and may even be said to tread in the very footprints, of this remarkable man,—a man great in his conceptions of material nature, great in his energy, great in his estimate of the power of fear and money over the human mind; but not great enough to estimate the truth and power of the spirit of liberty. It is almost a necessity of his nature, that man must estimate men by the measurement which exists in his own heart; and although Napoleon could adjust the measurement of selfishness to tyranny, and of tyranny to universal empire, he had no capacity within him which enabled him to solve the problem of such men as Vane and Hampden, as Lafayette and Washington.

It is said, by some commentators, that Virgil in the first book of the Æneid was aided in his exquisite description of the gulf in which Æneas took refuge after a violent storm, by his recollections of the Spezian Gulf. I can easily conceive that it might have been so, although there is no island here which would correspond to the island he has described. No one can doubt that, in its combinations of land and water, it is a place worthy even of Virgil's pen. If poetry could become embodied, and take up its residence in person, I think it would reside somewhere in this neighborhood. The views, as we passed around the head of these waters, were beautiful as imagination could well conceive.

On leaving this place we ascended gradually a long reach of rough and lofty hills, and came down on the other side, into the picturesque valley of the Magra. The Magra is a short river, formed by the smaller rivers and torrents rushing from the neighboring mountains, which seem to be branches from the Apennines. It is generally fordable; but when swollen by heavy rains, as it was at this time, it fills a channel of a quarter of a mile in width, and rushes towards the Mediterranean with great impetuosity. We were all taken by surprise by this sudden apparition of foaming waters. A ferry-boat, however, soon received us and our baggage. The boat seemed to be a memorial of departed generations. It was certainly a very old thing, and so much broken on one side as to invite, at every inclination in that direction, an additional freight from the river. With much noise and much tugging, the honest boatmen, who seemed to constitute a considerable portion of the inhabitants of this mountainous region, conveyed us over the main channel; but in default of wharf or other suitable landing-place, they thrust the head of the boat into a sand-bar about fifteen yards from the shore, and then, seizing each of us, individually and bodily, and without giving us time to consider or remonstrate, carried us in their strong arms to the bank of the river. I called them honest boatmen; but, out of regard to strict veracity, I ought, perhaps, to make an exception of the person or persons who took advantage of our peculiar situation and confusion to steal a carpet-bag.

The next considerable town was Sarzana. As we thus travelled along, admiring nature's beauty at every step, and estimating men and institutions as well as nature, we came in sight (and for this also I was unprepared) of the marble mountains of Carrara. An Italian gentleman, whom we had taken into our company at Spezia, pointed them out. He was a dealer in marble, and was going to Leghorn to arrange shipments for New York. I saw their white caverns in the distance, and I could not but remember that these mountains had been associated with the history of art for more than two thousand years. I was informed that no other quarries furnish marble of the same whiteness and purity. Thus it is that, in the combinations of infinite wisdom, nature and mind are made to correspond to each other. That which is finite must work upon that which has form and solidity. If there had been no Carrara, there would have been no Michael Angelo, no Canova. What can a workman do without materials? God only can work upon nothing.

The next considerable place upon our route was Pisa. It was formerly a large and flourishing city; and, notwithstanding the unfavorable changes it has experienced, it still numbers twenty-five thousand inhabitants. We stopped here a short time to look at the Cathedral, the Baptistery, the *Campanile* or bell-tower, better known as the *Leaning Tower*, and other objects of interest which usually attract the notice of travellers. The origin of the cathedral has an historical interest. In the year 1063, the Pisan fleet attacked a number of Saracen vessels, in the harbor of Palermo in Sicily, broke through the chain which the Saracens had thrown across the harbor for their protection, and returned home richly laden with the captured spoils. Devoutly ascribing their victory to divine superintendence, the Pisans resolved to erect a new cathedral, which should at the same time be a monument of their gratitude to God, and an honor to their country. And accordingly its foundation was laid in 1064; but it was not completed and consecrated until the year 1118;—a building which would be likely, even on the slight examination which we were able to bestow upon it, to give to many persons some new ideas of the energy and resources of the Italian states and republics of the Middle Ages. In the nave of this cathedral hangs suspended the bronze lamp which suggested to Galileo the theory of the application of the pendulum. The Campanile or Leaning Tower, to which I have referred, is fifty feet in diameter, and an hundred and seventy-eight in height. There are seven bells on its summit, the largest weighing twelve thousand pounds. With this great weight upon it, and rising in eight successive stories to such a height, it leans over, in consequence of sinking on one side, at the foundation, with an inclination at the top of thirteen feet from its original perpendicular position, producing on the mind of the beholder, by the combined influence of the beauty and greatness of the object, and its unexampled and perilous inclination, a very singular and powerful effect. Pisa is situated upon the Arno, one of the many rivers of Italy which have a classical celebrity.

Availing ourselves of the railroad which now connects Pisa with Florence in one direction and with Leghorn in another, we made a short excursion to the latter place, a journey of thirteen miles, and which was accomplished by railroad in thirty minutes. The traveller will be well repaid by taking it, although Leghorn is known more by its commerce than its works of art. We rode round the city, cast a glance upon its massive fortifications, and had the satisfaction of seeing the flags of different nations—among them that of America—floating peacefully together in the beautiful harbor. Leghorn, which, among the cities in this part of the Mediterranean, is second as a commercial place only to Marseilles and Genoa, contains seventy thousand inhabitants, eight thousand of whom are Jews. The Jews have their full share of the business of the city, and their richly-ornamented synagogue, to which we gained access without difficulty, will well recompense a visit from the traveller. In the Protestant cemetery, filled with memorials of the dead of different nations, we stood beside the dust of some of our own people who had died in this distant land.

Resuming our seats in the cars, and returning to Pisa, we proceeded immediately to Florence, which is reached by the railroad in a few hours. It is from Florence, the capital of the dukedom of Tuscany, that I date this letter; and here I rest for the present, though it is but for a short time. Inquiring of myself, as I went to my solitary room, what had been the effect of this journey thus far upon my own mind, I found that it had been to generalize my feelings, and to inspire them with a purer and deeper benevolence at the same time that it extended them. It was difficult for me before, except by a sort of abstract effort, to carry my feelings beyond America, and to bring them into a realizing sympathy with unknown races. I found, however, that there is a wide and great nation beyond that of any particular nationality. The sphere of humanity, the circle of divinely-united hearts, enlarged itself as I advanced; and I can say with Kotzebue and Mungo Park that in every land where I have been I have found evidences of confidence and of friendship.

To me this is a great deal. I value intellectual acquisitions; but still more do I want my heart enlarged to its utmost capacity. This train of thought and feeling recalled an incident which occurred at Pisa. Our little company were standing in the celebrated building called the Baptistery. In a little time our attention was diverted from the architectural skill displayed in the building to a religious ceremony which was about to be performed. Some poor people had brought a child to be baptized. We looked on, Protestants as we were, with those feelings of respect which are due from one form of religion to another. When the religious ceremony had been gone through, the poor Italian mother, in passing out of the building, came near the excellent lady who formed one of our little company, and entered into communication with her,—not by vocal language, because they could not in that way understand each other; but by that mysterious sympathy of souls which has a power above that of words. It was sufficient, though of different creeds and differently situated, that both were mothers. God and nature brought into harmony what lands and creeds might have separated. The American mother stooped down and kissed the little child of the Italian mother, and, seeing the evidence of their poverty in their poor and rude garments, added a present in money to this expression of her affection. This little scene of unaffected benevolence touched my feelings. It was the voice of humanity asserting its eternal relationships. The tear grew bright in the eye of the Italian mother, and dropped on the cheek of the infant; and I could see, in the countenance of the old priest and a number of poor Catholics who stood around, that a ray of mutual confidence and esteem was kindled in their hearts. And I could not but feel, if men would become better acquainted with each other and let the currents of love flow out, it would be a moral force greater than the sword, greater than dogmatical argument, in diminishing diversities of belief, in correcting errors, in harmonizing antagonistical systems, and in bringing in Christ's kingdom of universal peace.

(XXII.)

Situation of Florence—Origin of the Republic of Florence—Appearance and character of the people—Cathedral and church of Santa Croce—Dante and his writings—Milton—The Campanile, or bell-tower—The Uffizii and its works of art—The Medicean library—Re-establishment of capital punishment—Trial of insurgent republicans.

FLORENCE, DUCHY OF TUSCANY, SECOND LETTER.

THE present letter will be taken up with what has come under my notice, or rather with a part of what has been noticed, at Florence. The city of Florence is the capital of the duchy of Tuscany, situated on both sides of the Arno, which is spanned by four beautiful bridges. Surrounded by the villas which adorn the adjacent plain, with sloping hills and lofty mountains in the distance, it must be conceded that, in the merits of its natural position at least, Florence justifies the eulogies which have so often been bestowed upon it. And the beauty of the city itself, though it has lost something of its former splendor, corresponds well with the beauty of its situation.

The Florentines trace their history back to the time of the old Romans. And in support of this view they refer to the fact that they are mentioned in the Annals of Tacitus as having sent an embassy to Rome in relation to some matters which concerned their city. But their brilliant period—the period in which they have commanded their full share of the notice and admiration of the world—commences with the year 1250, when they arose and overthrew the nobles who had tyrannized over them, and established the Florentine Republic. Before this time they were subjects, and were treated as slaves; but, in the expressive language of one of their chronicles, they then constituted themselves a *people.*

The Florentines, whatever may have been their origin, are a select and noble race of men. I had no sooner entered their streets than I was struck with their appearance;—quite different from that of the people of some other cities which I had visited. Their well-built forms and expressive countenances, marked by thought and lofty independence, harmonized well with the idea that they were the descendants of a race who have achieved an honorable place in the records of men. Interesting in their political history, which shows their love of freedom, they are equally so in their relation to the development of the arts and in their contributions to literature. Works of art, exclusive of public buildings which display the genius of architecture, are found everywhere;—in their palaces, churches, public squares, and private residences. Peculiar circumstances, which it is the business of the historian to unfold, gave this direction to the great inventive capacity of the people.

It is the splendid edifices, however, which are likely to attract attention on the first entrance into the city. The cities and states of Italy have vied with each other in the erection of public buildings, particularly those designed for religious worship; and, although as Protestants we may well question their adaptedness in many cases to the purpose for which they were built, we cannot withhold our admiration from the genius which planned and the persevering energy which completed them. One of the most remarkable of these magnificent buildings is the Cathedral of Florence. In accordance with a decree of the city, which was desirous of erecting an edifice superior to any other then existing, the foundations were laid in 1298; and genius and skill, and labor and wealth, contributed to complete it. It is four hundred and fifty-four feet in length, with a transept of three hundred and thirty feet; and its height from the pavement to the summit of the cross by which it is surmounted is about three hundred and eighty-seven feet. The walls on the outside are cased with marble. The dome is said to be the largest in the world; and served as a model to Michael Angelo in building that of St. Peter's.

This great building, commenced at the time I have mentioned, was not entirely completed till the year 1446. Its interior is adorned with statues, bas-reliefs, busts, frescoes, and sepulchral monuments,—some of them, in the judgment of artists, works of great merit; but the pleasure of seeing them is somewhat diminished in consequence of their being so dimly revealed to the visitor by the feeble rays of light which fall through the small stained windows. Among the monuments in this cathedral is that of Brunelleschi, the great architect who built its dome, and who was buried here at the expense of the republic.

There is also a fine statue of Brunelleschi on the south side of the square of the cathedral; and near it the stranger is pointed to the spot, designated by an inscription, where Dante used to sit and occupy his imaginative mind in contemplating this vast edifice.

Among the numerous other churches which adorn the city of Florence, there is much to interest one in the old Franciscan church of Santa Croce. It was in the square of this church that the people assembled and took their decisive measures in the republican revolt of 1250. But to me this renowned edifice was an object of especial attraction; because, in common with every traveller who visits Florence, I here looked upon the tomb of Michael Angelo. The body which was once the residence of a mind of eminently great and original power reposes here. His tomb is ornamented with allegorical figures of the sister-arts of architecture, painting, and sculpture, in all of which he excelled. The marble bust, which is designed to perpetuate the outlines of the form that is crumbling beneath it, is regarded as a faithful likeness of him. In this church, which is sometimes spoken of as the Westminster Abbey of Florence, Marsuppini was buried, the secretary of the republic at an early period, and one of its eloquent and distinguished men. Here also are sepulchral monuments to Galileo, Dante, and Alfieri. The portrait of Dante was placed here by a decree of the republic in 1465. But the large and splendid monument to him, to which I have just referred, has been recently erected at the public expense.

It is evident that Florence cherishes the memory of her great poet,—great as compared with the poets of any other age or nation, and yet unlike all other poets. A country is nothing without its great names. And there are so many reminiscences of Dante here, that it may not be out of place to say something in relation to him. If no writer can be properly understood and interpreted separate from his age and country, this is especially the case with this remarkable poet. His conceptive power, which enabled him to imagine and to describe with so much exactness, was his own; but the subjects upon which he exercised it belonged to the incidents of his age, people, and religion. I never could well understand before, how a writer, no matter how great or how eccentric his genius, could think of going through hell, purgatory, and paradise, with a view to ascertain the locality, if I may so express it, of the spirits of the dead, and to announce to the world their respective degrees of reward and punishment, of hope and despair. But these ideas (I mean ideas which dealt with the unknown facts and incidents of man's disembodied destiny) were the ideas of the age of Dante. If a man died, and did not go straightway to heaven, (which was the happy lot of a few saints only,) the popular thought of that age, trained and established by its dominant religious ideas, at once assigned him an infernal or purgatorial locality. Books were written, and paintings sketched and executed, upon the basis of this prevalent mode of opinion and feeling. Michael Angelo himself was not free from this influence. And the interior of the cupola of the great Cathedral of Florence, which was the object of his study and admiration, is painted in fresco, with angels and saints in paradise, or with figures representing the sufferings of purgatory and hell. So that the remarkable work of Dante is really nothing more nor less than the poetical conception—which that great poet alone fully possessed—of the great religious thought of his age.

And, now that I am upon this subject, I may further add that some of the leading traits in the writings of our own Milton (I refer, however, particularly to the Paradise Lost) find an explanation, in part at least, in the same predominant ideas. He resided for some time in Italy, was perfectly acquainted with Italian literature, and with the religious thought and feeling which prevailed among the people. It has seemed to me, since I have been in Florence and other parts of Italy, that the hell of the Paradise Lost would not have been so clearly defined in his conception, and so accurately described, if Milton had not both heard and seen a good deal in relation to it on the banks of the Arno. Particular expressions and allusions also, full of beauty but evidently not of English origin, find their explanation in his residence here. Vallombrosa and the hill of Fiesoli are both in the neighborhood of Florence. And hence, in describing the prostration of the rebel angels, he says that they

> "lay entranced,
> Thick as autumnal leaves that strew the brooks
> In Vallombrosa."

And it is thus, with his mind filled not only with Italian scenery but with Italian art and science, that he compares Satan's shield to

> "the moon, whose orb
> Through optic glass the Tuscan artist views
> At evening from the top of Fiesoli."

The "Tuscan artist" is Galileo, with whom Milton became acquainted while he was in Italy.

Among other objects which the stranger can hardly fail to observe, and which he is not likely to forget, is the CAMPANILE, or bell-tower. Unlike that of Pisa, the Campanile of Florence stands erect; and is also much higher than the Pisan tower,—being two hundred and seventy-five feet in height. It is near the cathedral, and may be considered as a species of appendage to it. Its basement-story is ornamented with a series of well-executed reliefs, designed to represent the progress of civilization;—commencing with the history of Adam and the early patriarchs, and developing the leading events in human progress down to a late period. Rising in successive stories to its overtowering height, this remarkable structure is seen by a single glance of the eye, and stops the traveller and commands his admiration, at the very doors of the great cathedral, by that power of attraction which always belongs to simplicity when combined with grandeur.

The Florentine collection of works of art which is known as the Royal Gallery is one of the most valuable in the world. These works are deposited in the upper story of a large and fine building called the Uffizii, which was originally erected for the accommodation of the magistrates and tribunals of Florence. In this celebrated gallery nearly all the great masters of art, both of ancient and modern times, are represented. Here, among other works which have commanded the admiration of connoisseurs, is the Faun dancing, in marble; the celebrated group of wrestlers, writhing in sculptured strength and emulation; and the statue of the Venus de Medici, of which the world has but one. There were other works which were particularly interesting to me. Hardly anything which I saw impressed me more than the busts of the Roman emperors; authenticated as works of the date which is ascribed to them, not only by the circumstances of their discovery, but by their remarkable correspondence to those conceptions of the persons represented which an acquaintance with the past is most likely to suggest. They are a sort of resurrection of history. I looked again and again upon the furrowed but stern brow of Julius Cæsar; with anxiety, ambition, and intrepidity written in unchangeable lines. Here, also, living in the perpetuity of art, is the calm and intellectual look of Augustus. Esteeming its homage to the truth above everything else, the chisel of the sculptor has harmonized with the pen of the annalist in its Otho and Vitellius; and the very marble speaks in verification of our ideas of Trajan, whom history has praised for his wisdom, and of Nerva, who was styled The Good.

I have no time in a single letter to say anything of the splendid paintings which are to be found here and also in the Palazzo Pitti; nor of the treasures, invaluable to literature, which exist in the Medicean library. This library, rich in works in the Oriental languages as well as in Greek and Latin, contains more than nine thousand manuscripts. The oldest manuscript of the Pandects is deposited here; and I was shown what was said to be (and I believe the claim to its great antiquity is not disputed) the earliest manuscript of Virgil. The manuscript contains all the works of Virgil, excepting a small portion of the Bucolics.

This is only the beginning of what might be said, and of what came under my personal notice in Florence and its vicinity. Of course a mere letter-writer cannot say much; especially when travelling rapidly and in poor health. But I cannot close without referring briefly to its present religious and political condition. It is hardly necessary to say that in Tuscany, as in other parts of Italy, the Catholic religion is the religion of the State and of the people. Other forms of religion are tolerated for foreign residents and for those who have inherited, if I may so express it, and have been brought up in, a different religion. The Episcopal Church of England has its place of worship;—the Presbyterians also, in which religious service is performed in the French language in the forenoon and in the English in the afternoon. It was our privilege to worship on the Sabbath in this church, in company with Christians from different lands. But if toleration, kept within very strict limits, is allowed to existing forms of belief, it is limited, at least as far as the Catholics are concerned, *to what now is.* It does not admit of free inquiry nor of a change of religions. The Catholic who dares to inquire and think on the subject of religion, with a view to estimate his own form of religion as compared with that of others, is a marked and persecuted man. If he is led to change his religion, no matter with how great sincerity, the least he can expect is a long and severe imprisonment.

For nearly a century capital punishment has been abolished in Tuscany. It has very recently been re-established; so that Florence, which has its works of art, has also its guillotine. I was informed, on authority upon which I could rely, that no reason could be assigned for this unexpected measure, except what was found in the political state of the country. The object is, beyond all question, to strike terror into the hearts of the republicans, who are feared, and hated, and persecuted, with the exception of the constitutional monarchy of Sardinia, by all the ruling authorities in Italy. I shall endeavor to refer to this subject more particularly in another letter. But I cannot omit to mention an incident here, which affected my feelings much.

A few years ago the people of the Roman States and of Tuscany, inspired by a sense of right and by historical recollections, endeavored to recover their ancient liberties. They succeeded in part;

but, in consequence of the aid rendered to them by France, Austria, and indirectly by Russia, the rulers, whom they dispossessed for a time, have recovered their power. The consequence is, that throughout Italy (always excepting the dominions of the constitutional and patriotic king of Sardinia) the republicans, who obviously constitute a large portion of the people, are closely watched by the police;—many prisons are filled with them; and very recently a large number, including some patriotic Catholic priests, have been executed. While I have been in Florence, some of these persons, who believe, as we do in America, that man ought to have a voice in the government of himself, and who have dared to act in accordance with their convictions, have been under trial for high treason. As soon as I understood this, I lost no time in finding my way to the court of justice. I was not fully informed as to particulars. I can only say, therefore, that four men, who had been prominent in the republican movement, were undergoing a trial which in all probability was to have its termination in death, or in perpetual imprisonment. The men were guarded by soldiers. The place of trial was full of people; but the rich and noble were not there. I was pleased to see that the representatives of the masses were not absent,—the men of toil, of hunger and rags. Liberty has ever found its truest defenders and sympathizers among the poor. I looked with deep interest upon their hard hands, their sunburnt countenances, and their eyes sometimes filled with tears and sometimes kindling with the flashes of the old Etrurian and Roman fire.

A few women, some of them young persons, and some of them advanced in years, were there also; and I supposed, from the deep and changeless anxiety which they manifested, that they might be the near relatives, perhaps the mothers and sisters, of the men under trial.

With some difficulty I made my way through the dense mass of people, till I stood near the judges, and in full view of the prisoners. I understood that these men were not the leaders in the republican movement, but still were regarded as of sufficient importance to be offered up as the people's sacrifice. One of them, apparently a young man, seemed to be drooping and wasting away under the effects of the long imprisonment to which they had been subjected. Another, more erect, and possessed of more physical energy, cast a calm and intelligent look upon the judges and crowded assembly, which seemed to say, in its prophetic glance, that he feared nothing for liberty nor from the judgment of posterity. The others, with looks rendered intense and fierce by a sense of injustice, were like men who cared for nothing and asked for nothing but their old swords and another field of battle. Not doubting in my own mind that a great crime against humanity was about to be accomplished, I turned away from this painful scene with the sad reflection that, in a sinful and fallen world like ours, all that is good and true is established and sanctified by its baptisms of blood.

(XXIII.)

Departure from Florence—The ancient Clusium—Arrival at the Papal territories—View of Mount Soracte—Approach to Rome—Remarks on the political state of Europe—Strength of the Republican party—The forces arrayed against it—Republican meeting in London—Kossuth and Mazzini—State of things in Rome.

CITY OF ROME, DEC. 27, 1852.

WE are now in Rome. In coming from Florence to this justly-celebrated spot, we took the route of Sienna,—once a large and powerful republican city, and still an object of curiosity and interest to travellers. A few miles from Sienna is the town of Chiusi, the site of the ancient Etruscan city of Clusium, which was the residence of Porsenna. In passing the volcanic mountain of Radicofani, we left the frontier of Tuscany, and entered the territory of the Papal See.

Leaving the villages of Ponte Centino and Aquapendente, (the latter an interesting place, deriving its name from its waterfalls,) we rode for a considerable distance along the shore of the beautiful lake of Bolsena, which is supposed to cover a part of the ancient city Volscinium. It was in this vicinity that we had a distant view, for some time, of the celebrated Mount Soracte, now called St. Oreste. It rose in solemn grandeur from a distant part of the Campagna Romana. The Childe Harold of Byron has described it with the greatest accuracy, as "heaving from the plain, like a long-swept wave about to break, which on the curl hangs pausing." Horace in one of his odes describes it as white with snow; and the summit was covered with snow at the time we saw it.

As we approached near Rome, the object of many pleasant anticipations, our hearts were very cheerful; but our horses, unmoved by the inspirations of the place, were either very lazy or very weary, and, at the last stopping-place, which furnished relays, it was proposed by some of the company to increase our comfort as well as our motive-power, by changing the number which drew our VETTURINO from four to seven. As the proposal was an appeal to the principle of "humanity to animals," as well as of personal comfort, it met with no opposition. Everything was arranged accordingly; but not without exciting considerable movement and notice in the little town from which we started under these more favorable auspices. Everybody seemed to give care to the winds. The sun was bright above us. The postilions cracked their whips; the horses, as if conscious of this accession of strength, curved their necks and shook the little bells with which they were ornamented; the smitten pavements flashed fire; the dogs barked; and the very beggars shook their hats with jollity. It was thus, seated in the midst of this unusual locomotion, that we made our approach for the first time to the classic banks of the Tiber, to the ruined palaces of the Cæsars, and the memorable battle-fields of Garibaldi.

But I shall not undertake to describe what I see around me in the present letter. There is another topic to which I wish to advert. I have not as yet said much in relation to the political state of Europe. I have not considered the subject an unimportant one; but it is difficult at the present time to get at the precise state of things. Availing myself, however, of such means of information as I could command, I have been obliged to come to one conclusion, which, if it be true, is a fundamental one in the estimate of political probabilities, namely, that a very considerable portion of the people of England, France, Italy, Belgium, Poland, and Hungary, and perhaps in some of these states a majority, have adopted republican opinions. Nor is this the whole of the republican strength,—which is to be found also in part in other states and nations. The republican party of Europe, therefore, respectable, at least, both in its numbers and talents, and its courage and physical resources, is a permanent and important element in European affairs, which it would be useless to attempt to ignore, and which every wise statesman will not only be willing to recognize, but will be desirous to conciliate.

Of the republicans there are two divisions,—one which is desirous of leaving the establishment of the republican policy to time, and those methods of public enlightenment and of gradual political amelioration which time alone can bring. The other party, maddened by hopes long deferred, and by oppressions actually realized, carry the swords under their garments, and wait only for the day and the hour when they shall flash in open light on the field of battle.

Further, I think I can say this. No party will attempt to move now upon an irreligious basis; that is to say, with a disregard of those sentiments, everywhere implanted in the human mind, which recognize the existence of God, and the duties which are owed to him. Democracy, taught by the sufferings of her former blindness, has reassumed her respect for man's religious nature. This is right. Religion may be perverted; and its perversions may be tyrannical. But true religion is, by its nature, essentially republican. Patriarchs, prophets and apostles, and the early martyrs, were men, if I may so express it, who came up from the masses,—men who knew the people, men who sympathized with the wants of the people, and who labored and suffered for their good. The Sermon on the Mount is the great proclamation of human liberty,—a proclamation unequalled in its expression, as it is unequalled in the length and breadth of its just and generous sentiments. And I do not hesitate to say, that, in a true estimate of His character and teaching, considered in their relation to the universal establishment of human rights, Jesus Christ, as compared with any other reformer or teacher, ought to be regarded, and spoken of, and loved, as the true democratic leader.

The great republican leaders of the present time, unlike those of the period of 1790,—the Mazzinis, the Kossuths, the Cavaignacs, the Girardins and Lamartines,—understand well that religion is a necessity of man's nature, that it is the only sure basis of practical morals, and that liberty without religion cannot stand. This is a great gain to the republican cause; and I think it one of the most favorable omens of its ultimate success. And I do not doubt that the sympathies of a large body of religious and praying men, particularly in England, harmonize now, for the first time, with the republican ideas and position, as they are developed in one or the other of the republican sections to which I have referred. The moral influence of this significant alliance, which has greatly diminished and almost put an end to the cry of republican infidelity, is immense. And I think it but justice to say that in the republican enrolment there will be found to be—contrary to what in America is sometimes supposed to be the fact—a multitude of sincere and devout Catholics. So far as I can form an opinion, the republican position has never been so strong in Europe as it is at this moment. And no temporary disappointment, no sudden and midnight treachery, no defeat in the battle-field, no deferring, even from generation to generation, of long-cherished hopes, will be likely to alter this fundamental state of things.

It might perhaps be inferred, from this statement, that it is the object of the republican party, without making the proper and just discriminations, to overthrow the existing governments in Europe. But it would be better and nearer the truth to say, that their object, in any proper sense of the terms, is not to overthrow or to injure governments, but to establish the great and inalienable rights of humanity,—such as freedom of religious belief, freedom of political opinion and of the press, just laws and equality under the law, and especially the recognized and unchangeable representation of the people in all matters where the people are concerned. This they claim. For this they are organized. And this, if I am not mistaken in what has come under my notice, they are determined to accomplish. Any government that will so modify itself as to admit and establish what this great party regard as the rights of humanity, no matter whether it bears the name of a republic or a constitutional monarchy, will continue to stand and will be increasingly prosperous. And any governments which refuse this must take their chance of life or death in the great contest of opinions and of material forces which threatens soon to overtake them.

The wisdom of England, enlightened by her great and patriotic history, is steadily adjusting the ship of state to this new and fixed position of things; and thus there is reason to think that the flag which has waved a thousand years will yet triumph in any coming storms. Belgium and Sardinia (and I suppose it may be the same in a few other states) are taking the same course. So far is there from being any general hostility on the part of the republicans to these patriotic kingdoms, whose hospitality many of them have experienced in their sad exile from nearly every part of Europe, that they name them with pride and grateful affection, and quote them everywhere as examples of actual and progressive liberty,—broad enough now, and capable of expansion enough hereafter, to accept and conciliate the conflict of opinions, and to satisfy the reasonable demands of humanity.

I would say further, that the republican party is not a party which is circumscribed in its views by geographical limits. Its objects pertain to humanity. Its bond of union is the tie of human rights and affections. Its locality, therefore, is the world. It has those among it, as I have already intimated, who everywhere advocate its cause by the appeals of reason and love; men who do not cease to be men of peace because they are republicans, and whose declaration of independence is the "Sermon on the Mount," taken in its more literal and obvious import. This portion of the party, which embraces some names of great power and influence, is averse to war; though it is not on that account less true to its political principles, and is ready to sustain them by its testimony in prisons and on the scaffold. But the party has among its ranks also a still greater number, who, if reason and appeals to a kindred humanity shall fail to have a hearing, will unsheath the sword in the desperation of violated rights, and will either conquer or be destroyed.

But there is another side to this state of things. Face to face, in antagonism to this great and uncompromising party, who stand erect with their bosoms bare, ready to accept the charter of freedom or the baptism of blood, there are arrayed at the present moment the great empires and kingdoms of Russia, Austria, Prussia, and France, aided by Tuscany and Naples, and I know not how many smaller states, with a standing army of two millions of bayonets, and with cannon planted and with matches blazing from Paris to Moscow. It is thus beyond all question that the two great parties, with such modifications of thought and feeling as have been referred to, have taken their stand in fierce and fearful opposition; mutual in their defiance and mutual in their hatred; and each party apparently waiting for the signal of that mysterious Providence which rules the destiny of nations, and which destroys those who, in refusing to be just, refuse to harmonize.

Whether the two political parties which are thus arrayed in opposition to each other will come into actual conflict, is a thing which lies hidden in the future. It would be useless to conjecture. But this does not vitiate the correctness of the statements which have been made, nor alter the actual and imminent state of things which exists. Let us hope that sound reason will prevail; and that those who hold power against right, whoever and wherever they may be, if they fail to be moved by the sentiments of justice, will at least consult their own interests, by harmonizing with the claims of liberty.

I cannot close this letter without mentioning one or two incidents which have a little connection with it. I was in France at the time of the re-establishment of the usurped empire. Being in a certain town, a French gentleman invited me to the municipal hall. He led me to a corner of the large room where the town authorities were in the habit of assembling, and, taking the republican flag, on which were inscribed the large letters, "Liberty, Equality, Fraternity," he unrolled it and gazed upon it with deep emotion. Then, rolling it up, he returned it to its place; but not without giving me to understand that the hands which had unfurled it once, but from whom it had been deceitfully wrested, would unfurl it again.

In many other instances I found the same feelings expressed. At a certain time, stopping with my friends at an obscure village in Italy, the innkeeper, whose manners and whose open and intelligent brow indicated that he was not formed to be a slave, asked Mr. Thompson if he knew anything of the Italian exiles of America. And when he understood that he had seen Forbes, and Avizenna, and Garibaldi, and especially when he understood that we had both seen Mazzini in London, and that the great republican leader had lost neither heart nor hope for Italy, he was filled with wild delight. In a few moments the news was communicated to a considerable number of poor people around; and it was interesting to see how they gathered around our carriage as we departed, and lifted their hats in recognition of republican affinity, and earnestly gazed upon us with tears starting to their eyes, as if we had brought them news of a son or a brother, "who was dead and is alive again; who was lost and is found." And thus, in no small number of instances in France and Italy, we were able to ascertain the feelings of the people.

In London we attended the meeting of the Italian and other republican exiles. The room was capable of holding more than a thousand persons, and was full. And I cannot forget that this meeting, without spies to report or bayonets to control it, was held within the realms of Queen Victoria, who fears nothing from the republican sentiment, because the free constitution of government which she administers recognizes the just right which supports it, and provides, in one of its great departments, for its full and powerful manifestation. I never attended a meeting which evinced more settled principle, more fixed determination, more deep enthusiasm. Kossuth and Mazzini were there. And when they arose, embodying as they did in their own persons the hopes of nations, they seemed to me, as I associated them with the past and the future, like the strong but tempest-beaten landmarks of passing generations. They took each other by the hand, and in the presence of this large assembly mutually pledged whatever yet remained of life, fortune, and hope; and added, in the name of those who knew them and loved them, the still higher pledge of the blood of Hungary to Italy and the blood of Italy to Hungary.

On this occasion, and at the close of the meeting, I had the pleasure, in company with many others, of taking Kossuth by the hand, whom I had before seen in America,—the man invincible, not merely because of his vast powers of intellect and his generous and universal heart, but especially because he is a child of Providence, and is what he believes himself to be,—an instrument of God in the destiny of nations. I went also a few days after, in company with Mr. Thompson, and spent an evening in the humble and secreted room of Mazzini,—that great man, and true patriot and exile. We conversed with him; and it was from him that I gained some of the opinions and impressions which I have expressed. I saw in him, as I thought, the sincerity of conviction, the modesty of strength, a high trust in Providence, and the invincible will. It was nearly at the same time, and in the city of Paris, that I saw Louis Napoleon at the Tuileries. And I am obliged to say, that I felt a far deeper respect for the man who adhered to his principles and held the idea of a republic in poverty, suffering, and exile, than for the man who betrayed the people that trusted him, and rewarded himself with an empire.

Mazzini told us that blood was flowing in Italy,—

the blood of those who were dear to him. We soon afterwards had more specific confirmations of his remarks on the trying state of things in that country.

Before we left Sardinia, we learned, from a private but authentic source, the appalling news of the wholesale *massacres*—for such I think they may justly be termed—of suspected republicans in Austrian Lombardy. And since I have been in Rome I have been informed, on authority which I could not well doubt, that four thousand young men, republican citizens of Rome, are entered on the lists of the police as suspected persons,—that they are constantly watched, and are not allowed to be in the streets after certain hours of the day. And it is no small thing, that Rome itself, the land of the most celebrated names of freedom, is at this moment held in subjection, on account of its republican tendencies, by the bayonets of a foreign despotism.

It is thus that liberty, in the persons of those who love and cherish her, is everywhere proscribed. The heart mourns; but convictions are unaltered. The cause of freedom, like that of religion, has life in itself, and grows stronger and brighter in its trials.

The nations with ambitious mind,
  On wealth and warlike glories bent,
In strength alone had sought to find
  A true and lasting monument:
Alas! their early history's page
Foreshows the downfall of their age.

The grandeur raised by force or crime,
  In towers and walls and heaven-built spires,
Is like the mountain-height sublime
  That stands upon volcanic fires:
Above, 'tis seeming strength; below
An ocean's fiery billows glow.

But that which sinks, at last shall rise,
  Strong in the strength which cannot die;
The flames of that great sacrifice
  Have only power to purify:
The form may die,—the life remains;
Humanity survives and reigns.

(XXIV.)

First views and impressions of Rome—Porta del Popolo—Egyptian obelisk—Visit to the Capitoline Hill—Statue of Marcus Aurelius—View from the tower of the Capitol—The seven hills of Rome—The Coliseum—Arch of Titus—Remarks.

ROME, DEC. 28, 1852.

WITH the improved facilities of motion which were mentioned in the beginning of my last letter, we approached Rome by the old Cassian Way. The last place of much importance on our route was the town of Viterbo; the supposed site of the ancient "Fanum Voltumnæ," where the associated Etruscan States held their general assemblies. Passing the elevations of no great height which mark on that side the boundaries of the CAMPAGNA ROMANA, we descended into the plain of the Tiber, which flowed on, about four hundred feet in breadth, with a full and strong current,—not clear and sparkling like the Rhone, but with that dark and muddy appearance which I had noticed in the Saone and the Arno. At the distance of two miles from the city we crossed this celebrated river at the old Milvian bridge, the place where the envoys of the Allobrogi were intercepted in the time of Cicero, their letters taken, and Catiline's conspiracy discovered. At this bridge, among other places which witnessed their patriotic resistance, the modern Romans opposed the recent entrance of the French with no small share of the courage of their ancestors. Passing down on the north side of the river, we came into the city by the "PORTA DEL POPOLO," the Gate of the People.

One of the first things which arrested my attention, as we passed through the People's Gate, and into the great square into which it opens, was an Egyptian obelisk of red granite, towering to a great height and covered with hieroglyphics. This obelisk, which was first erected by Rameses, the Egyptian king who is known in Grecian writers under the name of Sesostris, stood originally in the city of Heliopolis, in Lower Egypt; and was brought to Rome by Augustus Cæsar after the battle of Actium. The sight of this striking object, the memorial of other ages and distant climes, vividly recalled to my mind that I had entered a city which more than any other had extended its influence either by arts or arms; the conqueror and the mother of nations; the mighty emblem of the rise and fall of greatness; the central point of profane history; from which, as if standing on the dividing-line of ages, the mind looks back to the beginning and forward to the end.

At the earliest opportunity I visited the Capitoline Hill; not only because it stood first and clearest in my historical associations, but because I had hoped by ascending it to gain at once a full view of the city, and in this way adjust and localize my remembrances. At the base of the steps which ascend this still imposing eminence, are two Egyptian lions of bronze granite. At their top are marble statues of Castor and Pollux with their horses; and in a central position, in the open place or square of the summit, called by the Italians the Campodoglio, is a bronze equestrian statue of Marcus Aurelius, elevated on a large pedestal composed of a single marble block. This is the only bronze equestrian statue which has come down to us from the times of ancient Rome. But this is not the only nor the chief circumstance which imparts to it an interest and value. I came unexpectedly in view of this remarkable statue, and stopped to look at it. It seized hold of my conceptions with a power which seemed to me a test of its excellence. Again and again I turned to examine it. The noble form of Aurelius is seated firmly erect. His countenance is imperial. His right hand is proudly extended, as if indicating the movement and destiny of nations. The horse on which he is seated seems to know that he bears an emperor. His form is the embodiment of energetic strength. His neck curves in the direction of his master's hand; and his large eye appears to glow, as it catches the meaning of its controlling power. Lifting his right hoof, he throws it firmly forward with a movement corresponding to the curvature of the neck and the stern direction of the hand of the emperor; and his broad and muscular breast swells with the impulse of his own fiery action. It is thus that I recall it to mind, as I am seated to write: a form true to nature; the action giving life to the form; and the life enlarged and glowing with greatness and fiery impulse. Such are the works of art which are everywhere found in Rome and in

Roman territory; so that, if it be true, that she is dead in the form of her ancient nationality, it is equally so that she lives, and will continue to live, in the perpetuity of her genius.

At the northern extremity of the Capitoline Hill, is the Franciscan church of Santa Maria d'Ara Cœli. As I looked upon this church, I called to mind a passage in the writings of Gibbon, which in early life had left a deep impression on me. It was here, as he himself tells us in his autobiography, "on the 14th of October, 1764, as he sat musing amid the ruins of the Capitol, while the bare-footed friars were singing vespers," that the idea of writing the "Decline and Fall of Rome" first occurred to his mind.

Leaving the area of the Campodoglio, and I know not how many works of art within and around it, I ascended the tower of the modern Capitol. Below me, including the Capitoline, were the seven hills of ancient Rome, so often mentioned by historians;—the PALATINE, once inhabited by Romulus and Numa, and in the later periods of the republic the residence of Quintus Hortensius and Cicero, now strewed with the fragments of the Cæsars' palaces; at a little distance, and reaching to the Tiber, the AVENTINE, which in other days had been surmounted by the temples of Diana and Minerva and a palace of Trajan, but now more destitute of edifices of every kind than any other of the seven hills; in another direction the CŒLIAN, the place of residence assigned to the ancient Albans, after the destruction of their principal city,—its extreme limit marked at the present time by the church of St. John Lateran; the ESQUILINE, situated to the north of the Cœlian, and extending with its gardens and its remains of ancient buildings to the city walls; the QUIRINAL, a long, narrow eminence, commencing at the Forum of Trajan, covered with buildings comparatively modern, and extending back of the Colonna Palace in a northeast direction; and the VIMINAL, between the Quirinal and Esquiline. These hills, of moderate height and extent, rising perhaps an hundred and fifty feet above the level of the sea, did not look to me like the hills which I had seen in America; but there is a greatness besides that which is physical, and history had magnified them; so that they filled a much larger space in my mind. Beautiful above was the clear Italian sky. In the valley below, skirting the Palatine and Aventine Hills, was the winding Tiber. Moving among the memorials of decay and dissolution, it seemed to have no death and no decay in itself; but still kept its triumphant march, as in the days of Romulus and Camillus, from its native mountains to the sea. Beyond the Tiber was Mount Janiculum. In the opposite direction was the mighty Coliseum. In the distance was the long line of the Apennines. Directly beneath me, in one direction was the steep Tarpeian rock, and in the other the old Roman Forum. Such were the various objects of interest around and before me. Having looked upon them for a short time, I came down from the Capitol.

I have mentioned the Coliseum, as one of the objects seen from the tower of the Capitoline Hill, —that great ruin of Rome and the world; and I am reminded now of my first visit to it. It was the evening of the day of our arrival in Rome.

The sky was cloudless. The moon shone brightly. That night, in company with the excellent friends who had accompanied me thus far, I went to visit this mighty ruin. The Coliseum (taking its name, as some have conjectured, from its great size) is an amphitheatre,—elliptical in its shape, six hundred and twenty feet in one direction, measuring from the exterior surface of the wall, and five hundred and thirteen feet in the other. The height of the wall is one hundred and fifty-seven feet. This immense edifice was commenced by the Emperor Vespasian and finished by his son Titus, ten years after his return to Rome from the destruction of Jerusalem. Capable of holding originally eighty-seven thousand persons, and built with all the strength which architectural genius and profuse expenditure could impart to it, it is now a great mass of ruins. We walked through the broken arches of this mighty desolation. The moon threw its light full upon the open arena, tinging the dewy grass and the clinging ivy which grew in the fissures of the walls. I remembered Byron's admirable description:—

> "I do remember me, that in my youth,
> When I was wandering, upon such a night
> I stood within the Coliseum's wall."

I subsequently visited it in the daytime. My mind had never been more deeply impressed by the greatness of man's works or the magnitude of their desolation; but the impression was subdued and obliterated by the recollection that this very spot had been the scene of one of the great contests of Christianity. Within these vast walls the Roman people, in the days of imperial enslavement and corruption, assembled to witness the contests of wild beasts and the dying struggles of gladiators. But this was not all. They looked with almost equal pleasure upon the shedding of innocent blood. A cross stands in the centre of the open space. As I fixed my eyes upon this significant emblem, I saw in my imagination the dying Christian. It was there he knelt. Perhaps upon the very spot where I stood, a mother or a sister looked down upon him, and prayed that his faith might not fail. He lifted his eyes to heaven. His body was torn by the wild beasts. His blood mingled with the sand of the arena. Perhaps it was Ignatius or Justin, names memorable in Christian history; perhaps some humble believer, unknown to the world, but dear to the Saviour. It was thus, in those days of fiery trial, that the old and young, the learned and the ignorant, the father, the mother and the children, perished. But Christianity still lives. When true to her principles of love, forgiveness, and willingness to suffer, she always conquers; and no defeat and no dishonor is recorded of her, except when, forgetful of the principles and example of her Master, she returns violence with violence.

There were but few objects in Rome on which I looked with more interest than the old imperial arches,—a number of which still remain. A triumphal arch, constructed in the manner of those at Rome, is susceptible in a very high degree of those architectural combinations which cause emotions both of beauty and grandeur. The eye embraces them in their general form at once, so that the emotion is not broken and diminished by that distraction of the attention which is caused when the mind contemplates an object which is much multiplied in its parts. At the same time, they are susceptible of minor decorations, which harmonize with the general outline. Erected in honor of distinguished names and memorable achievements, the principle of association also adds to the effect on the mind which the architecture itself is fitted to inspire. The arch of the Emperor Claudius, as appears from the fragments which yet remain of it, was erected in commemoration of his conquest of the island of Britain. The arch of Constantine —a truly magnificent structure, notwithstanding the injuries of time, and the loss of the triumphal car and the bronze horses which once adorned it—was erected in honor of the victory of that emperor over Maxentius. It has three archways, with eight columns of the Corinthian order, four on each front, and is ornamented with bas-reliefs. The arch of Septimius Severus, the model of the beautiful arch erected by Napoleon in Paris in the Place du Carrousel, which I mentioned in a former letter, commemorates the conquest of Parthia and Persia by Septimius and his sons. The arch of Septimius is in the northwest corner of the old Roman Forum. At no great distance, in the direction of the Palatine Hill, is the celebrated arch of Titus,—not so large and imposing as that of Constantine, but not less beautiful. It was erected by order of the Roman Senate in honor of Titus, and particularly in commemoration of his conquest of the city of Jerusalem. What affecting associations gather in the mind of the Christian as he views such a monument! In passing under the arch the attention is arrested by the bas-reliefs on the piers, which are still beautiful, though much injured. One of them represents Titus seated in his triumphal car, surrounded by Romans carrying the fasces, and drawn by four horses. But I looked with a different and much deeper emotion on the bas-relief on the other side, which represents the early emblems of our religion, taken from their sacred place, and carried in triumphal procession,—the golden table, the silver trumpets, and the candlestick of gold with its seven branches, and other spoils taken from the great temple of the Jews. Captive Jews, sad exiles from their native land, make a part of the procession. This bas-relief is regarded by Biblical archæologists as furnishing one of the most reliable and authentic representations of these sacred objects; harmonizing as they do with the accounts given both in the Bible and in Josephus.

The vessels of the Temple were taken away; but the Temple itself, the work of forty years, and unexampled in splendor, was levelled with the ground. The Temple of Jerusalem, with what was contained in it, represented, in the form of a great material emblem, those conceptions of the Deity and of the methods of approach to Him, which were suited to the capacities of the human mind in that period of the world. When the time came in which it seemed proper that the mind of man should be liberated from these limitations and raised to a higher and juster mode of thought, the ploughshare of destruction passed over it, and left no stone upon another.—The mysteries of Providence are unsearchable. They work out the problems of truth and freedom by destruction as well as by creation. Nations fall; monuments, temples, cities, perish; but principles and truths remain. And who knows, that the vast edifices of worship, which have since been erected in many places with more than Jewish architectural skill, and with but little short of Jewish splendor, tending as they do with the aids of statuary and painting to give a doubtful form to the unseen and unknown mysteries of eternity, and even to embody and localize God himself, may not be destined, in the convulsions of betrayed and struggling humanity striking at the same moment for civil and religious liberty, to a like sudden and terrible destruction? so that men, knowing God in his simplicity, shall understand at last the meaning of the Saviour's words, when he said, "Ye shall neither in this mountain nor yet at Jerusalem worship the Father; but the hour cometh, and now is, when the true worshippers shall worship the Father *in spirit and in truth.*"

Such was the thought that occurred to my mind when viewing the monument erected nearly two thousand years ago, in memory of a man whom God had mysteriously employed as his instrument in one of the most remarkable and terrible events in the history of the human race. It was a thought rather than an opinion. What is to be hereafter will be known when the mysteries of the future develop it. The calculations of human thought and philosophy are often baffled by the decisions of Providence.

One thing, however, is certain. The forms of

religion may vary. The exigencies of different periods may demand different methods of manifestation. What was once revered as an assistance by aiding the heart through the outward sight may require to be removed as an obstruction, because the heart has begun to see more clearly with the inward vision. But religion itself, in its essence, is always the same. Its office is to deal with spirit. "The kingdom of God is within you." In the day of his fiery coming and universal baptism, the Holy Ghost will not be bound. He will work not only in Jerusalem, in Rome, in London, but in Waldensian mountains and in American wildernesses. Mind and not marble will be his material. Working with the skill of the Godhead, which chisels thought and moulds affections, and adjusts the flowing outlines of freedom to the stability of Providence, he will sculpture the soul itself, and create immortal beauty from an immortal element.

(XXV.)

Departure from Rome—The Alban Mount—Lines to the morning star—The Appian Way—Principal towns—The Pontine marshes—Monument to Cicero—Arrival at Naples—Visit to Herculaneum and Pompeii.

NAPLES, JAN. 2, 1853.

SWEET morning star, with golden ray,
How clear thy gentle splendors shine,
To usher in the early day
Along the Tiber's winding way,
And o'er the Apennine.

Oh, thus, with smile as clear and bright,
In other lands I've known thy beam;

The lingering day delay'd its light,
But thou didst crown the distant height
That watch'd my native stream.

I met thee there, I meet thee here;
I loved thee then; I love thee yet;
And not the less, that thy bright sphere
Recalls the home, to friendship dear,
Which love cannot forget.

Oh no! And if it fits thy ray
The messages of love to bear,
Haste to that distant home, and say
That love may wander far away
And yet be always there.

Very early in the morning of the day after we left Rome, we passed down the side of the Alban Mount, where the ancient town of Alba Longa was situated, which was much older than Rome, and was destroyed by Tullus Hostilius. This beautiful eminence, gradual in its ascent and susceptible of being built upon and cultivated to its summit, answered precisely the idea of it which the descriptions of the Latin poets and historians had left upon my mind in early life. As I was observing, at the breaking of the day, the beautiful scenery which opened to my view, my eye caught the morning star shining with peculiar richness in the clear blue above the Apennines, not far distant. I had often watched its morning brightness from the hills of my own land: it reminded me so strongly of home, that I committed to its swift and beautiful rays the little message of the heart with which I have begun this letter, and which I trust will reach its destination in safety.

Our route from Rome to Naples was for the most part along the old Appian Way, built by the Censor

Appius Claudius, three hundred years before the time of Christ, and called by Cicero, with a good deal of propriety, "REGINA VIARUM." We entered on this road at Albano, on the Alban Mount, and left it at the river Garagliano, the ancient Siris. The principal places through which we passed were the city of Velletri, once the capital of the Volsci, but which has ceased to retain the splendor which formerly belonged to it; Cisterna, the location, according to antiquarians, of the Tres Tabernæ or Three Taverns, where the Christians of Rome are mentioned in the Acts of the Apostles as having met the Apostle Paul; the city of Terracina, originally one of the towns of the Volsci, known in the time of Horace by the name of Anxur, and which is described by him in his journey to Brundusium; the town of Fondi, which has some interest for the admirers of scholastic ingenuity as being the residence of Thomas Aquinas and the place where he gave his instructions in theology; the town of Itri, without any special historical interest, but encircled with hills which were covered with vines, fig-trees, and orange-trees; the town of Mola di Gaeta, from which we had a view of the beautiful city of Gaeta, situated upon the Mediterranean,—the same with the ancient Cajeta, which Virgil has celebrated in the seventh book of the Æneid; and the city of Capua, upon the river Volturno, the ancient Vulturnus, near which Hannibal defeated the Romans.

Between Cisterna and Fondi are the Pontine marshes, twenty-four miles in length,—once stagnant and unhealthy, but now drained and restored to fertility by canals. Large herds of cattle were feeding on them. At the western extremity of these marshes, stretching out into the sea, is the rocky and lofty residence of the ancient sorceress Circe, known at the present time by the name of Monte Circello, which the Homeric traditions have celebrated as the place where the companions of Ulysses were detained and made the subjects of her enchantments. On the portion of the Appian Way which passes through the Pontine marshes was the old Roman town of Appii Forum, which seems to have been a considerable place in the time of Pliny. The prevalent opinion locates it at the place in the marshes which is now called Casarillo, about fifty-six miles from Rome. "When the brethren heard of us," says the account in Acts, "they came to meet us as far as Appii Forum, and the Three Taverns."

Near one of the towns which I have mentioned —Mola di Gaeta—the great orator of Rome had a country-villa, to which he often retired for study and recreation. It was here that he had his meetings and conversations with Lælius and Scipio. When his inveterate enemy Mark Antony came into power, and the name of Cicero—a name equally dear to eloquence, philosophy, and liberty—was placed on the list of those who were proscribed, he fled to his retired residence, and had nearly reached it, when he was overtaken and put to death by his pursuers. It was with melancholy interest that we looked upon the lofty tower, still standing on the right hand of the road as it approaches Mola di Gaeta, which the affection of his freedmen erected to his memory on the spot where he was slain.

The road through the Pontine marshes is wide and level, and in many places planted with trees. Rich and various were the beauties of nature, appealing everywhere to man's heart and reading lessons on the goodness of Providence, as we passed onward to other places more diversified in their character. On one side were level and verdant plains and distant glimpses of the sea, and on the other hills and mountains; and everywhere, though it was mid-winter, were gardens, still bright with their flowers, and trees laden with fruit. Passing the river Vulturnus at Capua, now called the Volturno, I was much struck with the appearance of the rich and level plains, everywhere bearing the marks of high cultivation, which extended several miles from its banks. Situated in such a country, it is not surprising that ancient Capua had such attractions of magnificence and pleasure as to perplex even the strong mind of Hannibal, and that it stood second at one time only to Rome and Carthage. But while my heart paid homage to the beauties of nature, I could not conceal from myself that man, who should have been her glorious and crowning work, appeared in many instances sad, degraded, and suffering. The beggary which had afflicted us in other places increased in the variety of its forms and importunity, as we approached Naples. As I witnessed the rags and the sunken countenances of the poor creatures who continually surrounded our carriage and asked for the smallest pittance, it was difficult to realize that these were the descendants of the men whose genius has inspired the arts and literature of other nations, and who were once the conquerors of the world.

We left Rome the 29th of December, in the afternoon, and reached Naples on the 31st. On the next day, the 1st of January, we visited the remains of Herculaneum and Pompeii, and ascended Vesuvius. Pompeii was once a populous and beautiful city, some three or four miles in circumference, situated on the river Sarno, at twelve miles' distance from Naples. It was overwhelmed by an eruption of Vesuvius on the 24th of August, in the seventy-ninth year of the Christian era,—an eruption of terrible violence, in which the burning lava, boiling over the crater and carrying off large portions of the mountain, took the direction of Herculaneum and destroyed it, while immense masses of ashes and small stones, driven in another direction by the wind, overwhelmed Pompeii. The city of Pompeii, buried in this sudden and terrible manner, lay in its dark tomb of volcanic ashes, concealed and almost forgotten, for more than sixteen hundred years. In the year 1751, some peasants, who were employed in cultivating a vineyard near the river Sarno, discovered it. And since that time the excavations have been made; till at last a large portion of the city, in a state of wonderful preservation, has been brought to light.

On the first day of the year, and early in the morning, we entered Pompeii through the Herculaneum gate. With a map before us, and accompanied with a guide to give the necessary explanations, it may well be imagined that we walked with deep emotion through this city of resurrection, this disentombed memorial of a departed empire. The streets, which generally cross each other at right angles, are straight and paved with lava, and have on each side a raised footway. The houses are generally one story in height, strongly built of lava or other hard material, stuccoed, and frequently painted. As is common in this climate, they are so built as to enclose open quadrangular areas, in some of which are fountains supplied with water from the Sarno, which seems to have been carried under the city by means of subterranean canals. We rapidly examined many houses. Entering first the quadrangular space, we inspected successively the rooms of the house, which is built around the open square, which vary in number and size in accordance with the size of the house,—the parlor or sitting-room, the dressing-room, rooms for sleeping and bathing, the kitchen; and in some cases we noticed the small chapel which was appropriated to the Lares or household gods. The windows have the appearance of having been provided originally with wooden shutters. The floors are frequently a pavement of mosaic. The names and occupations of the inhabitants have been ascertained from the inscriptions in red paint on the exterior of the houses.

Some of the excavations are outside of the Herculaneum gate. The house of Marcus Arrius Diomedes is here. It is of two stories, and is the first which was discovered. Some of the rooms in this house are constructed with mosaic pavements, and adorned with fresco paintings. It has a garden, cellar, baths, and furnaces for heating water. In the cellar there still remain a number of large wine-jars partly filled and surrounded with ashes, and which, by a fusion of materials contained in the ashes, have become cemented to the wall. An incident occurred here, which reminded us of the dreadful nature of the catastrophe which overwhelmed this devoted city. We were pointed by our guide to the place in the cellar of this house where the skeleton remains of seventeen persons were discovered. One of them, adorned with gold ornaments, is supposed to have been the wife of Diomedes. One of the objects of special interest in the city is the house of Sallust, the Roman historian. It is a large house, situated upon the street by which we entered the city, and such a one as might be supposed to suit the taste and convenience of a man of wealth and a scholar. Art had contributed to adorn it with its statuary and paintings. Some of the paintings on the walls, to which our attention was directed, are still in a tolerable state of preservation; one in particular, a picture of Diana and Actæon. It is worthy of notice that this house has its little chapel for the LARES,—indicating that Sallust was not disposed to discredit or to treat with contempt the religious sentiments of his countrymen. The remains of four persons, who perished in the destruction of the city, were found here.

I could not have anticipated that anything which I should see at Pompeii would have any special personal interest for me. But the interest which we feel in the works of a man, whether of literature or art, naturally attaches to the author of them; and the interest which we feel in the man attaches itself again to his place of residence; so that in visiting the house of Sallust and going from room to room, I felt very much as if I were visiting the residence of some old friend, to whom I had been under personal obligations for his instructions and kindness. The residences of other distinguished Romans have been ascertained.

Among the buildings which have been excavated, are shops of various kinds,—wine-shops, barbers' shops, bakers' shops,—showing, as well as temples, theatres, and works of art, though in different ways, the necessities, employments, and character of the people. It is not to be supposed, however, that all which has been found at Pompeii exists there now. Among the ancient remains which have been dug up there, and which are still preserved at Naples, some of which we had an opportunity of seeing subsequently, are not only busts and statues and other sculptures, but household utensils, coins, weights and measures, surgical instruments, vases of silver and bronze, the various ornaments worn by females, such as rings, bracelets, ear-rings, sometimes enriched with pearls, also amulets of various forms and made of various rich materials, and exquisitely-wrought representations of birds and other animals in mosaic. I hardly know of any thing in the works of art which, in niceness of workmanship, and in the accuracy with which they represent objects, exceeds some of the mosaics which have been found at Pompeii.

(XXVI.)

Ascent of Mount Vesuvius—Narrow and precipitous paths bordered by a river of lava—Old Herculanean crater—The two craters now in action—The prospect in descending—Historical references.

NAPLES, JAN. 2, 1853.—SECOND LETTER.

RETURNING from Pompeii, we stopped at the town of Resina, which is built above the buried Herculaneum. We descended the excavation which leads to the celebrated Herculanean theatre, and afterwards visited another portion of the city, which has been excavated and remains open for inspection. At noon our party, including Mrs. Walcott, the enterprising and much-esteemed lady whom I have already mentioned as being one of our number, started from Resina on horseback, with the view of ascending Vesuvius, whose fires and ashes had caused the vast ruin of which we had just been the witnesses.

The route is on the western side of the mountain, the distance eight miles,—a continual ascent through ways narrow, rocky, and precipitous, but not without interest, bordered as they are with the habitations of men, and with gardens and vineyards, and often presenting wild and magnificent views. As we came near the mountain, which rose majestically above us, throwing out from its heated craters a column of smoke, we passed along the side of an immense river of lava, which had stopped in its burning progress and hardened into stone,—a perpetual monument, in its mighty and terrific desolation, of the terrible agency which has wrought in the bosom of this mountain. Having passed the rugged base and ascended to a considerable height, we found ourselves at last in the bottom of the great crater, from which are said to have issued the volumes of melted material which destroyed Herculaneum.

Standing in the centre of this old and mighty caldron, with its blackened walls of two miles in circumference, it was easy to go back, in imagination, to the time when its great heat melted earth and rocks, and when it boiled with its restless waves of flame. At this place, where the mountain becomes very precipitous and difficult, we were obliged to leave our horses. The remaining ascent was about a thousand feet, and could not have been effected by us without very considerable aid from others. Mr. Thompson, with the aid of the vigorous men who assisted us, ascended on foot. The others of our number, unequal to the attempt in any other way, were carried on chairs elevated on men's shoulders; and the whole distance was over lava and cinders. In this way, not without some trouble and perplexity, we reached the summit of the mountain of fire.

There are two craters, which are now slightly in action, not far from each other, and unequal, though not varying much in size. They seemed to be about three-fourths of a mile in circumference at the top. Their form is that of a hollow inverted cone. We walked to the edge of each of these craters. It was terrible to look down. The edge, which is distinctly marked in its outline, is a hardened and burnt crust; a fusion of the various materials thrown out from the vortex; black in color, but everywhere diversified by the pale yellow tint of sulphur. The craters, growing more and more narrow towards the bottom, are hundreds of feet in depth; and it is but natural to suppose that they are connected with other unknown depths in the vast burning caverns in the base of the mountain.

From the bottom the smoke ascended in columns of living and endless darkness. And the large dark mass from the abyss was increased by the numberless small wreaths of smoke which issued from the crevices in its scorched and sulphurous side. Repeatedly I placed my hand over these smoking crevices, which opened frequently on the edge of the crater, as well as on the side below, and felt great heat. Striking my foot upon the earth in different places, it emitted a hollow and ominous sound, which indicated that nothing but a heated and uncertain crust separated us from the unknown conflagrations below. Having sufficiently satisfied our curiosity in viewing this wonderful place, we were not slow in returning. And I think that most persons who have ascended Vesuvius will agree in saying that there is but little inducement to remain there for any length of time.

On coming down the side of the mountain, it was near the setting of the sun; and a scene of wide and diversified grandeur opened before us. In one direction were the Apennines with their tops covered with snow. In the other the bay of Naples, with the distant islands of Procida and Ischia, realized all that had been said of its wonderful beauty. Below us was the city of Naples, and other cities and towns as far as the eye could reach,—adorned with all that is rich and variegated in nature and wonderful in art. And the setting sun, illuminating the clear blue sky, glanced upon land and sea, upon mountain and valley, and wrote his farewell in letters of gold. And yet this expanse of inimitable beauty could not make us forget that we were on the sides of Vesuvius. It was a beauty around us, but not with us. The earth upon which we trod, in contrast with what we saw in the distance, was scorched, and black, and full of chasms. We could not forget that buried as well as living cities were at our feet. We were on the mountain of destruction.

I have already remarked that the eruption which destroyed the cities visited by us took place in the seventy-ninth year of the Christian era. Pliny the Younger, who was an eye-witness, has given a graphic and striking account of it in a letter to Tacitus. But Vesuvius did not exhaust itself at that time. There have been thirty-six recorded eruptions, some of them as terrible as that which destroyed Pompeii, besides those of which we have no account. The immense amount of ashes, lava, and cinders scattered over the whole coast—enough if collected together to form a mountain larger than Vesuvius as it now stands—is evidence of their number and violence. As the effects of these eruptions are essentially the same, differing only in degree, so are the circumstances which attend them.

Writers who have given accounts of them inform us that they often exhibit premonitory signs. The earth shakes. Beasts and birds, taught by their unerring instincts, scream with terror and flee away.

Murmurs and groans are heard, deep and terrible, as if uttering the agonies of a mountain laid upon a burning altar. The sea rolls back in agitation. Vast clouds of ashes, hovering high in the air, obscure the light of day. If the sun penetrates them at all, his rays are feeble and red, as if his brightness had put on mourning. Burning rocks in rapid succession are thrown high above the summit. Deep streams of lava, hundreds of feet in width, roll down the mountain's side in cataracts of fire, and in their restless march destroy everything that comes in their way. Man hides himself. Nature mourns. Desolation triumphs.

Such are the terms in which those who have witnessed these terrible scenes have attempted to describe them.

(XXVII.)

Tomb of Virgil—Capri, Scylla and Charybdis—Arrival at Malta—Shipwreck and journeys of St. Paul—Character of the Maltese—Churches.

VALETTA, ISLAND OF MALTA, JAN. 6, 1853.

A FRENCH steamer from Marseilles has brought us to this place. It has been pleasing to me to sail in a foreign vessel, because it furnishes a new chapter in the book of man's varied history and nature. We have been much pleased with the captain, sailors, and general arrangements of the ship. The zeal and native politeness of a Frenchman does not desert him when upon deck. But I must go back a little in my narrative, and say something more among the multitude of things which will be left unsaid.

I should not have pardoned myself, if I had left Naples without following the example of many others in visiting what is supposed to be the tomb of Virgil. The tomb, which bears the name of this great poet, is on an elevated spot near the road which leads to Pozzuoli and Baiae. It is a retired and beautiful place, affording a wide and variegated prospect. The tomb once contained a sepulchral urn supported on nine columns, which is now gone. The small monumental building which was erected around the urn still remains; but the greatest works of art, if they were here, could add but little to the interest with which the place is invested. Virgil was suddenly attacked with his last sickness, when travelling with the Emperor Augustus; and it is generally thought that he selected the place of his interment himself. There can be no doubt that the emperor, who esteemed and loved him, fulfilled his wishes, whatever they were. The common opinion, so far as I know, asserts this to be the chosen spot. It is such a place as might be supposed to suit a mind which loved retirement, and which was itself a receptacle and an emblem of beauty. Upon a marble tablet in the wall is the epitaph which he wrote for himself:—

> Mantua me genuit; Calabri rapuere; tenet nunc
> Parthenope.—Cecini pascua, rura, et duces.

Some poor people, who cultivate the grounds,—such humble people as he loved to describe in his inimitable lines,—live near his burial-place. Fragrant flowers and plants adorn the spot. The ocean-breezes fan it. The beams of the sun of Italy love to linger here.

In coming out of the bay of Naples we passed near the island of Capri, which separates the bay in one direction from the Mediterranean. It seemed nothing but a lofty rock, very little suited for the habitations of men. And yet this was the place selected by Tiberius Cæsar for his residence,—dark, solitary, rocky, shut out from every thing else, like the hardness and selfish seclusion of his own heart. Hating men, because his suspicions and injustice had made himself an object of hatred, he fled to this lonely and desolate spot, and made a palace on the rocks, but without ceasing to be cruel and without fleeing from remorse.

As we approached Sicily, we came in sight of the islands called the Lipari Islands, in one of which Virgil has located the habitation and caves of Æolus. One of the most remarkable of these is Stromboli,—a precipitous volcanic mountain, ten miles in circuit at its base,—a Vesuvius in the midst of the ocean. It is said that this volcano seldom ceases to give signs of action, so that in the night it is a light-house to the sailors in these seas; but, passing it in the daytime, we saw nothing but a heavy cloud of smoke resting upon its crater.

It is something for a man to say that he has passed safely through Scylla and Charybdis; but this has been done by us in our voyage to this place. As we passed along the coast of Calabria, we went into the beautiful harbour of Messina, in the island of Sicily,—formed by a narrow promontory of land running off from the east end of the city. This promontory contracts the straits of Messina at this place, and, combined probably with other causes, such as hidden rocks and caverns, causes a violent and irregular motion of the water. And this is the whirlpool, or rather a multitude of little whirlpools, of Charybdis,—less violent, perhaps, than it was once, but still not without its perils. Sailing-ships, in avoiding Charybdis, stand over to the Calabrian or Italian side, and are thus in danger, especially when the current and winds set in that direction, of running upon an elevated and rocky point of land at some distance in the narrowest part of the strait. This is the rock called Scylla; and near it is the modern Italian village of Sciglio. I am not at all surprised at the dread which these real dangers excited in the minds of ancient navigators. Brydone remarks that five ships were wrecked on the rock of Scylla, during the winter previous to his visit here some years since. Our excellent steamer of course carried us through without difficulty.

On arriving at Malta, we could not forget that this island was the scene of St. Paul's shipwreck, of which Luke has given so specific an account in his history of the Acts of the Apostles. I am aware that some writers have supposed that this shipwreck might have taken place on another small island in the Adriatic Sea. But the evidence in favour of Malta seems to me very decisive. The place, as designated by the traditions of the country, is on the north side of the island, about eight miles west from the city of Valetta. As our stay at Malta was short, we lost no time in visiting this interesting locality. We came in full sight of it on a height of land more than a mile distant, and were struck with its conformity to the description given in Acts. Here is the small creek where the sailors, in their perilous situation, would naturally endeavor "to thrust in the ship." On the left of its mouth is a narrow point of land projecting into the sea where the "two seas met;" or, what seems to be a better translation, "a place washed by the sea on both sides." On the point of land forming the other side of this natural harbor is the place to which the Maltese traditions assign the meeting of Paul with the "barbarous people who showed no little kindness." Publius, "the chief man of the island," is supposed to have resided at the old town of Citta Vecchia, a few miles distant.

On leaving Malta, after three months' residence here, the apostle sailed for Italy, touching at Syracuse in Sicily, and at Rhegium in Calabria. This last place, now called Reggio, we passed in coming through the straits of Messina. It is still a considerable town. His voyage terminated at Puteoli, now called by the Italians Pozzuoli. Puteoli was once a large and commercial place; and if it be true, as is stated by some writers, that it had much commerce with Alexandria, we see how it happened that an Alexandrian ship brought Paul here. It is an interesting circumstance, that a Christian church was established at Puteoli before Paul's arrival. At least such would be a natural inference from the fact that he met with Christian brethren there, and abode with them seven days. In visiting Puteoli, (which we did soon after our arrival at Naples,) we were influenced by a natural desire to see the spot which had witnessed the faith and prayers of Christians in the early days of Christianity, and where the apostle first set foot upon the land where he was to complete and crown his multiplied labors by a triumphant martyrdom. We had thought of him when travelling the Appian Road, and at Appii Forum and the Three Taverns; he had been recalled to our mind when visiting the Mamertine prisons in Rome and the dungeons of Nero on the promontory of Baiae; and in looking upon the fragments of the Cæsars' palaces on the Palatine Hill, we had not forgotten that this too was the scene of his prayers and toils, and that among the devoted ones who had been blessed by his labors were some of "Cæsar's household." He was put to death in the city of Rome. But, though history records the fact, no historian undertakes to state the precise time of his execution, nor the precise spot on which his blood was shed.

We have enjoyed much our short visit in this island. The truth is, that Malta, in many respects, is a very remarkable place,—remarkable in its location, its physical and geological formation, and in its long and varied history. A mere calcareous rock in the ocean, covered with so little soil that its industrious inhabitants are obliged to increase it by importations from Sicily, it is rendered important by its geographical position, in consequence of which it has long been one of the great naval stations of the Mediterranean. And it is an evidence of the value which is attached to it, that it has passed successively, in the course of its history, into the hands of the Phenicians, Carthaginians, Romans, Arabians, French, Spaniards, and English who now hold it.

The city of Valetta is the capital of the island of Malta, built upon a small rocky peninsula, which is washed on its two sides by two parallel arms of the sea, running some distance into the land, and forming two large and secure harbors. The fortifications of these harbors, and of other parts of the island, are of immense extent and of vast strength. The ditches surrounding the city, which are of great size and many miles in length, are cut out of the solid rock.

The Maltese have long had the reputation of being a peaceable and industrious people; and we saw nothing which led us to doubt the correctness of this opinion except the contests among the boatmen, which may be ascribed chiefly to the rivalship of necessity rather than to evil disposition. Their religion is Roman Catholic, and there is more appearance of sincerity and devoutness than we had noticed in some parts of Italy and France. They have numerous churches; the largest and most splendid of which is the cathedral church of St. John, which is distinguished, among other things, by its costly sepulchral monuments to the Masters and Commanders of the Knights of Malta. In our visit to this church we were shown three keys, taken at different times from the Turks by the Knights of Malta, and which are said to be the keys of the gates of Jerusalem, Acre, and Rhodes. Of the paintings which it contains, the most remarkable is the beheading of St. John, by Caravaggio. The church itself, like other Catholic churches, is on a scale of size and magnificence which is not often witnessed in Protestant countries; and which is hardly consistent with, or at least is not required by, the simplicity of Protestant worship.

(XXVIII.)

Coast of Africa—Reminiscences of Italy and its works of art—Of some frequent and obvious defects in them—Statue of Moses by Michael Angelo—Statue of Christ in the church of St. John Lateran—The Christ of Corradini in Naples—The Laocoon—The dying gladiator—American artists.

FRENCH STEAMSHIP ALEXANDER, OFF THE COAST OF AFRICA, JAN. 10, 1853.

WE left Malta on the seventh. In the course of the voyage, which is not yet terminated, we have sailed a considerable distance along the coast of Tripoli. And here, for the first time, we came in sight of the Great Libyan Desert, which stretches westward from the banks of the Nile. On this coast was the ancient city of Cyrene, the residence of the Cyrenians mentioned in the New Testament. We passed in full sight of the city of Derne, which was once in the possession of the United States during their troubles with Tripoli. It is still a considerable place. Vast desert plains and arid mountains have been in sight.

With the leisure now afforded I wish to say something further of what came under my notice in Italy. In one sense Italy is a land in ruins, and yet it is a land on which is deposited everything which human art and genius can effect. Works of art are found in England and France, in many of their principal places,—in Oxford, in London, in Paris, and other great centres of material and intellectual wealth. But in Italy, either in the form of ancient remains or as the result of modern skill, they are to be found everywhere. Temples and statues are in her dust. In repeated instances our attention was called to columns, capitals, sculptures, which in America would be regarded as great treasures, scattered in the fields and gardens, lying about in the streets, and sometimes built up in the rude stone walls which the people had erected around their cultivated places.

It would be pleasant, undoubtedly, to give some more particular account of the works of art which we have seen; but their number renders it difficult to do so in the course of a few letters; and, besides, it is hazardous to offer statements and critiques upon art when there has been but little time for examination and study. I give, therefore, impressions and not criticisms. Man is not born a critic, which implies culture, as well as elemental power; but he is simply born a man; and therefore, though I make no pretensions to formal criticism, founded upon any special knowledge of the arts, I cannot deny the power of perceiving and feeling, because this is common to humanity. It must be conceded, I suppose, that the world nowhere else exhibits what is to be seen in Italy, either in the number, the greatness, or the excellence of her works. To this general praise she is entitled; and it would be as little to a man's credit to deny the unsurpassed literary excellence of Cicero, Virgil, and Tacitus, as to deny a like completeness and excellence of the Italian genius in the various departments of art. And yet it must be confessed that the impression which is left upon the mind (I mean a mind which perceives and feels without pretensions to a scientific criticism) is not always favorable. In the great edifices which attract notice, the churches, palaces, and other public buildings, the most frequent defect which occurs is the want of apparent unity of purpose and plan. It may be thought perhaps, by some, that vastness and unity cannot be combined; but this is an error. One of the first feelings which a person has in contemplating St. Paul's church in London, or the church of St. Genevieve in Paris, or St. Peter's in Rome, is that one mind, animated by one leading artistic conception, presided over their construction, and harmonized their various parts. The same may be said of the Coliseum at Rome, and of many other large edifices. They are single thoughts,—the vast conceptions of the inward intelligence taking an outward form, and raised and brought into shape and harmony in sculptured stone and marble.

But still the defect to which I have referred—namely, the want of unity—is frequent. The circumstances under which many large edifices have been built is probably the explanation of this frequent defect, in part. The addition of building to building, carried over a large extent of ground, erected at different periods of time, with different styles of architecture, and with various and conflicting objects, may constitute an edifice which will astonish by its vastness and splendor, but which can hardly fail to be wanting in that obvious and controlling unity of conception which is essential to the completeness of architectural beauty. But it ought to be added, that these remarks may be true in regard to many public edifices, while at the same time the subordinate parts are finished with an excellence of art which cannot be surpassed.

Another defect in many of those public edifices, to which the particular notice of the traveller is invited, is excess of decoration. Art, not satisfied with the natural limits of its own power, has gone on exhausting itself in repetitions, and in worse than useless attempts to give additional touches to beauty which did not need them. Nothing seems to be left for the mind to fill up. Wherever there is a place for ornament it seems to be occupied, as if there were no power and no beauty in simplicity. This excessive decoration is probably owing in some cases to the zeal of unregulated piety, as much as to defective taste.

In the countless statuary which came under our notice, the defect which seemed to me most frequently to occur, was the failure to harmonize expression with character. If it is true that every man has a character of some kind, it is also true that every character, which is only another name for the predominant dispositions of the mind, has its appropriate expression. A sculptor may give the great outlines of the head of Nero or of Caligula; but if he adds the comparatively mild and just expression which characterizes the features of Antoninus or Nerva, he violates both history and nature. I am not certain that I shall make myself understood, but it seems to me that the celebrated statue of Moses by Michael Angelo may properly be regarded as an illustration of this remark.

In looking upon this great work, which occupies a place in the church of St. Peter IN VINCULIS in Rome, we felt no disposition to detract from its acknowledged and obvious merits. In all the attributes of art, with the exception, as it seemed to me, of the relation between expression and character, it is a work eminently worthy of its distinguished author. We could not fail to recognize the creative mind of the artist at once. But, naturally forming our ideal of Moses from our early readings in the Bible, we were led to inquire,—Where is the other mind which the mind of the artist has undertaken to represent? Where is the mind of Moses, which it should have been his first object to gather up and combine from history and re-establish and make alive in marble? Where is the expression of that humble and meek disposition which his history and his writings have led us especially to attribute to him? We certainly failed to recognize it in that stern and angry grandeur which characterizes the countenance of this statue.

In many of the numberless paintings and statues of the Virgin Mary which we everywhere saw, there was this painful failure of appropriate expression. Art has exhausted itself in drawing the outlines of her beauty; but they are not inlaid with those revelations of holy thought and feeling which her personal history has led us to expect. And still more is this defect seen in the statues and paintings of the Saviour. The predominant dispositions of the Saviour in his humanity were meekness, benevolence, pity, and perfect faith in God,—traits which were not overcome or obscured by man's unbelief and persecutions, nor by the inward trials to which his heavenly Father sometimes left him. He had nothing in himself, but all things in God. And, being a "partaker of the divine nature," he loved as God loves, and communicated himself to others in all the appropriate sympathies of humanity. His love shone in his tears. His faith was not shaken when the powers of darkness were let loose upon him.

In Paris, in Florence, in Rome, I looked upon painting after painting and statue after statue, and in almost every instance missed something of that divine expression which should have stood out as the interpretation and the symbol of his character. The works in other respects were often admirable. There was symmetry, intelligence, beauty, such as we often see in the statues and portraits of good and distinguished men, but still an absence, in a greater or less degree, of the true and Christ-like disposition.

I saw a painting in the Vatican, by a painter not much known, which is exempt in a great degree from this defect. It does not fully give the idea of Christ's intellectual power; but the expression of his affectional nature, of those heavenly dispositions which I have mentioned, leaves nothing to be desired. In the church of St. John Lateran we were shown a recumbent statue of Christ after his crucifixion, which produced upon us a similar effect. The countenance, as it appeared to be made present in marble, had not lost the look which was appropriate to its humanity; but a mingled expression of sympathetic sorrow and triumphant peace seemed to ally it both with earth and heaven. But I think I never saw the character of the Saviour, the outline and filling up of his inward and sacred disposition, so perfectly sculptured in the countenance, as in the marble statue of Christ in death, which we were shown in the church of St. Mary in the city of Naples. This extraordinary work was designed by Anthony Corradini, a Venetian artist of high reputation; but in consequence of his death it was executed by Sarumartino, an artist of Naples, to whom a large share of its perfection is to be ascribed. Christ is laid in the tomb *veiled.* The veil is wrought in the marble with immense care and labor, and with such skill that the form of the body, and even the muscles, are seen through it; and, what is remarkable, it is made to appear by the artist as if it were slightly moistened by the perspiration of death. But this veil does not obscure in any unfavorable degree the expression of the Saviour's countenance, which is full of resignation, sympathy, peace, and triumph. My heart, which had long dwelt upon the inward image, was deeply affected in the presence of that triumph of Christian art. The divine countenance, which it had embodied in marble, seemed to come like a revelation from another world, and was present with me many days after. So perfect was the expression of the Christ-like attributes,—it harmonized so completely with the impression left by the frequent reading of the Scripture narrative,—that I could hardly help saying to myself, that I had seen the Saviour.

It may be laid down as a general principle, that an artist can embody in the forms of art only what he has in himself. If he has powers of intellectual conception, he will make the marble or the canvas conform to the intellectual idea. But if, with these requisites of art, he is wanting in true and good dispositions, if there is nothing benevolent, just, and noble in his character, his hand will tremble and grow weak under the want of an inward inspiration and guidance, and will betray the imperfection of the artist's nature. I might almost say, since such is the general result, that the canvas and marble, as if unwilling to violate the tendencies and laws of universal nature, will refuse to honor that which is not honored in itself.

If this view is correct, I think we may partially understand the secret of the frequent failures in the artistic representation of Scripture subjects and persons. The artist must have some elements of sympathy with that which he undertakes to represent, or he will not be likely to succeed. And it is easy for me to believe that the artist who executed the admirable statuary to which I have last referred had much of the spirit of Christ in his heart; and that he was thus assisted in representing it in marble.

In passing through the galleries of art, the traveller is not to expect that he will find everything equally perfect. Some works are much mutilated, and are retained chiefly on account of their antiquity, or because they throw light upon some doubtful fact in history, or upon some obscure passage in ancient writers. Of those which are retained exclusively on account of their merit, some will be found to possess much more excellence than others. So that in rapidly passing through the immense and numerous galleries which are found in Italy, many works of art will justly claim and will be likely to receive only a slight notice. Others will stand out as their own commentators, and will make their own powerful appeals.

I shall not easily forget the emotions I experienced, when, in the palace of the Vatican, I stood for the first time in the presence of the Laocoon,—styled, by Michael Angelo, "the wonder of art." Different from all other works of statuary in the subject which is represented, and exceedingly difficult from the peculiar nature of the subject, it left upon my mind the impression that it must stand alone and unequalled in its execution. What a subject!—a father with two sons, enveloped in the folds of an enormous serpent, and yet so grouped and so developed from the marble, that each object is distinctly exhibited, and each in character. Central to the eye and heart of the spectator is the strong and muscular form of the father, rendered doubly strong by parental sympathy and fear, his body twined around by the serpent, his convulsive hand grasping his terrible folds, and straining with the anguish of despair,—a father mighty in his agonies. With sad and tortured countenances, turned upward towards the father, as if to catch a gleam of hope from him, his two sons, one on each side, are twined and compressed and crushed by the same terrible folds, but still struggling and beautiful. Youth, beauty, strength, age, a child's affection, a father's love, pain, sympathy, despair, horror, the death-struggles of the body, the agonies of the mind, each perfect in itself, all united in one group, all born as it were out of one solid piece of marble, and all grasped and wounded and crushed in the successive and endless windings of the inexorable monster:—such is the subject and the execution.

I wandered through the Museum of the Roman Capitol—another of the great receptacles of the works of art—with all those feelings of deep interest which are due to the place and the rich treasures it contains. We could give but little more than a passing look. Each successive work, so far as it had relation to the æsthetic nature, was allowed to tell its own story and produce its own effects.

Many things were seen and briefly examined with more or less care and passed by, leaving but feeble impressions. They had value, but not power. But it was not so when I came to the Dying Gladiator. The relation of this work of art to the operations of the human mind is definite and complete; and the result on the feelings is as certain as the laws of nature. The celebrated English anatomist, John Bell, who visited Italy some years since, asserts, and goes into particulars in support of the assertion, that the anatomy of this remarkable figure is exceedingly perfect. There is no doubt of the truth of this. But I must confess that I thought but little about the anatomy as a separate subject of consideration. It was the dying man which occupied my thoughts, or rather the dying body sinking slowly to the earth with its relaxed and recumbent limbs, and yielding up in expressions of sadness and agony the unconquerable spirit to another life. It was the sculpture of life and death in actual conflict, and both conquerors; death conquering the body, but life escaping from the drooping eye and asserting its immortality in the fortitude and mournful memories which still lingered upon the fainting countenance. Byron, in his Childe Harold, has referred to this wonderful piece of sculpture in a touching and graphic stanza:—

> "I see before me the gladiator lie:
> He leans upon his hand; his manly brow
> Consents to death, but conquers agony,
> And his droop'd head sinks gradually low;
> And through his side the last drops, ebbing slow,
> From the red gash fall heavy, one by one,
> Like the first of a thunder-shower; and now
> The arena swims around him. He is gone,
> Ere ceased the inhuman shout which hail'd the wretch who won."

I ought not to omit to say that we found a number of American artists at Rome. These young men go to Rome to contemplate ancient genius and to gather inspiration from the minds of other days still living in their works; as in earlier times, and under the same impulses of the love of truth and of honorable ambition, the artists and philosophers of Rome went to Athens, and the distinguished men of Athens went to Memphis and Thebes. We were kindly received in the studio of Mr. Story, the son of the eminent American jurist of that name; and our feelings were touched at witnessing the efforts of the artistic genius and filial piety of the son, in erecting, in the sculptured statue upon which he is employed, a worthy monument to his distinguished father. In the studio of Mr. Crawford, another American artist of justly-established fame, we spent an interesting hour in viewing the works of which he is the author, or which he has gathered around him. Mr. Crawford has been many years in Rome; and has made his way to his present high position as an artist, by the impulses of true genius, directed and aided by a just estimate of the cost of artistic skill, and by persevering and self-sacrificing industry. He is employed at the present time, by the State of Virginia, in making an equestrian statue of Washington.

(XXIX.)

Arrival at Alexandria—Cleopatra's Needle—Pompey's Pillar—Palace of the Pasha—Character of the population—Mahmoudie Canal—Commencement of voyage up the Nile—Character of the boat's crew.

EGYPT, NILE-BOAT LOTUS, TOWN OF ATFEH, JAN. 14, 1853.

We reached Alexandria on the 11th of January. We came in sight of the city at dawn of day. It was a calm and beautiful morning. No clouds obscured the sky. The surface of the sea was unbroken except where at intervals it dashed its foam gently over the breakers. On our right as we approached the city, a long line of low, sandy hills was seen in the distance. Large sea-birds in great numbers came around us. They seemed to rejoice in our coming,—sometimes soaring upward far into the blue depths, and then descending upon their broad white wings, till they fanned the sails of the vessel. As we were looking at the city, more beautiful in the distance than on a nearer inspection, a boat was seen approaching from the harbor. A swarthy Turk, his head bound with a turban, came on board, whose business it was to act as our pilot. Under the direction of his dark and thoughtful eye, the vessel moved slowly along the narrow and winding channel. On our left was the isle of Pharos; on our right was the pillar of Pompey. The harbor was full of merchant-vessels, steamers, and ships of war. The flags of many nations floated around us. The rising sun, gilding with light the objects which it touched, gave new splendor to the scene. For the first time I saw the crescent flag unfurled. It floated broadly and proudly, the emblem of Mohammedan power.

We had no sooner come to anchor than a number of boats made their appearance around the ship. They were manned by Arab sailors, clad in a rude dress, which but partially covered their sunburnt bodies; and, speaking in an unknown language, they were clamorous for the privilege of conveying us on shore. Through narrow streets, which bore in general the marks of poverty, we were conducted to the quarter which is inhabited by Europeans.

At an early opportunity, as we had but little time to spare, we made ourselves acquainted with what is to be seen in the various places of the city. Such have been the vicissitudes of commerce, and the ravages of time and war, that but few objects of special interest remain. One of them is the beautiful obelisk in the eastern part of the city, called Cleopatra's Needle, seventy feet in height, and covered with hieroglyphics. It appears, from the hieroglyphic inscriptions on the obelisk itself, that it was the work of Thothmes the Third, the Egyptian king who ruled in the time of Moses, some portions of whose history have been brought to light in the numerous hieroglyphical monuments of Egypt. It was originally erected at Heliopolis, and was brought down to Alexandria in the time of the Ptolemies. It is as high, wanting a few feet, as the obelisk of Luxor, which I had seen in the Place de la Concorde in Paris. Near it is another large obelisk, lying upon the ground, and at the present time nearly covered with earth.

In another part of the city, favorably situated on the summit of a small elevation, is the beautiful column called Pompey's Pillar. It is said to have been the centre of the ancient city, which extended in this direction towards the lake Mareotis. Different opinions are entertained as to the time when it was erected. But as I travel for health chiefly, I am obliged to leave antiquarian inquiries to others. It is ten feet in diameter, and ninety feet in height, exclusive of its Corinthian capital. It is a very striking object; beautiful in its position, as well as its symmetry and great height. At the foot of the gently-rising hill on which it stands, is an extensive Mohammedan graveyard, filled with its rude white monuments.

Among other objects and places of attraction, we found time to visit the palace of the Pasha, which overlooks what is denominated the "old harbor," and were pleasantly surprised at the taste and elegance with which it is fitted up. It was the varied and gorgeous richness of Orientalism, with scarcely a violation of a just and severe simplicity. Surrounded with gardens filled with the ever-blooming trees and flowers of the East, it reminded one of those enchanted palaces which Oriental poets and romancers love to describe.

It must be admitted that Alexandria, at the present time, is far from being what it was once. In the period of its early prosperity, it was fifteen miles in circumference, and contained six hundred thousand inhabitants, including slaves. At present, its population is said to amount to sixty thousand. Some writers place the number higher. It has long ceased to be the emporium of commerce and the seat of science and the arts. Comparative poverty has taken the place of the immense wealth which it once gathered from the contributions of many nations. The high civilization which in the days of the Ptolemies attracted the notice of other states and communities has gone back, at least among considerable portions of the people, to a state of semi-barbarism. But humanity, with its good and evil, is not extinct. The Turk, though a follower of Mohammed, is still a man, and not without man's capabilities of intellect and feeling; and I think I may add, that in his calm countenance, and ample forehead, and dignified manner, he leaves an impression which is much in favor of the prevalent opinion of the original capacity and power of his race. The poor Arab beneath his rude garment bears a heart which has been described as treacherous and cruel, but which I am obliged to say exhibited kindness to me. Much of the beauty of outward nature still remains; and, amid many things which are strange, amd some things which are unpleasant, there is not a little which is fitted to please both the eye and heart.

I walked through some of the bazaars. Much business is still done in them. The Turkish merchant, meditative, and never in a hurry, sits cross-legged, seldom without his pipe, and tenacious of the dignity of his flowing beard and turban. Various are the dresses and languages. There are traders from different nations, and, in the persecutions to which they have been subjected at home, many Italians have found their way here. Many of the streets are narrow and dirty, but there is a clear blue sky above them. Carriages there are none; but men and veiled women are riding on diminutive donkeys. Camels with heavy burdens, reminding us of the days of the patriarchs, march slowly through the streets.

On the third day after our arrival, we sailed in a beautiful boat, called the Lotus, on a two months' voyage up the Nile,—the great river which has not only fertilized Egypt, but nourished humanity. We were four in number; the same little company who have traversed together France, Savoy, and the different States of Italy, and who have found the attractions of travel enhanced by the pleasure of each other's society. We started from the south side of the city, with a favorable breeze, on the Mahmoudie Canal, which connects Alexandria with the Nile at Atfeh, the place from which I date this letter. The part of the city which extends in the direction of the canal, and which may be said to rest upon it, contrasts advantageously with the other parts. There are many good buildings in this part of Alexandria, and a higher cultivation. By the side of the streets, and on the banks of the canal, are the palm-tree, the sycamore, and the acacia with its "yellow hair." It was here that we heard for the first time the noisy wheel of the sakhia, by which the water is drawn up from the canal for irrigating the lands. The large and well-watered gardens are rich with the productions of the climate, and gorgeous with the hues of Eastern flowers.

The canal connecting Alexandria and the Nile is a little more than forty miles in length, and is ninety feet wide. This canal is undoubtedly an extraordinary work for modern Egypt, where there are so few evidences of practical energy and improvement. A hundred and fifty thousand men, called from all parts of the country by the despotic will of the late Mohammed Ali, were employed in its excavation. It was excavated in a single year, but at the sad cost of some thirty thousand workmen, who perished through want, fatigue, and cruelty.

In going through the canal, we have passed numerous boats from ten to thirty and forty tons' burden. They are on their way to Alexandria from different places on the Nile, and are loaded with the products of the country, particularly wheat and cotton. We have had thus far a favorable breeze, and our boat, throwing out her large lofty sail, has advanced with good speed. The crew are in excellent spirits. With the exception of our pilot, they all seem to be of Arabic descent. Many of them have friends at the different towns and villages which we expect to pass. Our captain lives at Gheneh, nearly opposite the celebrated Denderah, and more than five hundred miles above Alexandria. He has reason to be cheerful. His wife and children are there. Our pilot is a Nubian. His name is Hassan. He is not swarthy like the natives of Egypt, but black of the deepest hue. His full muscular form is in perfect proportions. He walks erect, and with a natural and firm step. His countenance is open and generous. His eye is darkness lighted. When he speaks, he accompanies what he says with a natural movement of the hands and body, which is full of dignity and grace. No one can see him without feeling that he has a capacity above his situation. He has a wife and children at Assouan, near the first cataracts of the Nile.

When I look upon these people, and study their characters and little personal histories, I cannot harmonize with those persons who speak contemptuously of them. There is something in them which interests me. I have seen enough of them already to know that they have the ties and sympathies which humanity recognizes, and which religion sanctifies. If science, exiled by a haughty despotism, has been compelled to neglect them, nature has not forgotten to be their teacher. Their affections are not buried in the ruins of the intellect. They all of them have a spot which they call their home. The past lives in their memories, and the clay-built hut of their fathers is still dear to their hearts.

After waiting an hour and a half for the passage of other boats, we have just gone down the locks. We are now on the broad bosom of the Nile, or rather on one of its branches, which, however, is a mighty river, about three-quarters of a mile in width. The flag of America is floating over us. We are sailing under the town of Atfeh, which is at the termination of the canal, and on the high, rich banks which overlook the river. And it is at

Atfeh that I date and close my letter, as I look around me upon the land of Goshen, and cast my thoughts forward to Cairo and the Pyramids, to Denderah and Thebes.

(XXX.)

Delta of the Nile and the land of Goshen—Villages and inhabitants of the Nile—Camels, oxen, and flocks of sheep—The passage of the Nile by a herd of oxen—Condition and character of the Arabs of Egypt—Incident illustrative of their kindness—City of Rameses—Bridge across the Nile—Wailing for the dead—Arrival at Cairo.

CITY OF CAIRO, EGYPT, JAN. 24, 1853.

As I remarked in my last letter, we left the Mahmoudie Canal and entered the Nile at the town of Atfeh,—ascending it by the Rosetta branch. A little below the city of Cairo, this great river, as if desirous of rescuing a larger portion of fertility from the surrounding deserts, divides itself into two streams of nearly-equal size. One of them, the Damietta branch, flows in an easterly direction, and, passing by the considerable towns of Semenood and Mansoora, enters the Mediterranean near the city of Damietta. This city contains at the present time twenty-eight thousand inhabitants, but was formerly much more important than at present, and in the time of the Crusades was regarded as the entrance and the key to Egypt in that direction. The Rosetta branch flows in a westerly direction, and enters the Mediterranean not far from the city of Rosetta. The Rosetta and Damietta branches at their entrance into the sea are eighty miles distant from each other,—leaving between them the triangular tract of land, bounded on the north by the Mediterranean, which is denominated, on account of its form, the Delta of the Nile. The Delta was anciently much larger than at present. On the eastern side of it was the land of Goshen, which holds so conspicuous a place in the narratives of the Old Testament,—also the great Egyptian city of Zoan, frequently mentioned in the Scriptures likewise, which was situated on the ancient Tanitic branch of the Nile.

In ascending the Nile from Atfeh to Cairo by the Rosetta branch, we were frequently delayed by opposing winds. This was in some respects favorable. It gave us opportunity to visit many of the numerous villages which line its banks, and to notice the methods of living and sources of support. The people have a knowledge of a few domestic mechanic arts, such as the making of a coarse pottery, the weaving and coloring of cloths, boat-building, and the making of bricks. They mingle straw with the mud or clay from which their bricks are made, as was done in the time of the Pharaohs. But they find their principal support in the cultivation of the soil and in the keeping of flocks and herds.

The soil formed by the overflowings of the Nile is of great depth and richness. It is irrigated by water drawn from the Nile. The fields, waving with wheat, barley, lentils, and the other products of the country, are not enclosed by fences. Each man distinguishes his land from his neighbor's by the large stones placed in the ground, which serve as permanent marks and boundaries. The soil and climate are favorable for the raising of cattle. The camels and oxen and sheep, which we daily saw in great numbers, reminded us of the days of Jacob and his descendants, who occupied portions of this land. The sheep look like those which are seen in England and America, but the wool is coarser. The goats and sheep are not separated from each other, but go in flocks together, and are generally watched by little children, aided by a dog. I noticed that the sheep and goats are sometimes, during the night, penned together in a fold in the open field. But generally the sheep and other animals, cows, goats, donkeys, and camels, are driven into the villages at night. Each house had an enclosure attached to it, formed of mud or of stalks and reeds and open at the top, in which they are shut up. Sometimes they seem to be otherwise provided for. A number of times in the morning I saw the sheep and goats walking complacently about on the flat roofs of the houses. The houses are commonly made of unburnt bricks, hardened in the sun.

The oxen of Egypt—those which we first met with and which are much the most frequent—are of a large size, resembling somewhat in shape the buffalo of America, black in color with scarcely an exception, and with large crooked horns reaching back and depressed almost horizontally with the neck. I often saw them patiently turning the wheel of the SAKHIA, or drawing the plough through the fields. The plough is very simple in its construction, being hardly more than a sharpened stick of wood, though sometimes pointed with iron. It could not easily have been more simple in the days of the patriarchs. The oxen are very tractable. I have seen them with a string round the horn or neck, led home from the fields at night by little children.

At one time I noticed a herd of these animals, which may be said to make a part of an Arab's family, on the brink of the Nile under the care of two boys. It was just as the sun was setting. They belonged to a village on the western side, and were on their way home from a pasture-ground, where they had been feeding during the day. I noticed their appearance, because they stood crowded together, about twenty in number, silent and thoughtful, as if meditating some act of importance. The boys took off their clothes, tied them in bundles, and fastened them on their own heads. They then mounted the backs of two of the animals, gave the word of command, and the whole herd plunged into the river. They passed directly in front of the boat at a place where the Nile was running more rapidly than common. The boatmen suspended their rowing. Nothing was seen but their black heads and horns moving towards the other shore. The boys sat upright with the bundles of clothes on their heads. They made a singular appearance, moving rapidly over the Nile and apparently without any support, as the backs of the cattle were concealed under the water. They reached the other shore in safety. The boys put on their clothes. The cattle shook their wet sides on the sand, and they went together up the bank.

The inhabitants of the villages of which I am now speaking are for the most part of Arab descent. When the Arabs overran the country in the seventh century, they wasted it, and made great destruction of the people. The descendants of the original Egyptians are found, not among the Arab portion, but among the Copts, who are few in number, and generally reside in the large towns. They are comparatively intelligent and well instructed, and profess the Christian religion. The religion of the Arabs is Mohammedan. They are poor, uneducated, and scantily clad. But the climate is such, that they do not require much clothing. Though they are poor, there is not such suffering from poverty as is often witnessed in the large towns of Europe. They are superstitious, chiefly because they are ignorant. In repeated instances I saw the children assembled in schools in the larger towns, but did not notice any schools in the small villages. Mohammedanism is not favorable to intellectual culture. The people need the Christian religion. But the laws of the Koran and of the country are strict in the defence of the Mohammedan faith, and to become a Christian is to expose themselves to death. It seems to me, therefore, that there is but little hope for Egypt at the present time; at least for this portion of the people. It may be different with the Greeks, Armenians, and Copts.

I was favorably impressed with many of their traits of character. I judge of them from what I saw. They seem to have lost the active and fierce spirit which characterized their ancestors. They are timid, and make but poor soldiers. I am not prepared, however, to condemn that cowardice, if such it may be called, which shrinks from the taking of human life. As a general thing I observed no deficiency of industry; but there is very little enterprise. Their study is to live, and not to improve and advance. I cannot easily join with those who are disposed to make an impeachment of their honesty,—because personally I have had no evidences to sustain it. Nor have I seen evidences of inordinate suspicion, cruelty, and disposition to injure. I have been in their villages daily. The dogs, which guard every door, have sometimes attacked me. But the dogs were faithful to what they considered their trust; and I have no especial complaint to make of their somewhat premature and unnecessary zeal; and the less so, because in some instances the Arabs themselves came and drove them away. What may be true of the Bedouin Arabs inhabiting the deserts, who are of the same race but differently situated and under different influences, I am unable to say. Time will perhaps determine. But from the Arabs of the Nile I have received as decided marks of kindness as amid the civilization of Europe.

I will mention a single instance, which may be taken as an illustration of their treatment of me. One day the boat was fastened to the shore on account of a head-wind. I strayed away alone into the fields, as was sometimes my practice. Passing near the little hut of an Arab shepherd, who was seated at his door on a mat, he made signs to me to come and sit down. I accepted the invitation and sat down on the mat with him, and we began to converse in signs, aided by a few Arabic and Italian words which one easily picks up. I felt quite at home. In a short time he arose and went to his dwelling, which was a very simple enclosure formed partly by a mud wall and partly by a fence of long reeds which were strongly bound together, and which was covered at the top with a roof of cornstalks. Bringing out a jug of water and a wooden dish filled with excellent dates, he invited me to eat. I could not well refuse his hospitality. I was pleased, because I saw he had that faith which can take hold of the common link of human brotherhood. Looking up, I saw a little child peeping round the corner of the hut. This was a new incident. I made signs to it to come to me; but it was frightened at my strange appearance, and ran away. The father smiled at this, and got up, and ran after the child, and brought it back. I pacified it with a little present, and we soon became good friends. The result of this was, that in a little time all the children, some four or five in number, came round successively from an opening on the other side of the enclosure. After a little while the Arab's wife—contrary, I believe, to the usual customs among them—came also with an infant in her arms. The sun shone brightly; but we were on the shady side of the hut, and a gentle breeze made music in the reeds. It was quite a family meeting, and I tried to make them as well pleased with me as I was with them. I stayed half an hour, and know not how much longer the visit might have been prolonged; but our captain (the Rais, as the people of the country call him) sent one of his men, named Mohammed, to find me. He came with an amazing long club, to guard me, as he said, against the Arabs, which seemed to me a very unnecessary precaution. I left my hospitable entertainers, well pleased with my visit, and with sincere desires and prayers for their happiness,—and have often thought of them since.

It was to this region of Egypt that Pharaoh sent the brethren of Joseph; and it answers well the description given of it, as the "best of the land." And no one can visit it at the present time, without seeing that it is peculiarly suited to their occupation as herdsmen. It is at the head of the Delta on the eastern side, and probably a little beyond its present limits, that we are to look for the site of the ancient city of Rameses, from which the children of Israel started on their memorable journey in the wilderness. Rameses is spoken of as one of the "treasure-cities of Egypt." It probably had its palaces and architectural monuments; but, like many other great cities of Egypt, nothing now remains of it. At the head of the Delta is a long and beautiful bridge in the course of erection, extending over both branches of the Nile, a little below the point where the river separates. It is a very picturesque object as viewed by one in ascending the Nile. It is nearly finished, apparently a mile and a half in length, if we include the portion of the Delta which unites the two parts together, and will compare well in strength and beauty with other great structures of that kind.

I find that I have omitted many incidents of this little voyage; but I will mention one. At a certain time, walking near a little village, I heard a sad and piercing cry. It was the mourning-wail of the Egyptian women. They tossed their arms wildly, as if frantic with grief, and scattered dust upon their garments. It reminded me of the descriptions of sorrow and wailing which are given in the Scriptures. The occasion was indeed a sad one,—the death of a little boy, who the day before was drowned in the Nile. He lay dead in the house. The mourners were outside,—some standing and some sitting on the sand. As I stood near, a witness, and perhaps I may say a sharer, of their grief, I saw a company of mourning friends and relatives coming from another village. The Arab loves his children, and his grief is bitter when they die. The voice of anguish sounded from village to village, and from one side of the Nile to the other.

But the traveller stops neither for joy nor sorrow. His sympathy, ruled by the occasion, may harmonize with either, but it passes on. He gives a smile or a tear, a just tribute to a common nature, and then goes forward to his own place.

In eight days from Alexandria we arrived at Cairo. Our boat stopped at Boulak, which is the harbor of Cairo. The bank of the river at Boulak is steep and rocky. For a mile or more it was lined with the large boats of the Nile, a number of which bore the American flag. We saw signs of activity, wealth, commerce, intelligence. Cairo is only a mile and a half distant, and is so connected with Boulak, notwithstanding the low sunken grounds between them, that in the eye of a stranger they are essentially one city. In coming back from Thebes we shall of course stop here, and I shall therefore speak of it now only in a few words.

Cairo contains two hundred thousand inhabitants, divided and characterized by descent, history, and religion,—Arabs, Turks, Armenians, Greeks, and Copts. Here also are the Nubian and the European. The number of the old Egyptian or Coptic race, of whose situation and prospects we hope to learn something further, is said to be sixty thousand. It is through them, as it seems to me, that we must look for the religious recovery of Egypt.

The streets of the city, the buildings and gardens, the dress, manners, and occupations of the people, all remind us that we are in a great city of the East. We are in the midst of Oriental civilization without the modifications which in Alexandria it is constantly receiving from the West. Knowledge has a different language. Art has a different eye. We perceive more and more, and not without painful emotions, that we are in a land of a different religion. The lofty minaret of the mosque of Mohammed Ali glitters in the sun.

Nature also, still more than at the mouth of the Nile, puts on a new dress. It is a land of flowers; and I might almost say every flower has its singing-bird upon it. The palm, the acacia, and the orange, are here. We have come once more to the region of mountains. I look upon them with the emotions of one who has loved them from childhood. But they are not the mountains of our own land. Back of the city, and guarding it from the Syrian desert, are the bare, broken, and lifeless heights of

Mokattam. Embosomed in the Nile are the beautiful gardens of the isle of Rhoda,—the place where, according to the traditions of the country, the infant Moses was exposed in the bulrushes. On the opposite bank of the river, near the site of the wasted and buried city of Memphis, are the pyramids. They stand alone, with the sandy billows of the Libyan desert breaking around them, like the peak of Stromboli in the midst of the sea.

But it is dangerous to get the first glance of such an object when one is closing a letter. There are no pyramids in America. Mountains and mounds, the monuments of a departed race, are there; but not the pyramids of Egypt.

(XXXI.)

Arrival at Benisooef—Convent of St. Anthony—Mohammedan mosque—Visit to a Bey of the Pasha—Picturesque appearance of the villages of the Nile—Birds of the Nile—Gebel-E-Tayr—The wounded eagle—The crocodile—The blind boy.

EGYPT, TOWN OF GHENEH, ON THE NILE, FEB. 15, 1853.

WE sailed from Cairo on the twenty-fourth of January with a favorable wind. Passing by the isle of Rhoda, and the town of Old Cairo on the left, and the town of Geezeh on the right, and village after village in continual succession, we reached on the fourth day the large town of Benisooef, which is distant from Cairo seventy-seven miles. This town is one of the principal places in Upper Egypt, and is the residence of the governor of the province of which Benisooef is the capital. Numerous boats, moored under the steep banks, lined the shore, indicating that it is a place of considerable commerce. It has manufactures of silk and cotton, recently established. Anciently it was famous for its linen-manufactures.

From Benisooef, commencing on the opposite side of the river, is the road which leads to the celebrated convent of St. Anthony in the eastern desert. The general course of the road is through the great valley called the Wady-el-Arraba, which runs between the two limestone ranges of mountains bearing the name of the Northern and Southern Kalalla. The convent, built at the foot of the Kalalla and surrounded with gardens, is within eighteen miles' distance of the Red Sea. I mention this convent the more particularly, not only because it is a place of considerable resort, but because it is the principal convent of the Coptic Christians. The patriarch of the Copts is elected by its members. The convent is of great antiquity, and possesses some historical interest. The cavern is shown near it in which the celebrated St. Anthony passed a portion of his days in religious retirement.

Leaving Benisooef after a slight examination of it, we reached the pleasant town of Minieh, on the west bank of the Nile, a hundred and sixty miles from Cairo, on the 2d of February. One of the objects which attracts notice in approaching this town from the water is a shekh's white tomb, situated upon the rising ground, and overshadowed by a large sycamore-tree. We visited the large and ancient mosque which stands upon the bank of the river. We found there a number of Mohammedans going through with their devotions. Within it are marble and granite columns with Corinthian capitals, which originally belonged to some building of earlier times. The modern cemetery of Minieh is on the opposite side of the river. The dead are ferried over in boats. The custom of burying their dead on the opposite bank, which is often easily explained in connection with the natural features of the country, existed in ancient times, and gave rise to the legend of Charon's boat.

Modern improvements on a limited scale have found their way to Minieh. The Pasha of Egypt has established a large sugar-manufactory here, which is in successful operation. Although we were entire strangers, we were kindly invited to go through it and examine it. We had repeatedly passed large and flourishing fields of the sugar-cane. The culture of the sugar-cane, and also of cotton, has recently been introduced.

A bey of the Pasha, resident at Cairo, was on a visit at Minieh when we were there. We understood that he had been sent up the river on a tour of inspection, but with particular reference to the manufacturing-establishments. His boat lay very near us. We called upon him in the boat. Seated on a divan in the Oriental manner, he bade us a cordial welcome, and, ordering coffee to be brought us, politely answered our questions, and made on his part many inquiries in relation to America. His countenance indicated that he possessed good powers of mind. And I have rarely seen a man more truly dignified and at the same time more kind and affable in his manners.

It is the small villages, however, rather than the large towns, which constitute the marked peculiarity of the Nile, and which constantly arrest the attention of the traveller. It is undoubtedly true that they lose much of their attraction when closely inspected; but they are certainly very picturesque when seen in the distance. For hours I have sat in the boat and looked upon them. There is poetry in their very location. They are almost always built in a grove of palm-trees. The palm-tree itself is a very impressive object. Tall, straight, crowned with a tuft of long waving leaves, it has a lofty and meditative aspect, as if it were conversing with the spirits of the air. In front of the villages is the Nile; and south of Cairo they have a background of mountains. The eastern mountains, with rugged but imperishable walls, guard them from the Syrian desert. The mountains on the western side protect them from the encroachments of the deserts of Libya. Many villages have canals near them, running back from the river towards the mountains. Their high banks form a road. Oxen, camels, flocks of sheep and goats, are constantly passing and repassing. Narrow paths lead from different parts of the villages to the water. Women and girls are seen going to and from the river with water-jars on their heads. They are dressed in simple but decent garments of blue cotton, and are modest and cheerful in their appearance. In many instances they are adorned with necklaces, ear-rings, and bracelets. There are folds for the sheep and cattle in the villages, and in nearly all of them are large dovecotes. The doves in countless numbers are flying about. Dogs are keeping sentinel on the flat roofs of the houses. Oxen are turning the wheels of the SAKHIA, by which the fields are watered. At times is heard the sound of the mill-stone, which is turned sometimes by oxen and more frequently by hand. Groups of unwashed children with their loud laugh are playing in the dust of the lofty banks or at the brink of the river. Such is the scene which repeats itself almost every hour.

One of the features of the Nile is its numberless beautiful birds,—not only those which haunt rivers and display their tall forms upon the water's brink and scream among the reeds, but the birds of song and bright plumage which haunt the tree and forest. The trees in the small gardens of the villages and larger towns are alive with them. A stone thrown into a wheat or bean field at a distance from the towns often starts up a cloud of them which fills the air. The Egyptians, either for want of fire-arms or for some other reason, do not seem disposed to injure them; and hence they have become exceedingly tame. I have seen a crow—a bird which is generally not very familiar in its habits—sitting quietly on the mast of our vessel. The sparrow was almost constantly hopping about on the deck, picking up the seeds which were there. Not unfrequently large birds are seen, seated much at their ease on the back of an ox or camel. Repeatedly I saw groups of pelicans, with their long snowy necks, walking on the banks of sand in retired places. Wild ducks are without number. At night flocks of geese, uttering their shrill cry, are seen flying over the river,—extending in long and marshalled array from one bank to the other. Eagles make their nests in the chains of mountains which bound the valley of the Nile; but we saw them frequently near the towns and villages.

One evening, just as the shades of night were falling, I saw an immense flock of birds pass near the boat and light upon the lofty side of a rocky mountain under which we were at the time. They were of considerable size, but I could not tell of what kind they were. In a few moments they all disappeared in the multitude of crevices and excavations which are found there. Here were their nests; and, as they were adjusting themselves for their night's repose, they set up that sort of social congratulation which is common with them at such times. Nothing was seen but the bare rugged face of the mountain; and yet every crevice and fissure and cavern was suddenly endowed with vocality. The echo of these hollow and rocky recesses increased the sounds to the loudness of the human voice. They were like an army of men that were talking loudly. I sat upon the deck and looked, but saw nothing. The illusion was complete. The whole mountain-cliff, as if it were a thing of life which had just waked out of sleep, seemed to forget its usual solidity and silence, and to become lightheaded, and to laugh, and to chatter and make merry.

I had written this before I was aware of the fact that one of the rocky heights on the eastern side of the Nile and above Benisooef is named GEBEL-E-TAYR, which means the "mountain of the bird;" and that a singular tradition is connected with it. The tradition is, that all the birds of the country round about assemble at this mountain once a year. They then hold a grand consultation for the purpose of selecting one of their number, whose duty it is to remain in the mountain till the next year. The birds then fly away into various and distant parts; but return again at the appointed time to the "mountain of the bird," for the purpose of releasing their comrade and appointing another in its place.

Travellers on the Nile frequently go ashore for the purpose of shooting. The sound of their guns was not pleasing to me. It seemed to me to be cruel. I cannot see the good sense, the humanity, or the religion, of taking away that life which God alone can give, for the gratification of a useless and momentary pleasure. Hearing a gun one day, I looked up and saw a dove winging its way heavily towards the boat. Its slow, irregular motion attracted my attention. The blood dropped from its breast. It struggled, but still descended nearer and nearer to the water. Its strength failed. Its white plumage sank in the dark wave. Near Minieh a wounded eagle fell by the side of the boat, and was taken on the deck, and died. That dark straggling wing, now feeble in death, had power to climb the mountains. As the light faded from his dying eye, he seemed to utter a reproach, and to say that to destroy him thus was unworthy of man. I am not ashamed to say that I wept.

The crocodile, which was here in the time of Herodotus, is still an inhabitant of the Nile; not, however, of all parts of it. They are very seldom seen below the town of Minieh. We did not see them until we had ascended above the town of Girgeh, more than three hundred and forty miles above Cairo. We then saw them repeatedly for a number of days, and in nearly every instance sleeping on little sand-banks in the middle of the river in the heat of the day. In a number of instances we approached quite near them. The largest of them were about twelve feet in length. There were generally two together. They lay stretched out upon these banks, dark, rough, motionless, with their legs and feet projected at their sides and pressed into the sand. When the boat approached them, they moved slowly to the water's edge and plunged into the river.

Some people of the country, coming down in a boat, had taken a young crocodile. They gave it to our men. It was very small, about two feet in length. The men placed it in a vessel of water, and gave it food, in hopes to keep it alive. Apparently discontented and angry at being taken from its native reeds and waters, it refused to eat, and in a few days died.

Such are some of the scenes and incidents which characterize a voyage on this remarkable river,—in its natural features, its ancient remains, its history, the customs and character of the people, unlike any other river in the world. Of the remains of ancient cities and temples which are found on its banks, I will endeavor to say something in another letter.

I have referred in a former letter to the strength of domestic and family attachments in this people, particularly the Arab portion. I have seen nothing since which leads me to alter that opinion, but some things which seem rather to confirm it. Egypt has its afflictions. And among others is the prevalence of blindness,—a fact not easily explained, but which is often mentioned by travellers. But it was pleasing to see that the subjects of this heavy affliction were not deserted by their relatives and friends. One morning when the boat was lying under a high bank, and before we were ready to start, I heard a voice uttering a plaintive note. I looked out of the window, and saw a beautiful boy standing half-way down the shelving declivity. He seemed to be about twelve or thirteen years of age. And his sister, a little smaller in size and younger in appearance, stood by his side, holding his hand. I looked a moment and perceived that he was blind. I asked our interpreter what it was which he sang so plaintively. He said it was only a few simple words having reference to his situation:—

> "I am blind.
> My father and mother are poor;
> Give me some bread:
> I am blind."

I noticed, while the boy was singing, that he turned his calm but sightless face upward, as if beseeching the Almighty to inspire us with kind sentiments; but the face of the sister, full of anxiety and sorrow, looked downward towards the people of the boat. One of the sailors ran up on the bank and gave the girl a piece of bread; and they were about leaving. But they were requested to stop a moment, and another piece of bread and some money were sent to them. The little girl took the pieces of bread and the money and placed them in the hands of her brother, and then placed her arm in his and led him away. I cannot easily forget their pleased and grateful expression of countenance as they left us. The burden seemed to be lifted from the heart of the sister, as she saw the smile on her poor brother's face. Affliction seemed to bind them nearer to each other. And I have sometimes thought that even sorrow has its value, when it thus adds increased intensity and beauty to love.

On the 7th day of February we reached the beautiful city of Osioot,—fourteen days from Cairo and distant two hundred and fifty-three miles. But the wind, which had been much in a contrary direction, being favorable, we passed on. We hope to visit it on our return. We are now at the town of Gheneh, or Keneh, on the eastern side of the river, more than four hundred miles south of Cairo. This place is celebrated for the manufacture of the porous water-jars through which the water of the Nile is filtrated. The clay from which they are made is found in a valley to the northward of the town. From Gheneh a road runs through the eastern desert to the town of Cossair on the Red Sea; and by means of this route it keeps up a considerable commerce with Arabia. A provincial governor resides here.

Opposite to Gheneh is Denderah, with its celebrated temple. We have just visited it. It is two miles distant from the present bank of the river. It stands on an elevated spot, rising from the green plain around. We walked among its columns and descended into its darkest recesses,—a great monument erected partly in the time of the Ptolemies and in part by the Romans in the time of Tiberius Cæsar, in honor of the Egyptian superstitions,—interesting to the Christian as showing, by contrast, the simplicity, the purity, and the great and ennobling disclosures of Christianity; interesting to the lover of art for its massive and splendid architecture, the work in different parts of different ages and nations, and also for its sculptures and paintings, still fresh and lifelike; interesting to the philosophical historian as a memorial of the development of the human mind, of the affiliated relationships of the human race, the transmission of artistic and social ideas, the successive life and decay of nations.

(XXXII.)

Preparations for a visit to the mountains—The old man's donkey and daughter—The Plain of Thebes—The statue of Memnon—Medeenet Haboo—Temple-palace of Rameses III.—Statue of Rameses II.—Reflections.

THEBES, WESTERN BANK OF THE NILE, FEB. 22, 1853.

On Saturday, the 19th of February, we arrived at Thebes. We moored our boat on the western side of the river. The Nile flows on as beautiful as ever. The spreading sycamore shades its level banks. The mountains are seen in the distance. There is life and majesty in the river. There is grandeur in the mountains. But the eye looks in vain for the mighty city which dates its early glory in the very beginnings of history.

Early on Monday morning, after our arrival, we made preparations for a visit to the mountains,—the locality of ruined temples, and of the celebrated Theban tombs. The sun rose. It was the sun of Egypt,—a cloudless and living radiance in a clear blue sky, more clear and deep and vast even than the sky of Italy. A breeze from the north cooled the air. The shore, as we left the boat, was lined with men and donkeys. I found myself in the midst of a crowd, clamorous in an unknown tongue, each vociferating and urging his claims. I was somewhat perplexed in the midst of this confusion. But, seeing a feeble old man at a little distance, who seemed to be thrust aside by his younger competitors, I made my way to him and placed my hand on the donkey's saddle. The younger Arabs looked disappointed. The old man's donkey was not as good as theirs. But very soon, seeming to appreciate my feelings, they murmured their approbation.

As I held my hand on the saddle, looking at the varying countenances of the crowd, I felt it timidly and gently held from the other side. It was the pressure of the hand of a little girl, who seemed to say, with a half-beseeching, half-grateful look,—"We are poor; take *our* donkey, though the saddle is not very good." The old man smiled at this innocent manifestation of filial earnestness, and gave me to understand that the young girl was his daughter, and would drive the donkey to the mountains. I was entirely satisfied.

We made our way through the centre of an Arab village. The dogs barked, and the goats and kids looked down from the flat roofs of the houses. The little girl, to whose protection the old man had consigned me, had a small stick in her hand, with which she rather gently exerted her authority over the donkey. They appeared to understand each other very well. She wore a loose garment of blue cotton. Her feet were bare; but she was adorned with the necklace and ear-rings, of which the poorest Arab girl will not willingly be destitute.

After leaving the village, we passed two miles or more over the plain, taking the direction of the statue of Memnon. There were groups of people raising water from the reservoirs of the Nile and pouring it into the sluices which conveyed it over the rich soil. Camels and oxen and flocks were feeding. On one side of our path was the ploughman; on the other the reaper. On going through a dry channel, through which the Nile flows when the water is high, we passed a blind man. My little girl, who sympathized in his affliction, gave me to understand that he was a suitable object of my charity. He was affectionately attended and led about by a young woman, whom I supposed to be his daughter. My little attendant, who was almost daily passing and repassing this part of the plain, seemed to be well acquainted with her.

The plain of Thebes is wonderful. I gazed upon it from one of the mountain-heights, and also from the top of one of the temples of Carnac. From both places the eye easily reached its limits as they are defined by the mountains, though it is a circuit apparently of thirty miles. As viewed from the ascent in the mountains, the curving Nile, seen through the whole length of the plain and glittering in the sun, flowed through it like a river of gold. The plain waved with luxuriant vegetation. It is not surprising, that the first inhabitants, who viewed it in its primitive beauty, made it their stopping-place and laid the foundations of the great city. Thebes, unlike the cities of the East generally, had no walls. In the time of its greatness it probably occupied the whole plain. Reaching out from both banks of the Nile, it was guarded on all sides by vast deserts, and still nearer by the continuous line of mountains which intervened between the plain and the deserts. It had but little need, therefore, of walls. The hundred gates of Thebes mentioned by Homer were not gates, as is commonly supposed, which furnished an entrance through city-walls, but the gates of palaces and temples. And the Theban Gate, which is thus commemorated in early poetry, is not a mere portal, through which a man can scarcely enter, but a great architectural and historical arch, some fifty or sixty feet high, which, in its proportions, sculptures, and massive boldness, leaves Greece and Rome behind.

We were three days in the plain and mountains of Western Thebes. I mention what we saw during these successive days,—arranging it in the order suggested by the nature of the objects, rather than by that of the specific day or hour in which they were seen. I shall give but part, however, in the present letter.

We first came to the statue of Memnon; and we had opportunity to examine it again on another day. It stands at the extremity of the plain and at the foot of the Libyan heights, sculptured from the solid rock with a care which preserves grandeur without violating truth and simplicity. Rising from the base of the pedestal to the height of sixty feet, and with head and breast and shoulders and hands and feet all in proportion to the height, it had the appearance, as it rose up suddenly before us, of some mysterious and mighty apparition,—holding as it were the gate of the mountains and keeping the guardianship of temples and tombs.

The statue of Memnon is only one among many which formerly existed here. Another of equal size, but not of equal celebrity, is standing near; and others, at no great distance, in mighty fragments, like fallen giants with their limbs dislocated, lie prostrate upon the ground. The Memnon statue is the one so often alluded to by ancient writers, which was said to welcome with notes of music the first bright rays of the rising sun. We had the opportunity of listening to the sounds which probably gave rise to this interesting fiction. They are produced by striking on a hollow portion of the stone in the lap of the statue, which has the peculiarity of emitting a sharp metallic sound like that of brass when it is struck. The statue is seated, and is so large that the boy who ascended it and went to the farthest part of the lap for the purpose of producing the sounds was entirely out of sight; so that the statue itself seemed to have the power of uttering them.

Leaving the statue of Memnon, we next came to the place called MEDEENET HABOO,—the Arabic name which is given to a portion of the plain of Thebes, on the western side of the river. Among the ruins which are found here are the remains of the great "temple-palace," as it has sometimes been denominated, of Rameses III. There were other ruins around, some of them of Roman origin; but our attention was particularly directed to this. We were perplexed at first in forming a satisfactory idea of the plan of this great work. Our guides furnished us but little assistance. But we were able, after a time, and with some little effort, to ascertain, as we thought, the general outlines and position, with the successive entrances and courts; and thus, with what still remained of massive walls and splendid columns, to fill up mentally the original and grand conception.

This temple, which was the abode of royalty as well as of the Egyptian gods, may justly be regarded, in its objects, the style of its architecture, and its hieroglyphical sculptures, as one of the great monuments of primitive Egypt. Some of its columns are more than twenty feet in circumference. The scenes, deeply sculptured with great skill on the walls, are chiefly battle-scenes. Rameses is represented in one place as putting to rout his Asiatic enemies, who are in full armor, but in flight before him; and in another as smiting the captives taken in war in the presence of the god Amunre. War then, as now, when prosecuted successfully, constituted glory. There are some scenes, however, of a more domestic nature. Among the sculptures, for instance, on the walls of the private apartments of this edifice, is a representation of Rameses seated on an elegant divan, surrounded with female attendants, who wave their fans before him and present him with flowers.

In another place he is represented as seated on a canopied throne, which is borne by twelve Egyptian princes, and attended by officers, who carry in their hands the royal insignia and arms.

This temple or "temple-palace" dates back in its origin to the reign of its builder, Rameses III. This king began to reign in the year 1235 before the Christian era,—about three hundred years after the time of Moses.

There are interesting ruins at the Arab village called Goorneh or Koorneh, which is nearly opposite Karnac and not far from the bank of the river,—especially the remains of a large and beautiful temple older than the one I have mentioned. These remains are scattered over a large extent of ground, and bear the evidences of mechanical skill as well as of sublime conception which generally characterize the architectural remains found in this region. And not far from these ruins are other fragmentary remains of a temple which dates back to the time of the third Thothmes, the cotemporary of Moses. But I found myself more interested by the ruins generally but perhaps incorrectly known as the MEMNONIUM, which are found between Medeenet Haboo and Koorneh.

The temple which bears this name was originally entered through the opening in the vast pyramidal towers, built of massive stone and covered with sculptures, which still stand as the magnificent front of the large area or court which first opens behind them. This court, which is more than two hundred feet in length by a hundred and eighty in breadth, was originally ornamented with a double row of columns on each side, some fragments of which only remain now. This large area opens into another court or area, a little smaller in size, which had lateral corridors of large circular columns. There were also rows of pillars of a different form at the northern and southern extremities of this court. The second court connects itself with a third, a hundred feet in length, covered with a solid roof, painted of a light-blue color and studded with stars. Forty-eight large columns of great beauty originally supported this roof, many of which are still standing, as also a considerable number of those in the second court. The twelve central columns in the third court are thirty-two feet in height and twenty-one in circumference. Some of the columns are prostrate. The remains of pedestals and statues are strewed around them.

The surfaces of these remarkable ruins are covered with hieroglyphical and other sculptures. Many of them seem to be historical in their character. Towns are taken. Chiefs are led captive with ropes about their necks. In one place a town, favorably situated on a rocky eminence, is defended with obstinacy, but at length overcome. Those who are able to interpret the hieroglyphical characters state that the towns were taken in the fourth year of Rameses II., who was styled the Great. He is the same with the Sesostris of the Greek historians. There are other sculptures of a different character. Some represent religious ceremonies. In one place is a procession of the sons and daughters of this Rameses.

One of the most remarkable things here is the statue of Rameses Sesostris. It lies near the entrance of the second court, prostrate and broken. Its estimated weight is a little less than 900 tons. It is sculptured from a single block of sienite. The passing traveller is obliged to rely chiefly upon the statements of others. I will only add, therefore, that those who have investigated the subject inform us that it was overthrown by the Persian king Cambyses, when he overran and conquered Egypt, so that it may be said to have taken a nation's strength to erect it, and a nation's strength to throw it down. The king, in the Egyptian idea of government, represented the state; and the statue which was erected in his honor may be said to have embodied the king. And as I stood beside the mighty fragments, and saw the head severed from the body and the face prostrate and hidden in the dust, I seemed to be looking upon a fallen empire.

A mere transient stranger in the land,—a sojourner of a few days,—I can of course see but little; but I have already seen more than I was prepared for. A new ray of intelligence has broken in upon the mind. I can understand now, better than I once could, why Greece, in her desire to obtain knowledge, came to Egypt. But where Egypt received her high civilization, and under what circumstances it was developed, is still a problem. Of the fact of such civilization, including both knowledge and art, the numerous monuments which still remain leave no doubt. So far as I could perceive, as I looked upon the standing or fallen statues and columns, and upon the numberless beautiful sculptures on the walls, and upon the paintings still fresh and distinct, they exhibited all the attributes of just conception and finished execution which constitute excellence in art. Of course, as there were many hands employed, there are different degrees of excellence. And it is true also, that the Egyptian idea of the outward or formal representation of works of art is different from that of the Greeks and Romans. But beauty is infinitely varied. Of all the numberless works of the Creator no two are entirely alike; and the power of genius is seen in retaining the essence and divinity of the thing (that which is its life and character) under a variety of forms. The eye of the Egyptian artist is Oriental; and, accustomed to scenery and life which are found nowhere else, it is filled with the forms of Oriental beauty. And that is not all which is to be said. What Egypt was, and what she was able to effect, is not to be estimated by European ideas, nor by the specimens of Egyptian architecture which are to be found from time to time in Europe and America. She is to be judged not only in connection with her Oriental position, which in part gives a character to her works, but in the light of her own intellectual and moral history, from her own massive ruins, and on her own soil.

What I have seen of these ruins is only the beginning. I can say nothing further at present. I will only add, that new forms of life are generated or take up their abode amidst destruction. I did not see the moss and the ivy growing upon the wall, as on the ruins of Italy and England. But these are not the only signs of change. What were once the palaces of kings or the temples of heathen deities have other inhabitants now. Aroused by the noise of our coming, a lizard thrust his head from a hole in a column. Countless birds flew around us from the crevices in the walls. A flock of sheep and goats came in from the plain, and reposed themselves in the shade of the towers and of the fallen statue of Rameses. Groups of Arabs were seated on the massy fragments. The noise of children echoed through the walls.

While my learned associate, Mr. Thompson, who added science to taste and industry, took measurements and made notes, I sat down on a broken column and meditated. "It is thus," I said to myself, "that the works of man perish." Among human works there seemed to me to be nothing greater than that which I then witnessed; but that which is greatest in grandeur is greatest also in desolation. But nature lives, because the life of God is in it. There is beauty in the Theban plains. There is grandeur in the Theban mountains. Truth lives also, because truth can never be separated from eternity. Love lives, because without love truth ceases to be beautiful, and because, without love to give it life, eternity itself becomes an infinite wilderness of desolations. Desolation, therefore, speaks. Its language is, that everything which is not of truth and love is false,—false in position and false in nature. And everything which is false, though in its power and pride it may call art and genius to its aid, only builds its own tomb. Man learns wisdom in the midst of ruins.

I was aroused from these contemplations, which the place and the objects could hardly fail to inspire, by my little donkey-girl. She had her own thoughts,—her own sorrows, cares, and joys. She had begun to think of her father's humble home, and gave the signal for our departure by pointing to the setting sun.

(XXXIII.)

Luxor—Palace of Amunoph III.—Dromos and Sphynxes—Temple of Carnac—Night-scene—Tombs of the kings and queens—Ideas of the Egyptians on the subject of immortality—Poetry.

THEBES, EASTERN BANK OF THE NILE, FEB. 25, 1853.

HAVING thus spent successive days on the western bank in the examination of various objects of interest, we passed the river to the village or town of Luxor, in Eastern Thebes. Luxor—"the place of palaces," as the name means, in allusion, probably, to the ruins which are found in it—is a considerable town situated on a small hill, with fertile valleys around, and pleasant residences and gardens. The population is mixed,—Arabic, Turkish, Coptic, and some Europeans. In all the important towns on the Nile we found resident Italians in greater or less numbers, who had fled from the oppressions or the revolutions of their unhappy country; but in Luxor and its vicinity there are attractions which, independent of the influence of any such necessity, are likely to induce the temporary or permanent residence of a few strangers. It is foreigners, and not the natives of the country, who bring to light and appreciate and explain the Egypt of ancient times. We were happy in making the acquaintance of a French gentleman, who is employed by the Egyptian Government in superintending the excavations which are still in progress here.

On the rising ground, and fronting the Nile, which flows by in unequalled beauty, a row of columns of great size, and finished in the highest style of Egyptian art, indicate the locality of another vast temple. Here again, carried back in imagination to its historic date of more than three thousand years, (the period when its foundations were laid,) we stopped in silent admiration of the genius which conceived and the power which executed these great works. This temple, as appears from the inscriptions upon it, was commenced by Amunoph III., who seems to have built the original sanctuary and the apartments connected with it; and was completed by Rameses II., who added a large court with its pyramidal towers, obelisks, and statues. If we can rely upon these statements, they carry us back to nearly fourteen hundred years before the Christian era. As I have already said, however, the passing traveller can only give the statements of others.

It is true that all can see and admire the beauty of the remarkable inscriptions which ornament the Theban walls, and which enclose, in the elegance of their sculptured outlines, the suggestions and truths of a remote history. Of the multitudes, however, who thus behold and admire, few only have the power to understand and interpret their meaning. But science, as well as curiosity, has trod among these ruins. Denon, Champollion, and Wilkinson, have been here. And we owe it to the patience of the laborious antiquary and the man of science, that we can thus associate results with historical persons, and skill with epochs of time.

This temple will be better understood, when the excavations to which we have already referred as being in progress shall have been completed. And yet, as it now exists, with large portions buried in the dust, it repays all the interest it excites. Among other fragments which indicate its ancient splendor, there still remains, though not without defacements and injury, a magnificent gateway, with its vast and lofty towers. The sides of these towers are covered with hieroglyphics. Before this large and imposing entrance are gigantic statues, which the labors of the learned antiquarians whom I have mentioned have ascertained to be the statues of Rameses II., one of the great men and memorable names of ancient Egyptian history. But these too, though once supposed to have the power of perpetuating the features and the honors of a king so illustrious, are defaced and broken. Here, also, were originally two obelisks, covered with inscriptions deeply cut in the solid granite,—inscriptions which are nearly as distinct now as when the rock first yielded to the chisel. I have looked upon both of them. But one of them only remains here. The other, removed a few years since at great labor and expense, adorns the city of Paris.

From the PYLON or great gateway of the temple of Amunoph, and from the obelisks which stood in front of it, there is a DROMOS or narrow road, enclosed originally on each side by a row of colossal sphynxes, which extended nearly two miles to the great temple of Carnac. Many of these sphynxes have disappeared under the changes of three thousand years; many are much injured; but others still remain, with much of their original vastness and magnificence.

Of the great temple of Carnac I feel unwilling to speak, because I know it would require little short of a life's labor, instead of a visit of a few days, to estimate it in the details of its origin, of its various and sublime architecture, and of the historical records which are concealed under its obscure but countless symbols. Volumes have already been written; but the subject is not exhausted.

Imagine a level expanse, beautiful in its situation, and a mile and a half in circuit. In the early days of Egypt and of the human race—as early as the period when Joseph, the son of Jacob, had authority—the king of that time erects a small but beautiful sanctuary near the centre of this plain. It still exists, definable and separable, without much difficulty, from all that is around it; but it exists in ruins. Its sculptures tell its history. It is the work of Ositarsen I. Other kings in after-times, and often at long intervals, Amunoph I., the third Thothmes, Osirei, and Rameses III., animated by sentiments of religion or of personal glory, add other courts, temples, corridors, walls, gateways, obelisks, colossal statues, which entirely fill up the circuit which has been mentioned; all having a combined but definite relation to the little central temple from which they have their origin, and also to the temple of Luxor on the eastern side and to the temple of Goornah on the western side of the

Nile. So that temple may be said to look upon temple; and the numerous objects of worship, which occupied their sanctuaries, or were sculptured on their walls, as we recall them in the days of their idolatrous supremacy, seem to utter voices of mutual recognition and encouragement from one side of the Nile to the other, and from mountain to mountain.

On all sides of this vast pile of buildings are gateways with lofty towers, some of them in a state of remarkable preservation,—so beautiful, so immense, that human art furnishes no other equally striking examples. In that part of the temple called the grand hall, which is more than three hundred feet in length by a hundred and seventy in breadth, are columns twelve feet in diameter and sixty-six feet in height, exclusive of the pedestal. The height of this hall from the pavement to the top of the roof is stated to be eighty feet. In all parts of this immense edifice, and on the obelisks which remain, are hieroglyphics and pictorial representations, which illustrate the customs and manners of the people, their political history, and their religion.

We visited these ruins by night as well as by day. The moon shone brightly. Silence reigned in the midst of desolation. It was an impressive scene,—art and genius struggling against time. In one of the areas a lofty column stood alone, like the palm-tree of the desert, and in its solitude seemed to look with sorrow upon its fallen brothers, which were broken at its feet. In another place I looked with amazement on two of these mighty pillars, which had started from their foundations apparently at the same time, and had met and embraced each other in their fall. There they stand, folded as it were in each other's arms, struggling together against the footprints of ruin, yielding a mutual and sympathetic support, and awaiting in some epoch of coming ages a mutual destruction.

On leaving these interesting places I must refer briefly to the tombs. They are in the mountains on the western side of the Nile,—in retired places and difficult of access, amid the stillness of perpetual solitude, and where nature's surrounding desolation, shapeless, discolored, and without verdure, is a fitting emblem of this great empire of the dead. We spent among them a large portion of two successive days. The tombs of the kings and queens, without a parallel in any other place or nation, are of immense size,—cut from the solid rock. Some of them, consisting of successive chambers, are more than three hundred feet in length. They are adorned in some instances with niches and statues, and with columns of great beauty, and might well be denominated the palaces of the dead. Not only the sculptures with which they are covered, but the paintings also, to a considerable extent, are exceedingly distinct and fresh in appearance. In a number of the tombs there still remain SARCOPHAGI, hewn from granite, and of very great size. On the lids of the sarcophagi are the sculptured figures of the monarchs whose dust they were destined to contain. One of these figures, well sculptured and in high relief, is that of Osirei II.

Many of the sculptures on the walls obviously

have relation to great moral and religious truths. We could not well doubt, from the inscriptions and figures which we saw, that the Egyptians, though much perplexed on the subject, had a dim belief in the immortality of the soul. How could the thoughtful and inventive minds which projected and carried into effect these remarkable works believe or think otherwise? Or what motive could they have had to stimulate them in these great exertions, if they had supposed that the death of the body is the absolute extinction of existence? In the farthest chamber of the tomb of Rameses VII., on the wall beyond the massive sarcophagus which encloses the ashes of the dead, is sculptured a winged globe, in the centre of which is a little child, intimating that from beyond the tomb there arises a new and higher existence. The sculptured representations, which are intended to set forth the examination and trial which the dead are required to undergo in passing from this life to another, involve the idea of the continuance of being.

If we adopt the supposition that their own minds were incapable of originating the doctrine of immortality, we may perhaps account for its existence among them in another way. To the distinguished men of the Israelites, Jacob and Joseph and Moses, and many others who resided in Egypt at different periods, but whose names are not handed down to us, this idea was familiar. They learned it from the God of their fathers. And with such dispositions as they possessed, they could not fail on favorable occasions to communicate it to others. From Egypt, which may be regarded as the first great school of the civilized world, it spread to other nations. Egypt was the teacher of Greece. Plato, with a mind thirsting for all knowledge, resided a number of years on the banks of the Nile, pursuing his studies in the renowned schools of Heliopolis. He is said to have visited Thebes. And a mind like his, which conversed with men, with history, and with nature, heard also and understood the voice from the tombs. He had an eye for the beauties of art; but, knowing that there is a science above that of the beautiful, he made it his worthy aim to become acquainted with the moral and religious ideas of the people; and, while his great and thoughtful intellect rejected their mythology and the puerilities of their unworthy worship, it accepted and defended the fundamental suggestion of an immortal existence.

Walking among the repositories of the dead, in the mountains of Thebes, the memorials sometimes of pride and ambition, and sometimes of domestic affection and of dim but struggling religious hope, and reflecting upon the character of the people with whom they originated, so ingenious and meditative, and in general so pacific in their dispositions towards other nations, my mind was profoundly affected. Especially when I saw them groping after the truth but still sinking into darkness; multiplying gods under the names and forms of Horus, Athor, Anubis, Osiris, Isis, Pthah, and I know not how many others, and yet rejecting or not seeing God in his truth and simplicity; unable to crush the desire of immortality and yet not understanding the time, the method, or the source of its realization;

demonstrating that the greatest human wisdom, without God to guide it, is but a light to error and a beacon to destruction,—I felt grateful that God, the only source of true guidance, had made himself known to the world, and had put an end to doubt. Clasping to my bosom that Bible which from early life had been my instructor and my consolation, my joy in prosperity and my hope in trial, I felt it to be more precious than ever; and I recognized anew, in the humble Son of Mary, a greater teacher than the masters of Roman, Grecian, or Egyptian wisdom.

Thus the time allotted us has passed. There are monuments of art and attractions of nature still higher up this river of rivers. But they are not for our eyes; and Philæ, with its broken and its standing columns, and the sounding cataracts, and Nubia, not unknown to history, cannot be seen by us. The rais of our little boat, instructed by the winds, has given his orders. The sailors, with their rude song upon their lips, are already seated at their oars.—Time is the controller of action. Each moment has its own history, and issues its own commands. I gave a parting look to the mighty architectural monuments of a buried nation, and saw for the last time the mountain of tombs.

LINES WRITTEN ON LEAVING THE TEMPLES AND TOMBS OF THEBES.

The oar is dipping in the waves
  That bear me on their watery wings.
Farewell to Egypt's land of graves!
  Farewell, the monuments of kings!
They died,—and changed the living throne
For chambers of the mountain-stone.

I trod the vast sepulchral halls
  Design'd their lifeless dust to keep,
And read upon the chisell'd walls
  The emblems of their final sleep,
And learn'd that, when they bow'd to die,
They hoped for immortality.

Dark was the way. They knew not how
  That other life would come again,
To rend the flinty mountain's brow
  That overlooks the Theban plain.
But if aright their hearts they read,
The rocks at last would yield their dead.

Oh, yes! The instincts of the heart,
  In every land, in every clime,
The great, ennobling truth impart,
  That life has empire over time.
Death for eternal life makes room,
And heaven is born upon the tomb.

They saw the end, *but not the way*,—
  The life to come, but not the power;
And felt, when call'd in dust to lay,
  The doubt and anguish of the hour.
O Christ! By Thee the word is spoken;
The power is given; the tomb is broken!

(XXXIV.)

Arrival at Osioot—Its situation—Coptic Christians—Mountain of Osioot—Tombs in the mountain—View from the summit—The desert—John of Lycopolis—Extract from Gibbon—Commotions in Upper Egypt—Affecting death of an Arab girl—Ruins of Abydos—Poetry.

OSIOOT, UPPER EGYPT, MARCH 7, 1853.

In coming down the Nile we have reached, after a passage which has been somewhat delayed by unfavorable winds, the pleasant city of Osioot,—the residence at the present time of the governor of the Thebaid, or Upper Egypt. and which may be regarded as its capital. It is situated about two miles from the river, under the shadow of a lofty mountain of limestone, which guards it from the sands of the Libyan desert. The flourishing village of El Hamra, upon the bank of the river, is its port. There is a large canal, which conveys the water of the Nile into the city, and into the fields and gardens around it. Portions of the grounds within the city and in its immediate neighborhood are low, and are inundated in the annual rise of the Nile; but a communication is kept up at all times between the Nile and the city, and between the city and the plain at the foot of the mountain, by means of a large dike, which is well built, and is richly ornamented with trees. The city is said to contain twenty thousand inhabitants, of whom one thousand are Christians, chiefly Copts.

In this place, and still more in other places, we have made some inquiries in relation to this Christian sect. They claim to be the descendants of the old Egyptians; and intellectually they seem to possess much of that power which gave such an ascendency to their ancestors. But deprived of the means of education, inheriting a system of forms and ceremonies which seemed to us in its tendencies to perplex rather than to enlighten and encourage the true religious spirit, and crushed by arbitrary power and the dominant influence of Mohammedanism, their condition is discouraging, and almost hopeless in their own view, as it seems to be in the view of others. They answered our inquiries promptly, and appeared to be grateful for the interest and sympathy we expressed. Their history, their character, their present prostrate condition, give them a claim upon the aid, the prayers, and the sympathy of Christians in other lands.

One of the objects of interest at Osioot is the lofty and picturesque mountain which overhangs it. It is steep and difficult of ascent, but well repays the labor of the traveller in the wide and rich prospect which it presents from its top. In its side are rows of tombs excavated in the rock, differing much in size, and rising one above another almost to the summit. In the days of early persecution under the Roman emperors, they are said to have furnished a place of refuge and of residence to the Christians of Egypt. We have occupied a short time in examining a number of them. In some of them are inscriptions upon the walls, which may yet repay the labors of the Egyptian antiquary. Portions of the mummies of human bodies are scattered upon the ground. And repeatedly we saw what we had seen nowhere else,—the mummy of the wolf, which was once regarded as an object of special veneration, and probably of worship, in this region. It was owing to this circumstance that the Greeks gave the name of Lycopolis to the city:—*the city of the wolf.* Some of the tombs are quite large, and would be regarded as objects of great interest in other countries; but they are so far inferior to the tombs found in other parts of Egypt, that the traveller looks upon them for a few moments and then passes on.

With some difficulty we reached the summit of

the mountain. A little below it, as we were clambering along among the rocks, two eagles, disturbed by the unusual sound of human footsteps, suddenly flew out of one of the smaller excavations. The summit of the mountain, which we judged to be some five or six hundred feet high, presents an enchanting prospect of very great extent. It is true, it does not differ much in its general features from what we had witnessed in some other places; but it is richly varied and heightened in particular elements of beauty; the rich Nile flowing for many miles in its magnificence,—the blooming gardens in the city and in its environs,—the fields, as far as the eye can reach, green with perpetual vegetation and traversed everywhere by flocks and herds,—the mountains which enclose the plain on every side with their lofty white walls,—the clear blue sky resting upon them; and on the side of the city the straight tall minarets, and the outlines of the city itself, mellowed and beautiful in the distance, without anything seen or experienced from the crowded bazaars and narrow and circuitous streets which might otherwise detract from the favorable impression. Repeatedly had we witnessed such scenes in Egypt. My experience has not been very wide, and therefore it might be more proper for others to make comparisons. I can only say, I have seen nothing which exceeds these wonderful panoramas in other countries, except perhaps the unexampled view from Richmond Hill in England, which has equal extent with increased elements of interest.

Turning from the valley of the Nile, we looked

in the other direction upon the desert. The contrast was as great as imagination could well conceive. But the desert also has its power over the human mind. If it is not beautiful, it is not without sublimity. Stretching in every direction, like an illimitable sea, it produces an impression profound, grand, sublime. Does philosophy undertake to explain it? The thing itself is both its cause and its explanation. How is it possible for vastness to be without sublimity? Magnitude of the thing, even if it be the magnitude of desolation, gives magnitude to the thought and feeling. There must be something ultimate. The vast power of such a scene is, and must be, inherent in it, by its own nature. True philosophy describes, when it has no further power to analyze. The desert, therefore, utters its own voice,—is sublime, if we may so express it, by its own declaration, because it is sublime in itself.

We saw the remains of ancient buildings on the top of this mountain. It was in this place, a spot peculiarly favorable to retirement and meditation, that we are to look for the residence of the celebrated eremite, John of Lycopolis. Shut out from the world by a voluntary and almost inaccessible seclusion, he may be said to have looked down upon it; and the suggestions of so grand a scene could hardly fail to have aided that communion with God which was favored by retirement. This remarkable man spent a great portion of his time in private worship; and such was the prevalent opinion of his sanctity and of his intimacy with the Divine Mind, that people came to him from a great distance, and even kings sent to him, to learn his opinion on the great matters of morals, religion, and providence. It is to this man—whom some people will call superstitious and others will describe as devout, but whose personal history is involved in so much obscurity and is perhaps so much exaggerated by fiction that all judgments upon it are liable to more or less of error—that the historian Gibbon refers in a passage which may properly be quoted here. Speaking of the Emperor Theodosius, he says:—

"Before he performed any decisive resolution, the pious emperor was anxious to discover the will of heaven; and as the progress of Christianity had silenced the oracles of Delphi and Dodona, he consulted an Egyptian monk, who possessed, in the opinion of the age, the gift of miracles and the knowledge of futurity. Eutropius, one of the favorite eunuchs of the palace of Constantinople, embarked for Alexandria, from whence he sailed up the Nile as far as the city of Lycopolis or of Wolves, in the remote province of Thebaid. In the neighborhood of the city, and on the summit of a lofty mountain, the holy John had constructed with his own hand an humble cell, in which he had dwelt about forty years, without opening his door, without seeing the face of a woman, and without tasting any food that had been prepared by human art. Five days of the week he spent in prayer and meditation; but on Saturdays and Sundays he regularly opened a small window, and gave audience to the crowd of suppliants who successively flowed from every part of the Christian world. The eunuch of Theodosius approached the window with respectful steps, proposed his questions concerning the event of the civil war, and soon returned with a favorable oracle, which animated the courage of the emperor by the assurance of an infallible victory."

At the very hour in which I am writing this letter, there is great commotion in Upper Egypt; probably greater than has existed for a considerable period. It is not, however, so much the commotion of political excitement and rebellion, as the general outbreaking of individual and domestic sorrow. This unhappy state of things, of which it would have been difficult for me to conceive if I had not witnessed it, originates from the recent order of the Pasha of Egypt for a new and universal levy of troops. The shekhs or subordinate governors of the small districts, who exercise authority under the Pasha and are dependent upon him, are required to enforce this military mandate; so that it is now taking effect in selecting and enforcing its victims in all the towns and villages. I refer to this subject in part, because it throws light upon the domestic habits of this people.

When we were at Thebes, as we went into the western mountains to visit the tombs of the kings, it was painful to see in repeated instances tombs and caverns and difficult places on the heights, occupied by large companies who had fled from the conscription. They preferred a military execution or starvation among the rocks in sight of their own homes, to an exile—which would be the result of their falling under the levy—of five and perhaps seven years, in Cairo and Alexandria, or on the borders of Syria. At every town where we stopped in coming down the Nile to this place, we heard the agitation and outcry of this universal sorrow. It is the same here.

As we came down from the mountain of Osioot, and were passing along the raised dike which connects the region of the mountain with the city, my attention was called to a sorrowful group of people. A guard of soldiers was conducting a young conscript to the city barracks. He was bound with cords, and closely followed by a blind old man, who was attended by two women, one on each side of him, whom I supposed to be his daughters. The faces of the women were soiled with dust. Dust was scattered upon their heads, and they uttered often a loud, wailing cry. Advancing a little farther, we found that there was a great number of conscripts in the city, who had been brought in from the neighboring villages. They were collected at the different military depôts, which were surrounded with large numbers of their relatives, who gave expression to their deep grief in the Oriental manner. I am not aware that any adequate explanation can be given of this general opposition to the levy on the part of the remote population, except their strong attachment to their families and homes. I could mention a number of additional facts in support of this view; but I will give only one, which has left upon my mind a painful sorrow.

On our return from a visit to the ruins of Abydos, where we had witnessed some remarkable remains of Egyptian art, and as we were passing over the beautiful plain which connects Abydos with the city of Girgeh, we met a number of men carrying a dead body on a rude bier. They appeared very sad, as they stood silently on the side of the road while we were passing by. And, as we had seen nothing of this kind before,—a lifeless body carried to its place, with mourners but apparently without any relatives present,—we took the liberty to make some inquiries. We learned from them that it was the corpse of a young woman who had been killed but a little while before, and that they were carrying the body to the place where she had lived. Her brother had been taken as a conscript and forced from his home. The sister whose affections had been united and nurtured with his in their solitary residence followed him with her lamentations, till the officer, under whose authority he was taken, exasperated by her uncontrollable grief, drew his pistol and shot her dead. The lifeless body was before us; and such was the story of her death, as I gathered it through our interpreter.

In a moment all the beauties of nature around me, which had filled my heart to overflowing, were covered with a cloud. Thought, imagination, consciousness, seemed to be absorbed in this painful event. I heard her lamentations; I saw her life-blood flowing. I followed the corpse to the old father's home. He was an old man unknown to me. I never entered his hut. I never saw his gray hairs. But still the sympathy of a common nature placed him before me. Imagination saw him in his sorrow. He stood bending over his staff. The corpse was brought to his door. He saw its blood-stained features; and the deep cry which he uttered went forth upon the winds. It was the shrill, hopeless cry of a broken heart.

There is but one consolation in such sad events. They are solemn protests against error and crime,—not the protests of calculation and of argument, but the higher and juster protests of the unconquerable instincts of the heart and of life itself. In the early times of the Roman republic, the blood of woman, in more instances than one, consecrated rights and truths; and history has done her justice. And the sacred blood of this poor Arab daughter and sister, (shed, if I may so express it, because her full, beating heart could no longer hold it,) the blood of this untaught but true-hearted child of the desert, has consecrated and ennobled the great truth, that affections are the life of the soul, and that man cannot understand the principles and worth of his existence till strife shall cease, and he shall "love his neighbor as himself."

I have referred in the course of this letter to our excursion to Abydos, which lies back at some distance from the river and about ten miles from the city of Girgeh. We were there on the 2d of March. There is an Arab village not far distant; but the site of the ancient city, which among the cities of the Thebaid is said to have been second only to Thebes itself, is buried deep in recent accumulations of sand, so that in walking over it we ascended a considerable distance and easily placed our feet on the sculptured roofs of the splendid temples which were once its ornaments. With no small difficulty we descended into them, and admired anew beautifully-colored sculptures and columns of nearly three thousand years' antiquity, as perfect as if but yesterday from the hands of the architect.

We are once more starting for the Pyramids and Cairo. We hope to be able to stop a few hours at the celebrated tombs of Beni Hassan, some of which were excavated in the time of Joseph, and which are represented as being covered with well-executed paintings, illustrative of Egyptian manners of that early period. It is there that Doric columns are found; differing but little from those of the Greeks, and sculptured and erected in these distant regions before the Doric name was known. But strange is the power of saddened associations. The poor Arab girl is still before me. The monuments of Egypt cannot drive her from my mind. And I will close my letter with a stranger's humble tribute to her sad but noble memory.

LINES COMMEMORATIVE OF AN ARAB GIRL SLAIN NEAR GIRGEH IN CONSEQUENCE OF HER INCONTROLLABLE AFFECTION FOR HER BROTHER.

Beneath the palm-tree's lonely shade
His flock the wandering shepherd leads;
'Twas there in early life they play'd
Around their lowly hut of reeds.

Oh, how she loved him! On the plain,
That stretches from the mountain-rock,
Twas theirs to watch the waving grain
Or guard the footsteps of the flock.

He was her brother. But the hour
Which tore him hence has hasten'd on.
Taught by affection's mighty power,
She felt that bliss and hope were gone.

Frantic, she could not let him go;
  The arms were clasp'd which would not part:
Oh, blame her not! Thou dost not know
  The pangs which rent that sister's heart.

But what against tyrannic wrong
  Are woman's griefs and feeble cry?
But woman too is sometimes strong:
  The Arab girl had strength to die.

Too weak to break her brother's chain,
  But strong in love, she bled and fell.
Child of the desert, not in vain
  Thy lips breathed out that sad farewell.

Oh no! Thy blood has made it true
  That despots cannot break or bind—
Though they may pierce the body through—
  The loves and memories of the mind.

(XXXV.)

Tombs of Beni Hassan—Columns and inscriptions—Arrival at Ghezeh—Excursion from Ghezeh to the Pyramids—Size of the Great Pyramid—Impressions left upon the mind—The colossal Sphynx—Memphis—Return to Ghezeh—Cross the Nile at the isle of Rhoda—Reach Cairo.

EGYPT, PYRAMIDS OF GHEZEH, MARCH 17, 1853.

We realized the anticipated pleasure to which I alluded in my last letter, in stopping at the tombs of Beni Hassan,—eighty miles below Osioot, where I last wrote. These tombs are interesting on account of their antiquity; it being conceded, I believe, by those who profess to be learned in early Egyptian history, that some of them were excavated in the time of Ositarsen I. I have already had occasion to intimate that it was in the reign of this king that Joseph and his brethren came into Egypt.

On entering the tombs of Beni Hassan, which are found at a little distance from the Nile, on the side of a high hill which overlooks the ruins of an Arab village, we noticed the deep square pits which we had seen in other places. They are not found, however, in all the Egyptian tombs. They are cut with great exactness and care in the rock, without any fixed relative position, but often near the centre of the great sepulchral chambers,—about six feet square, and varying in depth from twenty to forty feet. The bodies of dead persons—probably those not entitled to the highest degrees of honor—were deposited in them.

The sepulchral chambers in this place are not so large as those of the kings and queens in the mountains of Thebes; but it can hardly be said, I think, that they are inferior in architectural beauty. Certainly the proportions of the rooms and the beauty of the columns with which they are ornamented indicate artistic conceptions which could hardly be expected in the very early age which is assigned to them. The shafts of some of the columns are fluted polygons of sixteen sides, differing in style from any we had noticed elsewhere; and, from the similarity which they bear to columns of later date in other countries, it may well be supposed that the architects of Egypt, whose elaborate works could not exist without being widely known, furnished suggestions which had their influence in the progress and perfection of Grecian art.

The tombs of Beni Hassan are especially remarkable for the character of their sculptures and paintings, which are occupied almost exclusively with domestic scenes, and with the scenes and arts of common life. Mingled with representations of dancing and hunting, are other representations of men employed in agricultural pursuits, in manufactures, and in various other ways, such as watering flax, manufacturing cloth from flax, fishing with nets, making bread, feeding cattle, playing games of ball, making pottery, blowing glass, taking inventories of goods, inflicting the punishment of the bastinado, and performing various active and athletic feats. There is a difference in the execution; but some of the paintings, estimated on any just principles which are known to the art, must be regarded as admirable. Some of the figures are in perspective, and are executed with skill in that respect as well as in others.

In wandering a few months ago through the excavations of Herculaneum and Pompeii, I felt, as I trod the very dwellings they had inhabited, that I knew, from what I saw around me, much more than I could learn elsewhere of the domestic occupations, habits, and life of the people. They were records which could not be mistaken. And the sculptures and paintings in the tombs of Beni Hassan have left a similar conviction in respect to ancient Egypt. Dead in fact, and dead in the ordinary forms of history, it may still be said of Egypt —what can hardly be said of any other nation— that she still lives in her own burying-place.

We are now amid different scenes. In seven days from Beni Hassan and nineteen from Thebes, —a voyage down the Nile of unusual length,—we have at last reached the pleasant town of Ghezeh, directly opposite the town of Old Cairo and the enchanting island of Rhoda. From Ghezeh to the celebrated pyramids of Memphis, the ancient capital of Egypt, but which are now generally described as the pyramids of Ghezeh, is a distance of six miles. When the country is overflowed by the Nile, the route is circuitous and is longer.

The excursion from Ghezeh to the pyramids is a pleasant one. Skirting the town of Ghezeh, and on the edge of its wide and fertile plain, is an immense forest of palm-trees, regularly set out, and all of them of great height. Standing erect, and destitute of branches, excepting the long feathery limbs which fan the air at their top, they have the appearance of tall and majestic columns. The limbs at the top, reaching out towards each other, form a roof overhead, excluding the light and heat of the sun, and inviting the foot of the traveller to its shade. We passed through the edge of this forest. On leaving it, we proceeded over a plain of great fertility and high cultivation, which bore marks of being overflowed in the inundations of the Nile. It is the lower portion of the old plain of Memphis. The city of Memphis, of which scarcely a ruin now remains, was situated a little higher up the river. In two hours we reached the base of the Great Pyramid.

This pyramid, which has in its immediate vicinity a number of others of smaller dimensions, is four hundred and fifty feet in height, with a square base of seven hundred and forty-six feet on each side, and is said to cover twelve acres of ground. According to the statements of ancient historians, it was twenty years in building, and required the labor of three hundred and sixty thousand men. On the summit is a level space of about thirty feet square. Mr. Thompson was the only one of our party who felt able to ascend to the top. He represented the view which was presented from the summit as exceedingly extensive and beautiful.

A thousand questions arise on looking at this great work. Where were these immense stones cut? By what means were they transported to this place? By what skill and appliances of machinery were they raised to their position? What was the object of the mysterious chambers in its interior? Who was buried in the sarcophagus? The mind is bewildered in conjectures; but the pyramid itself is a reality, which sets conjecture and scepticism at defiance, as it defies time, tempests, and the Libyan sands.

It is difficult to exaggerate the impression which this enormous pile of stone makes upon the mind when it is seen for the first time. But while the emotion is powerful beyond what is experienced in other places, perhaps in view of any other mere work of man, it looks so much like another useless and heaven-defying tower of Babel, the monument of mere human pride and ambition, that the feeling of humiliating sadness is hardly less strong than that of admiration. Nor will the friend of humanity and of human rights forget that these pyramids stand the perpetual memorial of what political tyranny, grasping at power and trampling on rights, has done in past ages, and will continue to do, so long as it exists, in all ages to come. If there were no historic testimony to that effect,—if the Cheops of Herodotus, who is said to have been the builder of the Great Pyramid, were not historically commemorated as a tyrant by the father of history,—we must necessarily have come to the conclusion, from the work itself, that it was built at the price of the most unjust exactions, and had its foundations laid in blood.

At a little distance from the Great Pyramid is the colossal sphynx, which no traveller willingly leaves Egypt without seeing. Its enormous body is partially buried in the sand; but its head and majestic features are still erect and lofty. The sphynx, which, in its design, is a mystical emblem of the combination of intelligence and power, is a sculptured human form in its upper parts, attached to the recumbent body of a lion. The body is a little less than a hundred and fifty feet in length. The fore-legs and paws of the lion-shaped body extend to the distance of fifty feet. Such is the statement of its measurements made by travellers who have had leisure and opportunity to examine it carefully. The human breast and head, which lift themselves upward out of the immense sculpture which constitutes the leonine base, is more than sixty feet in height. The circumference of the head, around the full, projecting forehead, is a hundred feet,—all cut, with the exception of one or two small portions, from one solid rock.

No object in Egypt, among the multitude of its objects of interest, fixed my attention more deeply than this. So vast and so full of life, it had to me the appearance of some mighty existence, lifting itself by its own power from the deep bosom of the earth. Its features are worn and mutilated by time; but it requires no great effort of the imagination, aided by the mysterious power of what still remains, to call them back and to restore something of the original completeness of the mighty image. Its lips, diminished by the attrition of the sand and wind, were once full, and breathed their appropriate expression of wisdom and beneficence. Its calm, majestic eye, full of intelligence, but, in being robbed of something of its original power, apparently drooping with sorrow, looks out upon the wide level plain, the repository of unknown ruins, and seems to seek the men and monuments of other days. That benign but lofty look has watched the march of generations and nations. It saw the rising beauty of Memphis, and delighted in its matured and mighty magnificence. It looks at the present hour as if it still anxiously sought that image of beauty and greatness. It seeks it in vain. No wall, no tower, no palace, scarcely a broken column, is visible. It hears the sound of the camel's tinkling bell; it beholds the flock of the shepherd on the plain: but the queen of cities has departed; Memphis is no more.

Returning to Ghezeh on our way to the city of Cairo, which we reached the same day, we crossed the Nile to the pleasant and flourishing town of Old Cairo,—passing the southern extremity of the isle of Rhoda. The harbor of Old Cairo, which was crowded with the boats of the Nile, is formed in part by this island. It was here, according to the traditions of the country, near the southern end of this matchless island of flowers, that the infant Moses was concealed in the thick bulrushes on the banks of the Nile. It was here that the daughter of Pharaoh, whose name, according to Josephus, was Thermutis, found him. It was in this region, at least, and perhaps in the schools and palaces of Heliopolis and Memphis, now buried in the dust, that he was nurtured, under the care of a protecting Providence, for his high and mysterious destiny.

(XXXVI.)

Cairo—Excursion to Heliopolis—Name and scriptural allusions—Obelisks—Tradition of Joseph and Mary—Garden of Shoobra—Nilometer—Island of Rhoda—Religious ceremonies of the Dervishes—Slave-market—Citadel of Cairo—Tomb of Mohammed Ali—Divisions of the modern city—Condition and prospects.

EGYPT, CITY OF CAIRO, MARCH 26, 1853.

We are now once more in Cairo, which we reached on the 17th. We have been detained in making preparations for the journey of the long desert and Mount Sinai. In my former letter from Cairo, I intimated that I might write again on our return here from Thebes. We have been kept here longer than we expected; but this detention has furnished us with a better opportunity than we might otherwise have had of visiting the city and the interesting localities in its immediate vicinity.

In making excursions for this purpose we have met with no difficulty; but, on the contrary, every reasonable facility has been afforded. The hauteur and distance which were formerly ascribed to the Turks seem to have passed away. If this is not entirely the case, it certainly is so in a considerable degree. I ascribe this very much to their increased acquaintance and association with Europeans.

Among other excursions in the neighborhood of Cairo, we have visited the site rather than the ruins of the ancient Heliopolis, which was situated about six miles distant from the modern capital of Egypt. It was a city comparatively small in size, but of great celebrity, both on account of the Temple of the Sun, from which the city took its name, and also on account of its schools of astronomy and philosophy. It was here, as I have had occasion to remark in a former letter, that Plato resided and studied; and when in the reign of Augustus Cæsar the city was visited by Strabo, the geographer, a house was pointed out to him, in which the Greek philosopher was said to have lived. It was in Heliopolis, also, that Herodotus, who has been styled, with no inconsiderable reason, the father of history, spent a portion of his time when he visited these regions; and here, in conversation with the priests and other learned men, he acquired much of that knowledge which enabled him to write the affairs of Egypt. And it seems to me no unreasonable supposition, that Moses, at a still earlier period, who was *"learned in all the wisdom of the Egyptians,"* and whose writings, independent of what may be said of their inspiration, place him at the head of learned men in the attributes of knowledge, eloquence, and moral insight, studied in the same schools, and was the associate in *place*, if not in time, with the philosophers and learned men of Greece.

The ancient Egyptian name of this city, given in reference to its temple and the form of worship kept up in it, was EI-RE, which means the *house of the sun.* The Hebrew name applied to it by the prophet Jeremiah is Beth-Shemesh, which has the same meaning. It is hardly necessary to add, that the Greek name of Heliopolis, by which it is commonly known at the present time among Europeans, is similar in its import. In Ezekiel, in the prophetic announcement of the various desolations which were to take place in Egypt, it is called, by a rhetorical license of which we have other instances in the Bible, AVEN, or the city of falsehood or vanity, in allusion probably to the false worship established in it. In the opinion of many Biblical critics, it was the daughter of a priest of Heliopolis who was married by Joseph in the time of his great power and influence in Egypt. The hieroglyphical inscriptions which have been found there show that the city existed in his time.

I think the excursion to the site of this ancient and renowned city one of the most pleasant which can be taken from Cairo. It was a bright, cheerful day when we went there, which was not rendered oppressive, as was sometimes the case, by the heat of the sun; and the multiplied objects which presented themselves to notice harmonized in one great panorama of beauty. In approaching the place on which the city was built, we passed a large level plain, and I observed numerous camels and horses upon it, and that it was occupied by a multitude of tents, which made a picturesque appearance. They were the tents of Mohammedans, who were assembling in great numbers from various places on the Nile, preparatory to a pilgrimage to Mecca. Reaching the site of the city, we did not find, nor did we expect to find, many ruins. The natural effects of time, the inundations of the Nile, and the ravages of conquering armies, have accomplished their work of destruction here, as they have done at Memphis and other places. And there are now but few ruins remaining. We saw, however, a number of very large blocks of hewn stone, covered with sculptures which belonged to some ancient Egyptian building; also, mutilated sphynxes.

From the position of these ancient remains, partly covered in the earth, and with mounds of earth around them in some places, it was natural to suppose that other and more extensive ruins still exist under the ground, and may hereafter be discovered.

The site of the Temple of the Sun, which is particularly mentioned by Strabo, was easily indicated to us, in the midst of the trees and blooming shrubbery which now cover it, by the lofty obelisk which still stands. The earth had collected around this obelisk at its base to the depth of five feet above its pedestal, but had been partially removed so as to bring the pedestal in sight. The height of the column, exclusive of the pedestal, is sixty-eight feet; but it does not differ in its general form, and in the great number of its sculptures, and in the skill displayed in them, from other works of this kind which we have seen. It is, perhaps, proper to add, as indicating something of the primitive splendor of Heliopolis, that there were originally four obelisks here. One of them is said to have been destroyed by the Arabs; but at what time, and under what circumstances, I am unable to state. Two were carried to Rome by Augustus Cæsar after the battle of Actium. One of them I mentioned in my letter from Rome, as particularly attracting my attention as we entered the great square in the neighborhood of the PORTA DEL POPOLO. The other remains here, where it stood more than three thousand years ago,—a magnificent but solitary monument of a ruined city and a departed civilization.

It is said, among the traditions of the country, that this city was visited by Joseph and Mary with the infant Saviour, when driven into Egypt from Judea by the persecutions of Herod. I am aware that there is much difference of opinion in relation to the value which is to be attributed to traditions. I do not attribute any inordinate worth to them. And still it will always remain true that the history of traditions is a part of the history of the human race, and that they furnish suggestions and open up trains of thought which sometimes throw light upon history, and, still more frequently, upon the varieties of men's ideas and affections.

But here, in this singular land, the present and the past, the living and the dead, all epochs of time and all varieties of civilization, seem to be mingled together. In one of the excursions in the neighborhood of Cairo, desirous of seeing the Egypt of the present as well as of the past, we visited the palace and gardens of Shoobra. They are four miles from the city, in a northern direction. The ride for a great part of the distance is over a wide avenue, raised a number of feet above the verdant plains and gardens around it, and protected by its greater elevation against the overflowings of the Nile. In its whole length it is lined on both sides with very large acacias, which bend over so as almost to embrace and intertwine each other with their magnificent canopy of shade. It was filled with multitudes of people going in different directions, and with caravans of loaded camels. At its termination is the garden of Shoobra. Laid out perhaps with too much regularity, but still rich in the beauties of art and nature, this celebrated garden has its palace and fountains as well as its shrubbery and flowers. The birds have found out the beauty of its cool retreat. So numerous do they nestle in its thick green shades, that every branch and flower seems to utter its song. Near its centre is a large marble fountain, surrounded with a covered corridor, at the four corners of which are rooms richly fitted up with divans in the Turkish manner. The stranger, satiated with the beauties of nature, is invited to repose himself here, if he chooses. And yet, with a greater expense of the labors of art, the garden of Shoobra had less attraction for me than the quiet and varied beauty of the gardens of the island of Rhoda.

It was a matter of course that we should visit the Nilometer. It is opposite Old Cairo, in the island of Rhoda. We passed in a boat the branch of the Nile which separates the town from the island. Built by one of the Caliphs in the beginning of the ninth century, it once had its dome and its historic inscriptions. The most that is seen now is a large and well-built square chamber, which connects with the waters of the Nile. It has a graduated pillar in its centre, by means of which, at the time of its annual inundation, the rise of the Nile is ascertained. A proclamation of the exact advance of the river, as ascertained in this way, is made every morning by public criers, appointed for different parts of the city.

The island of Rhoda is little more than a mile in length. Not far distant from the Nilometer, and at the southern end of the island, is the palace of Ibrahim Pasha. Our little party were readily admitted into this palace and shown through its richly-furnished apartments. The southern side of the palace rests upon piles of solid masonry, which form a bulwark against the strong currents of the Nile. We wandered through the delightful gardens connected with the palace, to which I have already referred as being more attractive in some respects than the garden of Shoobra.

I hardly know by what impulse of the heart it was that the same excursion which carried us to the flower-garden and the palace of the island of Rhoda found us also in the large circular hall at Old Cairo, in which are celebrated the mysterious ceremonies of one of the sects of the Mohammedan Dervishes. Entering this building under the direction of our guide, we took a seat on the mats and cushions placed around its interior. On the wall were hung the badges of the society, and implements of war. On the side opposite to us, a circle occupying about a third of the space was formed of cushions and rich skins spread upon the stony floor. Soon after we had taken our seats, the Dervish who presided at the ceremonies on this occasion entered this circle, and seated himself at the place where it touched the wall. He seemed to be a man of about forty years of age, with a form erect and symmetrical, a countenance open and intelligent, an eye large and dark. As the other members of the company came in, those who seemed to be the more important members were received by him with a kindness and politeness which showed that he was not ignorant of the forms of polished society. This man, whose manners and physical completeness indicated a mind above the common rank, attracted my attention much. There was a hidden language in his intelligent countenance, in general carefully repressed, but which at times seemed to say, "My nature does not correspond to my situation. It is a hard or a sad necessity—that of sincerity building upon error—which has placed me here."

The members of the society were at first seated. For a time they seemed to be occupied in serious meditation. Then they rose. Sounds of rude music were heard. Standing in a circle, they began their singular ceremony, which they regard as a special act of religion, with a slight but regular motion of the head. The bowing of the head soon became more rapid, and with a deeper inclination. Then came exclamations and deep groanings. This went on progressively, till the regular and prescribed motion of the company was broken in upon by the unrestrained motion and contortions of individuals. The rapidity of the motion, continued in this way for a long time, caused a rush of blood to the head. They lost all control of themselves, and a number of them fell upon the floor in convulsions. One of them fell at my feet; and, as I saw him thus, deprived of consciousness, and his body writhing convulsively, I felt that superstition, in whatever country and under whatever name, is dishonorable to God, and a hard and cruel burden to man.

At another time we witnessed another painful scene,—that of the slave-market at Cairo. We had previously visited the slave-market in Alexandria; and, whatever opinions may have been entertained or expressed to the contrary, we saw enough to convince us that in Egypt the traffic in slaves continues in much of its original vigor. The greater number of the slaves whom we saw were boys and girls from ten to fifteen years of age, brought from Nubia, and other countries on the upper parts of the Nile. Sad in countenance, and half-naked as they were, they flocked around us with some appearance of animation and zeal, as if desirous or hoping to be purchased. Their conduct seemed to indicate on their part a conviction, the origin of which they might perhaps have been unable to explain, that their misery could not well be increased, and might be alleviated by some such change.

Among the objects especially worthy of being visited in Cairo is the Citadel,—a lofty, fortified rock in the south part of the city, overlooking the city in its whole extent, and furnishing a view of the valley of the Nile, and of its towns and villages for many miles southward, and north as far as the head of the Delta. It seemed to us, as we stood upon this elevated position, wonderful in itself and memorable in its history, with the Nile before us and mountains behind, with a hundred minarets at our feet, and the vast pyramids full in sight, that no other spot in this vicinity opened such an impressive view. One of the remarkable curiosities within the limits of the citadel is the celebrated well of Joseph, excavated in the solid rock to the depth of two hundred and sixty feet, with a winding staircase leading to the bottom. Day and night strong oxen are turning the wheel of this deep excavation, and pouring out the water from its inexhaustible fountain. This well, the history of which has been the subject of much discussion, is generally conceded to be one of the works of the ancient Egyptians; but at what period it was made is not known.

Within the limits of the citadel is one of the numerous palaces of the Pasha of Egypt, and also the new mosque commenced by the late Mohammed Ali. This structure, enriched on every side with Oriental alabaster, is one of great size and beauty, though still unfinished. Within its walls is the tomb of Mohammed Ali, whose ashes have found a resting-place here; one of those men who leave their mark in the annals of ages, by seizing power at any hazard and expense of benevolence and of right, and then by employing it, with almost the same energy and the same disregard of right, for what they choose to consider as the general good. These men are the Cæsars and Napoleons of history, renowned but problematical characters, who forget that success cannot justify crime, and that a man of a true spirit, and, most of all, a man of a truly conscientious and religious spirit, rejects and abhors all favors and all goods which are offered him as the tyrant's compensation for the loss of a just and honorable liberty.

There are two Egypts,—the Egypt of the past and the Egypt of the present. The Egypt of the past is a mighty wreck, and her mutilated limbs are scattered all along the banks of the Nile, from the Delta to the mountains of Nubia. And the traveller seeks a knowledge of her greatness at Thebes, at Denderah, and at Beni Hassan, rather than at Cairo. The modern Egypt lives in the modern city. Its representative and its life is Cairo. The stranger who visits it is soon satisfied. He passes through the narrow and crowded streets, amid the agitations of passion and the urgencies of business. He sees different and unknown races of men, coming from distant regions, and variant in costume and manners. He hears languages which he does not understand. The community of the intellect, and especially of the heart which needs language for its expression, is obstructed and weakened. And in the midst of a multitude he often feels himself to be in the solitude of the desert.

The city of Cairo is divided into different Quarters, as they are termed, which have their separate enclosures and regulations. Having seen the mechanic trades and the shops in these Quarters,—the Jews' Quarter, the Copt Quarter, the Armenian Quarter, the Frank Quarter,—and having visited the public gardens and the Citadel, and a few ancient and rich mosques, which have their painful associations for the Christian, the traveller finds but little either to gratify or excite his curiosity. There are gatherings of the populace around jugglers and mountebanks; but there are no places of public resort which are suited to the wants of a serious and intelligent man. Mind is not the growth of Cairo. The large public libraries which are found in the cities of Europe and America, many of which are easily accessible, are unknown here. There are no reading-rooms worthy of the name, no public lectures, no places and assemblies where great questions of a political, moral, and constitutional nature are discussed. The Nile still flows, but thought is stagnant. No Plato studies and meditates at Heliopolis now.

The form of government, the predominant religion of the country, and, to some extent, the habits and prejudices of the people, are all averse to inquiry and mental improvement. Their government, which is of the nature of an absolute monarchy, may be characterized as the tyranny of the body. Their religion, which proscribes religious inquiry and all change of religious opinion, may be described, with hardly less truth, as the tyranny of the mind. Science demands liberty, and liberty demands Christianity. And it seems to me that, in the present enlightened period, they demand, not the Christianity which, starting with good intentions, has become incarcerated and fixed in the formalities of ages, but rather the free, simple, believing, and loving Christianity of the pure and primitive days of its history.

In leaving these scenes, therefore, where there has been so much to interest and please, I am obliged to say that there is much of a different character,—much to discourage the patriot, much to try the faith of the Christian. But the light of truth comes through the instrumentality of prayer; and error, which stands in the way of all true progress, can be corrected only by light and love. The Christian should never forget that God reigns; and it is the privilege of the eye of faith to behold the triumphs of the future, while the natural eye, incapable of seeing things invisible, closes itself in despair.

(XXXVII.)

Departure from Cairo for the desert—Village of Bedouin Arabs—Desert of Suez—Its solitude and silence—Night-scene—El Mugdala, or Migdol of the Scriptures—The camel—Suez—An English steamer—Cross the Red Sea—The sirocco—Arrival at the wells of Moses.

WELLS OF MOSES, EASTERN *SHORE OF THE RED* SEA, APRIL 1, 1853.

We left Cairo on the twenty-eighth day of March,—our destination Mount Sinai and Palestine. The din of the crowded streets of the city soon died upon our ears. The direction which we took led us in the neighborhood of the lofty tombs of the Mameluke kings, often denominated the tombs of the Caliphs. We had already visited them; and we only gave them our parting look. They are situated beyond the numerous tombs of the people which crowd the space around the city gate,—standing with dome and pointed minaret under the silent heights of Mokattam. Their architecture is Saracenic; and, though they are lofty and elaborated structures, they give but slight indications of the vast resources and genius which characterize the Egypt of the days of Joseph and Moses. All monuments, however, have a degree of value, and th[illegible] contain the dust of kings and conquering warriors, whose individual history has an interest; but they are still more interesting as the memorials of the changes of dynasties and of the vicissitudes of nations.

To the left of the tombs, and not far distant, is one of the numerous palaces of the Pasha of Egypt. This, too, we had already seen. Viewed at a distance, it makes a fine appearance,—bearing the marks of modern European art. At a little distance farther on, and on the very edge of the desert, is a small village of Bedouin Arabs. Their huts, similar in structure to those of the Arabs of the Nile, are built around a circular area. I gazed a moment upon this novel scene. Wonderful are the sympathies which bind man to man. I had seldom heard this people mentioned, except in terms of distrust and condemnation. But I found my heart strengthening and widening within me, as if to understand and embrace to its centre, notwithstanding these unfavorable intimations, this new feature of a common humanity. An old man with gray hairs addressed me. The women, occupied in their humble employments, were seated at the doors of the huts. The children were noisy and playful in the open space. A camel, reposing its wearied form on the sand, occupied its centre.

I passed on, casting a parting look at the long line of verdure which marked in the distance the track of the Nile. The vision, filled with new and strange views of life and manners, had closed. In a few hours we left all behind.

We form a caravan of more than twenty camels. We carry our food and water with us. A vast expanse of uncultivated wilderness is before us. Gardens and trees, and fountains and flowers, and singing-birds, are gone. Day after day passes on,—monotonous, but still not without interest. He who has not been in the desert has not known all that the heart can feel. It is the great prerogative of our nature to unfold itself anew in every novelty of circumstance and situation. The desert speaks. It has a voice for the heart; and the heart answers.

The desert from Cairo to Suez is not in all respects so destitute and lonely as the vast desert on the eastern side of the Red Sea. There is something left. Absolute death cannot be predicated of anything except annihilation. From time to time are seen shrubs and tufts of coarse grass; but they furnish but a slight relief to the general character of the scene. I was surprised and pleased to find in some places a green plant, which bore pods of an inch in length, and which on pressing and breaking them were found to be full of water. At the distance of forty miles from Cairo, we sat down under a large acacia-tree,—the first tree which we had noticed for that distance. It is difficult to understand the secret of its growth in such a place. Such exceptions cannot make these vast solitudes otherwise than a desert.

Animal life dies as well as vegetable. It is true that it is possible in the course of some days to get sight of a snail, which is found in some localities and which has discovered the secret of attaching itself to the few shrubs of the region and extracting their moisture; or to cross the path of a beetle groping its way in the heated sand; or to startle the solitude of a lizard, which has contrived to live among the rocks. But in general the desolation is perfect. Locality exists. Life is in exile.

Marching over wide and arid plains, and with hills and mountains of rock and sand in sight, we go on from day to day. The eye rests upon *forms*, not upon life; but forms are the background of beauty; and imagination sometimes fills up the picture. Successive hours tell our progress. The march becomes wearisome; but the setting sun brings rest. Turning from the narrow beaten paths which constitute the roads of the desert, and seeking a retired and sheltered place, we pitch our tents for the night. This also is a new scene; but it has the associations of antiquity and religion. The patriarchs dwelt in tents. Paul was a tent-maker. As we hear the sound of the hammer, we know what it is when it is required of Zion "to lengthen her cords and strengthen her stakes." The Arabs shelter themselves under the piles of luggage. And if the evening is cool, they build a fire. They form themselves in little assemblies; and if they travel in comparative silence by day, they are noisy as laugh and song can make them, in their social groups, in the early part of night. The camels, weary with the heat and toils of the day, lie down at their side and are fed. They then prepare their own humble meal.

It was thus day after day and night after night. At a certain time, being little inclined to sleep in the novelty of such a situation, I walked out at midnight. The moon was in all its brightness.

The sky, without a cloud to suggest the idea of form or limitation, seemed vast as eternity; and, being studded all over with stars, it was bright with the brightness of God. The camels, stretched out at length upon the ground, were large dark shadows in the moonlight. The men slept at their side. There was no sound. But the soul heard the silence. I have stood at the foot of Niagara; I have listened to the deep moaning sound of the vast forests of my native land; I have been on the ocean when each wave had its voice and that voice was thunder; but these great voices entered less deeply into the ear of the spirit than the mighty silence of the desert at midnight. At such a time the soul opens its capacities. It magnifies and expands itself in the greatness of its dilated conceptions, and takes hold of eternity; and in the voice which is then sent forth,—a voice uttered in brightness without a shadow, in vastness without limit, in harmony without variation,—it hears the proclamation, so dear to every holy soul, of the unutterable tranquillity of God.

At the distance of sixty-four miles from Cairo, we passed the place called El Mugdala, supposed by many to be the Migdol of the Scriptures, which is mentioned in connection with the departure of the Israelites from Egypt. History always adds interest to a place. I stopped a moment to look at Migdol, if such it was; but it was only a repetition of desolation. I noticed no buildings at the place,—nothing but two barren hills of considerable size. We passed on. The Red Sea is not far distant. Our course from Cairo to Mugdala had been nearly east; but the road after leaving these hills runs in a southerly direction towards the sea till it reaches Suez.

The line of our route was marked from time to time with the bones of camels. This too brought with it its train of thoughts. God, who made the desert, fitted the camel to it. I will not assert that the camel is beautiful; though on the principles of Hogarth, who justly ascribes so much attraction to a curving outline, he ought not to be wanting in beauty. His large spongy hoof is suited to the sand and gravel. He eats but little, and carries his own supply of water. He bears immense burdens over the burning sands, and is generally tractable in his disposition. When his master loads him, he utters an amicable growl in protestation against any oppressive adjustments; but with a fair load and kind treatment he rises manfully to his task and patiently bears the heat and burden of the day.

The Bedouin loves his camel. When we started from Cairo, a large number of camels were brought out, which we were to try by riding, and were to make a selection from them for ourselves. I told our shekh that I should leave the selection of mine to him. With the true spirit of an Arab, who never fails to return all the confidence which is given him, he assigned me one of the best among his own. Repeatedly I saw him in the course of our journey turn his own wearied feet aside and gather the coarse grass of the desert, and then come and feed his camel from his hand, and utter words of recognition and kindness which were well understood between them. I could easily understand that there was a relationship of hearts, as well as of interests.

The camel, like everything else, has his history, —his place, his habits, his labors, his sorrows, his youth, his age. He labors faithfully. In his old age he lays down his burden, and turns aside to die. He says to his master, with all the power of utterance which a camel possesses, "My hour is come. I shall no longer bear my master's burden, nor sleep beside his tent. Dying, I remember the hand that fed me. Let me go to my last rest." His master's heart understands this sad language; and he takes the cord from his faithful servant's neck. Wearied and staggering, he gets away to a retired place under the mountains, eats something which he finds, or if he does not find it, he patiently does without it; and in a few days, or even hours, he dies. When I saw his bones, scattered on the sands and beneath the mountains, I felt that I knew something of his history. His master goes home to his hut; he tells the old camel's fate to his children; they have seen him for the last time. He has died, but he is not forgotten.

A little beyond Migdol the Red Sea came in sight. Narrow, and lined with sands often of a reddish color, it runs back into the desert on the easterly side of Suez some eight or ten miles. Between this portion of the Red Sea, and the lofty barren mountains which turn down from the pass of Migdol on its western side, is a large level plain, not less than twelve miles in circuit. In the opinion of some learned men, it was on this plain that the Israelites were hemmed in between the mountains on one side and the sea and the vast burning deserts on the other, with the king of Egypt and his furious chariots in the rear. If so, the Lord opened the sea, for the passage of the Israelites and for the destruction of their pursuers, not far from Suez. It is the opinion of other Biblical archæologists, that this great occurrence took place some ten or twelve miles lower down, opposite the wells of Moses, where the sea is wider and deeper. At one of these places it is generally conceded that the miracle took place. His people cried unto the Lord; and the Lord heard them. In the language of Scripture, the Lord triumphed gloriously. The horse and his rider were thrown into the sea.

We found Suez a place of some business. Much of the travel between the East Indies and England passes through it. There were many vessels here of small size. An English steamer, which had arrived two days before, floated proudly a few miles below. We passed the sea at Suez in a boat. Soon after landing, and when we were hardly seated upon our camels, the wind began to rise,—the wind of the desert, the much-dreaded sirocco. In the course of half an hour, it increased to a whirlwind. The agitated sea was hidden from our sight. The barren mountains on the left were no longer seen. The violence of the wind lifted the vast masses of sand, and they rolled by in torrents. The faithful camels, true to their duty and their destination, struggled on. The cry of the Arabs encouraged them; till, blinded with dust, and overcome in this unequal effort, we were glad to find a stopping-place and a place of refuge at the Wells of Moses.

We left Cairo on Monday, the 28th of March, and reached the Wells of Moses on the afternoon of Friday, the first day of April.

(XXXVIII.)

Arrival at the Wells of Moses—Gardens and fountains—Next day's encampment—Sabbath in the wilderness—Religious emotions—The bitter fountain of Marah—Valley of Elim—Wadee Ghurundel—Meeting with an old Bedouin—Ascent of Sarabiet-El-Khadem—Egyptian temple—Mount Sinai—Reflections.

DESERT OF THE RED SEA, PLAIN OF EL-KHADEM, APRIL 6, 1853.

I WROTE, in my last letter, that we had reached the Wells of Moses. This is the name given to what has the appearance of a little village,—consisting of a number of gardens and small houses, fenced with an enclosure made partly of stones and in part of stalks and reeds. They occupy a rising piece of ground, nearly a mile in length by less than a quarter of a mile in width. The gardens are watered from the remarkable fountains which are found there. The fountains, as we were informed, are seventeen in number; and probably the number might be increased by additional excavations. The water is brackish, but is used by the people of the place. In the gardens are cultivated the vegetables which are common in Egypt. A few flowers were in bloom. The trees are acacias and pomegranates, with a few palms. Some of the palms are outside of the enclosure. The white sand of the desert had drifted around them. They do not rise high and throw out their lofty and waving tufts like the palms of the Nile. It was pleasant, however, to see a tree or flower, even with diminished beauty. As I walked in the gardens, I heard once more the singing of birds. It reminded me of the gardens of Cairo.

In this interesting spot, associated with the name of the great leader of the Israelites in their memorable march over these very places, we were glad to find a refuge from the storm of scorching wind and sand which I mentioned in my last letter. The place is in sight of the Red Sea,—situated on its eastern shore, and twelve miles from Suez. On the opposite side of the sea, and in full sight of the place where we lodged, are lofty mountains, with a pass between them through which the sea can be approached. It was Friday when we reached there. The next day we marched twenty miles farther, and pitched our tents in a little valley,—the Red Sea a mile and a half distant on our right. It was a solitary place,—no vegetation, no dwellings, no man or woman out of our little circle, no beast or bird, no flowers, no trees. The Arabs drove their camels to another place, where they expected to find something for them to eat.

We spent the Sabbath here. It was a good Sabbath to me. Is it wrong for me to speak sometimes of my religious emotions,—and to say in connection with them that God dwells in the desert,—and to rejoice that my soul, cut off from some of its dearest earthly sympathies, had sweet communion with Him, —the *nothing*, if I may so express it, with the All and the Universal, the finite with the Infinite? How could it be otherwise? God, who is a present and living Spirit, always speaks; and if there is not communion with Him, it is because the heart is too dull to hear. It is true, He speaks in the "still, small voice," and very often the noises of the world, the contentions within and without, prevent his being heard. But what noise is here? Even the sound of the cricket's note is banished. The desert is the empire of silence. The heart, keeping pace with the eye, widens with the immensity around it. The mind is open to the slightest influences. The smallest whispers of the Almighty come distinct to the soul. And I should do injustice to the instincts of remembrance and gratitude, if I did not say, that I found them the whispers and the divine accents of love.

The cold by night, the heat by day,
  The feverish pulse, the aching head,
Let these or other ills array,
As thus I trace the desert's way,
  Their thorns around the path I tread.

But never, never may I know
  That grief of deepest agony,
Which carries with it more than woe,
The spirit's hopeless overthrow,
  The grief *of being left of Thee.*

We were now on the track of the Israelites as they went from Egypt to the promised land. The next day, about noon, we came to Marah, and drank of its bitter fountain. It is known to the people of the desert by the Arabic name Ain Howarah. This is the place spoken of in the book of Exodus:—"And when they came to Marah, they could not drink of the waters of Marah, for they were bitter. Therefore the name of it was called Marah." The fountain of Marah is in a rock on a small hill, with other large scattered rocks near. It is a picturesque place. There are a few trees and shrubs around. The camels browsed among them. The trees are small in size,—chiefly acacias, and of that hardy and durable species called the SONT acacia. We all drank of the water. It is brackish, like the water of the Wells of Moses; but it has also a bitter taste. This is one of the places where the people murmured against God. How hard it is, even amid the most wonderful manifestations of the power and goodness of God, to learn the lesson of simple and unwavering trust!

Next day, at a little less than twenty miles' distance, we came to Elim. This also is one of the places mentioned in the Scriptures, in the account of the departure of the Israelites. It is a long and pleasant valley, with numerous palm-trees, generally small in size, and with fountains of water; but only a few of the fountains are open and accessible. The water is good,—unlike that of Marah and the Wells of Moses. The statement in Exodus is this:—"And they came to Elim, where were twelve wells of water, and threescore and ten palm-trees; and they encamped there by the waters." There is said to be another place, not far distant and still more pleasant, which has its claims to be regarded as the Elim of the Scriptures.

The next day we came into a rocky and mountainous region, destitute of trees and with but little water,—a sort of entrance-porch to the wild mountainous region of Sinai. In all these regions there are wide mountain-passes, running in different directions, the origin of which may perhaps be satisfactorily accounted for on geological principles, but which, viewed in another and not less interesting aspect, may be regarded as left open by the foresight of Providence for the convenience of man.

Without them the region would be impassable. In a region so difficult or so desolate that a bird is scarcely seen to fly there, man has great need of such natural openings. Sometimes they are steep and narrow. More frequently they are wide and level, easy to the foot of the camel, and presenting, in the rocky and richly-diversified ridges that border them on both sides, a ceaseless source of pleasure to the traveller. The direction which we took led us through one of these wide mountain-roads, called the WADEE GHURUNDEL.

We had learned that in one of the mountains situated in the vicinity of the pass of Ghurundel were still to be seen the remains of an ancient Egyptian temple. Meeting an Arab who was coming through the pass, we learned from him that he was acquainted with the locality of these ruins. This man lived among the rocks. He looked as wild and desolate as the places where he lived. His feet were bare. The sun had burnt blackness into his countenance. He had a gun in his hand; and part of his dress was a sheepskin. Under the leadership of this wild-looking but faithful old Bedouin, I went with Mr. Thompson in search of this old Egyptian temple. Our friends, Mr. and Mrs. Walcott, proceeded on to the place of our encampment.

We first ascended the side of a mountain for a considerable distance, and then, passing the head of a deep gorge, reached the side of another mountain. Here we ascended still higher, but with great difficulty,—sometimes obliged to creep along on our hands and feet on projecting points of rock, not more than two or three feet in width, over precipices hundreds of feet in depth. Repeatedly we passed from mountain to mountain at the head of deep gorges, which rose successively one above another. As near as we could judge, we proceeded in this circuitous and perilous way a distance of two miles. The scene was as terrific as deep caverns, and rocks piled one above another, and blackness and desolation and the intensity of silence, could make it. Through excessive fatigue we were inclined at times to abandon our enterprise and go back again; but our old Bedouin, feeling that an Arab's honor was at stake, encouraged us to proceed. At last we reached the summit of the mountain. And we felt at once that we were repaid for our trouble.

Such a place, with such monuments and associations attached to it, could not be without a name. We learned that it is called, by the Arabs, the mountain of Sarabiet-El-Khadem, but without ascertaining that the name throws any light on its history. A pile of rocks in the sky, overlooking the surrounding heights, it presented, as we looked with wonder on every side, a prospect of great sublimity. It was here, on the long level space on its top, remote from human footsteps and which the eagle's wing did not fan, that we found the remains of the Egyptian temple which had been the object of our search. It was a temple erected to the Egyptian god Athor, whose "graven image" we had so often seen in the sculptures on the temples of the Nile. In long ages past the hammer of the workman had been here. Excavated in part from the solid rock, it was originally an edifice of very considerable extent; and it still exhibits in its finely-sculptured walls and its remaining columns the art and the untiring industry of which we had seen such striking evidences in other places.

It was to me an affecting thought, that the blindness of superstition, groping after the truth but unable to find it, had thus climbed these almost inaccessible heights.

In connection with this temple we noticed what we had not observed elsewhere. Erected at short distances from each other were numerous tablets of stone, from four to five feet high, straight at the sides and oval at the top, and covered with hieroglyphics. This remarkable place has been visited by travellers learned in Egyptian antiquities, though but very seldom. Judging from the inscriptions which have been found upon its walls and upon the tablets connected with it, among which are discovered the names of Ositarsen and Thothmes, they appear to have come to the conclusion that this temple existed as far back as the time of Moses, and probably at an earlier period.

But this was not the only object which arrested our attention and which gave a character to our thoughts here. Far beyond the intervening mountains, the lofty peaks of Sinai rose sublimely in the distance. God has never deserted the world, and never ceased to be merciful. In all ages of the world he has spoken to men, in order that they may have wisdom. It was on the sacred heights of Sinai, now seen by us for the first time, and in view of the temple and the worship where we stood, that Jehovah, speaking in flame and thunder as well as by the voice of the Hebrew shepherd, condemned, not

Egyptian art, but Egyptian idolatry, not Egyptian genius, but Egypt's debased and cruel superstition, and all idolatry and all "graven images," and all gods that are not the "true God," in all countries and in all ages. The place, the recollections, the vast antiquity sculptured and living in the rocks, man's mingled greatness and weakness, the light and skill of science and art overshadowed and dishonored by the groping darkness of the religious affections when God does not guide them, heathenism in its best estate and heathenism judged and condemned, the past uniting itself with the present and reaching forth to the future, time with its changes and eternity with its immutable relations,—such various objects and reflections, crowding upon the mind at once, could not fail to excite within me conflicting and strong emotions.

It was near the close of the day when we began to come down. We ascended in part by a nearer route, and over still more precipitous places. The sun, hidden by the lofty cliffs, shed his parting rays. Long lines of shadow stretched darkly from the rocks. Our camels awaited us at the foot of the mountain. It was now dark. Our Arab, who was familiar with these places, knew the way we were to take. Thought took the place of conversation. We followed in the silent starlight the track of our friends who had gone before us. It was pleasant to see once more the light of our encampment.

(XXXIX.)

Arrival at the Shekh's village.—The Shekh's son—Shepherd girls—Character of the Arabs—Pass of Niekeb Hawy—Plain of El-Rahah—Peak of Sussafeh—Arrival at the Greek Convent at the base of Mount Sinai.

GREEK CONVENT, BASE OF MOUNT SINAI, APRIL 9, 1853.

In my last letter I gave a concise sketch of our journey from the Wells of Moses to the plain of El Khadem. A little before we left our little caravan for the purpose of ascending the mountain of El Khadem, it turned off in another direction towards a large plain not far distant. Our shekh, whose name is Seelyman, resides on the edge of this plain. He is the shekh or hereditary chief of a tribe of the Tor Arabs, who hold all the country in the vicinity of Mount Sinai,—in subordination, however, to the Pasha of Egypt. It is in the little valley on the borders of the plain that the Arabs of Seelyman have their principal village; where they find water and a little herbage for their sheep and goats.

The communication had gone in advance of us, that our company was approaching. The shekh, who is a man of moderate size, but, like every other Bedouin, walks erectly and with a firm step, felt the dignity of the occasion, as well as its domestic interest. At the head of the expedition intrusted to his care, which magnified itself in the eyes of these poor Arabs, he put on the long red robe which he had bought at Cairo, as he came near to the tents of his people and the home of his wife and children. With his girdle around him, his short sword at his side, and his white turban, and turning neither to the right hand nor the left, Shekh Seelyman passed in front of his people's humble dwellings to the place which his foresight and a regard for our convenience had selected for our encampment. The women stood at the door of the tents, and were glad to look upon the faces of their husbands and brothers. They too had hearts. To them, who had never left the shade of the neighboring hills, Cairo was a distant place; and the absence of their friends had been long. The children too shared in the joy of this beneficent and unusual advent. The little boy of the shekh, about ten years of age, with a mild but beautiful countenance, and dressed especially for the occasion, was placed upon the back of a camel and carried in triumph to the encampment.

As I mentioned in my last letter, those of our party who had ascended Sarabiet-El-Khadem arrived at the encampment after dark. I was not present, therefore, when the shekh reached the village of his tribe, but learned what I have now said from our associates who had gone before us. The shekh, however, called upon us in a few moments after our arrival in the evening. His little son, whom I have already mentioned, was with him. The just pride of a father glistened in the eye of Seelyman as he brought his boy to our tent. We had the pleasure of being introduced to him, and looked with no small interest on this young eagle of the desert, as he stood modestly but firmly before us. What thoughts, what feelings, what destinies, if I may so speak, were hidden in the mind of this small boy! In these still solitudes, unknown to generous culture, he will grow up, without books, without a knowledge of the name of Jesus Christ, under influences the power of which it is difficult to estimate,—the subject of hopes and joys, of sorrows and passions, both good and evil, which constitute him a world in himself,—a world which not only has its beginning, but its progress and its immortality. As I beheld his intelligent countenance, and as my imagination unrolled the uncertainties of the future, it was natural that I should feel a sympathy in his situation and a sincere desire for his welfare. Two young girls, who had been absent during the day on the side of the mountain, were returning home with their flock of sheep and goats when our tents were pitched. One of them was a relative of Seelyman. They turned aside to participate for a short time in this new and exciting scene, influenced perhaps by the novelty of the occasion, as well as by affection to their friends. They had ornaments on their arms and heads; and, as they looked once more upon those whom they loved, they seemed to be conscious that beauty has power even among the sands and rocks of El Khadem. That night the fires shone brightly and beautifully in all the tents of the tribe. The stars above them were not brighter. There was joy in the hearts of the people of Seelyman.

I have repeatedly had occasion to speak in favorable terms of the Arabs into whose company we fell,—both those of the Nile and those of the desert. Intellectually, it is true that the Arab race may properly be regarded as inferior to the other races which are found in these regions.

Their countenances are less intelligent than those of the Copt, the Turk, and the Armenian; and their national history, though not without its distinguished names in science and literature, is characterized more by the achievements of war than by the trophies of art and knowledge. It is not easy to look upon the remains of Arabian or Saracenic architecture (terms which in the history of the nation are often used as convertible) without feeling that they are works, as compared with the remains of Greek and Roman and also of Assyrian and Egyptian art, which indicate less greatness of conception, and less simplicity and purity of taste. But the Arab, if inferior in quickness and breadth of perception, so that he has found it difficult in the most favored periods of his national history to reach the highest achievements of science and art, possesses, nevertheless, a generous sociality of nature. His domestic affections are strong. He loves his own family; and he does not appear to be wanting more than others in the love of his neighbor. Everywhere and in all places, if you penetrate the depths of his nature so as to find the secret sentiments which are lurking there, you will discover also a strong sense and spirit of independence. His very being opposes itself to that form of authority which circumscribes and trammels liberty. Undoubtedly the Bedouin Arabs, who inhabit the deserts and live a wandering life, give sufficient evidence of wild and untractable dispositions; and I am obliged to admit, that it would not be easy to measure them by the common standards of civil and political legality. The Bedouin, perhaps more than almost any other race of men, has the eye and the step of a freeman. And, I must confess, there is something which pleases me much in this indomitable spirit, which prefers the rock and the cavern, with liberty, to the cultivated field and the palace without it. But neither the Arab of the city nor of the desert, so far as I can perceive, can be rightly charged with the injustice, cruelty, and faithlessness, which have been so freely alleged against him; and certainly not to the extent in which the charge has been made.

It is not always safe to judge of men from the representations of others. In order to judge them accurately, we must know them. But knowledge is the result of intercourse and confidence. In order to know them, therefore, we must love them. Let the Arab be judged by these tests,—fierce and jealous as his comparative ignorance and poverty have contributed to make him,—and it will be seen that he has his good as well as his unfavorable traits, and that hearts can be found beneath the dark tents of the Bedouins, which can be trained to virtue and be ennobled by affection.

I hope you will excuse this irregular and incidental method of writing. We spent the night on the plain. Early the next morning we started for Sinai, whose lofty peak we had seen from the top of Sarabiet-El-Khadem. Our shekh had directions to take the short route, which would enable us to approach Sinai through the plain of El-Rahah. Leaving, therefore, the course which would have brought us to Sinai through the comparatively pleasant route of Wady Feiran and Wady Esch

Shekh, we followed the rugged and difficult mountain-pass of Niekeb Hawy; which means, I believe, the Pass of the Winds. We had reasons which justified us in taking this route; and if it is attended with much fatigue and some danger, I think it can be justly added that it amply repays all by its wild and stupendous scenery. The first day we passed over a portion of the desert marked by its usual characteristics of heated sand and gravel, without water, and without tree or flower. On the second day, after a few miles' travel, we entered the mountain-pass which I have mentioned, and were shut in for some eight or ten miles by vast rocks on each side piled one above another, immense, rugged, and rising so high that they shut out the light of the sun. For a long time the winding path which we took kept continually ascending; but, while we went up, the mountains around us did not seem to diminish their elevation, but kept pace, if I may so express it, with each step of our own ascent, and rose higher and higher; while deep caverns began to open at our side and below us. The foot of the camel trembled on the edge of precipices; and the admiration which we could not help experiencing was sometimes mingled with the sense of danger. At last the door of this great mountain-cavity opened before us, and with slow and cautious steps we descended from its lofty and rugged bosom into the memorable plain of El-Rahah.

The plain of El-Rahah, which has become an object of much interest to travellers in consequence of its connection with Biblical history, is two miles and a half in length by an average of three-fourths of a mile in breadth; uneven in some places, but generally level; having a little herbage and some shrubs upon which camels and goats can feed; and suitable by means of its hard surface of clean gravel for the encampment of a people dwelling in tents. It is bounded at its southeastern extremity by Mount Sinai, where it is approached and entered by the wide and level wady which bears the name of Esch Shekh. The Israelites, in their memorable march through the wilderness, having met and defeated on their way the warlike Amalekites, appear to have entered the plain of El-Rahah through this wady, filling not only the whole plain but some of the neighboring valleys, in front of that dark and lofty mountain which was soon to be robed with the lightnings and to be shaken with the voice of God.

It was into this plain that we had now descended from the rocky bosom of Niekeb Hawy. Mount Sinai was before us. With such remembrances, and in the sight of such localities, the mind would not be true to itself, if it did not turn from the outward to the inward. On the side of the plain a flock of goats was feeding. Here and there a camel plucked the thistle that grew in the crevices of the cliffs. But the eye and the heart seemed to be closed to outward nature. Silent we rode over the plain, and in sight of this sacred mountain; listening to the secret aspirations of our immortal natures; thoughtful as if its fires were yet burning and its mighty voices were even now sounding in our ears. Such a moment, striking deep by its suggestions and sympathies into man's moral and immortal nature, is an era in his life. If he is a Christian, he knows that the announcements made from that mountain and in the presence of the vast multitude assembled upon the plain which he is traversing have connections with his own destiny which his own limited mind cannot penetrate, and which are deep as the bosom of the Infinite.

It was at the close of the day when our camels came under that portion of Sinai which bounds the southeastern extremity of the plain. This part of Sinai, lifting itself perpendicularly above the plain, constitutes a distinct and lofty elevation. The Arabs, in allusion to a few willow-trees which grow near it, have given it the name of the Peak of Sussafeh. The last rays of the sun glittered on its rocky summit. Advancing a little farther, we descried at a small distance an opening in the mountains, which gave signs of the residence of men. That night, for the first time since we left Suez, we did not sleep in tents. The piety of primitive ages, holding in veneration the locality which God had honored, had erected a habitation. Entering the narrow valley between the eastern base of Sinai and the mountain E-Dayr, which bears the name of the Valley of Shu-Eib, we made our way to the ancient Convent of St. Catherine. Its solid walls reminded us of distant ages, when man had less confidence in his fellow-man. The monks opened its doors; and, wearied by toils of the body, and hardly less by memories and emotions of the mind, we found a place of rest.

(XL.)

Greek Convent—Situation and extent—St. Catherine—Of the use of the terms Horeb and Sinai—Visit to the Valley of El-Leja—Sinaitic inscriptions—Rock of Moses—Ascent of Mount Sinai—Grotto of Moses—Chapel of Elijah—Remarks on traditions—View from the summit of Sinai—Descent from Jebel Musa or Peak of Moses to the Peak of Sussafeh—The giving of the Law—Return to the Convent.

GREEK CONVENT, MOUNT SINAI: SECOND LETTER.

In my last I mentioned that we had reached the Greek convent at the foot of Mount Sinai. Its location is in the narrow and comparatively fertile valley of Shu-Eib, the place which an old tradition designates as the residence, or rather one of the residences, of Jethro, the father-in-law of Moses. The convent is situated, therefore, on the eastern side of Sinai, and between Sinai on one side and the high rocky mountain E-Dayr on the other. It is surrounded by a high and thick wall, with towers; and it seemed to me, with the great strength of its enclosure and with here and there a projecting cannon frowning darkly upon those without, to be as well adapted, and perhaps more so, to military than to religious and economical purposes.

Within the limits of the convent, which is quadrangular though somewhat irregular in form, and about two hundred feet in extent on each side, are a number of small open areas or courts, in some of which vegetables and flowers are cultivated and a few trees are growing. Around it on the inside, and in different parts of the building, are the small cells which are occupied by the monks. Contracted in size, and almost entirely destitute of furniture, they are undoubtedly suited to the limited wants and the unambitious life of their occupants; but they can be considered comfortable only by those who accept of inconveniences as a means of the fulfilment of a supposed duty. In the upper story of the building are rooms on a larger scale for travellers, fitted up with low divans running round three sides, and with a pleasant piazza in front of them. Attached to the convent on the north side, and entered by a low passage which leads under the northern wall, is a well-cultivated garden, running a little distance down the valley of Shu-Eib. This garden, with its almond and apricot-trees, its mulberries and its tall dark cypresses, is an attractive object as it is first seen by the traveller when he comes in from the desolate country around.

The monks, who are few in number at the present time, received us kindly, and assigned us such rooms as are usually appropriated to visitants. They showed us their church,—an ancient building rich in architectural ornaments,—and whatever objects they considered of special interest connected with it; such as the tomb of St. Catherine and the reputed place of the burning bush mentioned in Exodus. The convent, venerable by its antiquity and its historical reminiscences, bears the name of St. Catherine. This is the name of a rich and noble lady of the city of Alexandria, renowned for her learning as well as her devoted piety. She was one of the early worthies of the Greek and Roman churches, who suffered martyrdom for her religion; and her memory is cherished with distinguished honor. The origin of the convent which bears her name is involved in some obscurity; but it is generally understood to have been founded by the Emperor Justinian. Its location, its structure, its associations, all render it an object of interest. The monks, who are under the direction of a Superior residing here, probably do not differ much from the same class of persons found in other situations. They have the appearance of being assiduous and sincere in the performance of the religious duties prescribed by the Greek faith, but without giving evidence of much intellectual culture. But this is probably the fault of their situation as much as of their dispositions. One of them complained to me that they had but very few books of value, though I noticed in one of their cells a few volumes of the Greek Fathers.

It may be proper here, in order to avoid confusion hereafter, to make a single remark in relation to some of the geographical terms which I may have occasion to employ. I refer particularly to the terms Horeb and Sinai. I think there is ground, without stopping at this time to give reasons for it, for regarding Horeb as a general term, somewhat indefinite in its use, but still particularly applicable to the group of mountain-heights in the immediate vicinity of El-Rahah, and of course including Mount Sinai. The name Sinai, as it seems to me, should be employed in a more definite and limited manner; and as applicable, not to a series or group of heights occupying a considerable extent of country, but to the one immense mountain which has so long borne that name, and to the subordinate but lofty peaks which shoot up like towers and battlements from its base and sides. According to this view, Sinai, properly so called, is the lofty and irregular mountain-pile which occupies the space between the valley of Shu-Eib on the east and the valley of El-Leja on the west; terminating at its highest point in Jebel Musa or the peak of Moses.

In consequence of the ill health of Mr. Thompson, on whom the interest and success of our visits and inquiries very much depended, we delayed the ascent of Mount Sinai for a short time. Meanwhile I employed myself, as far as my strength and our limited time would allow, in examining the noble plain of El-Rahah, and the deep gorge or valley of Horeb between Sinai and St. Catherine, called the valley of El-Leja. The excursion to El-Leja will well repay the traveller for his trouble, especially if he keeps in mind that it has some historical as well as natural interest attached to it. I was accompanied in this excursion by Mr. Walcott. We left the Convent of St. Catherine, situated, as I have mentioned, in the valley of Shu-Eib at the base of Sinai, and, proceeding a little more than a mile, turned to the left and passed for some distance under the sharp lofty peaks which overlook the plain of El-Rahah. We left the wady of Esch-Shekh on the right. The projecting and comparatively elevated point of land between the valleys or wadys Esch-Shekh and Shu-Eib is the traditional place occupied by Aaron while the people at a little distance on the plain of El-Rahah were dancing in honor of the golden calf he had made. And it was here, in accordance with the same traditions, that Moses, on coming down from the mountain on that occasion, encountered Aaron, and gave utterance to his dissatisfaction and rebukes.

Proceeding a mile and a half, we entered the valley of El-Leja. In the excursion up this wild and rocky valley, and soon after entering it from the large plain, we were gratified at the sight of gardens with fruit-trees and other trees growing in them. These gardens are said to have been the sites of the ancient Convents of St. Peter and St. Mary, which have now passed away. It was obvious to me, that the valley of El-Leja, impressive and even sublime by the lofty walls of rocks on both sides of it, was susceptible at the same time, in many of its small nooks and recesses, of profitable cultivation. It was perhaps owing to this combination of qualities and attractions,—solitude, silence, sublimity, and the means of a limited but not self-indulgent support, and all beneath the mountain rendered sacred by hallowed memories and by clouds and fire,—that it became a favorite resort, in the early centuries of the Christian era, of those Christians who adopted, as the anticipated means of their greater progress, the silence, the privations and hopes of a solitary life. In the upper part of the valley the Convent of the Forty Martyrs still stands. The cave of Onuphrius, who had previously dwelt near Thebes, is found here. It was in this valley that the justly-celebrated John Climachus spent a considerable portion of his life; but whether he dwelt in a convent, or in some solitary cavern, is unknown at the present time.

In this valley are said to be found, although I noticed none in that part of it which I visited, some of those celebrated Sinaitic inscriptions—the written characters of a language now unknown—which have excited so much interest and inquiry among antiquaries. They are found, however, in greater numbers in other places in these regions. A few have been discovered in the rough mountain-pass called Niekeb Hawy. And they are very frequent in the vicinity of Mount Serbal, and also on its sides and near its summit,—a celebrated mountain, some thirty or thirty-five miles distant in a northwest direction from Sinai. It is not unreasonable to suppose that these inscriptions, in the new developments which time is constantly making, may yet throw some light upon the events which have occurred here.

In the central part of this valley, and not far from the base of Mount St. Catherine, is the rock, according to the traditions repeated and preserved here, that was smitten by Moses, and from which he miraculously brought the water which supplied the thirsty Israelites. So much has been said of this rock, that I looked upon it with much interest. It stands on the Sinai side of the valley, with a watercourse before it, through which at certain seasons of the year the descending water flows from the mountains around towards the plain of El-Rahah. It is separate from the other rocks around,—a hard, reddish piece of granite, about ten feet in height and twelve or fourteen in length, and slightly curved at the top. It is certainly an object worthy of the traveller's notice, although it might not be safe to assert its identity with the Mosaic rock. On the side facing from Sinai towards the watercourse of the valley, it presents a flat surface; and on this surface, rising one above another, are long indentations, which suggest the idea of having been left there by a succession of blows powerfully impressed upon it. There is also an opening in the rock, which easily reminds one of the sculptured openings or mouths through which the water is sometimes seen to gush out in large artificial fountains. The rock also has a discolored appearance in some places, —such as one naturally supposes might have been occasioned by the flowing of water.

The position of the rock in relation to the plain where the Israelites were assembled at the giving of the Law is not at variance with its traditional reputation. It is true they were not encamped, at the time of its being smitten, on the plain, but at Rephidim, which Biblical geographers locate in the valley of Esch Shekh. But it is worthy of notice, that the valleys of Esch Shekh and El-Leja are closely connected; so much so that the waters of El-Leja, which collect there at certain seasons of the year, find their outlet through Esch Shekh. And Rephidim also, though located in the wady or valley of Esch Shekh, is understood to have been at no great distance from the Horeb Mountains, to which Moses was expressly sent forward on this occasion. And soon afterwards the whole people moved onward to the plain of El-Rahah, and took a position at the foot of Sinai; which I understand to be one of the group of mountains to which the more general name of Horeb is applied.

After the favorable results of a day or two's rest, the whole of our party were in a situation to attempt the ascent of Mount Sinai. The mountain is an immense pile of broken granite, rising steeply and ruggedly to the southwest of the convent. Without the assistance of the Arabs, who were employed for that purpose, it would have been difficult for me to have reached its summit. The mountain corresponds to the associations which are connected with it,—vast, lofty, unchangeable; suggestive of the greatness and immutability of God. It has long seemed to me to be difficult for a man to live among lofty mountains and be an infidel. I say this in view of the impressions which they have oftentimes made upon my own mind. Suggestive by their vastness of the ideas of causation and power, they can hardly fail to nourish religious thought and sentiment. If all things which exist are God's, there seems to be reason for saying that the mountains are *peculiarly* His. They are His, not only by creation, but by the impressive attributes which pertain to them,—by their vastness and fixedness, by the permanency which they give to the rock-ribbed earth, and by the changeless sublimity of their solitude and silence. But more than this can be said of Sinai, which is His, not only by its rocky base and its towering summit, which exceed human power and are almost beyond human conception, but is His also by special manifestations and by holy history.

We stopped and rested a short time, after having ascended no small distance, at the grotto and fountain which is called the grotto of Moses. This is the name which was given to the place by those who attended us up the mountain. It is a small, circular chamber, opened and rounded in the rocks,—beautiful in its form, a protection from the heat, refreshed by living waters, and undisturbed by the noise of men. It is evidently no work of human art, but fashioned by the hand which made the mountain itself. I was taken by surprise in finding so delightful a place, suited as it seemed to be not only for quiet and repose, but for religious contemplation and for the nourishment of high and holy purposes. It seemed to me altogether probable that, in this very place, the inspiration of the Almighty, which could not be absent from a heart devoted and consecrated like his, had given rise to many of the thoughts and purposes which have stamped an immortality on the writings and the history of the great Israelitish leader.

Other names besides that of Moses have been associated with these memorable places. It is related in the book of Kings, that the prophet Elijah, after the destruction of the prophets of Baal, fled into these regions. As we advanced farther up, perhaps thirteen or fourteen hundred feet above the valley of the convent, we came to a small plain or basin, in the elevated bosom of the mountain, near which we were shown a large cavern bearing this prophet's name. A small chapel, called the Chapel of Elijah, is built over this cave. Ascending hundreds of feet higher, and very near the summit of the mountain, our attention was directed to the cleft in the rocks in which Moses is said to have hid himself when the glory of the Lord passed by.

It will be understood, of course, that many of these things depend upon tradition; but tradition, without always being accepted as the truth, may still have a degree of truth for its foundation, and may sometimes be an innocent and even a profitable helper of the imagination. Tradition often localizes and clothes with particular incidents a general and indefinite transaction. We do not necessarily accept of the traditional part as a truth or fact; but if it be not contradicted from other sources of evidence, we admit it as announcing what is possible and in some cases probable. The imagination seizes upon this probability or even possibility. And the result is, that the fact, which we never doubted in its general aspect, becomes more of a practical reality, binds itself more closely to the soul, when, without ascribing any undue weight to traditions, we are able by their aid to assign to it the length and breadth and height of a probable, or even a possible, particularity. But I ought to add, that the imagination hardly needed this aid here. That Moses trod these rocks, and that God walked with him and talked with him on these wild and solitary heights, I could no more doubt, than I could doubt the existence of the rocks themselves. It is true the footsteps of the prophet could no longer be seen; but it was enough for all the purposes of thought and of the heart, to know that those footsteps had once been here. This strong conviction, sustained by the present reality of the things around me, annihilated ages. The proximity of space destroyed, if I may so express it, the separations and distances of time; and Moses, who had become comparatively dim in the distance of ages, seemed to be seated on the rocks or walking by my side, as I was climbing over the heights of his own rugged and solitary mountain.

We at last reached the highest part of the mountain, and looked abroad from its elevated summit under the light of a clear blue sky. The extreme summit, more than six thousand feet above the level of the sea, is an immense rock,—or, more accurately, a number of large rocks slightly separated from each other; furnishing an irregular area of some eighty or a hundred feet square. The rock is a gray granite. On the eastern portion of it is a small building of great antiquity; which was once used as a chapel. With some assistance from the Bedouins who attended me, I was enabled to ascend upon its top. Remaining for some time on this dizzy height alone, I contemplated in silence the magnificence of the scene around me.

There has been no accurate survey of this region, and a glance even from this towering eminence could give but an imperfect idea of the relative position of surrounding objects. But still, although Mount Sinai is shut in with other mountains, it seemed to me pretty well defined. I looked to the southwest, and below me was the deep, narrow valley of El-Leja, which I have already described as holding in its bosom the smitten rock of Moses, and as being in ancient times the residence of many religious anchorites and the location of a number of ruined convents. Beyond the valley, in the same direction, is the lofty and magnificent peak of St. Catherine. I looked down the immense perpendicular wall on the southern side into the valley of Sebahyeh. There is a small opening there at the foot of the mountain, which seemed to me worthy of special examination. Perhaps it will at some time give a new phase to the history of this wonderful mountain. I was desirous to know more about it.

But the head grew dizzy in the attempt to ascertain, even in the most general manner, its features and extent. In the northeast direction the rocky heights of E-Dayr expanded their broad and level summit beyond the valley and gardens of Shu-Eib, from which we had ascended. In another direction was the peak of Sussafeh, and other lofty peaks overhanging the great plain.

Even natural greatness has power; but it was not the mere physical expansion and wildness of the scene which left its deep impression on the mind. That principle of association, which attaches deeds to places, and magnifies the one by the magnitude of the other, added the greatness of character and events to the greatness and sublimity of physical nature.

The principal summit of Sinai, called by the Arabs Jebel Musa, or the Peak of Moses, rises solitary and apart. It was this peak which we had now ascended; but it is worthy of notice, that, about midway or perhaps two-thirds of the way from the valley of Shu-Eib towards the mountain's top, the Jebel Musa subtends a large and irregular base towards the west. I did not notice this so much in ascending the mountain as in coming down. We descended the narrow and precipitous path perhaps a thousand feet; although I ought to repeat here, what I have intimated in another place, that I do not profess to have the means of entire accuracy in distances. The mountain at this distance from the top, as if seeking to lay down a part of its mighty bulk on the neighboring plain, widens its vast granite base in the direction of El-Rahah; throwing itself into many varieties of form and aspect; sometimes rising in sharp pointed cliffs, and sometimes sinking in ravines and small valleys.

At this place Mr. Thompson and myself separated from the rest of our party, and came down to El-Rahah and the Greek convent by the way of the peak of Sussafeh. The way was wildly romantic, and in general rocky and barren. From time to time, however, we passed over small level patches of ground, bearing a species of coarse grass and a few trees. Repeatedly a cold clear fountain sparkled from the foot of a rock. We passed over this part of the mountain for more than a mile. This struck me as being a remarkable place,—the chosen residence of solitude and silence; and yet a degree of beauty, shining in the ripples of a fountain or in a tree or tranquil flower, diversified and softened its solitary and silent grandeur. There are many caverns here. The fragmentary remains of some rude stone edifices are also to be found.

There was something in this singular place, so unique, so shut out from the world, so fitted to solitary contemplation, that it not only seized hold of the imagination, but had its marked attraction for certain tendencies and moods of the heart. It was once the residence undoubtedly of that class of men, commemorated in history and poetry, whose life of lonely prayer possesses, in these speculative and practical days, the aspect almost of religious romance.

"Far in a wild, unknown to public view,
From youth to age a reverend *hermit* grew;
The moss his bed, the cave his humble cell,
His food the fruits, his drink the crystal well."

It was in such a region as this—a region which finds in its want of fertility and its difficulty of approach a security against the influx and presence of mere men of the world—that this class of persons dwelt; and in few places did they reside in greater numbers than in the valleys and wild mountain-recesses of Sinai. Soon the mountain begins to rise again; lifting itself up gradually and slowly in its massive majesty, and terminating at a point where it looks directly down, at the height apparently of some twelve or thirteen hundred feet, upon the large and tranquil plain of El-Rahah. This is that peak of Sussafeh, the Peak of the Willow, which I mentioned in my last letter as having particularly attracted our attention when we came down into the plain of El-Rahah out of the dark and lofty bosom of Niekeb Hawy.

I think that this peak may be called, with scarcely an impropriety of speech, the tribune or pulpit of Sinai. Its position, its solitary grandeur, its historical associations, seem to me to entitle it to that appellation. I have seen the rock in which it terminates; and therefore speak with the greater confidence. I have stood upon it; and shall ever remember it well. And if the impression which can hardly fail to be left upon those who visit the spot be a just one,—then what scenes, unequalled in the history of man, have been enacted at this place! It was there that the visible and the invisible, that earth and heaven, may be said to have met together. It was there that the Almighty came down, and planted His foot. His form of Infinitude embodied, if I may so express it, rested upon the peak of Jebel Musa, which rose behind him. His arm extended itself over the plain that lay beneath him, and over the countless multitude who filled it. A thick cloud was around him; and flaming fire was at his feet. The trumpet sounded. The mountain trembled. It was at that hour of mingled grandeur and goodness that the word was spoken which unveiled the foundations of error. And truth, which had been obscured and distorted or had been wholly driven away from the habitations of men, was led back again by the hand of the Infinite, and restored to its primitive position and power.

I shall look for a description of the scene and associations of this remarkable place from the learned and eloquent pen of my companion. I listened to the reading of the law from his lips on this portion of Sinai. The words of those great instructions were heard again upon the rocks. It is hardly necessary to say that it was a deeply-interesting and impressive moment.

There are two great publications of truth, for which I find no parallels in human history, and which will never cease to stand pre-eminent both by their nature and by the circumstances under which they were made:—the law of Sinai and the Sermon on the Mount. The law of Sinai is essentially a republication of those great principles of natural religion which are engraven on the human heart, but which sin had obscured and almost obliterated. It places in an objective or outward position that which had been written within; and rewrites in letters of fire, and on mountain-tops, and in sight of the whole world, that which had grown dim and illegible in the subjective chambers of man's erring and fallen spirit. It is one of the fatal attributes of sin that it makes men blind and puts them to sleep; so that they do wrong almost without knowing that it is wrong. But the law of Sinai is a trumpet-voice, waxing louder and louder, which rends the rocks and wakes the dead; but, uttering its declarations in the form of prohibitions rather than of precepts, it only wakes them to a sense of their deadness, without giving them the living principle of a renovated life. So that in giving moral light and in verifying to men's stupid consciousness the facts of their multiplied transgression, it may be said to slay, rather than to make alive. But still, considering the condition of the human race at the time it was given, the moral ignorance, the idolatries, and the crimes which everywhere prevailed, it was a declaration which was essential and indispensable in the progress of man's restoration.

As my footsteps trod upon the peaks of Sinai, I looked, therefore, upon the scenes around me with the deepest interest and the sincerest gratitude, because I felt that they were theatres of necessary transition-points in that great history of Redemption which, beginning with the promise that the "seed of the woman should bruise the serpent's head," terminated in the crucifixion of the Virgin's Son. Law, however, is not LIFE. The true progress of man's restoration is from the outward to the inward, from the law which restricts action to the principle of holy love which inspires it. It is through the crucifixion of Christ and his resurrection from the dead, and in conformity with the Sermon on the Mount, that the true life comes,—that life of faith and holy affection which makes man like his heavenly Father. This is the little leaven, spoken of in the Scriptures, which leavens the whole lump; which, gradual but sure in its progress, restores the individual and reforms and improves society; which breaks down and equalizes the enormous distinctions resulting from selfishness,—consolidates brotherhood, humanizes and elevates humanity, and makes God ALL in ALL.

In coming down from the peak of Sussafeh into the plain of El-Rahah, I was greatly exhausted, after having travelled all day in feeble health. The descent is exceedingly steep,—requiring strength as well as great care in those who come down. Indeed, it would have been hardly possible for me to have made the descent and to have returned to the convent that day without the personal and persevering assistance of two Bedouin Arabs, to whose kindness I have already had occasion to refer. Night was rapidly approaching, and in more than one instance they took me in their arms and carried me. They supported me down precipices where a false step would have dashed me to pieces. In the rude and solitary tents of El-Khadem and El-Leja, they may cease to think of me,—because they might have found nothing worth remembering except my infirmities; but I should think unworthily of myself if I ceased to retain a recollection of the kindness of these untutored but warm-hearted men.

They came with me slowly along the foot of the mountain; and we turned again into the valley of SHU-EIB. We passed very near an Egyptian encampment. I heard the sound of fife and drum. The sound seemed strange and mysterious here. The mists and shadows were gathering upon the valley. The drum rolled again, and its sound was echoed from the rocks. It was natural that I should say to myself, in the words of Joshua to Moses, uttered not far from this very place, "There is a noise of war in the camp." The signs and voices of human strife have reached even these solitary places. That tide of desolation which has overwhelmed Europe, and which at different periods has rolled along the banks of the Nile, has driven its fiery wave across the sands of the desert also, and has dashed itself against the foot of Sinai. Depravity hardens itself in defiance of the law. Will it not yield to the self-sacrificing spirit of the gospel?

There is something within me which bids me go hence. It is not safe for weak and erring humanity to stop at Sinai. I will endeavor to find a teacher and a guide greater than Moses. Following his footsteps on the banks of the Jordan and on the shore of Tiberias, in the garden of Gethsemane and on the hill of the Crucifixion, I will hope, in the greatness of my own weakness and wants, to catch something of his benevolent spirit. I will listen to that voice of angels which still echoes over the plain of Bethlehem:—"Peace on earth; good-will to men."

(XLI.)

Departure from Sinai—Last view of the great plain—Group of Arab women and children—Wady Esch Shekh—Route from Esch Shekh to the Elanitic Gulf—Mountain-scenery—Wady Hudhera—Elanitic Red Sea—Idumea and Mount Hor—Eziongeber—Arrival at Accaba—Shekh Hassan—Leave for Niekel and Gaza—Fortress of Niekel—Amalekite territory—Beersheba—Reach Gaza—Historical references.

GAZA, PASHALIC OF SYRIA, MAY 7, 1853.

WE left Sinai on the 13th of April on our way to Palestine. When parties set out upon the long journeys of these deserts, it requires some time to adjust the baggage to the camels, and in general not less to settle the rivalries and jealousies among their owners. During the time when things were thus in a process of preparation for our departure, I occupied myself in going a little distance up the steep granite side of Mount E-Dayr, and took a last view of the walls and gardens of the ancient convent, of the rugged and towering heights of Sinai, and of the great historical plain below me; and felt once more that I stood in the midst of scenes which had witnessed events and were associated with names as memorable as any in history.

As I stood thus, I noticed at a little distance, huddled together in the sunless clefts of the rocks, a number of Arab women with their little children around them. They were the wives and children, I supposed, of the Arabs who had gone up with us in our ascent of Mount Sinai, or of those who were preparing to conduct us on our journey. Knowing that I had come from a distant land,—a land less poor and desolate and suffering than their own,—

they extended their hands and uttered in their own language their petition for some small present. This was not unexpected to me, because it is the custom among them,—a custom which is, in some degree, justified by their necessities. I saw them seated among rocks which the ploughshare does not enter, and where wheat does not grow. I saw that they were ragged; and I could hardly doubt that they were hungry. The women in their poverty and ignorance, and differing also in race and in religion, were nevertheless my sisters. Christianity required me thus to regard them. The children were everybody's children who has a heart to love them; and I could not believe, although I might differ in this from the opinion of other travellers, that it would hurt either my pocket or my heart to give them the small sum which they asked.

When the camels were ready, we mounted and set out. The course which we took led us through a portion of the beautiful wady Esch Shekh, which I have already had occasion to mention. I speak of the wady or valley which bears this name as beautiful, because, contrary to the anticipations which one is apt to form, there is sometimes surpassing beauty in the physical aspects even of these desolate regions. The succession of lofty cliffs, through which Esch Shekh passes, forms, in this direction, a sort of outworks and entrance-gateway, if I may so express it, to the secluded and mysterious region of Horeb, of which Sinai is the centre. After leaving this wady at the end of a few hours' march, and altering our course with a view to reach the Elanitic Gulf, we passed through other wadys and mountain-gorges, which continued to gratify in a high degree that sentiment of the beautiful and sublime which is natural to man, and which, in its wonderful power to mark and to reflect the numerous and minute aspects of surrounding objects, may be said to exist like a living mirror at the bottom of the human heart.

Our route, after leaving Esch Shekh, led us through Orfan, Murrah, and Hudhera. In many places in these wadys, which form portions of the more common route from Sinai to Accaba, the mountains rise abruptly on both sides, leaving a narrow path between them, and with such distinctly-marked relations on the corresponding sides that they have the appearance of being worn down or cut in two in the centre. Layers of rock of every variety of kind and color, granite, sandstone, limestone, greenstone, intermixed with slate and veins of porphyry, attracted a degree of notice which in other countries would have been given to the beautiful varieties of trees and flowers. No earth covers them. Washed occasionally by the rains, and polished, if I may so express it, by the blazing contact of sunbeams, they sometimes shine like gems. In some instances the forms were as remarkable as the colors; and the rocks were worn by the action of the elements into variegated shapes of beauty, which reminded us of the columns, statues, and temples of human art. It was often a magic scene, a wilderness of enchantments, probably unseen anywhere else,—which recalled, while it may be supposed to give an explanation in part of the gorgeous fictions of the Arabian tales.

It may be proper to say here, that the wady Hudhera, or rather the fountain of Hudhera in its vicinity, is supposed by Biblical geographers, and for reasons which have much weight, to be the Hazeroth of the Scriptures. If this view should generally be adopted as the correct one, it will be found important as indicating with great exactness the first portion of the route of the Israelites from Sinai towards Palestine.

Reaching after a number of days the Elanitic branch of the Red Sea, we encamped at night on its shores, and were refreshed by its welcome breezes. The transition to this novel scene was pleasant, although the desolation on both sides of the gulf was not less marked and complete than that of the regions behind us. But there was this difference. There had been unbroken silence before. Day had succeeded to day, without a sound to break their stillness; but now the voice of the waves, as they dashed gently on the shore, was like sweet sounds of music. This gentle and refreshing voice from the ocean seemed to have a power over the heart unknown before. But this was not all. In the barren region from which we had just emerged there were neither trees nor flowers to attract the eye with their verdure and variegated beauty; but scattered along the shore of the sea there were numberless sea-shells of exquisite tints and of every variety of form. Often we stopped to gather them; and we found a new species of companionship in the suggestive power of their beauty.

Continuing along the western side of the sea, we now proceeded, by an easier march of a number of days, some fifty or sixty miles to Accaba. In only one instance, when a mountainous rock came jutting down upon the water, were we obliged to leave the level shore and take a more difficult route. The sea, or gulf as it may be as properly called, varies in its upper portion from five to twelve miles in width. Such, at least, is the opinion which one would be likely to form in estimating it by the eye alone. On the side opposite to us, lofty and barren heights touched in some places upon the water, and suspended their huge cliffs over it. This rocky and mountainous region extending along the eastern shore—a region which includes Mount Hor within its limits—is the ancient land of Idumea,—the residence of the descendants of Esau, and the burial-place of Aaron.

At the head of this branch of the Red Sea were once towns of importance, which have now passed away,—particularly Eloth mentioned in the Scriptures, which is the same, I suppose, as the Aila or Aela of the Romans, and Eziongeber, the port of Solomon. David, the father of Solomon, had conquered the Idumeans; and the possession of this port, which was the channel of Arabian and Indian commerce, was a principal source of Solomon's wealth. It is stated of this king, that he "made a navy of ships at Eziongeber, which is *beside Eloth*, on the shore of the Red Sea, in the land of Edom." The site of Eloth was two miles south of Accaba. The latter is a modern Turkish town of small size, with fortifications of considerable strength, and is the residence of a governor. Reaching it in safety, but not without considerable fatigue, we pitched our tents on the plain of Accaba and near its walls, with the Red Sea in front and the mountains of Edom behind us.

The arrangement which we had made with our Arabs for our conveyance terminated at Accaba. We could not advance farther without the assistance and aid of Shekh Hassan, the chief of the Alloween Arabs. We waited for him some time. He was absent in the Idumean Mountains, which are inhabited by his people, and did not come to us till after the lapse of seven days. He gave explanations of his detention, which seemed due to the patience with which we had waited for him so long on the burning sands. We were glad to see the old chief, though he brought us unfavorable news. Shekh Hassan has often been mentioned by travellers. We were seated beneath some palm-trees which overshadowed our tents, when he made his appearance. He is an old man, seventy years of age; but with no want of elasticity in his step, and with no dimness in his keen, piercing eye. Dressed richly in the Oriental manner, and seated erect on a fine horse, which bore him majestically from the mountains behind us, he wheeled slowly and proudly into our presence. As he rode he bore a beautiful spear in his right hand, some twelve feet in length. He held it gracefully and proudly, as if conscious of elevating upon its sharp and glittering point both the emblem and security of his barbarian power. He was accompanied by his brother and son. He heard our story, and promptly returned his answer.

He informed us that, in consequence of some very recent difficulties which had sprung up among the Arab tribes, it would be impossible, in accordance with our original intention, to reach Palestine by the way of Hebron, and would be very difficult to advance even as far as Petra, the ancient capital of Idumea. We knew something of the power of this Edomite chief, and that we could not go without his assistance. And although we offered him inducements and made various propositions, he still insisted that the attempt to reach Hebron, in particular, would be at the risk of property and lives; and, with an honorable frankness, he declined entirely the responsibility of conducting us.

Under these circumstances we were obliged to give up some of the objects we had in view,—especially our visit to Petra, which was but a few days' distance from us, and whose remains of dwellings, tombs, and temples, excavated with taste and skill in the lofty rocks which overhang its narrow valley, have been the admiration of travellers. Altering the plan of our route with the view to reach the shore of the Mediterranean, and in the expectation of entering Palestine by the way of the old Philistine town of Gaza, we at once made preparations for our departure. The old Alloween chief, who showed in his intercourse with us that he was neither wanting in kind feelings nor in a good share of practical shrewdness, readily furnished the requisite camels and men. The Bedouin Arabs, under whose guidance we were now placed, have the reputation of being among the rudest and wildest of this peculiar and remarkable race of people. Their appearance, as they came around us and took possession of our tents and baggage, was not at variance with their reputation. The chief Hassan, thinking it unnecessary to attend us in person, or perhaps called to more urgent duties somewhere else, committed our escort to the charge of his brother.

A few moments before we started, I was interested to see this old man, the head of a fierce and powerful tribe, call around him those of his people who were to attend us. Their rude and coarse garments showed their poverty; but each one, I believe, or with scarcely an exception, had a gun in his hand. At the voice of their leader their discordant clamors were hushed. The aged chief took an elevated position on a rock; and the men seated themselves in a circle in front of him on the rocks and sand. Standing but a few feet back of the enclosure formed by the Bedouins, I was able to hear what was said, without understanding its import. I learned, however, from our interpreter, that he gave them advice as to their conduct; and certainly the propriety and earnestness of his gestures, and the falling tear that shone in his eye, and the visible effect upon the men, showed that even the fierce chief of a rude Arab tribe feels something of the obligation to be the father, as well as the leader and governor, of his people.

We left Accaba on Monday, the 25th of April,—retracing for a short time our steps around the head of this branch of the Red Sea, till we reached, in the mountains on its western side, the great pass which is annually trodden by the caravans between Egypt and Mecca. Turning into this pass, in which there are obvious traces of an old Roman road, we ascended for a long distance with mountain-heights on each hand, and amid that peculiar mountain-scenery which I have already mentioned. Arrived at the summit of this long and difficult ascent, we once more cast a look upon the waters which once floated with the navies and riches of Solomon, and upon the lofty mountains of Edom on the other side of them. We then, without descending into valleys again as we naturally anticipated, passed over elevated plains of vast extent, of a hard and pebbly surface, and blackened by the sun; and I think we found no part of these great deserts more destitute of vegetation and of every form of life than this. In four days' travel from Accaba, and at the distance of about ninety miles, we reached the village and fortress of Niekel.

The country around the fortress of Niekel, unable to supply with provisions even the little community here, is a wide, sandy desolation, not less barren than the country we had passed over. So that both the fortress and the little village connected with it draw their supplies from distant places; and chiefly from Suez and Cairo. A few artificial wells and fountains, however, are found here; which is a great convenience to the travellers and pilgrims that pass this way. The fortress of Niekel is not far from the borders of the Pashalic of Egypt, in the direction of Syria, and seems to have been established with the combined object of keeping the neighboring Arabs in awe, of protecting and aiding the caravans between Egypt and Mecca, and of indicating the fact of Egyptian authority exercised in full power at no great distance from the lines of a distinct and rival dominion.

There were sounds of music in the village and fortress on the night of our arrival there. It was an hour of feasting, and of that rude joy which in these regions accompanies the ceremonies of marriage. I sat in my tent and heard it at a little distance, and was not sorry to know that human sympathies may exist amid the desolations of nature, and that love has a place even in the sands of the desert.

We spent the Sabbath here, and on the next morning, the 2d of May, renewed our march towards the shore of the Mediterranean. At this place we ceased to be conveyed by the camels and Bedouins of Shekh Hassan, and came under the protection and were conveyed by the men of another tribe. This change in the men who conducted us had been the cause of some delay.

As we advanced from Niekel towards Gaza, we passed through a portion of the territory once occupied by the Amalekites,—an ancient and warlike people, whose power seems to have extended from the plains and valleys of Philistia to the mountains of Sinai. Their fierce wars with the Israelites are known to the readers of the Bible. Our course led us a little to the south of the ancient Beersheba, and at no great distance from it. Beersheba, which still retains its ancient name, and whose wells and scattered ruins indicate its position, is situated upon the southern border of Palestine. It was at one time the residence of Abraham and Isaac. Passing onward in a southwest direction, and going through what we supposed might be that portion of the

Philistine territory which bears in the Scriptures the name of Gerar, we reached in five days' travel from Niekel the shores of the Mediterranean, and were lodged in the quarters of the quarantine of Gaza.

In our approach to this city, and at the distance of about twenty miles, we began to pass from the unbroken sterility of the desert to lands susceptible of cultivation. The heart harmonizes with nature, and is gay or sad in correspondence with the joy or sadness of that which is without. I cannot forget the delight I felt when we came to a small brook. Grass and reeds grew upon its banks; and, as it played with its pebbly channel, its prattling music seemed to have a voice of social welcome in its sound. We saw once more flocks of sheep and goats, and the playing children who watched them, and droves of camels going to the watering-places, and husbandmen gathering in the barley from the fields. Life, that had been buried in the sands, was again struggling upward into form and beauty. Flowers unknown in colder climates sprung up by the wayside; and, as I gazed upon them with continual delight, it seemed as if I had known nothing of their radiance before. They seemed, to my pleased imagination, to vindicate to themselves the principle of life, and to arise from the earth like conscious and social beings desirous of expressing their joy. They revealed, in their pure and bright expression, a religious import. Is it not true that the glory of God is written on the leaf of the flower? Or is it the state of the mind, writing the inward beauty on the outward object, which makes it shine so brightly?

We are now in Gaza in quarantine. And it is here that I am writing, or rather finishing, this letter, which I had begun during our seven days' stay at Accaba. The detention here I suppose is necessary, or at least is deemed to be so. I have no fault to find with our accommodations. And the harmony of our little company, strengthened by piety, and cheered in Syria, as on the Nile and in the Desert, by woman's presence, has made every situation pleasant. I can see, from the windows of the rooms which we occupy, the site of the old city of Gaza. The ancient city, situated at the distance of a mile and a half or two miles from the modern Gàza, was a place of no small note as far back as the time of Joshua and the Israelitish Judges. Its position in the vicinity of the Mediterranean was favorable to it; and commerce enriched it and gave it strength. Its site is now covered by an immense pile of sand, so wide and so deep that the traveller who seeks for some memorial of its former greatness can scarcely find the fragment of a broken column.

That lofty pile, which the winds and waves of ages have drifted together, and beneath which the city and its gates and temples are buried, is a sort of monumental pillar of that which is passed away and gone. The pride of the Philistine states, the city of Gaza at successive periods was the place of commerce, arts, battles, sieges. It withstood for a long time the fierce attacks of Alexander the Great, who found it standing in his way in his triumphant march from Egypt to Phenicia. And at an earlier period it had a connection, in various ways, with Scripture history. It was the gates of Gaza which

Samson, in his contests with this people, took away at night and set upon a distant hill before Hebron. It was here that he was destroyed. And this is the scene, therefore, of one of the magnificent poems of Milton.

It is thus, wherever our journey leads us, that past deeds and generations spring up at our feet. As I am seated at my window and let my eye roam over these scenes,—that eye which becomes also a window to my heart and lets in the flood-lights of memory,—I call to mind the names of the men of distant ages,—the son of Manoah, the Hercules of the wild and heroic age of the Scriptures, who fought with Dagon and subdued him; of the Macedonian conqueror, the mighty but wayward child of a mysterious Providence, who has led onward to the destruction of cities in fulfilment of the denunciations of the Hebrew prophets; and of the wonderful bard of the Isle of the Ocean, who was illuminated with a brighter light when he became blind, and who, in his Samson Agonistes, has poured forth a song of sorrow and of triumph which matches the noblest melodies of Greek and Roman fame.

The story of Samson is one of the touching and instructive passages of Biblical history,—varied and wonderful in its conflicting aspects, and not unworthy of the sympathetic remembrances and the sublime song of the great English poet. Strong in his earthly passions, strong in his love of God, but vacillating from heaven to earth and from earth to heaven, he was an object which angels might look upon with pity,—sad and terrible in his inward conflicts. When he looked upon Delilah, he fell prostrate to the earth. When he remembered the prayers and faith of his father and mother, and of the ancient and great men of his people, his soul gained strength, and soared upward to celestial regions. And it was thus, not firmly fixed to the Central Life, and rent asunder by attractions from different sources, he passed and repassed from heights to depths, from good to evil. But God, who loved him, closed his earthly sight, in order that the eye which was closed and dark to earth might be open and illuminated from heaven. With light came strength; and the influx of strength into his soul gave strength to his physical nature. His hour was come. He was ready to die, because death, which is only a method of transition, is the gateway of the resurrection. But in that final conflict between the true and the false, between the perishable and the eternal, his arm grew mighty in God; he shook the strong foundations and pillars of falsehood; and the idol and the temple "crumbled into dust."

(XLII.)

Quarantine—Its occupants—Thoughts on experiences in the wilderness—Poetry—On President Edwards's system of pure or universal love—The slain lamb—Achmed the Syrian—The bird of Accaba—The tame fishes of Hingham—The little girl—Poetry.

PASHALIC OF SYRIA, QUARANTINE OF GAZA: SECOND LETTER.

My last letter found me in Gaza. I date the present letter from the same place in quarantine. The prevalence of pestilential diseases in the countries of the East renders establishments of this kind necessary. The quarantine buildings are erected around a square open court. One side of this open area is adorned with shrubbery and flowers. They are watered from a large well which stands in the centre of the court, and around which persons are constantly gathered. People from different countries, detained for the reasons which detain us, are assembled within these walls,—travellers to Jerusalem, traders from Cairo, Arabs from the desert,—and all differing from each other almost as much in their situations in life as in their habits, dress, nationalities, and language.

At a little distance from the room which we occupy there is a company of slaves. They were brought down the Nile from Nubia, sold to a slave-purchaser in Cairo, and are on their sad and desolate way to the interior of Syria. In another part of the building, as if in contrast with this scene of degradation and suffering, is a party of young Englishmen, full of activity, joy, and hope; among whom are students from the University of Oxford. Beyond the walls, but in sight of our room, which is the higher story of the quarantine building, a large company of Bedouins have just come upon the wide and beautiful plain which extends to the south and west of the city. They have pitched their dark tents. Their children are at play. The camels, relieved from their burdens, are strolling around. The smoke of their fires is ascending.

But I will let these things pass now, and permit my thoughts to take another direction. I will go back again for a short time to the wilderness; and the reason is, that the detention of a number of days at Gaza, under the restrictions and confinement of a quarantine, has afforded an opportunity, not only to give an outline of our journey to this place, but to record some of the thoughts and feelings to which it has given rise.

I have left the remarkable scenes of the desert; and in all probability have left them forever. But I hope it will not savor of affectation when I say, that my intercourse with this extraordinary and memorable locality has been an intercourse of the affections as well as of the senses. Such certainly has been the case. Leaving, therefore, its geography and geology to other and more appropriate hands, at least in their more specific and particular aspects, it will be enough for me, in the circumstances of physical weakness in which I have come here, merely to give an account of the general appearances of the country and some little record of my feelings. So that my descriptions, such as they are, may be expected to take their character in some degree from the heart as well as the sight.

A man never knows the length and depth of his own nature who lives in one place and deals with one class of men alone, but must expand and explore himself—must both enlarge his capacity and must understand his capacity—by exploring and exhausting many varieties of situation. And when he is wandering in places desolate and without an inhabitant, it will not be surprising if, in the yearning of his heart to find some object that can meet its wants, he should learn to love the fountains and even the rocks. A tree or a flower, so frequent in his own distant land as to diminish in some degree the sense of their value, will wake up an enthusiasm of thought and feeling which he had hardly known before. Flowers have no tongues, and therefore have no outward speech; but I think they may be said to speak with the heart; and sometimes they utter or suggest thoughts and enter into little affectionate conversations which are quite interesting. Some of the weary hours which were occupied in traversing the peninsula of Sinai were relieved by these little soliloquies. Allow me to give you an instance; which, for the sake of your younger and less critical readers, I will put into verse.

One day in the desert
  With pleasure I spied
A flower in its beauty
  Looking up at my side.
And I said, "O sweet floweret
  That bloomest alone,
What's the worth of thy beauty,
  Thus shining unknown?"

But the flower gave me answer,
  With a smile quite divine;
"'Tis the nature, O stranger,
  Of beauty to shine.
Take all I can give thee,
  And when thou art gone,
The light that is in me
  Will keep shining on.

"And, oh, gentle stranger,
  Permit me to say,
To keep up thy spirits
  Along this lone way,
While thy heart shall flow outward
  To gladden and bless,
The fount at its centre
  Will never grow less."

I was struck with its answer,
  And left it to glow
To the clear sky above it,
  And the pale sands below;
Above and around it
  Its light to impart,
But never exhausting
  The fount at its heart.

There is a system of philosophy supported by a great and memorable name—and none the less memorable because he who bore it pursued his sublime and difficult studies in the woods of America—which maintains that "virtue consists in the love of being in general." That, I believe, is the form of expression—or very nearly the form of expression—in which its leading doctrine is conveyed. It condemns isolation. It frowns upon selfishness. Like the Sermon on the Mount, which indeed may be supposed to have suggested its leading principles, it looks favorably and earnestly in the direction of wide and universal attachments,—not excluding even our enemies. It is a sublime doctrine, and indicates the thoughts and experiences of a far-reaching mind. Supported by its precepts, which anticipate and require the restoration of universal harmony, I am unwilling to set narrow limits to my sympathies. And certainly, if I thus felt sympathy with inanimate nature, the alliance of primitive harmony, if I may so express it, with the rock, the fountain, and the flower, I could not feel less with anything and everything which has life in it. And when at intervals I saw a bird flying in the air, or even a lizard basking upon the heated noonday sand, or a mole excavating its dim mansion under the starlight, I recognized that great and sacred tie, too long sundered, but still reclaimable, which binds together all existences. I will give one or two incidents in illustration of my feelings.

When we entered upon the elevated plain extending to the southwest of the Elanitic Red Sea, I noticed a little lamb following our caravan; at first led by some Arabs, and then left by them to follow at his own will. I loved it as soon as I saw it. It will be remembered that we were in the desert. And there is only one solitude which the soul cannot bear,—that which is destitute of any object of affection. For some time this little lamb, which had thus suddenly established a place in my affections, gave me some trouble, because I was afraid it would stray away and be lost. And I sometimes allowed my companions to advance, while I lingered behind and watched its motions. But my anxiety was perhaps unnecessary. It would stop, and go aside from the path among the rocks, and try to find something which it could eat; and then, looking up, and seeing the company at a distance, it hastened with all the speed of its little feet to rejoin it. I thought of the time when God brought the creatures he had made to Adam; and he "gave their names to the beasts of the fields and the birds of the air." A long way in the wilderness did the lamb travel in this manner. At night it slept, like a little child, by the side of our tents. There was something plaintive in its bleat as it ran along through the day by the side of our camels, as if some feeling or presentiment of sorrow mingled with its affection. When we arrived at Niekel, which I have mentioned in a former letter as one of the frontier-towns of Egypt, the lamb was killed. It had followed us a long way over the desert. It came sadly but confidingly to the place of its destruction. It loved the hand that slew it. And I felt that a tie of the heart was sundered, when I saw its blood in the sand.

In referring to these feelings, which I might not have noticed so much at another time, they do not seem to me to be at variance either with philosophy or religion. The love of our Maker is one of the first principles of practical religion. But is it possible for man to love God as he ought to love him, without at the same time loving, in an appropriate manner, all the creatures he has made? Perhaps it may be ascribed to emotional weakness; but still it is difficult for me to conceive of a man as bearing fully the divine image, who has so little sensibility that he mars the face of nature by needlessly crushing a flower; and still more difficult, if he dishonors and offends God by causelessly diminishing the happiness of any sentient being, however insignificant it may be, which is capable of happiness.

Now that I have availed myself of the broad title which I have given to these letters, and have ventured incidentally upon this subject, I will venture to give one or two more illustrations. We have in our company a Syrian, whose name is Achmed. His home is in Beiroot; but he has come with us from Cairo. He has with him a two-barrelled gun, which he uses with skill. And while we were in the deserts, if a bird or any living thing appeared, he endeavored to shoot it. I strove to make him understand my feelings; but it was to little purpose.

All I could do, when I saw him aiming his gun, was to give a signal by voice or action to the devoted bird, or whatever animal it was; and this I did not fail to do, although at the expense of incurring his displeasure. We were very good friends, however, except in this matter,—in which we found it impossible to agree.

At Accaba our tent was pitched near the Red Sea; and daily two large, beautiful birds sailed in the air above us. I was delighted with them. One day the report of a gun was heard. One of the birds fell upon the shore dead; and Achmed brought his trophy to our tent. I was offended. I knew that not a sparrow falls to the ground without God's notice. I stood silent. I could not praise his marksmanship. He soon took the bird and carried it away, not very well satisfied at his reception, and threw it down under the walls of Accaba.

I can hardly explain upon what motive or principle I acted; but I soon went away to the place, and sat down upon the sand amid a ragged group of Arab and Turkish children. They were not strong enough to use guns, and were not old enough to lose their natural sympathies. We sat there for a little time, admiring the yellow beak of the bird, its fading eye, and its long white wings; and not without a feeling of common sorrow. And I must confess that my feelings of regret and grief were not diminished when I looked up and saw its mate soaring above us with uneasy wings. I suspected the object of his visit. His eye caught a sight of his dead companion. He stooped his flight, and, passing directly above us, uttered a low, moaning sound, which was full of sadness; as if he had said, "Farewell, companion of the rocks and waves! Farewell, the light and joy of my heart! Our nest is desolate; and the life of the living is more sad than the death of the fallen:—

> "I see thy heaving heart with throbs dilate;
> I mark the shadows of thy closing eye;
> Yes, thou art fallen low, but shalt not die
> Without a friend to mourn thy cruel fate."

When there is so little life in the desert, either of man or animals, why should man hesitate and be unwilling to let it live? I hope I shall give no offence in saying, that both my instincts and my convictions attach a sacredness both to life and to all the innocent and right enjoyments of which it is susceptible. Man, and the beasts of the field and the birds of the air, once constituted but one family. And man cannot be restored to a millennial state without the restoration of the family in all its parts. The bird shall sing to cheer him; the beast shall feed from his hand; "the lion and the lamb shall lie down together;" and even the fishes of the river and sea shall again hear man's voice in their deep habitations, and shall enter once more into the circle of human sympathies. Allow me here to forget that I am on the borders of the Mediterranean, and to return in memory for a few moments to America.

A few years ago I read in a newspaper in America, that the fishes in a certain pond had been tamed, and brought back again, at least in some degree, into the original association with humanity. Being at leisure at a certain time, and having some curiosity to ascertain the truth of this statement, I embarked in a boat in Boston harbor, and in the boat I went down to Hingham. It was near night. Next morning, and quite early in the morning, I went towards the pond which was said to be the theatre of this interesting and unprecedented state of things. I recollect that I went through a long piece of woods, which was without habitations, and which, in its tranquillity and beauty, was favorable to benevolent dispositions and thoughts. The early sunbeams were playing with the dew-drops, and the birds were singing in the branches. After passing through the woods and coming in sight of the pond of water, I went to a farmer's house not far from it. I knocked, and a good-looking woman, with that intelligent and benevolent aspect which marks the women of America, came to the door. Making such apology as I was able for a visit so early, I remarked that I had come for the purpose of seeing the fishes in the neighboring pond, which were said to be tamed. Readily accepting my explanations, she pointed to a place on the brink of the water, and said that one of her children would soon come down there.

I had not stood there long before a little girl, apparently anxious not to detain me, came running down. She seated herself on a rock on the shore and looked into the mirror of the morning waters, which reflected back the delightful image of her innocent beauty. She called to the fishes; calling them sometimes by the names of their tribes and sometimes by particular names which she had given them. There was one, a large one, which she called Cato. But Cato was in no hurry to come. She said it was rather early for them. They had not yet left their places of slumber. But, repeating still more loudly the invitation of her sweet voice, they began to make their appearance. The smaller ones came first, and then the larger ones of many varieties; and at last Cato, who was a sort of king and counsellor in this finny congregation, came among them. Delighted with this renewed visit of their virgin queen, although they seemed to be conscious it was rather early in the morning, they thrust their heads above the water; and she fed them from her hand. And I fed them also.

Observing something peculiar at a little distance in the water, I was surprised to see two turtles making their way towards her. Her voice of affection had penetrated beneath their dark, hard shells. And I noticed that they came with great effort and zeal,—as if afraid of being too late at this festival of love. One of them, as soon as they reached the shore, scrambled out of the water, and climbed upon the little rock beside her. And she fed them both. I shall not easily forget this interesting scene,—this little episode of millennial humanity.

It will not be considered surprising, I hope, that I entered into conversation with this affectionate and charming child. In the course of our conversation, she told me she once had a brother, a little older than herself, who had aided her in taming the fishes. But he was now dead. This too touched my feelings. "How sad it was," thought I to myself, "for such a sister to part with such a brother!" But she spoke of her brother in such a way, that his benevolent spirit seemed to be not far distant, but to fill the air and to be with us and around us where we stood. The expression she employed was, that her brother was dead. And that is the way in which we are accustomed to speak of those who are taken away from us. But I always have a feeling that it can be said, with much propriety, that there is no death, and no possibility of death, to those who love. But it must be acknowledged that this depends in part upon what we understand love to be. Practically it seems to me to be a heart, or rather a tendency of the heart, in harmony with the happiness of all existences,—a benevolence which does not save one and smite another, but accepts and saves everything which does not reject and spurn its offers of affection. This is the doctrine, I suppose, of the distinguished American philosopher to whom I have already referred. Such a principle, having for its basis a correspondent *faith*, a principle which can call down the birds of the mountain and tame the fishes of the lakes and sea, and when clothed in song can make the very trees dance around it, according to the old Orphic melodies,—and, what is more, can make the lofty mountains move from their places, according to the doctrine of Jesus Christ,—such a principle, in passing upward through successive heights of glory, can change its form, but can never lose its immortality.

Selfishness may perish. Indeed, it is dead already. But love can never die. Poets say so. Prophets, who are poets gifted with religious insight, say so. Humanity, which in its better moments embellishes poetry with the inspirations of prophecy, says so. Love not only *recognizes* life, but *is* life. He who does not know how to love does not know how to live. His life is the negation of living. The true life is not in him.

But this is a digression. My apology is that I am in a prison, which is called, by a free license of speech, a quarantine. The sight has its limitations; but thought, which employs itself with that which is beyond the reach of the senses, is not bound. And this reminds me of a stanza of one of the touching poems of Madame Guyon, written when she was in the prison of Vincennes:—

> "My cage confines me round;
> Abroad I cannot fly;
> But, though my wing is closely bound,
> My heart's at liberty.
> My prison-walls cannot control
> The flight, the freedom, of the soul."

America is a great way from the wilderness of Sinai and from the sandy ruins of Gaza. The memory of the beautiful apparition, the loving and lovely daughter of the American woods, who stood upon the water's brink and charmed its pleased and obedient inhabitants, does not restore the slain lamb of Niekel or the wounded and dying bird of Accaba. But in the great law of progress mercy is preceded by suffering; and truth is established on the falsehood which it destroys. Perhaps some flower of the desert will spring up from their blood.

LINES WRITTEN ON THE MAIDEN FISH-TAMER.

> O maiden of the woods and wave,
> With footsteps in the morning dew!
> From oozy bed and watery cave
> The tenants of the lake who drew,
> Thy voice of love the mystery knew
> Which makes old bards and prophets true.
>
> They tell us of that better day
> When love shall rule the world again;

When crime and fraud shall pass away,
  And beast and bird shall dwell with men;
When seas shall marry with the land,
And fishes kiss a maiden's hand.

The iron age has done its best
  With trump and sword and warriors slain,
But could not tame the eagle's nest
  Nor lead the lion by the mane:
With all its strength and all its woe,
There was an art it did not know.

'Twas fitting that a maid like thee,
  In childhood's bright and happy hour,
Should teach the world the mystery
  That innocence alone has power;
That love the victory can gain
Which is not won by millions slain.

O man, if thou wouldst know the art
  The shatter'd world to reinstate,
Like her put on a loving heart,
  And throw away thy guile and hate!
A maid shall tell thee how 'tis done,
A child shall show the victory won.

(XLIII.)

Reference to Egypt—Topics omitted—Wilderness of Sinai—The historical and literary interest which attaches to it—Early history of Moses—Scholars of the desert—John Climachus—Analysis of the influence and love of solitude—Personal recollections—Poetry.

QUARANTINE OF GAZA, PASHALIC OF SYRIA: THIRD LETTER.

You will not expect me, while shut up in these narrow walls, to give very extensive details of what I am seeing; but rather, if I write anything, of what I am thinking. It does not follow, because the sight is restricted, that the principle of thought is restricted and bound in an equal degree. And I find that this season of detention, in refusing to gratify the outward curiosity, is, on the whole, favorable to inward reflection.

In justice to myself, and still more in justice to the memorable scenes through which we have so far passed, I ought to say something in the way of apology. In passing through Egypt, I wrote a number of letters from Thebes and other places, in which I gave a brief account of some of the numerous objects which came under notice, and of the impressions which they left upon the mind. But, for reasons which it is unnecessary to detail, I was obliged to leave many things unsaid, to some of which I will take this opportunity briefly to refer, —not with a view, however, to fill up the deficiency at the present time.

And one of the subjects thus passed over is the primitive religion, or rather the system of religious opinions, which prevailed in ancient Egypt. This subject, it is true, is briefly mentioned in the histories of ancient philosophical opinions; but it seemed to me that it ought to be more fully meditated and studied. And this more complete examination of it can be made to the fullest advantage only in one place, namely, in its own appropriate locality, among the mountains and tombs of Egypt, and in the presence of the hieroglyphics and symbols which show the hopeless but great struggles of that remarkable people to ascertain those moral and religious ideas which throw light upon man's position and destiny. Another topic, which I was compelled to pass by without remark, but which can hardly fail to force itself upon the attention of every traveller who is capable of serious reflection, is the perplexed and obscure question of the origin and history of Egyptian culture. From what lands did this people come? What earlier civilization was the parent of their own? Did it find its way along the course of the Nile from those distant Ethiopians who are celebrated for their noble qualities by Homer? Or did it come more directly from some Oriental source? There is also another subject, on which I have omitted hitherto to remark; I mean the peculiarities of Egyptian art, and especially as compared with Grecian, Roman, and modern art. Any view of Egypt which is unattended with some suggestions and explanations on these subjects must fail of giving full satisfaction. But one who knows the difficulty of such subjects, even with the aid of leisure and books, will hardly expect me to make the attempt under the existing unfavorable circumstances. And perhaps it may be thought with reason, by some, that such discussions, involving as they do mental problems as well as material and historical facts, are more suited to philosophical treatises than to the slight memoranda of journalizing and letter-writing.

In my last letter I substituted for my usual narrative of our progress from place to place some little memoranda of my personal feelings. In this letter, also, I do not propose to continue the narrative of our journey, but shall occupy it with a few things which I might forget or omit to say at another time. In my last letter I said I had left the desert; but it was in person and not in memory. I had something to say of the desert then; and I have something further to say now. The word desert is a very general term, including more than one locality which is characterized by barrenness. The country from Cairo to Suez is a desert; but it differs much in its characteristics from the desert of the peninsula of Sinai, and has less interest for travellers. The peninsula of Sinai, which, in reaching this place, we have crossed in two directions, is formed by the two arms of the Red Sea,—the Gulf of Suez extending north, and the Gulf of Elan extending east. Remarkable in its natural features, the wilderness of the peninsula of Sinai is remarkable, as it seems to me, for other reasons. I cannot deny that the desolate regions over which we have so far passed have to me something of the claims and the aspect of "*classic ground*." They are the locality of Moses; and, associated as they are with his achievements and purposes, they are hallowed by the memory of great deeds and of a great name. Possessed of a mind above the ordinary degree of human intelligence, the Hebrew legislator and moralist was instructed in the best institutions of Egypt. It is not beyond the bounds of reason and of probability, that he studied in the schools of Heliopolis,—unless there were others at that time which boasted a higher learning and were more adapted to the children of the families of kings. The book of nature also, laid open in its fairest characters on the beautiful banks of the Nile, was exposed to the meditations of his thoughtful mind,—a book full of positive and suggestive revelations. And here also, on the banks of the same wonderful river, were the treasures of art,—the conceptions of great minds, shaped into stone and marble in the hope of giving perpetuity to thought and affection. On the lofty columns and walls which existed even in that primitive period, he read the records of early history,—and the lessons also of domestic affection and of moral truth,—mingled and deformed, undoubtedly, with the imperfect ideas and the struggling but disappointed hopes of a debased idolatry. "Learned in all the wisdom of the Egyptians," he had read the hieroglyphics before they were read by Champollion.

And it may be added that his Egyptian training, whatever it was, did not prevent his acceptance and mastery of that other and higher culture, characterized by its Aramean origin, which had quietly established and perfected itself among his own people. There was learning in the land of Goshen; and Moses was not ignorant of it. The Hebrew culture was religious; and, aided by the inward presence and teachings of the God of his fathers, it placed him upon that higher and better position which enabled him to understand and appreciate the truths and errors of other cultures. Placed in the most favorable position, and prompted by the highest inward inspirations, he beheld all, knew all, appreciated all.

An Egyptian by adoption, but a Hebrew by birth and by nature, it was natural that his heart should be kindled with generous and zealous sentiments in favor of his own people. Baffled in his early efforts to instruct and deliver them, because perhaps his wisdom and charity were not yet developed in proportion to his zeal, God saw fit so to order his providences as to drive him away into this very wilderness.

One day, as I was travelling in the wilderness, I saw a small Bedouin village in the midst of high hills, skirting and overhanging the level plain over which we were passing. It is but reasonable to suppose that this little community, like all others, had its ruler, a man unknown to the world, but still the father and chieftain of his small but solitary people,—the Jethro of the desert. At a little distance was a watering-place: flocks and groups of camels were standing near; and the maidens of the village drew water and they drank. It was to such a place that Moses fled,—exchanging the fertile valley for the arid plain, the rich Nile for places without rivers, the recorded instructions of towering monuments for the suggestive eloquence of lonely mountains, and the teachings of priests and the wise men of Egypt for the conversations of a shepherd and a patriarch in the wilderness, and for woman's love. Jethro had daughters. The Hebrew exile saw, loved, and married. He who, with man's energy and unchastened passion, had slain an Egyptian in Egypt, became a little child in Midian. He who had trod the pavements of palaces and had been in some sense the heir of kingdoms was willing to dwell in tents, to carry the crook of a shepherd, and to follow after the flock. It is in such transitions from glory to obscurity and silence, from riches to desolation, from the city to the desert, that men learn the great lesson of the relation of human actions to God's oversight, and that there is a power above us which shapes our existence and is the master of our destiny. Napoleon was a wiser man on the rock of St. Helena than he had been in the palace of the Tuileries. And Moses, who had slain an Egyptian and hid him in the sand, experienced the inspiration of higher and better thoughts when he watered his flocks and camels in the wilderness, or was seated on its solitary rocks by the side of those whom he loved.

To what precise part of the peninsula of Sinai Moses went, is uncertain. The country of Midian, which is mentioned in connection with his place of exile, seems to have extended west of the Elanitic Gulf as far as the region of Horeb. If this view is correct, it would harmonize with one of the traditions still repeated at Sinai, that Jethro, his father-in-law, resided in the narrow valley of Shu-Eib, which runs between Sinai and the heights of E-Dayr.

Many years he dwelt in these wonderful solitudes, —recalling the memory of his ancestors, reducing to form in the beautiful language of his own people their unexampled traditions, pondering the problems of Providence, studying minutely the geography of that wide wilderness which he foresaw was to be the theatre of great achievements, and awaiting that mysterious hour when God speaks and man is silent. God spake to him in the burning bush. The Greek monks who still linger in these regions pointed out to us the traditionary place. It is within the limits of the convent of St. Catherine. It is not especially important whether we suppose that the burning bush was here or in some other valley or plain in the vicinity of the great mountain. Its blaze must have ascended somewhere in this region; and though it has gone out in the wilderness, and darkness has gathered upon its place, it may be said to exist and to burn forever in the locality of memory; and the great words which were uttered in its fires are still sounding in all lands. It was no false god of Egypt or Syria, no Osiris or Thammuz, but the God without form, the I AM, who spake.

In the fulfilment of the great mission which the God of his fathers had assigned him, he set out for Egypt. He had fled into exile alone; and he returned alone. He had learned in the wilderness that affection can grow up among the sands and rocks. He left behind him his aged father-in-law and his wife and children, who fed his flocks, and kept the fires of his tent burning, till he who went forth as a father should return a father, a lawgiver, and a prophet. He planted his foot on the banks of the Nile. He came back to the palaces of Memphis. He said what God gave him to say. He who speaks for God has no other than God's message. Kings trembled. The nation mourned. The Nile ran blood. The chain of the people of his fathers was broken.

I think, therefore, there is no impropriety in speaking of the peninsula of Sinai, though a land without rivers or verdure, as classic land. In these solitudes was written a code of laws differing from any other, but still remarkably adapted to the times and the people, which places their author in the records of civil and political history by the side of Solon and Lycurgus. The learned commentaries of Michaelis will justify a remark which might otherwise seem an exaggeration. In these regions, stretching from the Nile to the Jordan, were written those remarkable annals of the beginnings of the human race, which are the starting-points and the foundations of human history. As a moralist, he spake as no one had spoken before him; and as a poet, touching the varied strings of human passion, he has passages which remind one sometimes of the tenderness of Virgil, and sometimes of the sublimity of Pindar.

In these regions, thousands of years later, but still in a venerable antiquity as compared with the present time, have resided no small number of Christians,—some of whom fled from persecutions in Egypt and other lands, and others sought these remote solitudes with a view to greater retirement from the world and more intimate communion with God. Strange as it may seem, it is undoubtedly true that men of distinguished talent and learning have formerly dwelt in these places. Sometimes they resided in convents, the ruins of which are still found in the gorges of these mountains; and not unfrequently they took up their solitary abode in lonely caverns, excavated by nature or by the hand of art. Among the residents who once gave a celebrity to places which are now scarcely trodden by human footsteps, some of whom were named in a former letter, mention is made by ecclesiastical historians of Sylvanus and Nilus,—names worthy of remembrance, but better known to Catholics than Protestants. Either in a cell in the rocks of El-Leja or in a small convent of that valley, a few miles distant from the convent of St. Catherine, the celebrated John Climachus spent many years of his life. It is difficult to conceive how he could have developed the powers of his mind under such circumstances; but he was favorably known as a scholar and a writer. His "Ladder of Christian Perfection," originally written in Greek, has been translated into other languages,—a work which discovers great insight into the human heart, and which, in some of its passages, will compare favorably with the celebrated "Imitation of Christ."

An interesting literary and ecclesiastical history might be written of the men who resided during the first centuries of the Christian era in the mountains and rocky gorges of the Thebaid and of the peninsula of Sinai. And it is in the history of these men, and of others similarly situated, that we find one of those problems of human nature which suggest inquiries and furnish food for reflection.

On what principle is it that men in all ages of the world, men of great capacities and the finest sensibilities, have valued much the places and hours of retirement, and have loved to be alone? In some cases such persons have chosen solitude as a necessary condition of an ascetic life: with them solitude is a means to an end. They have first chosen suffering, and then have chosen solitude as an auxiliary of suffering, and both as an expiation for their personal sins, and as a means of propitiating the divine favor. The sincerity of these persons, though it may lay a claim upon our charity, furnishes no reason for an acceptance or mitigation of their error. It is not wisdom on the part of man to undertake that which is appropriate to a divine nature. The Lamb of God, "slain from the foundation of the world," is slain forever. The expiation is made; the door of entrance is opened; God wants and asks no other atonement.

Others, again, without any idea of meriting heaven by asceticism or by any form of human suffering, have fled into the wilderness, to avoid the temptations of great cities and of too much intercourse with the world. In the desert they supposed that riches could not tempt, that honor could not allure, that beauty could not entice them. The desire of finding a place in which he should be exempt from temptation seems to have been the principal motive which influenced St. Jerome when he left Italy and the palaces of the imperial city for a residence in the Syrian desert. And this is a motive, certainly, which is worthy of respect, though not without its dangers and its disappointments.

And there is something further. To thoughtful and expansive minds, whatever may be the peculiar incidents of their situation, solitude is to some extent a *necessity*. Oftentimes, in the case of such men, the harmonious development of their own thoughts and feelings is perplexed by the discordant alliances and claims of society; and they seek retirement as a necessary means to the proper adjustment and perfection of their inward nature. In solitude they escape the storms around them; and outward harmony is the precursor of inward peace. The history of the distinguished men of all ages will illustrate and confirm these remarks. It is in the reflections which are engendered in solitude that the soul, turning in upon itself, discovers the endless filaments of its mysterious destiny, and unites itself with God in uniting itself to everything to which God is related. It goes down into the depths and it finds him there; it ascends into the heights and it finds him there; it turns in upon its own centre, and in the spirit of penitence and of faith it finds him there also.

And on this subject I may perhaps claim the liberty of saying something from experience. It is still true, as it was in the times of the ancient prophets, that there is a voice in the wilderness. It is still possible for the soul, in some of its aspects, to be nurtured in solitude and among the rocks. The mighty desolations through which we have passed, operating upon the heart as well as upon the intellect, have sometimes called out spiritual tones and harmonies from the soul's depths, and have filled the whole mind with various and high emotion. The desert, which may be regarded as the imperfect hieroglyphic of the great Thought which made it, presents, in its first impression, the idea of vastness in chaos. And when we were working our way through sands without verdure, and among immense rocks piled together in mysterious confusion, it sometimes seemed to me as if we were carried back, by a transposition of places and ages, into the primitive workshop of experimental creation. The hand of the Almighty, as mountains from summit to base were opened before us, appeared to be laying the foundations of some mighty habitation. And then again, seeing in other places the adjustment of rock to rock, and of the successive strata and layers in which the earth's materials arrange themselves, I discovered the beginnings of order growing out of confusion, and had new conceptions, both of the world's strength, and of the strength and wisdom of its great Architect. And if the mountains and the rocks gave the idea of power in action, the vast, arid plains, wide as a bright and motionless ocean, gave the additional conception of power and majesty in repose,—the one being the image of God in agency and the other of God in rest.

I am obliged to say, therefore, that a journey through the wilderness of Sinai, which brings with it so many great thoughts as the product of its chaotic vastness, not only furnishes no apology for irreligion, no apology for atheistic unbelief, but, on the contrary, proclaims hostility against a light and irreverent spirit. God is there. His footprints are in the sand. His voice is heard in the winds. His name is written with sunbeams on the rocks. The very silence utters him.

I wanted repose; and I found it in the desert. I wanted communion with God; and I found it there. I found it in the day, in the vastness of its objects and its silence. I found it still more in the night, when magnitude enlarges itself and silence becomes more silent. I found it in the earth beneath, and in the heavens above. Often I watched the stars. Beautiful as the heavenly mansions, they looked out from their blue abodes, clear and lovely as if they were the eyes of that great Being who fills their urns with light. There was one with its large angelic eye that came with peculiar sweetness. It danced upon the mountain-tops. It had no audible utterance; but there was a divine language in its smile, which spoke of heavenly peace. It was in the desert of Sinai that I gave it a place in my memory. It was in the vast wilderness which had inspired the prophetic impulses and the songs of

Moses, that I watched the mild splendor of its beams, and endeavored to record the emotions excited by its mysterious but lovely presence.

LINES WRITTEN IN THE WILDERNESS OF SINAI.

I mark'd the bright, the silver star,
That nightly deck'd our desert way,
As, shining from its depths afar,
Its heavenly radiance seem'd to say,
"Oh, look! From mists and shadows clear,
My cheering light is always here."

I saw thee. And at once I knew,
Star of the desert, in my heart,
That thou didst shine, the emblem true
Of that bright star whose beams impart,
From night to night, from day to day,
The solace of their inward ray.

There is a beam to light the mind;
There is a star the soul to cheer;
And they that heavenly light who find
Shall always see it burning clear;
The same its bright, celestial face
In every change of time and place.

Star of my heart, that long hast shone
To cheer the inward spirit's sky!
Illumined from the heavenly throne,
Thou hast a ray that cannot die.
'Tis God that lights thee. And with Him
No sky is dark, no star is dim.

(XLIV.)

Arrival at Askelon—City of Azotus, the ancient Ashdod—Territory of the ancient Philistines—Jaffa, the ancient Joppa—Biblical references—Town of Lydda—Town of Ramleh—View from the Tower of Ramleh—Valley of Ajalon—Kirjath Jearim—Arrival at Jerusalem—Poetry.

PALESTINE, CITY OF JERUSALEM, MAY 13, 1853.

We left Gaza on Tuesday, the 10th of May, and arrived at the city of Jerusalem on the 13th. After leaving the place of quarantine, where we had been kept four days, we went into the modern city of Gaza, which is a mile and a half distant from the site of the ancient Gaza, and spent a short time in its bazaars and streets. We could only look and pass on. But, judging thus, it had the appearance of being a place of considerable enterprise and business; though, like the cities of the East generally, it is but the shadow of the greatness of the ancient city. In leaving the city we passed numerous gardens in a high state of cultivation. These gardens were protected for the most part by the high natural fence formed by the intertwining branches and the large leaves of the prickly pear. The gardens were succeeded at a little distance from the city by a forest of olive-trees, the most of them very old, which extend a number of miles.

We reached, about the middle of the same day, the city of Askelon, another of the Philistine cities, and spent a short time in wandering among the numerous scattered columns and broken walls and arches which testify strongly to a former period of wealth and power. Like Gaza, it is on the shore of the Mediterranean, and was once a place of commerce. Askelon is often mentioned in the history of the Crusades.

About sunset of the same day we came to Ashdod. It was to this place that the Ark of the Lord, after the defeat of the Israelites in the time of Samuel, was brought, and was placed in the house of Dagon, the god of the Philistines. This town, called in the Old Testament Ashdod, is the Azotus of the New Testament. And hence it is said of the Apostle Philip, after his separation from the Ethiopian eunuch, that he was found at Azotus. The country around Ashdod is not without fertility, and appears to be well cultivated. As we approached it, we passed through large fields of grain, occupied by busy reapers. In a wide open space near the entrance of the city were numerous piles of wheat and barley; and oxen, generally four abreast, were treading out the grain after the Oriental manner. In a grove outside of the city we pitched our tents and encamped for the night.

It seemed obvious to me that the territory of the ancient Philistines, though of very limited extent, was originally of great fertility and capable of sustaining large numbers of people. Some of the passages of the Old Testament which refer to them imply that they had a knowledge of the mechanic arts. They were certainly a powerful people at an early period; and their wars with the Israelites, in which, in the confidence of their strength, they defied the armies of the living God, are familiar to the readers of the Bible. The character and location of the country, considered in relation to the territories of the Israelites, and the location of the principal cities so often mentioned in the Bible, are such as to strengthen one's confidence in the exactness of the scriptural narratives.

From Ashdod, which we passed through without stopping, but which had the appearance of being a populous and comparatively flourishing town, we proceeded early the next morning on our way to Jaffa, the ancient JOPPA. Deviating from the direct route to Jerusalem, we reached this city the same day. Jaffa is situated on a rocky eminence overlooking the Mediterranean, and, seen at a distance, had an aspect beautiful and imposing, but which failed, however, to be realized when we had entered its narrow streets. It is a walled town with fortifications. It once had a good but small harbor, formed and protected by the natural sea-wall of a continuous line of circuitous rocks; but the depth of water is so diminished by accumulations of sand and other things, that large vessels anchor beyond the rocks in the open ocean. The steamers from Beirout to Alexandria and Marseilles touch at this place. A small portion of the inhabitants of this city profess the Christian faith. The American consul at Jaffa is a native of the country, and in his religion an Armenian, but of that class of Armenians now known as Bible or Reformed Armenians. He is a man of intelligence and wealth, and insisted on lodging us at one of his own beautiful residences a little out of the city. He seemed to understand and appreciate the rising wealth and power of the American States, and spoke in high terms of the character and influence of the American missionaries in Syria, with whose labors he appeared to be well acquainted.

This city, which holds a conspicuous place in political and military history, has also its Biblical and religious associations. Only about forty miles distant from Jerusalem, it has always been regarded as the seaport of that city. The wood of Lebanon, used in the great edifices built in the time of Solomon, was brought in "floats by sea to Joppa," and transported from Joppa to Jerusalem by land. It was to this place that Jonah came, and from which he set sail for Tarshish, in disobedience to the command which required him to go and preach against Nineveh. It was here that Dorcas resided,—celebrated for her good works, and who was restored to life by the Apostle Peter. Here was the residence of Simon the tanner, whose "house was by the sea-side," and with whom Peter "abode many days."

We reached *Joppa*—if I may be allowed to use the ancient and historical name—on the 11th, and proceeded the next day to the pleasant and flourishing town of Ramleh,—visiting on our way the village of Lyd, the ancient *Lydda*, mentioned particularly in the Acts of the Apostles. It is said of the Apostle Peter, that "he came down also to the saints which *dwelt at Lydda*." It was here that he miraculously healed Æneas, a man who had been eight years sick with the palsy. And it is added by the historian, in speaking of Æneas, that "all that dwelt at Lydda and Saron saw him and turned to the Lord." Lydda is spoken of as being "nigh to Joppa;" and Peter was here preaching the gospel to the people when the people of Joppa sent for him on the occasion of the sickness and death of Dorcas. Christianity was early established in this retired place; and the probability is, that it was sustained and that it flourished here for some time. There are still to be seen the beautiful remains of an early Christian church.

Accepting and valuing the Bible as revealing the foundations of Christian hope, I cannot express the satisfaction I feel in finding everywhere the confirmations of its truth. I found these confirmations at Rome, at Naples, at Malta. And on the Nile which washes the land of Goshen, and at the Red Sea which was divided by the rod of Moses, and in the deserts of Sinai, and among the mountains of Idumea, these confirmations have been repeated. They are written, as a part of a nation's history, on the walls of Thebes. They are inscribed, in fulfilment of prophecy, on the fallen columns of Askelon. I find them here.

Proceeding from this early scene of the Apostle Peter's preaching and miraculous labors, we reached the town of Ramleh on the afternoon of the same day,—which, indeed, is but a short distance—some three or four miles—from Lydda. It is a walled town of considerable size. It was near sunset when we arrived. At the distance of half a mile from its walls there stands a lofty and lonely tower; a memorial of past ages, but with a history unknown. It is a hundred and thirty feet in height, and is erected of hewn stone in successive stories, which diminish in size as they approach the top. Around it at no great distance are vaulted sub-structures, which will probably be found to have a connection with its history, when that history shall be ascertained. It already threw its long evening shadow; but we had time to ascend it, and in the last rays of the setting sun to witness the wide and varied prospect from its summit. It was a scene of surpassing beauty, —the land of fields and gardens, of the fig-tree and pomegranate, the "olive and the vine." The shepherd was returning with his flocks from the fields. The fertile territories of ancient Philistia were beneath us. The eye rested upon the vales of Sharon, whose bloom has not yet withered. The rocky heights of the "hill-country of Judea" were in sight.

On the morning of the next day, and only at a few miles' distance from Ramleh, we passed in sight of the valley of Ajalon,—the scene of the hard-fought battles and the stupendous miracle of Joshua. "And he said, in the sight of Israel, Sun, stand thou still upon Gibeon; and thou, moon, in the *valley of Ajalon*." And it was thus, from this time onward, that almost every mountain and valley had its scriptural associations and interest. After a few hours' travel farther, we stopped again for some time at the ancient town of Kirjath Jearim. Here also, as well as at Ramleh and Lydda, were what we supposed to be the remains of a place of early Christian worship. Situated on the side of a hill, this town is strong and imposing in its position, and has a picturesque appearance. The valleys below and the heights around are covered with groves of olives. The circumstance that for twenty years the Ark of the Lord rested at Kirjath Jearim gave it a peculiar interest.

We now rapidly approached the termination of our journey; or perhaps I should rather say, approached the principal object we had in view in journeying,—*the city* which embodies, to the Christian at least, more interesting associations than any other in the world. The city of Jerusalem is built upon a hill, or rather a connected range of hills,—the hill of Zion, the hill of Moriah, the hill of Acra. But, considered in reference to the lofty eminences around it, it seems to be almost in a valley. So that, in looking upon it, we readily felt the propriety of the expression of the Scriptures,—"the mountains are round about Jerusalem." We approached it over one of these surrounding heights, which is almost without trees and without verdure. It is thickly covered with rocks. And the narrow way which winds over it is exceedingly rough and difficult,—so much so as to perplex even the careful tread of the camel and the experienced foot of Syrian horses. As we passed the summit of this difficult height, which we were a long time in reaching, we came in view of the long irregular line of the city-walls. We met many poor people, for the most part women, returning to their homes in the neighboring villages. They had a cheerful aspect. It was near night. The shadows were settling in the valley of Jehoshaphat. We entered the city on the western side, over the hill of Zion and through the Bethlehem gate. This gate opens nearly under the massive tower of David. As I passed beneath its heavy arch I felt that the desire of a life was accomplished. What a scene! What associations! Other lands have their history, their character, their associations, their greatness. But Palestine, as compared with all others, is emphatically the *sacred* land,—the dwelling-place of patriarchs, prophets, apostles, the scene of visits and holy communications between heaven and earth. Every valley is a tomb, every mountain a monument. Wherever I turn my eyes, the dimness of distant history becomes actual vision. I look from my window, and my eye rests upon the hill of Moriah, upon the site of the Temple of Solomon, upon the

Mount of Olives, and upon the supposed place of the Crucifixion.

O land of men of other days!
  Where bards and ancient prophets trod,
The land of rapt Isaiah's lays,
The land of David's psalms of praise,
  Land of the men of God.

And if 'tis not enough of fame
  To be the home of prophets, then
From all thy hills and rocks proclaim
The higher and more glorious name
  Of *Him who died for men.*

In vain, like birds on ocean's foam
  When toss'd amid a troubled sea,
In vain the sad in spirit roam,
In search of resting-place or home,
  Who turn away from thee.

By thee the seal of doubt is broken
  Which long to human hearts had press'd;
By thee alone the words are spoken
Which "peace on earth" and love betoken,
  And give the weary rest.

The clouds of Sinai's mount proclaim
  The law that wakes the spirit's fears;
From Calvary's height the message came,
The law of love for that of flame,—
  Love for the coming years.

Land of the soul! forever dear;
  Wide o'er the world the words impart
Which turn to hope despairing fear,
Which dry the penitential tear
  And heal the bleeding heart.

(XLV.)

Excursion from Jerusalem—Village of Bethany—Tomb of Lazarus—Road to Jericho—Fountain of the Apostles—Bedouins—Mountain of Quarantana—Fount of Elisha—Brook Cherith—Modern Jericho—The river Jordan—The Dead Sea.

PALESTINE, CITY OF JERUSALEM: SECOND LETTER.

On Tuesday of this week, the 17th, we left Jerusalem on an excursion for a few days to Jericho, the Jordan, and other places of interest, from which we have just returned. I propose to give a little account of this excursion.

We left the city by St. Stephen's Gate, which is on the eastern side of the city, and is said to be the same with the "Sheep-Gate" of the Scriptures. Descending the steep side of Mount Moriah into the valley of Jehoshaphat, and crossing the brook Kedron, which flows through this valley, we went a short distance along the base of the Mount of Olives; and then, turning and passing its southern extremity, we came to the village of Bethany. This village is two miles distant from the city of Jerusalem by the route which we now took, although a little less, I suppose, by the more direct path over the summit of the Mount of Olives. The road which we took is the great road from Jerusalem to Jericho,—the same which was travelled in the time of Christ, and which had been travelled hundreds and perhaps thousands of years before. At the distance of about a mile and a half from Jerusalem, on a point of land projecting into a deep valley, and on the right of the road, we noticed the remains of an ancient village, which is supposed by some to have been the village of Bethphage. This village is mentioned in the New Testament in connection with Bethany, as being "at the Mount of Olives."

The village of Bethany was the favored place to which our Saviour frequently resorted. Situated in a retired spot near the base of the Mount of Olives, on its southeastern side, with a little valley below and the mountain rising gently behind it, and surrounded with groves of fig-trees, olives, and oaks, it had especial attractions, both in its natural aspects and in the peace and silence of its seclusion, for a serious and contemplative mind. Here dwelt the family of Lazarus and his sisters, whom "Jesus loved," and in whose company he found a confidence and sympathy suited to his social nature. What the precise appearance of Bethany was in the time of the Saviour it may be difficult to say. It is now a small village called by the inhabitants *Lazarieh*, or the place of Lazarus, containing about forty houses, inhabited chiefly by Arabs, who support themselves by cultivating small olive-gardens, or by feeding their flocks on the neighboring hills. In this village was performed one of the Saviour's great miracles,—the raising of Lazarus from the dead,—the last miracle, I believe, that is recorded as being performed by him. The tomb of Lazarus, in which he was placed after his death and from which he was called by the Saviour's voice, is still shown to the traveller. We descended into this tomb over a flight of steep and narrow steps which terminate at the depth of eighteen or twenty feet in a dark sepulchral chamber excavated in a rock. Early tradition, older than the time of Eusebius, assigns this as the tomb in which Lazarus was buried and from which he was raised; and the incidents of the place seem to favor the traditional opinion.

As I stood near the tomb of Lazarus, and as I went in silence through this small but memorable place, I felt but little disposition—as indeed I had but little strength for any such thing—for geographical and other inquiries; but my soul was full, and my affections meditated. The heart fed on the food of memory. "It was here," I said, "that the Saviour often came." I looked behind me and upward, and saw the nearer and more solitary path by which he was accustomed to cross the summit of Olivet. It was here that he composed and rested his weary spirit in the bosom of a beloved family. It was here that Martha "received him into her house," and Mary, her sister, "sat at his feet," and listened to his teachings, and chose that good part which could not be taken away. The walls of their humble mansion had crumbled; but the ground stood, and memory clung to the soil. The earth upon which I looked had been trodden by Him to whom divine grace and the experience of God's goodness and truth had taught me to give my own affections. And now a new link of union seemed to be established between those affections and their great and divine object; and He seemed nearer than ever. It was a scene and an hour never to be forgotten.

We had started early in the morning; and this visit to Bethany was in the early part of the day. We proceeded towards Jericho by the old Jericho road which I have already mentioned,—rocky and often precipitous, winding for a few miles among heights on both sides, on which camels and goats were feeding, and then descending into a plain. Near the head of this narrow plain, or, more properly speaking, valley,—for it was shut in by hills on each side,—we passed, on the right of the road, a large fountain. A drove of camels had come down from the hills and were standing near. A few women from the neighborhood were seated around it; and some were carrying away its waters in large jars on their heads. The place is attractive in its situation; the waters flowed fresh and full; and the tradition of the country is, that it was visited not unfrequently by the Saviour and his disciples: and this is a tradition which would harmonize well with the Scriptures. It is called the "Fountain of the Apostles."

As we proceeded towards Jericho we met with no incidents particularly worthy of being mentioned. Prospered by a kind Providence, which had followed us at every step, we did not "fall among thieves." From time to time we saw in the openings of the hills the dark open awning which generally forms the tent of the Bedouins. Their sheep and goats feed upon the coarse grass of the rocks. They offered us no molestation, but seemed to be pleased that we had come among them; for we were under an escort of their own people, who were faithful to us here as they had been in other places. The Arabs who attended us took a natural pleasure in occasionally displaying their skilful horsemanship before us, and were exceedingly happy when we were disposed to enter into conversation and to form something like an intimacy of acquaintance.

In the afternoon of this day, when we had entered

the edge of the plain of the Jordan, we passed the lofty and barren mountain of Quarantana, or Mount of Forty Days. It is perforated in many places with natural and artificial caverns, which in former times were the abodes of hermits, who in this desolate solitude spent their days in fasting and vigils. It is to this mountain—undoubtedly wild and desolate enough to have been the theatre of that remarkable portion of his history, and not unsuited by its position—that tradition assigns the locality of the Saviour's forty days' fast, and of his temptation by the devil. A large extent of country in the vicinity of this mountain is barren and mountainous, scarcely exhibiting anywhere the least signs of vegetation, and is called in the Gospel "the wilderness of Judea."

It was in sight of this mountain, and not far from its base, that, on entering the plain of the Jordan, we turned aside from the direct path to the modern Jericho, for the purpose of visiting the bright and beautiful fountain which was miraculously healed by the prophet Elisha. The prophet was tarrying at Jericho at that time. On hearing the complaint of the people of the city, who represented the water as not good, he asked for a cruse with salt in it. "And he went forth unto the spring of the waters and cast the salt in there, and said, Thus saith the Lord: I have healed these waters." It is now called the Fountain of Elisha. We went to its spring or source. Flowing suddenly up from the recesses of a large hollow rock on the side and near the base of a hill, it gushes onward in a clear swift current over a hard bed covered with stones and overhung with small trees and with shrubs in flower. The scene recalled the history of the prophet; and I recollected with gratitude the goodness of God in raising up from time to time teachers and benefactors who administered to the necessities of the people, at the same time that they gave them moral and religious instructions.

It was only an hour or two before that we passed the brook Cherith, which flows through a part of the plain of Jordan and empties into the Dead Sea. It was near this brook that the prophet Elijah, the predecessor and spiritual guide and teacher of Elisha, was commanded to hide himself; and it was here that he was miraculously fed by ravens. The channel where we crossed it was deep and of considerable width; but there is but little water in it at this season of the year, as it is fed from the rains, and by the springs from the mountains, which are now dried up. The Fountain of Elisha, on the contrary, gushing from the unknown riches of a rock, seems to flow with a source and a current always full.

From this remarkable fountain we proceeded—over a plain which was once exceedingly fertile, and is still profitably cultivated in some places—to the modern Jericho. The precise site of the ancient Jericho is unknown; but the mounds of earth in the neighborhood of Elisha's fountain exhibit appearances which furnish ground for conjecture that it may have been there. The modern Jericho is a large Arab village, full of people, with a small fortification near it which was occupied by a Turkish guard. It was dark when we reached it.

We were much fatigued with the day's journey, although the place is but little more than thirty miles from Jerusalem. The next morning very early, and while the stars still lingered in the sky, we completed our journey to the Jordan. We saw the rising sunlight shine upon its banks. It is very deep, and apparently a little more than a hundred feet in width, as it flows now within its lower channel. Rising in Mount Hermon and running from north to south, it passes through the lakes Merom and Galilee, and empties into the Dead Sea a few miles south of the place where we reached it. It rushes on with a swift, impetuous current, carrying onward at all times a large volume of water. Trees and shrubs grow thickly upon its steep sides; so that it is difficult in many places to reach the brink of its channel. We approached it where there is a bend in the river, and where the trees had been cleared away. But, at a little distance both above and below us, the waters were shaded by the thick foliage around it, the oleander dipped its flower in its wave, and countless birds, unseen and unheard in the desert, were singing in the overhanging branches and leaves. When the waters are high, and when it overflows its upper banks, it must have the appearance of a large majestic stream.

As far back as the time of Abraham, and down to the destruction of Jerusalem, the Jordan is closely connected with many of the interesting incidents of Biblical history. It is associated with the histories of Joshua, Elijah, and John the Baptist. And in the Psalms and the prophetical writings, like Hermon and Carmel and Sharon, it is one of those poetical elements which furnish food to the imagination and give harmony and beauty to truth.

To me the most affecting recollection connected with it was the fact that the Saviour was baptized in its waters. It was here that the "heavens were opened" and the mystic Dove descended; and here was uttered the voice from heaven, saying, "This is my beloved Son, in whom I am well pleased." It was immediately after the baptism of the Saviour in the Jordan, and the utterance of this heavenly declaration in confirmation and testimony of his character, that he was "led by the Spirit into the wilderness." As the rugged and barren "wilderness of Judea," including the desolate mountain of Quarantana, is in this vicinity and indeed in full sight of the Jordan, we find something in this circumstance in support of the traditionary opinion that this region, remarkably fitted by its wild and majestic desolation for such an experience, was the scene of the Saviour's seclusion, fasting, and temptation. The precise place of the Saviour's baptism is unknown.

After spending the early part of the day in the neighborhood of this river, to which so many and interesting allusions are made in all parts of the Scriptures, we went southward a few miles to the head of the Dead Sea,—an expanse of dark gloomy water, from seven to ten miles in width and forty in length, thrown into shadow by the mountains of Judea on one side, and the mountains of Nebo and Moab on the other, with no tree on its banks, no bird in its air, and no fish in its waters, but sad, silent, and motionless as the guilty cities which lay buried in its bosom. The water is salt and very unpleasant to the taste. A bituminous substance is found on its surface, and is sometimes deposited in small pieces on its shores. This dark sea, with its rim of barren rock or of burning sand, occupies the place of the lower portion of the beautiful valley of the Jordan. It is called by the Arabs of this region BAHR LUT, or Sea of Lot, and is the site of the ancient cities of Sodom and Gomorrah, of Admah and Zeboim. The subjects of the divine displeasure, and smitten and sunk from the sight of men, they are wrapped in its sulphurous and heavy winding-sheet; and everything around, without life and without a smile, has that sinister and gloomy aspect which is significant of a locality where curse and ruin have followed upon crime.

(XLV., CONTINUED.)

Leave the Dead Sea for the city of Hebron—The Gazelle—Convent of Mar Sabas—Valley of the Kedron—Reach the city of Hebron —Burial-place of Othniel—The king's pool—Cave of Machpelah —Burial-place of Abraham, Isaac, and Jacob—Plain of Mamre —Character of Abraham—Ain Simim—Pools of Solomon—Tomb of Rachel.

LEAVING the borders of the Dead Sea, we now directed our way towards the city of Hebron. As we entered again into the mountainous region, a wild gazelle started up on the side of a sloping hill, in the neighborhood of the brook Cherith. At the hotel at which our party stopped in Jerusalem, I noticed one of these beautiful animals. He wandered at will over the house; and I became well acquainted with him. But this was the first time that I had seen the gazelle in what may be called his native home. The sight was the more beautiful, because it was life, beauty, and motion starting up suddenly in the rudeness and barrenness of the desert. The gazelle is timid, but he curves his neck with pride; and nothing can exceed the brilliancy of his large dark eye. Swifter than the foot of the huntsman who pursued him, he bounded from rock to rock as if his little feet had wings.

We stopped, on the night of the second day of this excursion, at the Greek convent of Mar Sabas or St. Sabas,—one of the memorable and justly-cherished names in early religious history. This massive and well-built convent, founded in the sixth century, is situated on the side of the brook Kedron, which at certain seasons of the year is sometimes enlarged by heavy rains to an impetuous river, and finds its way from its source in the neighborhood of Jerusalem, through rocky and mountainous defiles, to the Dead Sea. At this place it has worn a passage by its impetuous and long-continued action through a rocky hill of great height, cutting it down perpendicularly from summit to base, and forming for itself a deep unchangeable bed, with walls on each side hundreds of feet in height. The convent is situated on the southeastern side, about half-way down. In company with my travelling-associates, descending through passages cut in the rocks and in part by means of a wooden ladder, I went down into the deep bed below, which was dry at this time, and, walking for some distance, it was with no small surprise that we saw, high in the wall of limestone which enclosed it, a multitude of excavations. Many of them were obviously artificial, and were opened in the rocks with great labor. Such was their number, and such the labor which had been evidently bestowed upon them, that they reminded us of what travellers have said of the rocky excavations of the city of Petra. It was remarked to us, but on how good authority the assertion was made I am unable to state, that in the early persecutions to which Christianity was subjected, many Christians fled to this deep and secluded valley of the Kedron, and concealed themselves in its rocky recesses and caverns. It is well known that John of Damascus, a monk of the eighth century, celebrated for the great powers of his mind and for his various learning, resided here. The Greek monks, who occupy the monastery at the present time, were attentive and kind to us,—showing us their church with its solid architecture and its rude fresco paintings, the tomb of Mar Sabas, and whatever else there was of interest.

On the third day, going nearly in a western direction, and leaving Jerusalem on the north, we reached Hebron. This city was originally a city of the Canaanites, and was called Kirjath Arba, in honor of Arba the father of Anak; and it is said in the book of Numbers to have been built seven years before Zoan in Egypt. Among the old cities of Palestine, Hebron, in the historical interest which attaches to it, stands second only to Jerusalem. For many miles, in our journey towards the city of Hebron, our road had led through a region very uneven and hilly, and for the most part unfruitful.

But in coming near to the city the aspect of the country round it changed very much. After the cultivation and the exhaustion of thousands of years, it is still exceedingly fertile. In coming up by the route which leads from the Dead Sea, and which connects with the road from Bethlehem, we entered the city from the north, passing through the long narrow valley of Eshcol, which now, as it was in the days of Moses and Joshua, is covered with vines, whose thick and heavy clusters attract the notice of the traveller. The modern city is built for the most part on the sides of two hills, which are separated from each other by the small valley between them. It is said to contain eight thousand inhabitants, the greater number of whom are Jews. Near the little grove outside of the city where we pitched our tents is the large excavation which has the reputation of being the burial-place of Othniel, who was in the army of Judah when that tribe first conquered Hebron, and was afterwards one of the judges of Israel. On entering this tomb, which was capacious enough to hold many people, we found it filled with Jews, who were occupied in reading the Scriptures and going through their forms of worship. In that sad blindness to which a retributive but just Providence has left them, they still cling in sorrow and hope to their native land. It was at Hebron that David was anointed king over Judah; and it is stated that he reigned there "seven years and six months." In going through the eastern or Mohammedan part of this ancient place,—the part of it which was the site of the city as it existed in the time of David,—our attention was directed to a large artificial pool of great antiquity, formed of hewn stone, and coated with cement. It is more than a hundred feet square, and at least twenty feet in depth, and is called to this day "the king's pool," in allusion probably to David. There can be but little doubt that it is the same pool which is mentioned in the second book of Samuel, where it is said of the murderers of the son of Saul, that "David commanded his young men, and they slew them, and hanged them up *over the pool in Hebron.*"

At a little distance, perhaps the third of a mile, from the king's pool, and on the side of one of the hills occupied by the city, is the "cave of the field of Machpelah," which was bought by Abraham of Ephron the son of Zohar. The field, of the purchase of which we have a particular account in the book of Genesis, was bought by Abraham at the time of the death of Sarah, who died in Hebron. Abraham, who seems to have left Mamre after the destruction of the cities of the plain, and to have been dwelling at this time in Beersheba in the land of Gerar, came to Hebron to "mourn and to weep" for Sarah. His conference with the sons of Heth and with Ephron in relation to a burying-place for her may be regarded, I think, as one of the most graphic and touching passages of the Old Testament. This cave, in which nearly four thousand years ago Sarah was buried, and in which Abraham and Isaac and Rebecca and Leah were afterwards buried, is now covered by a Turkish mosque, into which Christians are not permitted to enter; so that we could only go to the place which contained the hallowed dust of these early followers and friends of God, and walk around it without going into it. No sculptured tombs of Beni Hassan or Thebes had for me the attraction of this ancient burying-place of the patriarchs. Among the sacred remembrances which it suggested, I could not forget that it was the dying request of the patriarch Jacob, when he breathed his last far away in the unbelieving land of Egypt, that he might be buried "in the cave in the field of Machpelah," which he describes as the burying-place bought by Abraham of Ephron the Hittite. "There," he adds, "they buried Abraham and Sarah his wife; there they buried Isaac and Rebecca his wife; and there *I buried Leah.*"

In returning from Hebron, we left, for a short time, the main road leading to Jerusalem, with a view to reach by a nearer path the plain of Mamre, which for a long time was the residence of Abraham. In speaking of distances, I remark again that I do not profess to be very accurate, because I merely give them in many cases as they seemed to me,—judging from our usual rate of travel and the time occupied. But, judging in this way, the plain of Mamre at its northwestern extremity is, by the nearest path, two miles and a half or three miles from Hebron. In reaching it we passed over a portion of the vine-bearing valley of Eshcol, and then, going up a gradually-ascending height of land which was partitioned into small fields by terraces and walls of stone and everywhere carefully cultivated, we came, as we passed its summit, into the elevated and beautiful plain where Abraham is said to have dwelt. It appeared to be a plain on a mountain,—a beautiful place on earth, and yet expanding itself on such an elevated position that it seemed very near to heaven. The plain, sinking in its centre into a narrow valley where the waters collect in the rainy season, runs in an easterly direction, and then, turning southwardly, appeared to me gradually to descend and terminate in a level open space, which we had previously noticed to the south of and in sight of Hebron.

The tradition in relation to this plain is, that Abráham dwelt in the highest part of it; and we were conducted into a large square building, supposed to be of great antiquity, made of hewn stones of great size, which is shown as indicating the precise spot of his dwelling-place. But, however this may have been, we could not doubt that we were in the region where he spent no small portion of his life. His hand had cultivated this soil; he had been seated beneath these oaks; he looked upon these heavens filled at night with the stars which he could not number,—the bright emblems of his spiritual children in all ages and climes. It was here that he held that memorable conversation with God, when he pleaded so earnestly and eloquently for the wicked cities of the plain. Ten righteous men would have saved them, because Abraham, the friend of God, had asked it; but the ten were not there. The place of the "cities of the plain" is in full sight of the elevated plain of Mamre. In a direct line it is probably not more than twenty miles distant. With a mind filled with these great memories, I looked in that direction. My eye reached over the rocky hills of Judea, and over the dark sunken abyss which bounds them, and rested upon the mountains of Moab beyond. It was from the low level plain, overlooked by these hills and mountains, that the smoke ascended. It was in the sunlight of the morning when we stood on this memorable place; and it was in the morning—"*early* in the morning"—that Abraham arose and "looked towards Sodom and Gomorrah and towards all the land of the plain, and beheld, and lo, the smoke of the country went up as the smoke of a furnace."

And here I feel inclined to delay a moment, in a remark or two upon the great patriarch. There are some men whose thoughts and achievements, aided sometimes by the peculiarities of their position, have been such, that they may be said to fill the eye of nations,—and not more when they are living than when they are dead. They reappear and exist without cessation in the world's thought, which becomes so vivid and clear in its apprehension of them, that it illuminates the ancient night of ages, and restores the dead to life. And it makes but little difference whether they are men of great ideas or men of great actions; though the life which they thus live in the locality, if I may so express it, of the human mind, is more distinct and impressive, if their ideas have found an expression and a confirmation in their own personal history. The patriarch Abraham was such a man,—a man who knew the truth,—a man who illustrated the truth by his deeds.

We find him in early life on the plains of Chaldea. It was there that he first tended his flocks. Whether it was by means of religious traditions communicated through his father Terah, or that

God himself by a direct inspiration was the source of his great wisdom, it was at this early period that he became acquainted with some of those great religious truths (such as the unity of God and the relations of faith and love which ought to exist between God and man) which have always perplexed the best and most persevering efforts of mere human philosophy. In his journeyings from place to place, and from nation to nation, he went from Chaldea to Palestine, and from Palestine to Egypt, —but always in accordance with the openings of Providence, and always guided and sustained by the great religious truth, that God exists, and that he is the friend and rewarder of all those who are willing to believe on him. He was emphatically the man of faith. It was faith which gave strength to his purpose, which imparted purity to his inward nature. His great mind saw, intuitively, that the very idea of God imposes the obligation to believe. He had stood beneath the Chaldean stars; he had looked upon the broad Euphrates and the mighty Nile; he had crossed vast deserts and wildernesses; he had trod the majestic mountains of Palestine; and, as he cast his illuminated eye around and above him and perceived things in their greatness and in their relations, he felt deeply in his soul that there is no middle ground between the true and the false; that the negation of God is the affirmation of chance; and that the affirmation of chance is the inauguration of moral and intellectual weakness and wrong.

To accept God was a necessity. In accepting him, he accepted the faith which honors him. And on Mount Moriah, when called upon as a test of his faith to offer up his beloved son in sacrifice, he showed not only the truth of his own soul, but the truth and mighty power of a principle which elevates and saves humanity by bringing God and man into harmony. History is right, therefore, and honors the God who is the living and controlling power in the series of its own varied events, in taking such a man out of the common ranks of men, and in establishing him among the guides and teachers of the human race.

Leaving the plain of Mamre,—a place so closely associated with this great and remarkable man,—we regained in a short time the main road to Bethlehem and Jerusalem,—passing, at the distance of a mile and a half, the place called "Ain Simim," or the Fountain of Simeon.

There is a large stone building here, erected apparently for military purposes, and in its neighborhood are said to be some very ancient tombs excavated in the rocks; but we had not time to stop and examine them. The fountain gushes out from the side of a small hill on the right of the road; and directly opposite is the plain rendered memorable by a battle fought in 1192 between Richard of England and Sultan Saladin, in which Richard was defeated and driven back to Askelon. Going on about two miles farther, over rugged and rocky hills or along the edge of cultivated valleys, we came to the stupendous water-reservoirs called the Pools of Solomon. We had passed them in our journey to Hebron, but stopped to examine them more particularly on our return. There are other great "pools" or water-reservoirs in other places, the erection of which is ascribed to Solomon. There are three in this place, rising one above another on the side of a hill, and supplied by water from heights still more elevated; the largest of which is nearly six hundred feet in length by an average breadth of more than a hundred and fifty feet, and is fifty feet in depth. All of them are of solid masonry, and are coated with cement. They are entered by steps cut in the sides. The water, collected in the highest from the rocky eminences around, gushes from one to the other, and is then conducted by conduits under ground to the city of Jerusalem. I recollect in early life to have heard a person whose faith in the Scriptures had been shaken, objecting to the statements made in the Bible of the great wealth and power of Solomon; but he had not been in Palestine, and had not seen the works and the remains of works which furnish overwhelming evidence not only of the riches and power, but of the science, of that period.

Going a few miles farther, we came to the city of Bethlehem, the birthplace of the Saviour. "The Word was made flesh, and dwelt among us." But I must leave what I have to say of this city and of the events connected with it, to another letter.

At two miles beyond Bethlehem we came to the tomb of Rachel, the wife of Jacob, who is said in the book of Genesis to have been "buried in the way to Ephrath, which is Bethlehem." A pillar was erected over her grave by Jacob. He was journeying with her from Bethel to Bethlehem at the time of her death. The pillar of Jacob has disappeared. The present tomb is a Saracenic work; but there is no difference of opinion as to the place where she was buried. The burial-place of Rachel—where the traveller naturally stops to indulge in the recollections connected with her touching story—is on the side and near the summit of a hill, furnishing a wide and beautiful prospect. And he naturally thinks of the village with which her name is associated in one of the sad and bloody passages of history. It is to the northwestward of her grave, some three or four miles distant, that we find the village of Rama, to which reference is made in the second chapter of Matthew:—"In Rama there was a voice heard, lamentation, and weeping, and great mourning,—Rachel weeping for her children, and would not be comforted, because they are not."

Half-way between Bethlehem and Jerusalem we passed on our right the large Greek convent of Elias. It is on a hill. We did not stop to visit it. At a little distance from this convent, as we descended the hill towards Jerusalem, we came in sight of the plain of Rephaim, or plain of the Giants. It was on this beautiful plain, which was waving as we passed it with fields of wheat, that David fought twice with the Philistines, who seem to have become alarmed on account of his increasing power, and who had come up here to attack him after he had established himself in Jerusalem. The same night, crossing the deep rocky ravine called the valley of Hinnom, and then ascending the steep sides of the hill of Zion, we reached the city of Jerusalem, after an absence of four days. We entered it at the tower of David, by the Bethlehem gate,—which is also called the Jaffa gate.

(XLVI.)

Visit to Bethlehem—Appearance of the country round it—The city and its inhabitants—The convent and church of the Nativity—View from the top of the convent—St. Jerome—The grotto of the Saviour's birth—Reflections on the Incarnation—Poetry.

CITY OF JERUSALEM: THIRD LETTER.

In my last letter I gave a brief account of an excursion from Jerusalem to the river Jordan and the Dead Sea, and thence to the ancient city of Hebron. In the course of this excursion we had the satisfaction of visiting the city of Bethlehem twice. In going westward from the northern extremity of the Dead Sea to Hebron, by the way of the convent of St. Sabas, we found that Bethlehem was so nearly on the best and direct line of our route, that we took the road leading through it. As I remarked in my last letter, we spent a night at the convent which I have named. Starting early in the morning, and passing over a number of lofty and barren hills between St. Sabas and Bethlehem, we at last ascended from a picturesque valley, and, having passed through some comparatively large and well-cultivated fields on the sides and summit of the height, we arrived at the limits of the celebrated city where the Saviour of the world was born.

In coming from St. Sabas, we approached Bethlehem on the east. This was the first time that I saw it; and it seemed to me as if Jerusalem itself had not excited a deeper interest and a more profound emotion. But the view of the city was not very good. In coming from Hebron on our return to Jerusalem, we approached it on the western side. At this time the city was seen very distinctly on its lofty height at a considerable distance, and made a very impressive appearance. Our ascent to it in this direction was more steep and difficult than in our approach from the east. And again, on our way from Bethlehem to Jerusalem, which placed us upon its northern side, we often turned to look back upon it. There was an attraction in the name and in the histories connected with it, which we were not willing to lose. So that we had good opportunities, notwithstanding the short time which was left us, to see and to impress its interesting features upon the memory.

The country around Bethlehem, diversified with hills and valleys, had to my view a very pleasant aspect. I think it may be regarded as fruitful, even at the present time. And in former times, before the earth became exhausted by long and ill-directed cultivation, it probably was a very fertile region. The name Bethlehem, which means the *house of bread*, and the name Bethlehem-Ephratah, which was also sometimes applied to the city, and which means Bethlehem the *fruitful*, seem to indicate that such was the case. It was once a land of shepherds; and flocks of sheep and goats, and droves of camels, are frequently seen now. From time to time, we saw in all these regions the dark, open tents of the Bedouins. Their flocks are always near them. About a mile's distance from the city in an eastern direction, in a low green valley, is the place where the shepherds are said to have been watching their flocks when the Saviour's birth was announced to them.

The lofty limestone hill on which the city itself is situated runs from east to west. And on all sides the approach to it, with the exception of the route from St. Sabas, is abrupt and steep,—particularly on the northern and southern sides. These abrupt ascents are built up in many places with terraces, which are planted with flourishing fig-trees, vines, and olives. I have already referred to the general aspect of the city. On approaching it in almost any direction, it has quite an imposing appearance, though in different degrees. On entering it, however, it does not realize the expectations which are raised on seeing it at a distance. There are no evidences of wealth and splendor; nor, on the other hand, are there signs of great poverty. The houses are generally one story in height, and built of stone, —many of them with flat roofs; but frequently they are surmounted with a dome. As a general thing they have no windows towards the streets. Many of them are well built; and, notwithstanding the idea of almost entire seclusion which they are apt to suggest, they have an aspect of neatness and comfort which is seldom seen in these regions. Bethlehem resembles nearly all Oriental cities in the narrowness and irregularity of its streets. A few Turks and Arabs make their residence here; but the greater part of the people are understood to receive the Christian religion,—chiefly, though not exclusively, in the forms of the Greek and Catholic churches. The population is variously estimated from three to four thousand. We found the principal street, which leads from the open area in front of the church of the Nativity towards Jerusalem, occupied for some distance by a large number of persons, who had come in from the neighboring villages with vegetables, oranges, and other fruits of the country, for sale. Nor was there any want of traffickers in other articles,—particularly in rosaries and crosses, and representations of holy persons and places ingeniously carved in olive-wood and mother-of-pearl. I thought I could discover, as I walked through the streets and mingled with the people for a short time, the marks both of increased comfort and intelligence, as compared with what we had noticed in other places.

A portion of the eastern extremity of this rocky height rises steeply over the large and beautiful plain and valleys in that direction. A convent is built upon this part of the height. Its massive walls and battlements, like those of the monastery of St. Sabas, give it the appearance of a fortress. We entered it through a small, low opening in the bottom of the western wall. It does not belong exclusively to one Christian sect; but the different parts of it, including the church, are divided among Catholics, Greeks, and Armenians. Within the large area which is enclosed by the convent-walls is the church of the Nativity,—built in the form of a cross. It is said to have been built by the Empress Helena; though the origin of the convent-buildings around it is attributed to the pious zeal of a distinguished Roman lady by the name of Paula, whose tomb is still shown here. Passing through the large entrance-porch or vestibule of the church, we paused a few moments in the lofty nave, which is adorned with numerous Corinthian columns, and is architecturally an object of much interest. And from this place, under the guidance of men of the different religious sects who claim and hold possession, we proceeded to see and examine what is worthy of notice in this remarkable spot.

Ascending to the top of the convent, we had the whole city at our feet. We also had a fine view of the surrounding country,—particularly of the mountainous region in the direction of the Dead Sea. The lofty cone which has borne for many ages the name of the Frank Mountain was in sight to the southeast, and apparently not more than four or five miles distant. This mountain, including a portion of land at its base, is the supposed site of the ancient city and castle which was built by Herod, and which was called Herodium. The ruins which are still found on the mountain and in its vicinity support this view.

At a little distance south of the Frank Mountain is another lofty eminence, which is visible from this place. It is the ancient Tekoa, the birthplace of the prophet Amos, and the residence of the wise woman who was consulted by Joab in the case of Absalom. In coming from St. Sabas we passed these places on the left. The ancient Hebrew name of the Frank Mountain was Beth-Haccerim. Such, at least, is the supposition of some Biblical critics. It was upon such lofty heights that those flaming beacon-lights were kindled which gave notice to the surrounding country of approaching dangers.

Hence the expressions in the prophet Jeremiah:—"Blow the trumpet in Tekoa, and set up a sign of fire in Beth-Haccerim."

Going into the lower part of these ancient edifices,—into that portion denominated the Latin Convent,—we visited the place where the justly-celebrated Jerome spent a considerable portion of his life, and where his tomb still remains. The tomb of Eusebius, the ecclesiastical historian, is also here.

A peculiar interest, which the Biblical student will easily understand, attaches to the fact that St. Jerome dwelt so long in this place. And perhaps I shall be pardoned for recalling a few incidents of his life at this time. Born in the times of the Roman empire, and in a small Roman town near the province of Dalmatia, he was sent to Rome by his father, who was a man of wealth, in order that he might be early and thoroughly instructed in the literature, the arts, and the philosophy of that day. Aided by the best masters in the city of Rome, among whom was a learned grammarian by the name of Donatus, who is still known by his commentaries on Virgil and Terence, he soon became a proficient in Greek and Roman learning. Embracing the study and the profession of the law as a business for life, his great ability and high mental culture gave him reason to hope that he would ultimately reach positions of influence and honor,—such as would fully satisfy a high ambition. He soon found, however, that the world has its enchantments as well as its honors. The fascinating pleasures of Rome held out their allurements, and he had begun to feel both their power and their bitterness; but the lessons of piety which he had received in early life recurred to his mind, and a divine voice, perhaps in answer to a father's or mother's prayers, whispered to him the vanity of human philosophy and fame, and urged him to seek the knowledge and the honor which come from Christ. He was then in the midst of his travels in France, and still in the ardent pursuit of knowledge; but he had the wisdom to listen to this higher and better voice, and accepted the simple but sublime philosophy of Christ for that of the Grecian and Roman schools. In accordance with the ascetic principles and practices of his age, he left Rome, which seemed to him to present too many temptations to a young Christian, and, finding his way after some time into Syria, he took up his residence in a desert and solitary place near Chalcis,—though not very far from the city of Antioch and the banks of the Orontes. In this Syrian wilderness, which he has rendered celebrated in his eloquent writings, he resided four years. It was in the year 377 that he first came into Palestine; and after the year 386 he made it his permanent residence. He dwelt at one time on the Mount of Olives, but subsequently took up his abode at Bethlehem,—diligently pursuing his studies, as he had done during a large portion of his life, even in the deserts of Syria, and investigating with great zeal the various subjects which throw light upon the history, the persons, and the doctrines of the Bible.

I refer thus particularly to this distinguished man, so well known to Biblical scholars, because undoubtedly the locality of many of the sacred places in

Palestine, particularly in Bethlehem and its vicinity, is considered as settled, in concurrence with his opinions and authority. And when we consider the early period in which he lived, his long residence in Palestine, his great learning, and the deep interest which he could not fail to take in the subject, I think we may feel a good degree of confidence that many of the most important localities are satisfactorily known.

The reader of the Bible cannot forget that many events of interest have occurred in Bethlehem and its immediate vicinity, besides that great event which supersedes and overshadows all others. This is the scene of the beautiful story of Ruth and Naomi,—inimitable in its simplicity and touching pastoral allusions. Bethlehem is interesting also as being the birthplace of king David. He was the keeper of his father's flocks in the neighborhood of Bethlehem, which is spoken of as being at that time in the wilderness, when he was called to engage in contest with Goliath. It is still more interesting—perhaps we may say it exceeds all other places in the world in interest—in being the birthplace of the Saviour. The prophecies of the Old Testament—full of intimations and glimpses of the future—led the Jews to expect the birth of the Saviour in this place. "But thou, Bethlehem-Ephratah," says the prophet Micah, "though thou be little among the thousands of Judah, yet out of thee shall He come forth unto me who is to be Ruler in Israel; whose goings forth have been from old, from everlasting."

The church of the Nativity, which is understood to enclose the Saviour's birthplace, is built over a large grotto. Descending the flight of stairs which leads into it, we found it brightly illuminated with rows of costly lamps, which are kept constantly burning. Art, coloring, drapery, lend their aid to give beauty and impressiveness to the place. The figure of a large and beautiful star, formed of marble and jasper laid in mosaic, indicates the place where the Saviour was born. Golden lamps are suspended above this star, and throw their light down upon it. Around it, in the Latin language, are the words, HIC DE VIRGINE MARIA JESUS CHRISTUS NATUS EST.

I am not ignorant of the doubts and queries which have been started by the learned. And still the argument, depending upon facts and circumstances too numerous to be detailed here, which may be brought to bear in support of the identity of this part of the hill of Bethlehem as the birthplace of the Saviour, is so strong, that my mind found no difficulty in receiving it. It was here that the prophecies were fulfilled. It was here that the Saviour was born.

In giving myself up to profound emotion, I could not forget the accessories of that great event. I saw the wise men coming from the East, with their offerings of frankincense and gold. I remembered that the very heavens were bright with transcendent glory. I recalled the watching shepherds, and the song of the angels. But these were only incidents; and were important chiefly by the relations which they sustained. It was the event itself which absorbed memory, thought, emotion. I repeated to myself the expressions which seemed to me to describe that great occurrence. I said, "The

Divine Mind became embodied,—the Infinite reposed in the arms of the finite,—God manifested himself in the flesh,—*on the place where I now stand*."

I do not profess to understand precisely the import of these expressions, which may well be supposed to suggest thought rather than accurately define it. But it was through the medium of such emphatic and suggestive forms of speech, which could not fail to have an important influence upon early thought and belief, that I had been taught in childhood. It was thus, before I was capable of thinking for myself, that I had been instructed in distant America,—in her primitive and humble assemblies, and in the books which had come down from my Puritan ancestors. Undoubtedly a hereditary belief, though sanctioned by the wisdom of those who have gone before us, and taught in the young home which we always love, is a proper subject of re-examination and further inquiry. Such inquiry I have not been unwilling—and indeed have thought it right and proper—to give to the wonderful doctrine of the Incarnation. Considered in its time and its incidents, in itself and its relations, I have endeavored to compare the advent of the Messiah with other advents and manifestations of supposed power and greatness which men in their blindness have accepted and idolized; and, without professing to be aware of the full import of my own expressions, I am still obliged to say, not only because it is authorized by the Bible, but because all other expressions come short of the convictions and aspirations which struggled in my own breast, "*God was manifest in the flesh.*"

I am aware that human philosophy, reasoning more from the head than the heart, is likely to be perplexed on this subject. In its doubts and difficulties, it propounds the question, whether it is possible for the Infinite to embody itself in a finite form. I answer, if God is merely an impersonal infinite presence,—in other words, an infinite power, but not an infinite personal agent,—then I feel the pressure of this inquiry; but I do not feel it if He is what Christians suppose Him to be,—*an infinite personality*. In the view of the matter as it presents itself to my own mind, the incapacity to manifest himself in a form, in connection with which He should communicate with his creatures would be an imperfection.

And it is to me an interesting circumstance that all nature, I may perhaps say,—certainly all races of men,—demand such a manifestation. It is an instinct of the human mind,—demonstrated, as it seems to me, by the religious history of our race,—which requires that the Infinite should subject itself, at particular times and in particular forms, to the limitations of the finite, in order to satisfy the finite want and to perfect the finite communion. To one tribe, (I speak of those portions of the human race which are not enlightened by the Bible,) God is in the sun; to another He is in the moon and stars; to another He is embodied in the clouds, or floats in the rivers and the ocean. And others again find Him embodied and incarnate in some lower animal, which they fall down and worship.

God has done homage to the great instincts he

has implanted. He knew the wants of men and was ready to meet them, when man himself, disappointed in all false manifestations, had sufficiently recognized and felt those wants. He met them by his presence. But in coming into the world he gave the preference to the weak over the mighty. He paid homage to human wants, but not to human pride; and, passing by Rome and Athens, and whatever other names and places had dazzled by their greatness and splendor, He selected the little city of Bethlehem.

Philosophy, or rather imperfect *human* philosophy, perplexed in the fact of his coming, is equally perplexed in relation to the *form* of his coming. It thinks more of greatness than of innocence, and vainly imagines that a descending God cannot come in less than a king's chariot, and with the noise of trumpets, and with royal purple and gold. But such is not the expectation of that better and divine philosophy which attaches the highest value to purity and love. Divine wisdom, without stopping to inquire at the great schools of human learning, chooses its own form. And what form, helpless though it may be, is more beautiful in itself, or more significant and emblematic of truth and beauty, than that of an infant? Or what place is more fitting and suitable to such an advent and manifestation than a mother's arms?

And I may say, further, that I personally sympathize in those deep instincts of the human heart to which I have referred,—I mean those instincts which need and require the manifestation and presence of a divine nature,—and that I rejoice also in the manner in which these yearnings of the heart have been responded to. To those who are weak in spirit like myself, the manifestation of Divinity in humanity, so that in our helplessness we may feel the hand of the Infinite and be lifted up, is not only a possibility but a *necessity*. Believing, as I do, that in the name of Jesus the many evils which exist in the world are to be subdued, its sorrows ended, and its discordancies harmonized, it is not without emotion that I have come, from a distant land, to the place which the guiding-star has illuminated, and that I offer here the "myrrh and frankincense" of a penitent and believing heart.

The star which shines over this sacred spot—emblematic of the heavenly radiance—is to me the source of light. I endeavored in my early days to study the philosophies and to become acquainted with the masters and teachers of men. I felt that I needed illumination. But, standing as I now do on the hill of Bethlehem, and by the cradle of the manger, I am not ashamed in these last years of my life, and after the labor of many hopeless inquiries, to say that I accept of the coming of this infant Jesus, and that I am willing to be taught by a child.

LINES WRITTEN ON THE OCCASION OF VISITING THE BIRTHPLACE OF THE SAVIOUR IN BETHLEHEM.

Philosophers of other days,
  In learned schools, their wisdom taught,
And earn'd from human tongues the praise
  Of guides and lights of human thought:
But *here* an infant's lips declare
A wisdom which they did not share.

The kings and conquerors of old,
  Who march'd to power through seas of gore,

Rode in their chariots of gold,
  And crown and sceptre proudly bore;
But *here* an infant's sceptre bears
A weight of power, which was not theirs.

The weak are great in outward show,
  Magnificent in high pretence;
But God, descending here below,
  Appears in peace and innocence:
He seeks no power of arms or arts,
But that of conquering human hearts.

Temples and towers and thrones may fall,
  And learning's institutes go down,
But, in the wreck that sweeps o'er all,
  Christ shall come up and wear the crown;
And from their scatter'd dust shall spring
The empire of the infant King.

He reigns, to judge the poor man's cause;
  He reigns, tyrannic sway to bind;
He reigns, to renovate the laws
  And heal the wanderings of the mind,—
Restoring, in his mighty plan,
God's empire in the soul of man.

(XLVII.)

Introductory remarks—Visit to the Mount of Olives—Historical notices—Mount Zion—Valley of Hinnom—Church of the Holy Sepulchre—Hill of Scopus—Titus—Return from the mountain—Garden of Gethsemane—Poetry.

CITY OF JERUSALEM: FOURTH LETTER.

THE objects of interest in Jerusalem and its vicinity are very numerous. I shall not undertake a minute description, which is better left to those who have more time, and who come here with the requisite qualifications, and under circumstances which are more favorable to extended and specific inquiries. There is much work in Jerusalem and its vicinity for profound scholars, for painters, poets, historians,—a work which, it is very certain, cannot be satisfactorily performed, especially so far as relates to its controverted antiquities, by transient visitants. There are men, however, who in due time will be found adequate to the task. Without mentioning all the names which I now have in my mind, I will only say here that Dr. Robinson of our own country has made a good and very thorough beginning, which entitles him to the gratitude of the friends of Biblical science; and future inquiries, connected with the same ability and energy, will throw great light upon these interesting topics. At the same time, I think there may possibly be some value in those more general writings where the moral, social, and physical are mingled together. I shall describe, or rather make the attempt to describe, only generally and briefly.

I went one day to the top of the Mount of Olives, in company with my American friends. From this commanding position, we endeavored to arrange and fix in our minds the objects around us. With an estimated height of more than two thousand feet above the Mediterranean, carrying it high above Jerusalem, this celebrated mountain, which in itself is an object of great interest, was favorable to our purpose. Standing on that part of the summit which is occupied by the chapel of the Ascension, —so called because it was supposed by its builders to be erected over the place where the Saviour ascended,—we gazed with deep interest upon the various objects which here presented themselves to view. Looking in one direction, we had before us

Jerusalem, and the deep ravines which enclose it on the south and east, and the mountains which arise above it on every side. In the other direction was the rough and elevated region bounded by the valley of the Jordan and the Dead Sea, and by the mountains of Moab beyond.

But this first visit, which enabled me to fix in mind the outlines of objects, was calculated to satisfy the head rather than the heart. Perhaps I may more clearly express myself thus. The mind went out to the objects; but the influence of the objects had not time to come back and to write itself upon the mind. The Mount of Olives must take its own time, and have its visitant all to itself, in order to make present and to convey into the soul all that it is capable of revealing.

This, I suppose, will be easily understood. Places, as well as persons, have power. Thoughts, whose seeds are in the soul, are oftentimes the product and the outgrowth of *situations*. The influence which such situations or places possess over the human mind is very various in its origin,—sometimes from the greatness of nature and sometimes from the greatness of art,—sometimes from the power which they still hold, and not unfrequently from the power which they have lost,—sometimes from sympathy with the living, and sometimes from the memory of the dead. Many are the places which thus speak to the soul, either with a natural or associated power.

One of the many places which have this power in a remarkable degree—perhaps as much so, or with very few exceptions, as any in the world—is the Mount of Olives. Irregular in its surface, with here and there a few olives and fig-trees still growing among its projecting rocks, it adds to the impressions which naturally attach to its rough and majestic form, the power which it derives from its history, its associations, and its position.

I had gone through the streets of Jerusalem, and had rapidly examined, both within and without its walls, the various objects of interest which the pens of numerous travellers have sufficiently made known. But before our little company left the city on our way to other parts of Palestine, and on the route preliminary to our return to America, I felt a secret and strong desire to ascend once more the mountain where the Saviour had so often been, and, aided by its lofty summit, to look again upon the theatre of the great scenes and sufferings which the Scriptures record. On the occasion to which I now refer, which was a day or two before our departure, it was convenient for me to go alone. This solitary visit, like a visit to the tomb of a departed friend, harmonized with the state of my feelings; because my object was, not to converse with men, but with God, nature, history, and eternity. I easily found a secluded and lofty position suited to my object; and, as I looked abroad from that memorable height, I felt how one short hour could reproduce and live over again the growth and the decay, the agonies and triumphs, of ages.

Jerusalem, as it is now, and in its natural features as it always has been, was all before me,—a place more closely associated than any other with the destinies of men, and going back in its history to the early periods of the human race. Taken by

David from the Jebusites, and in the reigns of David and Solomon advancing to great wealth and splendor, destroyed by Nebuchadnezzar, rebuilt in the times of Nehemiah, captured and laid waste by the Roman armies under Pompey the Great, restored and beautified by Antipater and Herod, destroyed again by Titus and in part restored by Adrian, and at later periods successively captured and held by the Persians, Arabians, Turks, and Crusaders, it still stands, amid all these changes and revolutions, an object of deep interest and attraction.

Checking this natural tendency to indulge in historical recollections, that I might the better understand the place which gave rise to them, my eye first ran along the circuit of its beautiful but irregular walls, and then, glancing rapidly upon the valley of the Kedron and over the steep rocky heights beyond it, rested upon the magnificent mosque of Omar. This great structure, a sad memorial of the vicissitudes to which Jerusalem has been subject, is built within the present walls of the city, on the eastern side, and overlooks the abrupt, rocky valley of Jehoshaphat,—occupying the top of that Mount Moriah which is supposed to be the place where Abraham was directed to offer up Isaac. The place which is occupied by this imposing Mohammedan edifice is the precise spot which was occupied in other times, and under other and different influences, by the great temple of Solomon.

Imagination, which controls time as well as places, and has the power of changing and remodelling all things, was not slow in banishing the mosque and in remodelling and replacing the temple. "It was there," I said to myself, "that the wonderful structure stood, of which I had read so much in my childhood; and which, described in history and rendered visible in paintings, had become a part of my thoughts and dreams; on the place *which is now before me*," the place, ascertained and identified with the concurrence of all antiquaries, and which, as I looked upon it in its marked and imposing outlines, seemed to me to carry the evidence of its historic claims in itself. It was there, then, that the great edifice was erected,—the "Lord's house," shining in cedar and gold,—which required a nation's wealth in building, which held the ark and tables of the covenant and the cherubim of glory, and which, by its history, its position, and its rites and ceremonies, became the central and controlling element in that system of religion which was superseded by the mission and the doctrines of Christ. The subterranean crypts, arches, and gates, and the immense blocks of granite, constituting together the vast substructions which still remain,—some above ground and some below, —but which will be likely to be better known in the explorations of future times, furnish evidence that what is said in the Bible of the glory both of the first and second temple, and of the wealth and skill of the times of Solomon, is no exaggeration.

As the traveller stands upon the Mount of Olives, the ancient as well as the modern Jerusalem, at least in its essential outlines, is restored and made present to his eye. Following the attractions of sight and memory, and crossing the narrow Tyropœon valley, which, however, is now nearly filled up and is hardly perceptible from this elevated position, he next ascends the hill of Zion. Here, in the neighborhood of the Bethlehem gate, is the tower of Hippicus, standing in grandeur to the present hour,—whose strong foundations, hardly less immovable than the mountain itself, carry the mind back to distant ages. Some antiquaries assign the laying of these massive foundations to the historic era of king David. Beyond the wall, and within the court or enclosed area of a Mohammedan mosque, is David's tomb. "His sepulchre," says the Apostle Peter, "is with us unto this day." Around the tomb are small cultivated fields. The denunciations of prophecy are fulfilled. The ploughshare has passed over the summit of Zion.

It was here, in this part of Jerusalem, that the son of Jesse, the warrior and Psalmist of Israel, had his residence. This, then, is that hill of Zion which he describes, in his own matchless language, as "beautiful for situation, the joy of the whole earth." This is the place which for ages held the sword and the seat of empire. From this mountain-rock, which lifts its southern brow so proudly over the deep valley of Hinnom, the tide of aggressive war has been scattered and driven back. Conquering armies, proud to obey the greatest king of Israel, have stood upon its frowning height.

But, with all these lofty recollections thronging around this memorable place, I could not suppress the thought that this was not its chief honor. It is not the spear but the lyre of David—

"The harp the monarch-minstrel swept"—

which survives most deeply and distinctly in the

memory of later generations. The hill of Zion may perish, but I think it may be said of the songs of Zion—estimated by those who have the true insight of poetry as well as religious feeling—that they have a life which cannot die.

With such impressions, I must confess that my eye was not tired in looking upon the spot which gave origin to those divine songs and lyric odes which bear the Psalmist's name,—poems which embody with such mingled simplicity and power the various forms of natural and religious feeling, of natural and religious truth, that they descend to the level of the understanding and heart of a child, while at the same time, by their great thoughts and sublimity, they fill and satisfy minds of the greatest breadth and culture. It was there that he gazed upon those surrounding heights and mountains which still look down upon his burial-place. It was there that he walked forth at night, and looked again with his poetic eye upon the deep blue heavens which he had watched and loved when in early life he tended his father's flocks in Bethlehem. "When I consider thy heavens, the work of thy fingers, the moon and the stars, which thou hast ordained, what is man, that thou art mindful of him? and the son of man, that thou dost visit him?"

The hill of Zion is often regarded as the type or earthly emblem of heaven. And why should it not be? It is a place which is lofty and imperial; and the cavernous depths of Gehenna, hardly less terrible than when its fire and smoke ascended, are still far below it. But it is entitled to this distinction and lifts the mind to a better state of things, not only on account of its elevation, but still more because it is *the hill of song*. Song is truth, uttered in harmony. Heaven is what it is, because nothing enters there which "loveth and maketh a lie," and because the truth which enters and is embodied within it, in being always consistent with itself, has no discordant sounds, but is always uttering, by the very necessities of its nature, a voice which is full of melody. Heaven, therefore, whatever other attributes may attach to it, is the true locality of whatever is highest and best in the conception of poetic harmony. And hence it is natural that the place on earth which has breathed forth the sweetest and tenderest melodies should be the sign and emblem of the heavenly inheritance.

But what a contrast of associations, as well as of height and depth, may be seen at no great distance! As we approach the edge of the hill of Zion, we look down, almost with dizziness, into the deep valley which bounds it on the south and southwestern side,—the valley of Hinnom of the Old Testament, the Gehenna of the New. In this valley there was once an idolatrous image of the heathen god Moloch, who exacted from his followers the rites and sacrifices of his cruel worship. In those sad days it was truly the place of weeping and wailing. Gloomy and terrible in itself and terrible in its history and associations, it was afterwards the place where the useless and decaying impurities of the city, including the dead bodies of animals and malefactors, were collected together. And this was done so frequently, and to such an extent, that the fires which were rendered necessary for the purpose of consuming them were kept continually burning. This is no place of song. This is no emblem of the heavenly world. These masses of corruption, these ever-burning fires, and the columns of smoke continually ascending, furnish the terrible figures which are employed by the writers of the Bible to indicate the opposite of a state of blessedness, and to shadow forth the end and destiny of the wicked.

At some distance from Mount Zion, a little outside of the line of the ancient wall, which antiquaries profess to be able still to trace, but within the limits of the modern city, is the rocky height, surmounted by the church of the Holy Sepulchre, where the Saviour was crucified. This vast church, which in itself is a history, has been so often described in its length and breadth, in its towering arches and columns, that I will say nothing in relation to it so far as its architecture is concerned. The church is adjusted, in its foundations, to the hill and rock of Calvary. I had visited it before the time of which I am now speaking. I had ascended the successive flights of steps which led to the elevated platform covering the portion of the rock where the cross is said to have been placed, and where the Saviour was crucified. I had gone down into another part of the church at a little distance and seen the place where he was buried. A small chapel, not wanting in beauty, is built over it. And many are the pilgrims, from many and distant lands, that kneel beneath it.

At such a time, and amid such remembrances, I must confess that I had no disposition to think of painting or architecture, of Greek or Jew, of Saracen or Roman, of Helena or Justinian,—not even of prophets and apostles,—but only of that one good and innocent man—the child of Mary and the incarnate Son of God—whose blood, shed upon the elevated rock, may be said to have readjusted heaven and earth, by cementing once more the broken links of love, life, and immortality.

I am aware of the fact that some Biblical antiquaries have doubted whether the crucifixion took place on the site of the church of the Holy Sepulchre. I will not undertake to reconcile and measure the probabilities of a question which a life's labors would not be sufficient to exhaust. But seated as I am, on the summit of the Mount of Olives, with Jerusalem and the objects around it for miles in extent fully in view, I think I can say without impropriety, even if there is a foundation for the doubt to which I have referred, that my eyes have rested beyond a question upon the place where this great transaction actually occurred. Whether it was within or without the walls of the present Jerusalem, it was certainly within the field of vision, as I look outward and around from this overshadowing height. Situated as I now am, and looking upon the general aspect of things without always being certain of particulars, it is not necessary, in order to see the Son of God led to execution, to confine myself to the traditionary limits of the VIA DOLOROSA. I can behold the cross erected, whether it was within or without the measurements of the church of the Holy Sepulchre. My mind, without accepting or rejecting the glasses of tradition, avails itself of the aid which this lofty height affords me, to see by the light of its own intuitions, and to adjust its own localities. And seeing with the heart also, as well as with the outward sight, every thing becomes a reality. The Divine victim is before me. His gushing blood flows down. His dying voice exclaims, "IT IS FINISHED." I hear the rending of the vail of the temple. I see the quaking and the rending of the rocks.

The death of Christ was also the death of a great and venerated system,—a system which had its season and its uses, but which always proclaimed itself to be only the precursor of another state of things, less striking in the form but more efficacious in the spirit, and which should be better suited to the advancing intelligence of the human race. And that sad event, witnessed in the very place which my eyes now behold, while it swept away the priest, the altar, and the temple, was at the same time the building up of the inward temple and the inauguration of the reign of the Holy Ghost.

In the passing away of the old system, punishment found the fitting occasion to vindicate its claims and to adjust itself to crime. And a great nation, which had shed the blood of the innocent, was smitten by the hand of retribution; and the name of its greatness and power forever passed away.

I turned my eye away from the church of the Holy Sepulchre. I looked in a little different direction. I saw on the north side of the city, a little beyond the upper valley of the Kedron, and rising above the road which leads to Shechem and Samaria, a gently-ascending but lofty height of land, which is called the hill of Scopus. It was on that spot, according to Josephus, that Titus, who had marched into Palestine the fierce legions which his father Vespasian had left in Alexandria, cast his proud eye for the first time on the city of Jerusalem. This was that Titus under whose triumphal arch I had stood at Rome and saw on its sculptured sides the emblems of his victory. Seated sternly on his war-horse like the sculptured Aurelius in the Roman Campodoglio, he is worthy of our attention; and, more than that, he at once seizes and fixes our attention,—because he holds forth in his lofty front and his uplifted arm the marks of the man of providential destiny.

It is true that every man is a providence; that each one, whether great or small, fills a place which no other one can, and holds a link in the great chain of events which can be uplifted by no other hand. But it is not true that every man's providential position and relations are known; and, not being known, they are not the subject of specific thought and meditation. It was not so with the son of Vespasian. As he stands under the combined light of prophecy and history, he is exhibited to the world's view a providential instrument, an agent that fulfils purposes not his own, a man of inevitable destiny. Perhaps he knew not his own position; but the "blinded beast," says an old writer, "that turns the wheel of the mill, though it seeth not, neither knows what it does, yet doeth a great work in grinding the corn." Neither his knowledge nor his ignorance would have any effect in altering the plans of infinite wisdom, and in disturbing the connection of everlasting adjustments. The man, the hour, and the destiny had met. As he looked once more upon Jerusalem, and pointed out to his soldiers the walls and towers of the devoted city, he bore in that extended arm, feeble in itself but mighty in its relations, the hidden thunders and lightnings of God.

Such were some of the objects which were presented to my notice. Such were some of the reflections which arose in my mind. I had thus stood for the last time upon the mountain which looked down upon a vast panorama, not more of nature than of great and wonderful events. Resuming my way towards the city, I followed the narrow and winding path which has been trodden for ages. In coming down from the rocky height, I fell in company with a shepherd, who was driving before him a flock of sheep and goats. The keeper of sheep trod in the footpath of kings. It was over these heights that the exiled David fled from the triumphant Absalom. In a short time he drove the sheep into a rude sheepfold made of rocks. And again I walked on alone.

At a little distance from me I noticed the traditionary place where the Saviour is said to have wept over Jerusalem. Reaching the foot of the mountain, I stopped at the garden of Gethsemane. At a little distance on my right was the beautiful chapel and the sepulchre of the Virgin Mary. The traditionary belief is that the dust of the mother reposes near the garden which witnessed the heavy trials of her Divine Son. The garden of Gethsemane is now enclosed by a high wall, which overlooks the channel of the Kedron. I entered it and walked among the flowers which the hand of Christian veneration loves to cultivate on its sacred soil, and beneath the shade of the aged olive-trees, the growth of many hundred—perhaps of a thousand—years.

"And this," I said to myself, "was the garden of preparatory suffering,—the sad and memorable scene of one of the most trying periods of the Saviour's life. This was the place of his agony. It was here he kneeled and prayed, 'If it be possible, let this cup pass from me. Nevertheless, not as I will, but as Thou wilt.'"

The world of spirits took an interest in this great struggle. An angel appeared,—strengthening him. His prayer was answered. The will of his Father was accomplished. The Son of God was betrayed into the hands of wicked men. His blood flowed upon Calvary. Jerusalem was destroyed. But a world was redeemed.

LINES WRITTEN ON VISITING THE GARDEN OF GETHSEMANE, MAY, 1853.

Oh, let me not forget! 'Twas here—
  Earth of the Saviour's grief and toil!—
He knelt; and oft the falling tear
  Mingled his sorrows with thy soil;—
When, in the garden's fearful hour,
He felt the great temptation's power.

Here was the proffer'd bitter cup.
  "THY WILL BE DONE!" the Saviour said;
His faith received, and drank it up:
  Amazed, the baffled tempter fled,
Repulsed, with all his hate and skill,
Before an acquiescent will.

O man! In memory of that hour
  Let rising murmurs be repress'd;
And learn the secret of thy power
  Within a calm and patient breast.
"THY WILL BE DONE." 'Tis that which rolls
Their agony from suffering souls.

Such is the lesson that I find
  Here, in the Saviour's place of tears,—
The lesson, that the trusting mind
  Has strength to conquer griefs and fears,
And, doom'd upon the cross to die,
Finds death itself a victory.

(XLVIII.)

Departure from Jerusalem—Last view of it--Village of Beeroth—Spend the night at Bethel—Visit to the mountain east of Bethel—Well of Jacob--Christ's conversation with the Samaritan woman—Tomb of Joseph—City of Shechem.

SHECHEM, FOOT OF MOUNT GERIZIM, MAY 24, 1853.

WE left the city of Jerusalem, Monday, the 23d of May. We were delayed in our preparations; and it was near noon when we departed. Our object was to go into Galilee and the region of Nazareth. The direction of our route, therefore, was towards the northern part of Palestine,—the country of Ephraim and Manasseh, of Issachar and Zebulun. Soon after leaving the walls of the city, we passed through a large grove of olive-trees, in which we met from time to time with groups of people of both sexes, who seemed to enjoy its retirement and shade. At the distance of about a mile in a northwest direction, reaching a piece of rising ground which afforded a wide prospect, we stopped, and, turning and looking back, took a last view. The city with its walls and towers, the valley of the Kedron, and beyond it the Mount of Olives, were in full sight.

From no other point, with the exception of the Mount of Olives, had it appeared to us so beautiful. Was it strange that we stopped thus to gaze upon it?

Our visit had been short; but the scene had brought back so much of the past, and so vividly,—as if some beloved friend had arisen from the dead and spoken to us once more,—that we naturally felt sad at parting. But as the scene, rising above all ordinary forms of association and interest, had a relationship to the soul itself, it was easy to carry away its image in the heart. From that hour, unseen by the outward sight, it became the possession of the mind itself,—the living child of memory.

The road we took is called the Damascus road. It leads in the direction of that celebrated city. The same day in the afternoon, passing on our left the distant heights of Ramah and Nebi Samuel, we came, at the distance of eight or nine miles from Jerusalem, to the village of Beeroth,—called by its present Arab inhabitants Beereh. A copious fountain, which probably gave its name to the village, flows near it. In the neighborhood of the village are extensive ruins. We spent a little time in walking among massive columns and arches,—the remains and testimonies of the art and power of distant ages. The people of the modern village, which is situated at a little distance on a slightly-elevated piece of ground, came down to the fountains. It seemed to be the gathering-place of men and children. The young women also filled their large water-jars and carried them away on their heads. Camels and horses stood at the watering-troughs.

This place, rendered attractive from the earliest times by the abundance of its water and its fertility, is repeatedly mentioned in the Scriptures. It is situated on the road to Damascus, which is also for some distance the great road to Nazareth; and there is a tradition that it was here that Joseph and Mary, on returning from Jerusalem to Nazareth from the feast of the Passover, first discovered that the "child Jesus," who had tarried behind without their knowledge, was not in the company with them.

In accordance with the customs and traditions of the country, which make Beeroth the first stopping-place and the first day's journey from Jerusalem, the people who conducted us were desirous of remaining here through the night. But this was inconsistent with our arrangements and wishes, and we went on three or four miles farther, deviating a little from the main route, and pitched our tents, about the time of sunset, in a field in Bethel. The present name of Bethel is BEITEN,—the Arabic variation of the original Hebrew name. It was natural for us to desire to reach this place, which is associated with interesting names and incidents, and is often mentioned in the Old Testament, though I believe it is not mentioned in the New. The country around Bethel is uneven and rocky; sustaining in that respect the reputation which it seems to have had in the days of the patriarchs. It was here that Jacob, journeying from Beersheba, made at night a pillow of stones, and slept and dreamed, and saw in vision the angels of God ascending and descending upon the ladder of heaven. It was here that the Lord, who styled himself the Lord God of Abraham and Isaac, appeared to Jacob in this midnight vision of angels and of the opened heavens, and spake to him, and promised him the land on which his head was pillowed. And the place, which had been previously called Luz by the Canaanites, Jacob called Bethel or the Lord's house,—the name which it has borne since. We spent the night here, sleeping among the rocks.

Early the next morning we ascended a lofty hill about a mile from our encampment, which seemed to us to correspond to the description given in the twelfth chapter of Genesis:—"a mountain on the east of Bethel, having Bethel on the west and Hai on the east," and where it is said of Abraham, who also as well as Jacob had travelled through this region and at an earlier period, that he "builded an altar unto the Lord and called upon the name of the Lord." Here also are the fragmentary remains of buildings, which are worthy of the notice of the antiquary.

In the time of the Canaanites Bethel was a royal city and the residence of a king; and in the time of Jeroboam, after the revolt of the ten tribes, it obtained an unhappy celebrity as the place selected for idol-worship in opposition to the worship of Jerusalem. It is perhaps impossible at the present time to indicate the precise site of the ancient city. The footprints of a hundred generations have greatly disturbed and nearly obliterated the lines that were drawn around it. The massive hewn stones, however, which are found at intervals on the surface of the ground or projecting from mounds of earth, and the remains of buildings and other works which are found on the hill I have mentioned, or between it and the village which bears the name of Beitin, indicate the existence in ancient times of a large city in this vicinity. There is a large square pool or water-reservoir here, formed of hewn stones, similar in extent and solidity to the great works of this kind which are seen at Hebron and Jerusalem. We found this ancient reservoir, as we did in some other instances, destitute of water.

Pursuing our journey, we reached, on the afternoon of the second day from Jerusalem, the celebrated well which bears the name of the patriarch Jacob. Among the people of the country it is denominated to this day AIN YACOUB, the well or fountain of Jacob,—though it is sometimes called also AIN SAMARIEH, the well of the Samaritan woman. By order of the Syrian Government, as we understood, and for the purpose of preventing the injuries resulting in consequence of persons constantly crowding around it and into it, the top of the well has been closed for a number of years past by large stones placed over it. We found, however, a small opening, which enabled some of our party to let down a long measuring-line, and thus to assure us of the correctness of the Scripture statement, that the "well is deep." Before it was closed, this well had been repeatedly entered and examined by Christian travellers, who agree in ascribing to it a depth of about a hundred feet. Maundrell says of it, "The well is covered at present with an old stone vault, into which you are let down by a very straight hole; and then, removing a broad flat stone, you discover the well itself. It is dug in a firm rock, is about three yards in diameter, and thirty-five in depth, five of which we found full of water."

It was by the side of this well that the wearied Saviour, in his journey from Judea to Galilee, seated himself. And here, in conversation with the Samaritan woman, he uttered those memorable words:—"Whosoever drinketh of the water that I shall give him shall never thirst; but the water that I shall give him shall be in him a well of water, springing up to everlasting life." And it was here that he uttered those other words also, which are similar but still wider in their import:—"The hour cometh, and now is, when the true worshippers shall worship the Father in spirit and in truth; for the Father seeketh such to worship him. God is a Spirit; and they that worship him must worship him *in spirit and in truth.*"

How often have I thought upon these remarkable sayings of the Saviour, so far beyond and above the thoughts and anticipations of his age and his people, not knowing or thinking that I should ever stand upon the spot where they were uttered!

It was in this place it was announced, and from this time it was understood clearly and forever, that the true worship of God is mental rather than physical or local. In other words, it consists in the rectitude of dispositions. The homage which God loves is the soul's harmony with Himself and his infinite relations. The temple of Solomon, emblematic of the formal and restricted nature of the first worship, covered the small circuit of Mount Moriah. It fell at the bidding of Christ; and through its sundered columns this new Captain of our salvation led the emancipated world into the wide and great freedom of God's spiritual temple. The locality of God's temple, overtopping and outshining all human temples, is the infinity of space. It is not necessary to go over six thousand miles of ocean and over burning sands in order to find it. The place of the true worship, no longer exclusively at Jerusalem or Gerizim, is everywhere. Every valley where there is a soul to be tempted and to weep may be a Gethsemane. Every hill-top where there are hearts to rejoice and sing may be a Zion. Every town and secluded village, no matter in what land or beyond what ocean, may become a Bethlehem; and every mind of man which shall break the bonds of selfishness, and make room for his coming, may be a manger where the infant Jesus shall be born. This great announcement, this Magna Charta of spiritual freedom, was made here.

Jacob's well, which suggested this remarkable conversation, is not far from the narrow entrance which separates the mountains of Ebal and Gerizim. It is excavated in the solid rock on the side of a gentle elevation facing to the northeast, which gives a good view of the large and beautiful plain, generally understood to be the land "bought by Jacob of the children of Hamor." It was here that Jacob resided for a time; and there are but few places in Palestine more beautiful and more fruitful than this. It is watered by a large fountain, which flows at a little distance from the well of Jacob. Beyond this clear fresh rivulet, and less than a quarter of a mile's distance north from the well, is the structure which bears the name of the tomb of Joseph. That the body of Joseph was brought from Egypt and was buried in this vicinity, there can be no doubt. It is expressly said in the book of Joshua, that the children of Israel brought the bones of Joseph out of Egypt and buried them in Shechem, "in a parcel of ground which Jacob bought of the sons of Hamor." A square, stone edifice, open at the top, is erected around the supposed place of his interment. But at what time and by whom it was built is unknown. Within it is a small, unostentatious tomb, such as is frequently seen in Oriental burying-grounds, far different from the splendid tomb which I had seen in the rocky heights of Beni Hassan, overhanging the broad bosom of the Nile, and in which, according to the traditions of the country, his remains were deposited till the departure of his people from Egypt.

Leaving this interesting locality, and advancing again upon our journey, we passed at once between the lofty mountains of Ebal and Gerizim. These mountains are twenty-five hundred feet above the level of the sea, and nearly a thousand feet above the valleys and plains immediately around them. Their sides are rocky and steep; and they stand face to face, unchanged and unchangeable, as they stood thousands of years ago. In looking upon the rugged heights of Gerizim, I could not forget that they were anciently occupied by the place of Samaritan worship to which the woman of Samaria alluded in her conversation with the Saviour:—"Our fathers worshipped in *this* mountain.

At the entrance of the mountain-pass which commences near the Well of Jacob, the two mountains approach very near each other at the base,—so near that the human voice, as it seemed to me, might be heard without difficulty from one to the other. It was here, in the beautiful valley between them,—beautiful now, and still more beautiful then,—

that the Ark of the Covenant once stood, in the days of Joshua. Priests and Levites were gathered around it. The tribes of Israel, rejoicing in their victories over the Canaanites, and, if I may so express it, fresh from contemplating the great miracles of God, pressed with their thronging masses into the valley and on the sides of the two mountains. With half of the tribes on Gerizim and half of the tribes on Ebal, they stood and listened to the reading of the Law of Moses, and the blessings and curses of Jehovah,—blessings upon the good and curses upon the evil.

The sight of the mountains where these things actually occurred replaced this remarkable scene among the vivid pictures of imagination and memory; and it was not surprising that the mountains themselves, as we passed between them, should seem a sort of proclamation and testimony of the truth of the historical events with which they had been connected.

Proceeding a little farther, we reached the ancient city of Shechem, which is called Sychar in the New Testament. It is situated in a place in the valley where the two mountains recede a little more from each other,—a mile and a half distant from Jacob's Well, and in a direction nearly west. It is supposed to contain at the present time from six to seven thousand inhabitants. At the time of the Roman domination in Palestine, and about forty years after the death of Christ, the city was enlarged, and underwent so many alterations and improvements that it was called Neapolis, or the new city. It is from the name of Neapolis, which was given to it under these circumstances, that we have the name of Nablous, which is now commonly applied to it. The city of Shechem, if I may be allowed to substitute the ancient and Biblical name for that of Nablous, is often mentioned in the history of the Jews; and at the present moment I think it may be regarded as one of the most flourishing and interesting towns in Palestine.

In this city there are still to be found a few Samaritans,—the diminished and perishing remnants of a once remarkable people, who retain their primitive attachments to the Samaritan institutions and beliefs, and who are understood to be as far as ever from any harmony or any associations with the Jews. When the city of Samaria, in the vicissitudes of war and conquest, had lost its original importance and had gone to decay, it was natural that the Samaritans should select that city as their place of residence and as the centre of their religious authority and polity, which was nearest to the mountain where their fathers worshipped. They pride themselves that they hold to the doctrines and ceremonies of the books of Moses without accepting other portions of the canon of the Old Testament; and it is said that the smoke of their sacrifices even now may be seen ascending from time to time from the heights of Gerizim.

Earnestly did I gaze on the celebrated mountains which enclose the city on both sides with their lofty walls. Ascending a little distance on Mount Gerizim, I could not doubt, from what came under my own notice, that its accessible places had been occupied in early times by the habitations of men; and that the mountain, grand and imposing in itself, had been beautified by works of art. The heights above, massive and rugged with rocks,—the valley below, filled with shrubbery and flowers,—constituted a combination of beauty and grandeur which was not exceeded by anything that had fallen under our observation in any other places of Palestine.

It was at the city of Shechem that we spent the second night after leaving Jerusalem. The trees of the valley waved around our tent. I shut myself within its folds, to make some brief records or to commit more deeply to memory the impressions which had been made upon me. And in the silence of the night I did not forget those words which the circumstances of the day had brought so vividly to mind:—"*God is a Spirit; and they that worship him must worship him in spirit and in truth.*"

(XLIX.)

Arrival at Samaria—Its ancient greatness—Church of John the Baptist—Reach En-Gannim or Jenin—Proceed towards Tabor—Jezreel—Plain of Esdraelon—Arab horsemen—The Gazelle—Shunem—Village of Nain—Arrival at Mount Tabor.

GALILEE, BASE OF MOUNT TABOR, MAY 26, 1853.

ON the morning of the third day after our departure from Jerusalem, we left Shechem,—the Shechem of the Old Testament, but bearing in the New Testament the name of Sychar. We started early in the morning, on our way to another city of still greater celebrity,—the ancient city of Samaria. Our tents had been pitched on a beautiful plain at the foot of Mount Gerizim. Before the light of the morning sun had reached them, they were once more struck, our Syrian horses were saddled, and we went down at once into a deep valley. Through this valley, which greatly attracted our attention in consequence of its various enchantments, there flows a bright and musical stream. It scatters richness in its path. The trees and shrubs which spring up around it are such as are common in these regions,—pomegranates, almonds, olives, mulberries, the fig-tree, the vine, the orange, and the oleander. The valley, in its great fertility, seemed to be loaded everywhere with the yellow richness of its fruits and the varied hues of its flowers. The stars gradually retired from the sky. The golden sunbeams crept silently among the dewy branches. I listened to the voice of the rocky stream. The song of the morning birds answered to the song of the waters. Nature rejoiced and put on her ornaments at the sound of these sweet voices.

Proceeding thus some eight or nine miles in a northern direction through a country contrasting strongly in the whole distance with the barren mountains and plains which are to be found in many other parts of Palestine, we came to the city of Samaria. This city, situated on the side of a lofty but gently-sloping hill, with broad and deep valleys around it, was once the residence of the kings of Israel, after the revolt of the ten tribes against the kings of the house of David. Of the great wealth and splendor of Samaria, at different periods of its history, I suppose there can be no reasonable doubt. It is said in the book of Kings, that Ahab built a palace of ivory in Samaria; and prophetic denunciations, called forth by the luxury and oppressions of the Samaritans, are found in the book of the prophet Amos:—"I will smite the winter-house with the summer-house; and the houses of *ivory* shall perish; and the great houses shall have an end, saith the Lord." These expressions indicate with some distinctness the magnificence of the city of Samaria at an early period. It had its vicissitudes; but its wealth and splendor remained for many years. After the conquest of Palestine by the Romans, and during their authority here, Samaria was selected as a place of viceroyal residence, and was enriched and beautified by works of art. Herod the Great once resided here; and, expending upon it all the vast resources of his genius and tyrannical power, he gave it the proud name of Sebaste, in honor of Augustus Cæsar. Christianity also, at a later period, left the impress of its piety and genius.

Ascending the eastern brow of the Samaritan mount, one of the objects that first met our view was the lofty remains of a Christian church, said to have been built over the body of John the Baptist. Standing afterwards upon the western brow, at a mile's distance from this church, where the beauties of nature eclipsed those of art, I cast my eye along the valleys of Sharon towards the distant Cæsarea and the waters of the Mediterranean. The valleys and the waters live; but cities perish, leaving a sad memorial. All around us the dust was literally sown with columns,—some prostrate at full length on the ground; some partially buried and projecting from the side of the hill; some standing erect in rows and at stated intervals, but without capitals, like wounded and mutilated soldiers on the field of battle; some leaning towards the ground, as if they were borne down with hearts of sorrow, and were mourning the loss of their former greatness. They reminded me of those newly-ploughed fields in America, where the old stumps remain,—the rough and ancient masters of the soil,—refusing with stubbornness to be removed, and projecting raggedly and mournfully from the earth, in all diversities of position.

Art, genius, power, have been here,—idolatry with its abominations, wealth with its luxurious refinements, art with its creative and adjusting eye, tyranny with its kings, the just and purifying dispensation of the Old Testament with the denunciations of its Elijah and Elisha, and the peace, forgiveness, and purity of the New with its early and humble teachers. The weary foot of the Son of God, the teacher from another world, the man unknown, has left its pressure on these hills and valleys. He came from the Jordan to Jerusalem and from Jerusalem to Galilee; and he "*must needs go through Samaria.*"

In our rapid march, we may be said merely to have looked on this interesting place, and then to have departed. We directed our course towards Mount Tabor and the Sea of Galilee. In the afternoon we stopped at Jenin,—the Ginæa of Josephus, and the place which is otherwise called En-Gannim, *the fountain of gardens*. As usual, we pitched our tents outside of the place. Jenin is a considerable town, said to contain two thousand inhabitants, with some families of Greek Christians residing in it. Its houses are of stone; and comparatively it has a marked air of neatness and comfort. It has its bazaar, its public water-reservoir, and numerous gardens fenced in with the prickly pear. We walked through its streets, drank of its fresh and beautiful fountain, made some little purchases, formed the traveller's passing acquaintance with some of its inhabitants, but were not able to connect with it any scriptural associations, except that we here first obtained a sight, as we supposed, of the mountains of Gilboa.

The next day, going in a northerly direction towards Mount Tabor, we passed in the early part of the day the ancient Jezreel. Its modern Arabic name is Zerin, which is formed from the Hebrew by changing *El* into *In*,—a change frequently made,—and by dropping the Yod of the first syllable. It is situated on the eastern side of the great plain of Esdraelon. A few houses, located on a steep rocky eminence which projects from the mountains of Gilboa and overlooks the plain, but with nothing inviting or remarkable in their appearance, constitute all that now remains of this once considerable place. Travellers speak of a few ancient ruins here; but we did not go into the place, and, in passing it, noticed nothing but an old and broken sarcophagus by the wayside. The celebrated valley of Jezreel, which extends along the northern base of Gilboa, and connects with the great plain of Esdraelon, opens into the plain not far from the elevated site of the city of Jezreel. From this valley there are fountains—one of considerable size—flowing towards the Jordan. It was here, at the foot and on the sides of Gilboa, and at the junction of the valley of Jezreel with Esdraelon, and near the fountains I have mentioned, that Saul and Jonathan were encamped in their last disastrous battle with the Philistines.

The great plain of Esdraelon is bounded by Mount Carmel on the west, and by Tabor, Hermon, and Gilboa on the east. Proceeding over the plain in a north direction from Jezreel, we came, at the distance of four miles, to Shunem, the place of the encampment of the Philistines in the great struggle which was so disastrous to the Israelites, —so that the two armies were encamped in sight of each other. Shunem is now called Solam. Its situation is elevated and pleasant. This place was the residence of the Shunamite woman, with whom the prophet Elisha resided, and whose son he raised from the dead. From the high ground of Shunem there is a good view of this great plain in the direction of Carmel.

As we were passing this part of the plain of Esdraelon, our Arab horsemen had a good opportunity to exercise their skill in horsemanship, for which they are much renowned. Their horses are small, but full of life and exceedingly tractable. I am not prepared to say that they have all the intelligence which Lamartine and other travellers have sometimes ascribed to them; but, whether it be a part of their natural traits, or is owing to that early and familiar training to which they are accustomed, they certainly seem to have a strange perception of their position, and to sympathize with their masters in a remarkable degree. They are evidently susceptible of feelings of pride and mortification, and appear to understand very well that their master's honor is their own. They are well trained. Their riders are skilful. They move with great swiftness,—stopping at once in their rapid course at a single word. They wheel suddenly. The dust rises under their flying feet. They bound over the rocks.

When we were passing the part of the plain of Esdraelon which is between Jezreel and Shunem, and our Arabs in great spirits were showing the skill of their horses, they suddenly started a beautiful gazelle, that was feeding quietly on the plain. The fleetest Arab horseman at once gave pursuit. The gazelle crossed our path directly in front of me, taking a course over the partially-cultivated fields, bounding from furrow to furrow and from rock to rock. For some time it was a doubtful contest. After a time the gazelle suddenly stopped and looked around, as if to understand more fully the character of his pursuer. I involuntarily stopped my horse, and looked on with sad amazement at this apparently hopeless want of wisdom on the part of the poor animal. But in a moment, as if he had ascertained precisely the rapidity of his enemy's movement and the danger and necessities of his own position, he started again with renewed speed. Fear or hope carried him over the reeds and rocks as if his little feet trod on the wings of the wind. I must confess I experienced no small feeling of satisfaction when the baffled Arab wheeled around his panting and smoking horse and came slowly back to our company. The victorious gazelle, gaining the top of a rock on a little hill and lifting its sharp horn in triumph, looked round with innocent but indignant astonishment at this sudden and strange invasion of the realm which God had given and consecrated to its life, its beauty, and its freedom.

Shunem is situated at the western extremity of the mountain called the Little Hermon. Turning the western end of Hermon, we came about noon of the same day to the small village of Nain, on the northern slope of this mountain,—the place where the Saviour raised the widow's son to life. The touching and sublime narrative of the miracle performed in this ancient city gave to the place a peculiar interest. Its situation is pleasant,—so much so as probably to have given origin to its name, which means *the beautiful.* It is now small and decayed; but we saw enough in its present ruined condition to satisfy us that it might have been, and probably was, far different from its present state in former times. On the same side of Hermon, but farther east, and apparently a mile and a half distant, is the village (or perhaps I should rather say the *site* of the village) of Endor,—the residence of the strange and mysterious woman whom Saul in his troubles visited just before his final battle. Endor is in sight from Nain, on a gentle slope of the Little Hermon, but was more distinctly seen as we advanced farther upon the plain. Continuing our journey across the plain of Esdraelon in a northeastern direction, and passing the dry channels of small streams which seemed to be tributaries of the river Kishon, we have pitched our tents again, early in the afternoon of this day, (May 26,) at the base of Mount Tabor. Tabor is distant from Nain about four miles; and is sixteen miles, as near as we could judge from our rate of movement, from En-Gannim or Jenin,—the place from which we started in the morning.

At the base of Tabor, and at a little distance from our encampment, is the pleasant Arab village of Deburieh. It has its cultivated fields in front, reaching out into the great plain, its gardens around it with their strong hedges of prickly pear, and its full, sparkling fountain of water, the Ain-El-Sherar, which flows into the Kishon. By some persons, I believe, the fountain which rises here is considered the central and principal branch of that river. I have observed here, as almost everywhere else in this region, flocks of sheep and goats, and numerous oxen and camels. The people of the village, quietly pursuing their labors, are gathering in the products of the fields. In going through this town I have noticed in repeated instances large and deep excavations in the rocks beneath the surface of the ground, but without any suitable opportunity to make inquiries in relation to them. Undoubtedly the region at the foot of this mountain has teemed with population in former ages; but time, which erases the past in giving birth to the present, has left but few intimations and marks of their existence and history.

(L.)

Ascent of Tabor—Fortifications on its summit—Historical references—Death of Saul and Jonathan—Elegy of David—Remarks upon David—The Transfiguration.

GALILEE, MOUNT TABOR: SECOND LETTER.

SOON after our arrival at the base of Mount Tabor, we ascended to its top. Entirely separate from the other mountains, which are seen at no great distance around it, it arises out of the north-eastern part of the great plain of Esdraelon, in graceful and solitary beauty. Taking a circuitous route, which was rendered necessary by the steepness of the mountain, we were enabled to ascend the greater part of the way on horseback. There are a number of such winding paths leading from the base to the summit. Selecting that which commenced at the village near us, we followed the leadership of two Arab horsemen whom we had taken as guides, and who seemed to find, in the roughness and steepness of the ascent, something which harmonized with their own wild and unregulated spirits. Although the narrow way which we travelled was rocky and difficult, our small but well-trained horses had been so much accustomed to such rough places, that the ascent was completed in a little less than an hour. The sides of the mountain are everywhere covered with trees and clumps of bushes. The oak-tree is frequently met with. A tall, coarse grass grows among the rocks.

The form of the mountain is that of a sugar-loaf or of a truncated cone, and, standing apart from other mountains, and being clothed with trees and herbage to its top, it justifies, in its appearance, the celebrity which it has long possessed. Its height has been estimated at various times by travellers. It rises about eighteen hundred feet above the Mediterranean, (whose waters can be seen from its top,) and a thousand feet above the plain immediately below it. From the irregular and rocky edge of its summit we looked directly down upon our tents, which were pitched in a grove of olives at its base. The mules and horses of our little caravan were fastened under the trees. At a little distance from the tents the ancient Arab village of Deburieh, to which I have already alluded, was also in sight. It is from the centre of this village that the fresh and living spring of Ain-El-Sherar sends out its contributions to fertilize the surrounding plain, and to swell in the rainy season the waters of the Kishon.

The summit of Tabor is an oblong plain, nearly level, not far from a mile in circuit, and covered with tall grass, shrubs, and trees. The remains of ancient fortifications are found upon it, which appear to have been originally of great strength. It appears from the historical writings of Josephus, who held a military command in Galilee, that fortifications were erected upon this summit by his own orders, with a view to resist the progress of the arms of Vespasian. It had probably been held as a military position at an earlier period.

The prospect from the top of Mount Tabor can hardly be exceeded in extent and beauty. The region where the Saviour spent a large portion of his life was spread out in its length and breadth before us. In the eastern direction, and at a few miles' distance, is the Little Hermon, and beyond it the celebrated mountain-range of Gilboa. The city of Nazareth, not distinctly visible, on account of being shut in by hills, is in the west, and only at the distance of six miles. The sunken valley of the Sea of Galilee, with its hills and valleys around, is distinctly seen in the northeast. The vast plain of Esdraelon expanded itself at our feet. Here is the city of Shunem. Here are the sites of Megiddo, Jezreel, and Taanach. Here are the pathway and the waters of the Kishon.

The plain of Esdraelon, remarkable in its physical features, has other claims upon the traveller's notice. It possesses an historical celebrity which attaches to few other places. In the year 1799, a fierce battle was fought here between the French under the command of General Kleber, and a Syrian army much larger in numbers. Kleber was relieved from his perilous position, and the Turco-Syrian army was defeated, by the opportune arrival of Bonaparte, who thus brought his name, which fills a large place in the sanguinary and disastrous annals of men, into association with the names and places of Biblical history. This plain, at an earlier period, was the scene of the severe contest between Barak and Sisera, with which the readers of the Bible are familiar. Barak seems to have made his head-quarters near this mountain. The expressions in the Scriptures are, "Barak went down from Mount Tabor, and ten thousand men with him." Sisera was defeated; and the triumphal song of Deborah and Barak, with its highly-poetic allusions to Taanach and Megiddo and "the ancient river of

Kishon," its eulogy of Jael, and its graphic description of the mother of Sisera, celebrated a victory which gave rest to the land for forty years. It was here that the Jewish king Josiah was defeated and lost his life, in a contest with Pharaoh Necho, king of Egypt. And it was in a great battle with the Philistines, on the plain of Esdraelon and at the foot of Gilboa, that Saul and Jonathan were slain.

The story of the last battle and of the fall of Saul and Jonathan has a peculiar and melancholy interest. I had always felt the affecting sadness of its incidents, and my presence among the scenes where their death occurred renewed those early feelings. The monarch of Israel, standing face to face with what he felt to be the last and decisive hour of his destiny, experienced, in his want of faith, the loss and want of that moral strength which was necessary for the encounter. And, what a want, what a loss, was this! Man is so constituted that he must believe in something. Such is the innate sense of his own weakness when he is placed in difficult and trying circumstances, that he finds it a strong necessity of his nature which compels him to seek some support. And if he does not trust in God, he will naturally and almost necessarily look round for something else. Saul had ceased to place confidence in the God of Abraham and Isaac, and went to seek counsel of the Witch of Endor. The scene of this remarkable and unbelieving visit is all in sight. It was here—over these plains and around these mountains—that the humiliated monarch, shrouded in the darkness of the night and in the mists of the valley, found his way to her mysterious dwelling. Strange was the vision that met him. The earth opened, and an "old man came up." Terrible was the denunciation which was uttered.

> "Death stood all glassy in his fixed eye;
> His hands were wither'd, and his veins were dry;
> His foot in bony whiteness glitter'd there,
> Shrunken and sinewless, and ghastly bare.
> Saul saw, and fell to earth as falls the oak,
> At once, and blasted by the thunder-stroke."

The poetry of the English bard has not exceeded the simple but sublime and terrific statement of the Scriptures.

In deep astonishment and sorrow the Jewish king arose from the ground, on which he had fallen prostrate. He went back to the foot of Gilboa, where his soldiers awaited him. He again put on his armor; but military skill has no power against the decisions of Providence. God had left him. His spear, without a higher power to hold and direct it, was shivered in his grasp. And in dying he left a melancholy name, which has attracted the memory and the sympathies of men, because it was associated with that of Jonathan, and because it is celebrated in song.

As I stood upon the top of Tabor, and cast my eye towards the region where Saul fought and fell, I felt anew how genius consecrates place,—how mind immortalizes matter. I remembered the touching allusion to Gilboa in the sad elegy of David. I have already had occasion to speak of this great king and poet. And here also, amid the mingled scenery of plains and mountains which he has celebrated in his songs, he is once more brought to mind. In the overthrow of the king who persecuted him and of the king's son who loved him, unable to help, but with a heart full of pity, he could only pour forth his lamentations in such strains of tenderness and beauty as no other one could utter.

A great poet is necessarily great in his character,—and is great also, or is likely to be so, in the circumstances which surround him. David was a poet, because in his life and character he was himself a poem,—a great dramatic and epic history, reaching from the shepherd to the king, and filled up with thoughts, affections, and actions. And, worthy to be celebrated himself, he imparted immortality to others, because his intercourse with God had opened in his own soul the fresh springs of immortal life.

But if mind consecrates and immortalizes matter, it is equally true that material nature, in connection with the incidents of personal situation and relations, give a character and development to mind. The fact that the mind's inspiration, so far as it is really great and true, is from God, is not at all inconsistent with the additional and the obvious fact, that whatever is special in the character and mode of its action is from the subordinate providence of situation and circumstances. This whole region seemed to me to claim the great Jewish poet as a child even now. The mind of David, as it is recorded and represented in the Bible, shows, too distinctly to leave any doubt, in what land and under what influences of religion and of history it developed itself. If Homer, separated from his own enchanted Greece, could not have been Homer, but would have missed and lost the secret of his own powers amid the strange scenery and manners and the barbarous language of the British Isles, or of other rude and uncivilized places of his time, David could not have been what he was in any other country, among any other mountains, and under any other institutions and histories than those of Palestine.

This region is connected with another and far more illustrious name than those which have been mentioned. It was the scene of the early life, and, at a later period, of many of the miracles, of Christ. I can look from this spot upon the village of Nain, on the western side of the Little Hermon, where he raised the young man to life, the only son of his widowed mother. Brought up in Nazareth, and possessing a heart and eye open to the beauties of nature, it cannot be supposed that he was ignorant of the varied and beautiful scenery between Tabor, Nazareth, and the Sea of Galilee. In nature he saw and loved the God of nature. It reminded him only of truth and beauty, and not of sorrow and sin. He visited, no doubt, these very heights. He looked down upon this great plain. He beheld the rising and the setting sun here. His locks were wet with these morning and evening dews. To these interesting incidents, however, I may perhaps take another opportunity to allude, and shall leave them now.

Of one thing, however, I am obliged to speak here. "And after six days," it is said in the Scripture narrative, "Jesus taketh Peter and James, and John his brother, and bringeth them up into a high mountain apart, and was transfigured before them. And his face did shine as the sun, and his raiment was bright as the light." According to a tradition reaching back to the close of the third century or about that period, this was the mountain on which Christ was thus transfigured. The mere fact of such a tradition has some weight with me. As a general thing, traditions may well be supposed to have a basis in fact. The nature and instincts of the human mind require this supposition. It is undoubtedly true that traditions may be falsified, like everything else. But, if nothing specific and reliable can be said against them, the presumption, more or less, is in their favor.

One of the objections, perhaps the leading one, to the tradition that Mount Tabor was the scene of the Transfiguration, is the fact that its summit was at that time a fortified place, and that the presence of soldiers was inconsistent with that seclusion and silence which were appropriate to such an occurrence. To estimate accurately such an objection, a person must visit the mountain itself. It is probably true that soldiers were stationed in the fortifications the remains of which still exist on the summit of the mountain; but it is not very likely, under the strict requisitions of Roman discipline, that they were permitted to roam about very freely over all parts of the mountain. The base of the mountain is some six or eight miles in circuit at least; and any one who has been upon it must be satisfied, I think, that it would have been easy, in the vast circuit of its sides which fill up such an area, to find many places suited to religious retirement. The Transfiguration, witnessed only by a small number of persons, would not require a large place; and of all the mountains in this region, it will probably be conceded that there is no one which harmonizes so well in its attractive and imposing character with the sublime and joyful nature of the event.

In estimating this question, I think we should not forget the mutual attractions of the mind and of outward nature,—attractions which have a permanent foundation and are universal in their operation. Every inward mood of the mind may be well supposed to have its counterpart, its correspondence, in something which is external; and it is in connection with this mutual adaptation that these attractions exist. Accordingly, the mind in its sorrow seeks the shade; in its joy it seeks the garden of flowers; in its hour of contemplation it wanders into the place of silence and retirement; in its sociality it mingles with the companies of men. When the Saviour was baptized, and the Holy Ghost descended upon him and proclaimed him the "beloved Son," he stood upon the banks of the Jordan. The waters were an emblem of his purity. The balmy incense of trees floated around him, and flowers bloomed at his feet. When he was in the sorrow and darkness of his first great temptation, it was not by the river's side, but in the wilderness. He sought a place where desolation could harmonize with grief. He climbed alone some rugged height, —perhaps the traditionary Quarantana,—barren, dark, flowerless, where truth and beauty never come, and never had a disposition to come, except in the hour of trial and of tears. When he was about to be transfigured and to put on, though only for a short time and as it were experimentally, the clothing of his celestial glory, it was a natural instinct of his heart, a law of his inward perfection, which led him to ascend a mountain rather than go down into a valley, to go among flowers and foliage rather than among desolate rocks, and among all the mountains of his native Galilee to select that which stands apart from all others in its solitary but unexampled beauty.

Such were some of the recollections and thoughts which passed through my mind on Mount Tabor. We descended to our tents just as the sun was shedding his parting rays over the distant heights of Carmel.

(LI.)

Departure from Mount Tabor—Appearance of the country between Tabor and Tiberias—First view of the lake—Valley and city of Tiberias—Jews—The Mishna—Emmaus — Turkish regiment—Beauty of the lake—Country around it—Scriptural references—Poetry.

GALILEE, CITY OF TIBERIAS, MAY 28, 1853.

WE could have spent with much interest a longer time at Mount Tabor and in its vicinity; but the increasing heat, and a desire to reach Beirout as early as possible, did not permit us to delay. The remembrance of our own country, and the anticipated pleasure of once more meeting with our distant friends, began to mingle with our thoughts. We left the mountain on Friday, the 27th of May, early in the morning, on our way to the Sea of Galilee,—the sea, or more properly the *lake*, so often mentioned in the Scriptures, and associated with so many interesting events. We wished to see its celebrated waters, and to catch a view of the surrounding scenery, without being able to allow to it much time. Our destination, therefore, was Tiberias,—the principal town which now remains upon its banks. As we left the mountain, the beautiful hills of Nazareth, covered with groves of small oaks, were in sight.

The road from Tabor to the Sea of Galilee runs in a northeasterly direction, and the distance is not far from twelve miles. It runs at first along the lower side of the mountain, among cliffs and clusters of trees, and when it reaches into a more level country it is frequently broken and irregular. It passes over hills and rocky swells with names unknown to me, and over the plain El-Hamma, which extends in the direction of the Jordan. On our left, and not far distant from our route, there is a valley of some extent, which carries its waters westward into the Kishon. It is supposed to be the valley of Jiphtah, which is repeatedly mentioned in the book of Joshua. Our route, thus diversified with alternations of ascent and descent, of plain and hill, presented continually some new views of nature,—views, whatever may be their characteristics, which are always interesting to those who have seen the countries of the East for the first time. Leaving a number of high hills on our left, one of which was the hill or mount of Tell Hattin, to which reference is often made by travellers, we obtained our first distinct view both of the Lake of Galilee and of the city of Tiberias, from the brow of a lofty and steep eminence, over which the road from Mount Tabor approaches the lake and city from the west. We were at that time, as I judged, about a mile and a half distant from Tiberias.

The descent from the lofty hill which I have mentioned was over a long line of steep and irregular rocks, so dangerous, as it seemed to me, that I chose to walk a considerable part of the way rather than ride. I had experienced on one occasion, by the fall of my horse on a smooth and slippery ledge, that the good training of the Syrian horses, and a sort of instinctive foresight and carefulness which they manifest, are not a perfect security against these dangers. The view on the summit and side of this hill is exceedingly interesting. The eye first looks down upon the Lake of Galilee,—or the Sea of Galilee, as it is called in the Scriptures,—which is in view nearly in its whole extent. It is not a large body of water, being only sixteen miles in length by an average of four or five in breadth. I now saw it, with the exception of the partial glimpses from the top of Mount Tabor, for the first time. The sun shone brightly; there was scarcely a breath of air stirring; there was no cloud upon the sky, and, in the deep calm and silence of nature, the lake lay in the arms of the steep mountains around it, like an infant in the lap of its mother, and with an aspect of tranquil and almost sad repose. But when the heavy winds and storms which sometimes occur break over the mountain-tops and come down upon its calm and sleeping surface, it is easy to see that it might be suddenly and easily agitated and thrown into the white dashing waves of the tempest. Fleets have been built here, and naval battles fought upon its surface; but that was in the days of its ancient prosperity; and I saw only one small boat upon it at this time.

The hills recede from the lake on the side of Tiberias, leaving a pleasant plain or valley, though somewhat irregular in its surface, between the water and the base of the surrounding heights. There was every appearance to me that this undulating plain was once a place of great fertility. The site of Tiberias, in the centre of this once fruitful spot, was obviously well chosen. The city, which is surrounded on the land-side by a strong wall a mile and a half in circuit, is built upon the shore of the lake. It bears the marks and characteristics of antiquity and Orientalism, without any thing in particular which distinguishes it from the old cities of the East. We noticed, however, on the flat roofs of the houses, what we had not observed elsewhere, or but seldom, a sort of temporary tent, erected of long reeds and branches of trees, which seemed to be occupied chiefly as places of rest in the warm nights of the summer. Though the country around the city was once fruitful, it has now an aspect of want and desolation. I missed much the fountains, trees, and gardens which sometimes imparted an air of cheerfulness to other towns and cities. On the south side and near the sea are the remains of an old and strong fortification, which has been rent and shaken to its foundations by the earthquakes which have occurred here.

I will not undertake to say much in commendation of Tiberias, although the general impression I received was more favorable than that which has been left upon the minds of some other travellers. It cannot be denied that the aspect of an Oriental city has not much in its favor in the eye of a European or an American. There is not time to the passing traveller for the readjustment of old habits and thoughts. He is apt to forget that he is in another land and under a different climate. And hence, in judging of the large towns of the East, he is liable to make a very low estimate of them,—not only of their material comforts, but of their civilization and their social character. A closer examination might give a more correct estimate. Within the dark and mutilated walls of the houses which line their narrow streets, there is probably more intelligence, refinement, and comfort, than would be at first supposed.

There is a comfortable hotel within the limits of Tiberias, kept by a Jew; but, thinking it better for us, in the pleasant weather which we experienced, to remain in our tents, we pitched them outside of the walls; but we were permitted to enter and leave the city whenever we chose. The place is not large; the number of inhabitants is said to be two thousand; but that probably, judging from what came under our notice, is a low estimate. It has fallen into decay, but there are still some signs of business. The situation of the place is such, relatively to the other parts of Galilee, that it cannot altogether lose its importance. The river Jordan flows through the lake; and Tiberias is in a situation to command the region both of the Upper and Lower Jordan. We found a regiment of Turkish soldiers encamped here, a little to the south of the city. This was said to be in consequence of some disturbance among the people on the opposite side of the lake.

There are many Jews in the city. As I was walking along in one of the streets near the seashore, I addressed a man for the purpose of making some inquiries, whom I found to be a Jew, and who appeared to be a man of intelligence and culture. He was acquainted with a number of languages, and had some knowledge of the English, though he spoke it imperfectly. He conducted me into the Jewish Quarter, which is in the middle of the city, and into two Jewish synagogues, one of which had the appearance of neatness and even elegance. He seemed willing to converse, and I gathered from his conversation that the strong prejudices which formerly existed among his people against Christians were disappearing to some extent.

Tiberias is understood to be a favorite resort of the Jews. They attach to it, as compared with many other places in Galilee, a peculiar sanctity. It has also some interest with scholars, on account of the reputation it formerly enjoyed as one of the principal places of Jewish teaching and culture,—a reputation which it has retained to some extent even to modern times. After the destruction of the city of Jerusalem by the Romans, a number of eminent Jews collected together at this city and established a school of learning. Some of the teachers in the school or college which was thus founded were men of high reputation for knowledge. It was here that the Mishna was written,—a work containing the traditionary opinions of the Jews on matters of religious doctrine and practice. It was written or rather compiled near the commencement of the third century, by a learned Jew at the head of the school of Tiberias, and constitutes, with its continuation at a later period, under the name of the

Gemara, that celebrated Jerusalem Talmud which has had so great weight with the Jewish people.

At the distance of a mile and a half from Tiberias, and not far from the outlet of the Jordan, is Emmaus,—a place of some celebrity on account of its warm mineral baths. The name of Emmaus, which is descriptive in its meaning of the places to which it is applied, is given to other places which have warm mineral waters. The small stream which supplies the baths here issues from the base of the surrounding hills. This place, which is mentioned by Josephus and has had a long celebrity, was visited by my American friends, from whom I learned the most that I know of it. It was once a place of very considerable resort. Buildings suitable for bathing are still erected upon it. The water has been analyzed by chemists, but it is not necessary to repeat the results here. My friends found it of a very high temperature; so much so as almost to lead one to conjecture that it has a connection with those subterranean fires which from time to time rend and shake this volcanic region.

It was not convenient for me to go there, but this circumstance gave me a little more time to stroll along the lake-shore. There was no want of objects, either natural or artificial, to take up my attention. It was difficult for me to turn my eyes from this beautiful sheet of water, with the dark mountains hanging over it. I watched the ripples of the gentle waves as they fell softly on the pebbly bank. The water is as clear as a mountain-brook. I gathered beautiful shells. I saw flights of birds, such as usually make their haunts near lakes and rivers. I stopped to watch the multitudes of small fishes playing near the shore. The fish in this lake are abundant. A person cannot walk on its shores without seeing them in great numbers; so that it is not surprising that this place was formerly the abode of fishermen, as it is now, though in a less degree.

And then my attention was arrested by other objects. The drum beat here as I heard it in the deserts of Mount Sinai,—a sound which has its stirring but unpleasant associations. War is everywhere. My attention, therefore, was diverted from these objects of nature by the military manœuvres of the Turkish regiment already mentioned, which was stationed on the plain between the shore and the high hills that bound it on the west. The soldiers went through the formulary of military discipline; and afterwards, at sunset, I noticed that they repeated, under orders and drawn up in line, the prostrations and prayers of Mohammedan worship. And then I looked from the floating crescent, the symbol of Mohammedan power, to the mountains beyond. On the sides of the surrounding heights which overlooked the encampment of the soldiers are numerous excavations. The hand of nature and of human art has been there. We had not the time at command which was necessary to explore these dark excavations and to learn their history; but it is probable that some of them are the ancient tombs which have been mentioned from time to time by travellers. Undoubtedly, this remarkable valley and these rocky hills have been a great burying-place. Millions of inhabitants have occupied these now desolate places. Time, which completes the destiny of nations, has swept them away, and their record remains in part in the dust beneath the traveller's feet. As I walked along the shore, I noticed the remains of walls and columns which indicate that the ancient city, built or at least enlarged in honor of a Roman emperor, extended in the direction of Emmaus and of the outlet of the Jordan. These remains are sad but convincing evidences, which establish, beyond any reasonable question, the fact of its original wealth, refinement, and greatness.

Attempts have been made to compare the Lake of Galilee with other lakes. To me it seemed highly beautiful, but with such marked and distinctive characteristics that it would be difficult to bring it into comparison. Beauty, however, is the result of two forces or powers,—that which is found in the object, and that which is found in the heart which interprets the object. It thus has two eyes, if we may so express it, which look into each other and complete the image of its contemplation by their combined action; but when the veil of some inward sorrow or perverseness is upon the traveller's mind, one of the eyes of beauty is put out, and only half of her glory is seen. And thus there are differences of opinion, sometimes as to the fact of beauty, and still more frequently as to the degree. But, however this may be, eminent beauty has been here. No eye is so blind as not to see it. And yet it is necessary to add, amid the heavy blows of time, nature, and Providence, that it is beauty in its widowhood,—shining in tears.

I said it would be difficult to bring the Lake of

Galilee into comparison with other lakes. I have not been in Switzerland; but once in the interior of America—in my own land, in the wild mountainous region of New Hampshire—I saw a lake, of which I have been reminded by that of Tiberias. It bears the name of the Newfound Lake. As I was travelling, I came upon it unexpectedly. It is some eight or ten miles in length. It is near the head-waters of the beautiful mountain-stream which the primitive inhabitants called the Pemigewasset. Like Galilee, it is without islands, or nearly so. It lay dark and motionless in the bosom of barren and rocky heights; and I was much struck with its peculiar expression of thoughtful and solitary beauty.

This lake and the country around it is the scene of many interesting incidents mentioned in the New Testament. To the northwest, on a lofty eminence which rises some twenty-five hundred feet above the Mediterranean, is the city of Safed, to which the Saviour is supposed to have made allusion as the "city set upon a hill, which could not be hid." At the head of the lake, on the western and northwestern shore, and not far distant from each other, were once the ancient cities of Bethsaida, Chorazin, and Capernaum. The site of Capernaum has been ascertained with a considerable degree of probability by the learned American travellers Smith and Robinson; but the precise locality of Chorazin and Bethsaida, though we have reason to suppose it to have been on the same shore of the lake and not far from Capernaum, is not definitely known.

This lake was the scene of the miraculous draught of fishes. The traditional place where it occurred is still pointed out; and at a little distance from the shore, and in part in commemoration of this remarkable event, a Catholic church is erected, called the church of St. Peter. By some, however, this church is said to be built over the site of the house of Peter, who resided here,—with the design to commemorate the place of his residence. It was here, on this sea, that the Saviour sat in a boat and taught the thronging multitudes. It was here, among the fishermen who pursued their humble and laborious calling on these shores, that he selected a number of his disciples. "And Jesus, walking by the Sea of Galilee, saw two brethren, Simon called Peter, and Andrew his brother, casting a net into the sea, for they were fishers. And he saith unto them, Follow me, and I will make you fishers of men." It was here that he walked upon the waters. It was here, when there was a great tempest and the ship was covered with the waves, that "he arose and rebuked the winds and the sea, and there was a great calm." And it was probably upon one of the heights rising above these waters (an old tradition says upon Tell Hattin) that he uttered those remarkable sayings—without precedent in the annals of mere human thought and wisdom—which constitute the Sermon on the Mount.

At evening I stood at the door of our tent. The stars began to show themselves again. The lake was at a little distance. I heard its gentle voice. Excepting the sound of the waters, there was silence on the plain and on the mountains. One feeling occupied my heart. One thought subordinated all others.

LINES WRITTEN AT THE LAKE OF GALILEE.

Strange is the deep, mysterious tie
Which makes departed ages nigh:
But God has form'd it; and its power
Has mark'd with me this sacred hour.
'Twas thus, I thought, as thy bright sea,
Blue-tinted wave of Galilee,
With gentle sound and motion sank
Upon the bold and rocky bank.

O lake and land where memories last
Which link the present to the past;
Whose waves and rocky heights restore
Departed scenes and forms once more!
'Twas here He press'd the conscious earth;
'Twas here His heavenly thoughts had birth.
Oh, give me back, if yet ye can,
This "Son of God," this "Son of man."

He comes; He walks upon the sea:—
"Have faith," He says, "*and walk with me.*"
I go,—I sink; He takes my hand;
I, too, upon the waters stand.
But soon from cliff and mountain-side
The tempest sweeps the foaming tide;
The lightnings flash; the billows rise;
Storms lift and dash them to the skies.

'Twas to the weak His hand He gave:
And has He power the weak to save?
Fierce and more fierce the billows roll,
But FAITH has anchor'd in the soul.
Amid the clouds I see His form;
I hear His voice amid the storm;
The tempest listens to His will;
The winds are hush'd; the waves are still.

(LII.)

Departure from Tiberias—Reach Cana of Galilee—Miracle of the water and wine—Of other places said to bear the name of Cana—Village of Raneh—First sight of Nazareth—Its situation and appearance—Mary's fountain—Franciscan convent—Residence of Joseph and Mary—Joseph's workshop—Brow of the hill—Of Jesus Christ—His personal appearance—Christ as a propitiatory sacrifice—Christ as a moral teacher—Results of his teachings.

GALILEE, CITY OF NAZARETH, MAY 30, 1853.

WE left Tiberias on our way to "Cana of Galilee" and the city of Nazareth. Ascending the lofty hill to the west of the city, we took a last view of the distant Safed, of the plain of Genesareth, of the desolate sites of Chorazin and Bethsaida, and of the lake and its mountains. About noon we reached Cana,—known to the inhabitants at the present time under the name of Kefr Cana. Passing through the village, which covers a portion of a small hill, we stopped for the purposes of rest and refreshment in a grove of olive-trees at a little distance. This grove is on the side of the hill. A small brook, from which the village is supplied with water, flowed at a short distance below us.

It was at this village, if the common tradition is a correct one, that the Saviour performed the miracle of converting water into wine. And hence the brook or fountain which I have mentioned is an object of interest with travellers, as having furnished the water which was thus miraculously changed.

The place of this remarkable miracle is called, in the Scriptures, "Cana of Galilee," in order to distinguish it from another Cana near the Mediterranean, and within the limits of the tribe of Asher. There are other circumstances, in addition to its name, which aid in some degree in indicating its locality. When the son of a certain nobleman at Capernaum was healed, the Saviour was at this place. The nobleman came to Cana, and, desirous that Jesus should visit his son at his own residence, he besought him that he "*would come down*." And again it is said of the nobleman, in his return to Capernaum, "As he was now *going down*, his servants met him, and told him, saying, Thy son liveth." We found that these expressions correspond well with the situation of Cana as compared with that of Capernaum,—the site of the latter place being, in its relative position, much lower. It does not appear that there are many references to Cana in early ecclesiastical writers. It is mentioned, however, by St. Jerome, in a letter to one of his friends by the name of Marcella, as a place known in his time, and as being "*near to Nazareth*,"—expressions which also harmonize well with the locality of this village.

And yet it is possible, I suppose, that Kefr Cana is a comparatively new village, which has taken the place and which bears the name of some older and deserted village in the vicinity. Such, at least, is the opinion of some persons. Mr. Thompson and myself were taken, by a guide whom we obtained at the village, to a rocky hill, a mile and a half distant, where the remains of an ancient village may be seen, which the guide seems to have regarded as the original Cana. There is another place, to the north of this, which bears the name of Cana. It is situated within the limits of the large plain of Buttauf. This place is some six or seven miles distant from Kefr Cana. Only a few remains of buildings are now seen there. We intended to have gone to this ancient and decayed place, but, our guide professing to be ignorant of its situation, and being quite unwilling to attempt to find it, we gave up our purpose. The place last named was visited by our learned countryman, Dr. Robinson, who gives reasons which are worthy of much consideration, in favor of the supposition that the Cana of Buttauf is the true Cana of the Gospels.

A few of these questions remain to be settled by time and further inquiries. The resident people and Christians in Palestine, who have the control of the "sacred places," as they are called, seem to have decided in favor of the Cana which is nearest to Nazareth. It was natural that we should take much interest in this place, notwithstanding the doubts which attach to it. We were shown, accordingly, into the small but neat church erected over the traditionary place where the Saviour performed his first miracle. Like the other churches of Palestine, both Greek and Catholic, it is adorned with a number of paintings, which, however, are of no especial merit. We saw here also, in the interior of the building, and arrayed in a row on the side of the wall, a number of large water-jars made of stone and capable of holding from ten to twelve gallons each. Of the history of these jars, although they are regarded here as having some connection with the miracle, we could obtain no information which would be entitled to reliance. Large jars of this kind, some of them whole and others broken, were seen by us in the fields of this village and in the vicinity of its houses,—just as we had seen in other places the scattered and broken fragments of columns.

Resuming our journey, we went from Cana to Nazareth. Before reaching Nazareth, and at about two miles' distance, we passed a small, secluded village on our right,—beautified by its fountain and trees. There were many people at the fountain, watering their flocks and camels. This is probably the place which has sometimes been mentioned by travellers under the name of Raneh.

We approached the city of Nazareth over the hill, which lies to the south of it. It was from the summit of this hill that we obtained our first view. Immediately below us was a basin or low sunken valley, running in a northeast direction. It connects in that direction with the great valley or plain of Esdraelon. The eye could easily and accurately survey it for the distance of more than a mile. On the eastern and western sides were lofty hills, approaching each other at the base, but gradually separating to the distance of half a mile. The eastern hill is partially cultivated. The city of Nazareth is directly opposite, on the rocky slope of the hill on the western side. The deep valley, the precipitous rocks, the city, the hills, the lofty sycamores, the groves of olives, the green grassy spots upon which the flocks of goats and sheep repose, formed a wild but variegated and romantic picture which is not often seen.

At the base of the southern hill and on the western side of the valley we pitched our tents under the shade of some tall sycamore-trees. A little below the place of our tents there is a fountain, which flows through the valley towards the plain of Esdraelon. Many persons, chiefly young women, were almost constantly passing and repassing with water-jars on their heads. The fountain is called Mary's fountain, in memory of the mother of the Redeemer; and it is certainly a reasonable supposition, when we remember the customs of the country, that she often came to its waters in company with the "child Jesus." The fountain cannot have changed its position, and the customs of the country are the same that existed at that time.

The city, which is surrounded by walls, is at a little distance, occupying in all probability the precise place where it stood in the time of Christ. Bare, frowning rocks tower above it. To the top of these rocks we did not go; but it is said that their summit, rising some fifteen hundred feet above the sea, furnishes a very extensive prospect, reaching from the Jordan on the one side to the Mediterranean on the other. In the depths of the valley below the city, which is watered by the fountain of Mary, are gardens and groves of olive and fig-trees. Such is the place where the Saviour spent the greater part of his life. It is a place which is almost entirely secluded from the world, and thus is peculiarly fitted for the growth of a pure and contemplative mind. In natural beauty, however, notwithstanding its great seclusion, it is one of the bright and lovely places of the earth. In historical interest it is second only to Bethlehem and Jerusalem.

We reached this interesting place on the afternoon of Saturday, and remained there over the Sabbath. Soon after our arrival I left our tent and went into the city. In going through the streets I was cheered by the open and friendly countenances of many of the people, all strangers to me; and yet I could not feel that the heart was entirely a stranger. The name of Jesus, operating by the inspirations of confidence and love, constitutes the world into a family. And little does he know of the power of that wonderful name who has not experienced in himself a growth and expansion of the affections, such as can place the ties of humanity and of a common salvation above the differences of situation, history, and language. Mohammedans are found here; but the large majority of the inhabitants, estimated to be four thousand in number, are Christians,—chiefly Roman Catholics and members of the Greek church,—together with some Maronites. Differing from those whom I saw around me in various incidents of situation and of religious belief, it was natural, notwithstanding, that I should feel a new impulse of gratitude and love to God—a new strength of the bonds of the common relationship existing between man and man—when I met for the first time with groups of men, women, and children within the circuit of the hills which constituted the earthly home of our common Saviour.

One of the principal edifices of the present city is the Franciscan or Latin convent, which is enclosed with walls and is strongly built. It is on the eastern or lower side of the city, as it slopes down from the western hill, and not far from a steep descent into the lowest part of the valley. Within the walls of the convent is the church of the Annunciation, occupying the traditional place where Joseph and Mary resided. On the Sabbath I went there at the hour of worship. The interior of the church, which seemed to me a well-built and in some respects a rich and costly edifice, is adorned with paintings and hung with drapery. Many people, decent in dress and quiet and serious in appearance, were assembled. The place itself, independently of the utterance of religious truth and of the methods of worship, could hardly fail to excite sentiments of religious recollection and homage. There is truth, eloquence, and inspiration in the sound of the organ; but it seemed to have a new power of heavenly tenderness, as I heard it for the first and last time over the rocky cavern which is supposed to have formed a part of the home of the mother of Jesus.

We were shown in another place, at a little distance from the convent, a small chapel, which is said to occupy the site of the workshop in which Joseph pursued his trade as a carpenter. In another part of the city, and under the roof of a small chapel, we were conducted to a large piece of rock, twelve feet long by about nine in breadth, which derives its interest from the ancient tradition that it had been used by our Saviour and his disciples as a table from which they ate, both before and after his resurrection.

On one occasion, when the Saviour was preaching in the synagogue of Nazareth, the people were offended at the boldness and plainness of his instructions; and we are told by the Evangelist Luke that they "rose up and thrust him out of the city, and led him unto the brow of the hill, whereon their city was built, that they might cast him down headlong." There are a number of steep places in the vicinity of the city which would answer to the terms of this statement. The celebrated traveller, Dr. Clarke, who visited this place a few years since, thinks that a precipice a little beyond the limits of the city and above the Maronite church is probably the precise spot which is alluded to in this passage.

Such are some of the objects, natural and historical, which interest the traveller's attention in Nazareth. But I stop here, after what we have thus seen, both here and in other parts of Palestine, to meditate a moment upon the character of that wonderful Being whose history is closely associated with these places. We, who live in these later ages, have never seen personally this great friend and teacher of our race; but I suppose I may be permitted to say, in common with many others, that long and grateful meditations on his history have given an existence to his image in the heart. He lives in the soul,—always in the consolations of his sustaining and sympathetic presence, and sometimes in the brightness of that heavenly appearance, of that celestial personality, which imagination loves to originate and to ascribe to him. But perhaps I may justly add that these scenes, where he grew up from childhood, and where he toiled and suffered, have given him a greater distinctness in my thoughts, a greater nearness in my affections.

In the passage in the Antiquities of Josephus

where a reference is made to Christ, he is spoken of as a man of wisdom, as a teacher, and as a doer of wonderful works; but no reference is made to his personal appearance. Nor is there any account of his personal appearance in the more authentic record of the evangelists. There is a painted portrait, however, which is very ancient, and which purports, in the Latin inscription which accompanies it, to be a true portrait of the Saviour. This celebrated portrait, which was brought to Palestine from Spain many ages since, was formerly in possession of the Franciscan convent of Nazareth, and still belongs to it. We made inquiries for it, but learned that it had been taken for some temporary purpose to another convent. It would be interesting to know more fully the history of this portrait, which naturally attracts a considerable degree of curiosity.

There is also a letter extant, purporting to have been written during the lifetime of Christ by Publius Lentulus to the Roman Senate, which gives a description of Christ's person. He says, "There appeared in these our days a man of great virtue, named Jesus Christ, who is yet living among us; and of the Gentiles is accepted as a prophet of the truth, but his own disciples call him the Son of God." The writer goes on to describe him as curing all manner of diseases and as raising the dead. He then further describes him as comely or well formed, and somewhat tall in stature; with a serious expression of countenance, but such as is calculated to excite love as well as reverence. His hair, which is represented as being divided or parted on the forehead, varied in color,—being of the color of a ripe filbert on the head, but where it flowed and curled over his shoulders, of a bright or orient hue. He represents his forehead as smooth and delicate,—the face without spot or wrinkle, and expressive of innocence as well as of seriousness. He speaks of him as a man of great modesty as well as wisdom of speech, courteous in admonishing, solemn and impressive in reproof.

These and other things are said in this letter, which is admitted to be ancient, although it is not received by learned men and critics as having been written at the time claimed for it and by the person to whom it is ascribed. But, without being necessarily regarded as genuine in the matter of its authorship, it is not unreasonable to suppose that it may possibly embody some of the traditional ideas of the Saviour's personal appearance, which were handed down undoubtedly for many ages. Some of the great painters have been aided in their attempts to represent the Saviour's appearance by the ideas embodied in it.

I have been at the place where he was born and the place where he died,—to the river where he was baptized and the garden where he suffered his agony. It has been my privilege to visit that "well of Jacob" where he conversed with the woman of Samaria; and, in looking down upon the Lake of Galilee, I may be said almost literally to have seen the place of his footsteps on the sea. I am now in Nazareth. With deep emotion I look upon the place where he grew up,—a child among children, —the son of an humble and believing mother. It was here, on these hills and in this deep and secluded valley,—the playmate of the fountain and the rocks, —that he walked abroad in the evening shade or in the early morning ray. It was here, in the solitude of nature and in the divine stillness of the soul, that he listened to the holy revelations of truth and love. It was here that he "increased in wisdom and stature, and in favor with God and man." His story is in the Bible. The scene of it is in these regions, which we have thus been permitted to visit. Whatever doubts may now rest upon his personal appearance, none rests upon the great facts of his incarnation, his character, his labors, the scenes of his residence, and his history. Unchanging nature stands up in faithful confirmation of the historian's statement.

Jesus Christ came into the world a sacrifice for sin. He died that the world might be restored from sin by his sufferings and death, and once more brought into harmony with God. From the moment that he ascended the altar of sacrifice and was fastened there,—an offering so pure, so exalted, that all men and holy angels and all holy existences might see it,—from that hour of transcendent agony and of infinite victory all types and shadows and offerings and sacrifices fled away. The cross on the rock of Calvary was the last altar. Christ was the last victim. That great suffering reaches and heals all other suffering. Of its mighty power in purifying the soul from evil and in giving hope in sorrow and despair, what place, what country, what period of time, has been ignorant?

But Christ was a teacher also. From the beginning of time the question has been asked by wise men of different countries, What is moral goodness?—what is VIRTUE? Plato, instructed by the example of Socrates and by the priests of Egypt, and aided still more by his own reflections, made some approaches to the true answer, but spake nevertheless obscurely and with hesitation. But Jesus Christ, the child of the mountains of Judea, not educated in Grecian and Roman schools, but taught inwardly by the Holy Ghost, spake openly and clearly. He grasped the truth without reasoning upon it; because the truth, harmonizing with purity, and fleeing from everything which is impure, is the necessary development of holy hearts; and because it proclaims its nature and its name, where there are such hearts to receive and appreciate it, in the very fact of its existence. By his own nature, therefore, he was a prophet of the truth. Being born of God and taught of God, he had the truth in himself; it was incarnated in his heavenly nature; it lived in his life and spake in his voice; and he uttered it, therefore, not in the slow process of syllogisms, but by the intuitive impulse and necessities of inspiration.

If virtue may be described very properly as the highest excellence of moral beings, there is one thing, according to the doctrines of Jesus Christ, and only one thing, which can constitute it. He gave it a name on the Galilean mountains; and he illustrated its reality on the bloody rock of Calvary. It is LOVE;—not merely of father and mother, of brother and sister; not merely of those of our own name, language, and nation; but the love—*pure* by being unselfish—of all men, of all climes, countries, and situations; and not only of all men, but of all existences which are the appropriate objects of love,—a love which flows from God in its source, is sustained by God in its action, and attaches itself to everything of which God is the author and in which He takes an interest.

Such love is VIRTUE;—not merely the abstract conception of virtue, but its living essence. Being a life, it has life's mighty and living power. It unites God with the creatures of God. It unites the creatures of God with each other. It abolishes all exclusiveness and all limitations which are not founded in the highest wisdom and required by the highest good. And in its mighty power and vast extent, passing as it does from the centre to the limits of existence, it may be said to harmonize infinity.

It was thus that the babe of Bethlehem, the child of the hills and the fountain of Nazareth, without the learning of those who professed to be philosophers, and yet with a wisdom far above human wisdom, anticipated and expounded the doctrines of Augustine and Fenelon.

And yet it is worthy of notice, that he did not announce his doctrines, however novel and important they might be, with any of the forms and affectations of worldly ceremony. Brought up in the mountains, and not in palaces, he was no son of the Cæsars, but a plain humble man of the people. He spake "as one having authority," and yet without the badges of authority. He had no sword by his side, no diadem on his head, and wore no floating and decorated robe of office. The vaulted roof of his church was the clear blue heavens above him. His rostrum was a rock on the height of Tell Hattin, or a fisherman's boat on the sea of Tiberias. His audience was the universal heart of man embodied and represented in the poor and suffering multitudes of men, women, and children around him. Humanity with him was something which was far above the ordinary distinctions which separate man from man. His insight into the destinies of the future elevated the individual, and gave a vastness to his character by means of the vast sphere of development which expanded around him. He saw, in the small circle of man's present low estate, an infinity of progress. He saw in the poorest, the most ignorant man,—the man on whom power sets its heavy foot and crushes him to the earth,—if not the seeds and beginnings, at least the possibilities, of eternal truth, eternal good affection, and eternal glory. And therefore his heart of love was filled with the deepest sympathy: he recognized a bond of pitying and sympathetic union between himself and the greatest sinner; and whatever he had to say, flowing from the depths of eternal wisdom and goodness, was said in the spirit of self-forgetfulness,—without the artifices of a false rhetoric,—truly, simply, and feelingly.

But this is a subject on which more might be said, and perhaps more appropriately on some other occasion. I will only add a single remark. The truths of Christ—I mean those which go most deeply into man's nature and destiny—are beginning to have an effect which they have not had hitherto, because the day appropriate to them had not yet come. They are gradually, if not rapidly, altering the social and political as well as the religious condition of things. Jesus Christ, in the result of those great influences which must necessarily originate from him, will be found at last to be a king as well as priest. He came into the world not only to save individuals, but to hold the destiny and to be the Saviour of nations. And accordingly the secret but mighty virtue which is proceeding from the bleeding hands and side of this great leader of the people is breaking up old political systems which had extended their gigantic limbs over the world, and which age had strengthened into adamant. What means, during the more recent periods of human history, this falling of towers and Bastiles, unable to withstand the billows of the great masses of the world's population which are rising up from their depths and dashing against them? And, at the present moment, states, kingdoms, dynasties, no longer secured by the principles of hereditary authority, are rocking to and fro on their uneasy foundations. The instinct of a great fear, which foresees the coming of unknown confusions and overthrows, pervades the thought and heart of millions. It is a fear of that change, or rather of that destruction, of everything at variance with the best social and civil interests of man, which is embodied in the doctrines of Christ, and which cannot fail to come in its time.

The first contest is between the past and the present; between institutions and rights; between tyranny and freedom. But freedom, great and desirable as it is, is rather a condition than a principle,—is rather the capacity of life than life itself. And yet it is only in the wide area which the arm of civil liberty shall open and consecrate, that truth will be able to establish the great and final empire of LOVE. The battle-axe of the wars of freedom, lifted perhaps in the severe and forewarning spirit of John the Baptist, and sometimes striking without fully knowing its own object, is nevertheless hewing the way for Christ's entrance. Its heavy sound reminds one of that voice which was heard in the wilderness:—"Prepare ye the way of the Lord."

Everything indicates the voice and the stirrings of a great preparation for the coming of Christ. And he comes—whoever and whatever may be his precursor—to substitute his own principles for those of a different character, and to realize his own pure and pacific conceptions. He comes, therefore, not with the sword, but the olive-branch; not to reign by violence, but by the authority of wisdom and brotherly kindness; not to found dynasties, but to purify, elevate, and establish humanity. If old systems of law are abolished and constitutions of government pass away, if the discordant Babel of gray-headed antiquity is shaken to its foundations, the patriot of a single and exclusive interest and a single people, who sees no universe beyond the metes and bounds of a factitious nationality, will undoubtedly mourn; but the patriot after Christ's great model—the patriot of *all* interests and *all* nations—will put on heart and hope, because he foresees that the institutions of the past, which have always had selfishness and blood at their foundations, will be displaced and substituted by the great charter and kingdom of the Sermon on the Mount.

And here in the solitary valley of Nazareth, where the beauty and silence of nature come in aid of reflection and memory, it is not easy for the traveller to forget that the mighty Lawgiver, from whom these things proceed, sat in his mother's arms beneath this sunlight, was nurtured beneath these overhanging rocks, and spent the days of his childhood and youth by the side of this murmuring fountain.

(LIII.)

Departure from Nazareth—Mount Carmel—Arrival at Caipha—Ascent of Carmel—View from its summit—Carmelite convent—River Belus—St. John d'Acre—White Promontory—Phenician plain—Ras-el-Ain—City of Tyre—Historical notices—Remarks—River Leontes—Arabs.

SYRIA, BANKS OF THE LEONTES, JUNE 1, 1853.

WE left Nazareth on the 30th of May, on our way to Mount Carmel. In a short time we came again into the plain of Esdraelon. We had not proceeded far when the lofty and beautiful ridge of Carmel came fully in sight. Descending into the long, level plain which terminates on the Mediterranean at the bay of St. John d'Acre, we came upon the track of the river Kishon, which here collects its waters and becomes a considerable stream. This stream flows for some distance along the base of the mountain. The ridge of Carmel, covered with its groves of small oaks, rose above us on our left.

Carmel has its place in history and poetry. The events of which it has been the scene connect it with history. Its numerous caverns, which is one of its peculiarities, rendered it the abodes of men whose marked and towering characters necessarily made them historical. It was here that Elijah and Elisha, too stern and uncompromising for the smooth and vicious civilities of palaces, oftentimes made their residence. It was at this mountain that the contest took place between Elijah and the prophets of Baal, which may well be regarded as one of the remarkable historical incidents in the Scriptures. The graceful beauty of Carmel, rising at times into magnificence, connects it with poetry as well as history. Picturesque and often grand in its appearance, it is a mountain which is fitted to fill and delight a creative and imaginative eye. And accordingly references, such as naturally suggest themselves to a poetic mind, are made to it in the prophets Amos, Jeremiah, and Isaiah, and also in the book of Canticles. In those better days to which the people of God look forward with such great interest, the solitary place and the desert shall blossom and rejoice, in the language of the prophet Isaiah, "with the glory of Lebanon and with the *excellency of Carmel.*"

Originally it was very fertile and well cultivated. I am not surprised that the ancients, struck with its beauty and fertility, called it by the poetic name which it bears, and which means the "vineyard or garden of God." It has not wholly lost its ancient reputation. Unlike the naked mountains in the neighborhood of Jerusalem, it is covered with a variety of trees, such as oaks, olives, pines, and laurels. Odoriferous plants and flowers are found upon it. Without laying claims to its ancient fertility, it is still susceptible of cultivation in many places, and furnishes pasturage for cattle on its sides and summit. Flocks of goats browse among its cliffs.

The long plains which stretch from its base are fertile now, and formerly must have been so in a remarkable degree. In the rainy season numerous brooks rush down from its sides. These brooks, sometimes collecting in large pools at the base of the mountain, find their way into the Kishon. Clusters of bushes and flowering plants grow on the edge of their narrow channels.

Passing some six or eight miles along the base of these celebrated heights, with but little to diversify our journey except from time to time the sight of a small Arab village or a herd of cattle tended by the herdsmen on the reedy plain, we came at last to the pleasant maritime town of Caipha,—situated on a small bay by the same name, forming a part of the great bay of Acre. Without thinking it necessary to delay at this town, we passed on through an extensive grove of large and aged olive-trees which is a little beyond it. From this grove, whose grateful shade protected us for a time from the burning heat of the sun, we ascended the mountain by a steep and difficult path to the portion of the lofty summit which hangs almost perpendicularly over the sea. As we looked down, the sea was at least a thousand feet below us. We stopped and gazed intently upon the wide and magnificent prospect which was thus opened to our view. Along the shores of the bay of Acre, which is bounded on its southern side by the projecting heights of Carmel, the billows, with their hoarse and unchanging sound, fell heavily upon the sandy beach. The town of Caipha, to which I have already referred, was directly beneath us. The dark wreck of an English vessel, at no great distance, lay fastened in the sands and beaten by the waves. A few merchant-vessels, with their broad white sails, glittered upon the blue and unruffled ocean. St. John d'Acre, the ancient Ptolemais, was in sight, a few miles distant, on the other side of the circuitous bay. And leaning upon the vapory sky beyond the city were dimly seen the rough and misty heights of Lebanon and Anti-Lebanon.

Upon the abrupt and lofty eminence which we had thus reached, there is a Carmelite convent,—a large and convenient and even elegant building, erected and sustained by the contributions of pious Catholics in different countries. The material of which it is composed is a light-colored sandstone. Lofty in its position, and glittering in a bright Syrian sun, it made an imposing appearance. It has been erected within a few years,—and upon the site of an old one, which once occupied its place. This convent is understood to be one of the richest in Palestine; and everything which we saw tended to confirm its reputation in this respect. It bears the appropriate name of the convent of Elijah,—whose name and history are associated with Carmel as that of Moses is associated with Sinai. We were very kindly received within its walls. A monk, in the simple garb of a Carmelite, but with no want of propriety or even refinement of manners, showed us its various apartments and paintings. The circular chapel of the convent, into which we were conducted, is erected over a grotto, which religious tradition has consecrated as having once been honored by the residence of Elijah. Near the close of the day we came down from the mountain, and pitched our tents and spent the night in the vicinity of Caipha.

Early on the next morning, the 31st of May, we renewed our journey,—passing along the bay of Acre towards its northern extremity. Our path was upon the smooth sands of the beach. The waves dashed at the feet of our horses. Their heavy but regular and not unmusical sound is in strange contrast with the silence of the desert. We crossed the river Kishon near its entrance into the sea, and were thus reminded once more of the plain of Esdraelon and of Mount Tabor. At the distance of four or five miles beyond the Kishon, we crossed the river Belus,—a small stream, and at this time easily fordable, but which has some historical interest, in consequence of being connected with the discovery of the method of making glass. This river is supposed to derive its name from Baal or Bel, the deity of the ancient Phenicians. Leaving the city of St. John d'Acre on our left, which we had not time to visit, we pitched our tents at the close of our day's journey some eight or ten miles beyond it, on the shores of the Mediterranean.

St. John d'Acre, situated near the northern extremity of the large bay which bears the same name, is known under the name of Accho in the book of Judges, and under that of Ptolemais in the book of Acts. The latter name was given in honor of one of the Ptolemies. Its harbor is small, and unfavorably situated; but still it is a place of some commerce and much historical interest. It was taken by the Saracens in the year 636. In the year 1099, when Europe had become aroused by the sense of impending dangers, it was wrested from the Saracenic control by the efforts of the Crusaders, but afterwards, in 1187, was retaken by the Saracens under Saladin. It is connected, also, with the strange and bloody wars of modern history. In the year 1799, it was successfully defended by Sir Sydney Smith against the attacks of Bonaparte. It would have been pleasing to have stopped at a place which had become renowned by so many incidents; but we were obliged to pass on. The vicinity of Acre, however, reminds us that we are now entering upon the small but celebrated territory of ancient Phenicia. The sites of its great and ancient cities, Tyre and Sidon, are not far distant.

At the close of this day we are seated in our tents on the side of a gently-rising hill. A small, uninteresting village is at a little distance. Clustering trees wave above us. The sea breaks sadly and heavily upon the long, sandy beach.

In the morning, June 1, we resumed our march. We soon began to ascend rocky heights, which project from Anti-Lebanon and look directly down upon the Mediterranean. These heights are the Djebel Nakhura. Then we came, in the course of a few miles, to the celebrated place called the White Promontory,—the Album Promontorium of the ancient Romans. In order to furnish a passage here, a way has been cut with great labor over the lofty limestone rock, which overlooks perpendicularly the waves of the ocean. Both the ascent and descent are aided by these steps, which have given to the place the name also of the "ladder of Tyre." Ascending this worn-out and broken ladder, which time and constant travelling have altered very much from its primitive shape, we reached the summit at the height of some five or six hundred feet. The road goes upon the very edge of this terrible precipice. We looked down upon the dashing waves. The sea-birds spread their wings and screamed beneath us. A single vessel was in sight, on what was once the great highway of commerce. It was over this dizzy rock that Alexander led his forces to the conquest of Tyre.

As we approached the middle of the day, we came upon the celebrated Phenician plain, bounded on all sides except the west by the rocky heights of Lebanon and Anti-Lebanon,—a region small in extent, but renowned for its fertility, and rendered illustrious in history by the wealth, arts, and genius of its two great cities, Tyre and Sidon. The Phenician plain is thirty miles in length by an average of two or perhaps two and a half in breadth,—if we reckon it in the usual way as extending from the White Promontory on the north of Tyre to the small river called the Nahr-el-Auly, three miles south of Sidon. Before reaching the city of Tyre, at the distance of two miles and a half from it, we stopped at Ras-el-Ain, or the Fountain-head. At this remarkable place a subterranean brook, collecting its supplies of water probably from the base of the mountains not far distant, bursts out from the earth. The clear, pure water gushes up with much force, and is first collected in a number of large reservoirs composed of stones and gravel strongly united with cement. The reservoirs, four in number and varying from fifteen to twenty feet in height, are so constructed that we could easily ascend them and walk about on their broad, smooth tops. The water is raised by means of these artificial works to a considerable height, and anciently, through well-constructed aqueducts, the remains of which are still seen, was conveyed in large quantities both to the city of Tyre and over the surrounding country. At the present time a single mill is turned by the water which flows from one of the reservoirs. The water, which was once employed for purposes of irrigation by means of aqueducts and for the supply of the city, now flows off for the most part in a rapid brook towards the sea.

Having spent a little time in examining these remarkable remains, we advanced in sadness over the beautiful plain which was once covered with Tyrian magnificence. We could not help seeing that God, whose great artistic hand is everywhere building homes of beauty out of fragmentary earth and stone, had designed this spot between the mountains and the sea as the residence of a favored people and a great city.

Tyre, like Damascus and Thebes, was one of the primitive cities of the world,—one of the cradles of wealth, knowledge, and civilization. It is mentioned as a strong city in the book of Joshua. It is again mentioned in the time of Solomon. The minute description of the city in the prophet Ezekiel is particularly worthy of notice.

The harbor of Tyre, which reminded me, on a miniature scale, of that of Alexandria, was formed originally by an island, but was extended and completed by a sea-wall of immense strength. The ancient city, which is now all swept away by the destructive influences of war, barbarism, and time, was built chiefly upon the shore, and not upon the island. This old and flourishing place, renowned for its commerce and arts, was destroyed by Nebuchadnezzar, the Assyrian king,—or at least that portion of it which was built upon the mainland,—573 years before the time of Christ. A little more than two hundred years after, the insular city, or that portion which was built upon the neighboring island, was attacked and taken by Alexander the Great, after a siege of eight months. Making use of the materials of the first city, which were scattered in fragments upon the shore, he constructed a vast mole, two hundred feet in breadth, which extended from the continent to the island. The sands have drifted over this great work; and thus the ancient island, which is at the distance of a half or three-fourths of a mile from the shore, is converted into a peninsula, upon which the modern city of Tyre now stands. Treading literally in the steps of the Macedonian conqueror, we passed slowly over the isthmus and went through and around the city. There are still some remains of commerce here. A few small vessels were in the harbor. The tide had receded; and the rocks were laid bare. Upon these rocks the fisherman spreads his nets. All around the city, on the sandy shore and the sea-beaten rocks, were melancholy evidences of the wealth and gigantic labors of other days,—fragments of walls and of numberless large and beautiful columns, which seemed still to have a voice and to utter the story of their greatness and their degradation.

On this spot, before the city of Alexandria had a being, was the centre of ancient commerce. Tyre was the London of ancient days. Situated at the head of the great sea, midway between the old pillars of Hercules on the one hand and the Persian Gulf and the Indian seas on the other, she held her commercial dominion for nearly a thousand years. In these streets walked the merchants of Egypt. The loaded camels of Judea and Damascus kneeled at her gates. On these waters rose the masts of Lebanon; and the sea foamed under the stroke of oars made from the oaks of Bashan. The loud sound of her sailors' voices echoed over the great sea-wall of her harbor, as they came in from distant Spain and barbarous Grecian isles. Arabia poured her spices and balm and frankincense into her lap. The ivory and the costly woods of the Persian Gulf adorned her palaces. The mother of arts, she clothed the world in her linen and purple. The mother of knowledge, she sent her Cadmus to teach mankind the mystery of letters. States, cities, were born in her bosom. She built Carthage, the powerful rival of Rome, from the treasures of her wealth and love. And the cities of Cadiz in Spain and Utica in Africa were among her children. But to-day how changed is all this!

With deep interest the traveller looks upon the remains of this great but fallen city. He beholds it a mighty and a memorable desolation. It was predicted that it should be so. Speaking in the language of the prophet Ezekiel, God is represented as addressing Tyre in terms which indicate his displeasure:—"Behold, I am against thee, O Tyrus, and will cause many nations to come up against thee, as the sea causeth his waves to come up. And they shall destroy the walls of Tyrus, and break down her towers. I will also scrape her dust from her, and make her like the top of a rock. It shall be a place for the spreading of nets in the midst of the sea."

It is thus that nations and cities, one after another, have perished and passed away. Since I left Europe,—and Europe itself is only an exception in part,—I have found only desolate cities and nations. It might have been otherwise. At least it seems so to me. If any nation had in the beginning adopted the principles of the gospel,—the principles which are the opposite of selfishness, which bless them that persecute us and which do good without asking for reward,—its principles would have conquered the destructive tendencies of time, and, triumphing over death and decay, would not have failed to establish an immortality of beauty. Of this it is difficult for me to doubt.

Principles are the life of action; and if our principles are the old Tyrian principles of exclusive or selfish possession,—everything for ourselves, and nothing, or comparatively nothing, for others, with that watchful and contentious jealousy which always attends it,—in other words, if it be a principle or the shadow of a principle differing from that which measures the love of our neighbor by the love of ourselves, it is necessarily the principle of death;—in the first place, hostility and death to others, and in the end death to those who adopt it. It is this, and this only, which has spread desolation over the fairest portions of the earth, which has substituted on the banks of the Nile and the Euphrates the sandy plain and the barren rock for the flower-gardens of Eden; not antiquity, but *falsehood;* not time, which is only the measurement of bright, revolving suns, but the pride, luxury, and enmity which have resulted from not walking in God's glorious and everlasting truth.

And I ought to say something further. In going from country to country, I have mourned not only for man, but nature. Not only great cities, but the earth also is desolate. What was more beautiful once than the great Phenician plain? But now, like the cities which once adorned its bosom, how sad, how deserted! Nature, like nations, has gone to decay. She mourns and weeps, like a sad mother. She is silent, sorrowful, and sometimes fretful. She puts on sackcloth; she sits upon the rocks; she throws mud into her crystal rivers; she buries her flowers in the sand. But it is not time which has made her desolate; it is not the consciousness of guilt which has rent and marred her veil of primitive beauty: the cause of her sadness is in others more than in herself. She lives like one in hopeless widowhood, and turns away and hides herself, because man, her child, for whom she built the earth's beautiful home, has ceased to love. She laments the spirit of contention which has lacerated her heart in all ages. She mourns for the millions of her children scattered and bleeding on every shore.

And this is not mere imagination,—is not the playful or unmeaning metaphor of poetry. Man and material nature are parts of one great system, which are designed to harmonize with each other, not merely on the principle of adaptation, but on the principle of a true but mysterious sympathy; and accordingly there is a truth and life in nature resulting from its correspondence with man. Does not the fibrous root of trees and plants, as if it were a thing of thought and intelligence, seek the earth and water which are most appropriate to it? Does not the plant itself, seeking to realize the beauties and harmonies of growth, creep along the ground with the same object? Does not the flower turn towards the sun? Everything shows that nature has a true life, an instinctive but silent intelligence, and also a triumphant beauty, which crowns and perfects that life; though now, in consequence of the crimes and sorrows which she witnesses, she hides herself in her sad garments of barrenness and mourning. The divine principle of sympathy has been violated. She has been struck and wounded in the heart. Such, and so wide-spread, are the miseries which flow from sin.

And this also may be reversed. A disappointed, grieved, and bleeding affection is not necessarily a dead one. When man, from whose heart should flow out fountains of love, and whose face should beam with a brightness clearer than the sun's, shall be what he is yet destined to be, and what Christ's loving power shall yet make him to be, then shall nature restore itself from the silence and weakness of its mighty sorrow, and everything, as if touched with a divine consciousness, shall recognize man's presence: the leaves and branches shall strew his path and twine themselves about him; the flowers shall cease to weep, and shall grow bright with smiles; the very rocks shall utter a song of joy.

Such are my meditations, as I sit thoughtfully at sunset on the banks of the Leontes. To this place have we come after leaving Tyre. We stay here to-night. I suppose it to be seven or eight miles distant from Tyre. I love to spend the night at the foot of a mountain or on the bank of a river. I seek some solitary place, where man and his crimes are unknown. The silence sings. The stars dance upon the mountain-tops, or look up brightly and smilingly from the water. How beautiful flows this murmuring, rapid stream! The golden sunset throws the veil of its bright yellow over the blue waves. It is comparatively tranquil now; but in early spring it is covered with foam and is dangerous to travellers.

Rising in the neighborhood of the ancient city of Baalbec, it sweeps down through the valley between Lebanon and Anti-Lebanon. It waters the old romantic gardens and rude terraces of Cœle-Syria. It is spanned by a well-constructed bridge near the place of our encampment. A company of Arabs is encamped near us. This is a remarkable people. I love to gaze upon them. Their spears are long, their horses are beautiful; they stand erect, and look upon us, through their dark, burning eyes, with much curiosity. But, if I understand that dark look aright, I must describe it as the curiosity of indifference.

Old historians speak of the Leontes. But rivers never die. It flows now as it flowed a thousand years ago,—old in history, but young in its life of never-ceasing movement. At a little distance, on the side of a hill overhanging it, are some rude habitations. Its steep banks are covered with reeds and flowers. The light of its flowers, like the light of its waters, is bright in the radiance of the setting sun.

(LIV.)

Ruins of Sarepta—Scriptural allusion to this city—Reach Sidon—Its situation—Arrival at Beirout—American missionaries—Services on the Sabbath—Rev. Mr. Whiting—Dr. Eli Smith—Influence of Christian missions—Mount Lebanon—Its appearance—Its inhabitants—America—Thoughts on leaving Palestine—Poetry.

PASHALIC OF SYRIA, CITY OF BEIROUT, JUNE 8, 1853.

In going from the banks of the Leontes to the old city of Sidon, June 2, we passed over the site and among the ruins of Sarepta. Our course was along the shore of the Mediterranean, and over the plain between the mountains and the sea. The site of Sarepta is near the sea on the old Phenician plain which has already been mentioned,—eight or nine miles north of the Leontes, and seven miles south of Sidon. It was to the city of Sarepta, which is mentioned under the name of Zarephath in the Old Testament, that the prophet Elijah was at one time sent. Here he dwelt with a poor widow, whose meal and oil he miraculously supplied, and whose dead son he restored to life. In the command which was given to Elijah, and under which he acted,—of which we have the account in the first book of Kings,—it was said to him, "Arise, get thee to Zarephath, which *belongeth to Sidon*, and dwell there." The Saviour in the Gospel of Luke refers to the event mentioned in Kings, and says of this prophet, that he went to a widow in Sarepta, *a city of Sidon*. We passed directly over this spot. There was not much remaining of the ancient city, which, I ought to say, is to be distinguished from the modern Sarepta, at a little distance to the east, on the side of a hill. The site of the city is considered as well ascertained, not only by the unanimous tradition which reaches back to an early period, but by the fragmentary remains of streets and buildings which still exist, and by the allusions and statements of history. It is true that the ruins which now remain are comparatively few; but it is a matter of historical record, that those which existed in the thirteenth century were such as to indicate that it was once a place of much wealth and splendor.

It must be admitted, however, that the interest which attaches to Sarepta consists chiefly in the fact that it was the residence of a poor woman who had faith in God, and who furnished a home to one of His persecuted and exiled prophets. The Crusaders erected a chapel over the traditionary place of her residence; but her true memorial is in the Bible. The name of kings and conquerors is forgotten; but the memory of this poor woman, who in her poverty and suffering never thought of fame, is protected by God's providence, and is written in His imperishable records.

Our route was from the south to the north. On our left was the sea. On our right were the mountains. In some places the mountains came down near to the sea, leaving but a narrow space between them.

Following this route, we next came to the city of Sidon. This city was the mother of Tyre, as Tyre was the mother of Carthage; and, although the daughter's surpassed the mother's splendor, Sidon also had its wealth, its commerce, and its name of renown. The situation of Sidon is beautiful. And this I have had occasion to notice in relation to many of the old celebrated places. I have seen and heard of no great city of antiquity which did not vindicate the wisdom and the glowing heart of its founders, by its relations not only to the useful, but the true, the expansive, and the grand in nature. Sometimes they built upon mountain-tops, that they might look upon the clear sky above or upon the valleys beneath. Sometimes they built upon the banks of great rivers, like the Nile and the Euphrates,—which, flowing on forever, and scattering around them the seeds of fertility and beauty, filled the heart with great and glowing sentiments. Sometimes they selected a spot in the midst of mountain-rocks, with heights on either side, with a deep valley between and a gentle brook flowing through it, and there, amid the silence of nature, which is favorable to the activity of thought, made a new world for themselves in palaces and statues carved from the changeless stone. Sometimes they built upon the ocean,—in sight of its immense expanse and in hearing of its mighty voice,—but only where it had established, if I may so express it, an æsthetic or spiritual harmony with the shores, by moulding itself into those forms of beauty which appeal both to the eye and the heart.

Sidon is situated on a promontory running into the sea in a southwest direction. It is enclosed by a wall on the land-side. It was interesting to look upon this old town,—almost as ancient as the foundations of the world. The eye took in at a single glance the circuitous and beautiful harbor, which was once all that could be desired, but has been much injured from various causes. The rich environs of the city are occupied by numerous gardens, filled and blooming with the various fruit-trees and flowers which are common in this region. It has some remains of the skill and labor of other ages. Our attention was attracted in the distance to an old square tower forming a picturesque object on the southern end of the promontory. At what time and by whom it was first built is not certainly known. As we spent but a little time in the city, I will not attempt to speak more particularly of this or of other objects which claimed a slight notice. All I can say is, that we came, saw, and left it,—without time to make minute inquiries, and yet with time enough to receive the general outlines of its image upon the mind and heart. It has its convenient residences,—some of them built of stone and beautiful,—its flourishing gardens, its mechanic occupations and arts; and, though it is no longer the possessor of its ancient wealth and commerce, it is comparatively flourishing. Such was the impression left upon my mind in one of those rapid judgments which a person sometimes forms when merely passing through a place. It seemed to me that there are some distinct evidences of that recovery of wealth and strength which characterize Alexandria and Jaffa. At Sidon is an American sub-consulate; and the Americans have a missionary establishment there,—a branch, I suppose, of the important mission which has its central operations at Beirout.

Sidon, as well as Tyre, is repeatedly mentioned in the Bible. It is first mentioned in Genesis. In the book of Joshua it is called "*great* Sidon." References are made to it also in the books of Kings and Chronicles, and in Ezra, Isaiah, and Ezekiel. It is repeatedly mentioned in Homer. In the earliest times Sidon was one of the great centres of knowledge and the arts. Before the injuries to its once convenient and beautiful harbor, it was the seaport to the great inland city of Damascus, from which it is distant by a journey of a little more than two days. The route to Damascus leads in a northeast direction over Mount Lebanon, and then, passing through the intervening valley of the Leontes, crosses the more distant heights of Anti-Lebanon. The business-intercourse of Sidon with Damascus, the most of which is now transferred to Beirout, increased its commerce. Its harbor was once covered with sails. The vessel in which the Apostle Paul sailed from Palestine for Italy touched at Sidon. The Saviour himself visited this region. He had been teaching in the region of Genesareth, which is not far distant; and it is added by the evangelist, "Then Jesus departed thence, into the coasts of *Tyre and Sidon.*" It was here that he performed the miracle upon the daughter of the Syro-Phenician woman.

We encamped the night of this day, June 2, a few miles beyond Sidon. About the middle of the next day, we reached Beirout, the ancient Berytus. Before reaching the city, and at a few miles' distance, we passed the river called the Nahr-el-Tamour,—the same with the ancient Tamyras. The stream is rapid, and, when swollen by rains and melted snows, must be difficult to pass. We noticed, a little above where we crossed it, the remains of a stone bridge which had been swept away. Like the Leontes, its banks were lined with oleanders. The near approach to Beirout was through a long grove of pines, succeeded by cultivated gardens. Numberless mulberry-trees lined our path.

At Beirout I felt quite at home. The hotel at which I stayed had every convenience. The presence of the excellent American consul,* who had apartments in the same hotel, gave a sort of reality to the idea of national protection. At a little distance, the American flag floated over the consulate. The strong arm of a great though distant nationality, which is rapidly extending itself to every land and sea, placed itself around me.

I had with the place also some pleasant personal associations. This city had been the residence, a number of years ago, of a former friend and fellow-student, Rev. Mr. Bird, who labored here as a faithful and successful missionary. I was reminded of

---

* J. Horsford Smith, Esq.

him not only by the circumstance of his having resided here, but by an incident which recalled the memory of his self-denying labors. Passing one day a bookstore, I went in. The books were chiefly of a religious character. This led to some conversation with the bookseller, who could speak English, and to whom I found that no subject was dearer than that of religious truth and experience. In the great truths of the Bible and the great facts of religious experience we found a common ground to stand upon, broader than that of sect or nationality. He told me that it was Mr. Bird who many years ago directed his attention to these interesting topics, and who was the instrument under God of leading him to the study of religious truth, and to inward liberty and life.

On the Sabbath after our arrival, I went to the religious service in the American missionary chapel. The sermon, imbued with a pure and deep religious spirit, was preached by Rev. Mr. Whiting, whose long and arduous labors as a missionary are well known in America. The sermon was in that plain, simple language which befits great subjects,—full of well-digested thought, and practical and serious in its application. Christ was its theme. Redemption was its object. And it was pleasant to an American, from a land unknown when these great announcements were first made, to hear such a theme dwelt upon and such an object held up with sincerity and zeal on the shore of the Mediterranean and under the shadow of Lebanon.

In the afternoon of the same day I heard another member of the same missionary establishment, the learned and justly-celebrated Dr. Eli Smith, preach to a congregation in the Arabic language. I cannot be supposed to have understood the sermon; but the circumstances were such—the time, the place, the man, the audience, the language—that I felt its power in the heart, without the aid of any pentecostal miracle to interpret the unknown words in which it was uttered. Mr. Smith had the kindness, during my stay at Beirout, to take me over the large printing-establishment under the direction of the missionaries. The labors of this learned and devoted missionary are not limited to preaching. He has aided the great object to which he has devoted himself by the religious works which he has written in Arabic or has translated into that language. His geographical labors, the results of which are incorporated into the great work of Dr. Robinson, have given him a claim to the respect of scholars as well as of Christians. He appears to have a critical and entire mastery of the Arabic language. And it would not be hazardous to predict that his translation of the Bible into the Arabic—a work which is already considerably advanced—will increase the favorable opinion which already exists of his learning, untiring industry, and usefulness.

I should do injustice to my feelings if I did not here express my opinion of the favorable influence of the various Christian missions which are now established in many parts of the world. If I may be permitted to judge not only from what I have learned from others but from what I have myself seen, the real impression which the sincere and laborious men of these missions have made is much greater than is apparent to the public eye. From their gentle voice, uttered in conversation, in the pulpit, and in the silent announcement of the circulated tract, have gone forth, into the hearts of thousands and millions, the thought and the hope of a higher and truer life. The years which have been spent in missionary labor have not been lost time. Those who have died far away from their native home—the good and the beautiful, the men and women of the Christian faith—have not died in vain. The seed which has been sown on many a barbarous shore, in tears always and sometimes in blood, though it has sometimes lain long buried in the dust, is springing up at last in the blade and flower of a freer thought, a liberated hope, a more generous confidence, and a looking on every side, and often with an intensity of desire, for the coming of that kingdom of Christ, without sword or floating warlike banner, which shall bring with it not only individual restoration, but universal harmony and peace.

My health did not allow me to go into the mountains while at Beirout. I could only gaze upon them as they arose in majesty around the city. The great range of Lebanon, with its irregular and rocky surface, comes down upon the sea, on the north side of the harbor,—Lebanon, renowned of old, which has its interest for the geologist and naturalist, and which, by its rude grandeur, is the delight of poetry. Unchanging in its position and features, it is also a living and eloquent protest against scriptural infidelity. Although the mountain has a desolate appearance, the small patches of earth in its ravines and valleys, watered by the rills and brooks that find their way among the rocks, are everywhere cultivated. Scattered among the mountains are many small villages; and the general appearance of wild and rocky barrenness is relieved at times by clusters of mulberries, and of fig and olive trees.

The mountains of Lebanon consist of two great ranges, running nearly north and south, extending the distance of a hundred miles from the neighborhood of Tyre on the south, to the bay of Tripoli on the north,—parallel with the Mediterranean and parallel with each other,—with the valley of Cœle-Syria and the Leontes between them. The western range, fronting and overlooking the Mediterranean, is called Lebanon. The eastern range, including within its limits the snowy peak of the Great Hermon, (which is said to be ten thousand feet in height,) and overlooking a considerable portion of Palestine, is called Anti-Lebanon. The rock of these mountains is a whitish limestone; and it is either the white appearance arising from this cause, or from the snows which gather upon the high peaks, which has given them their name. Lebanon is a word of Hebrew origin, and means the White Mountain.

These mountains, which have now in a great degree a naked and barren appearance, were once covered with forests. Frequent references are made in the Scriptures to the fountains, forests, and snows of Lebanon. In these celebrated mountains were found the masts for the Sidonian and Tyrian navies.

Here were the cedars which were wrought into the temple of Solomon. In a distant and secluded part of the mountains a few cedars yet remain. The memorial of past ages, they still spread their aged arms upon the winds. Travellers of great enthusiasm, who have the requisite time, make it a point to climb over the rugged rocks and visit them, though they are few in number and are marred and changed by time.

The inhabitants of the region of Lebanon are objects of much interest. In these mountains, which I here look upon for the first and last time, as they thus overhang the city of Beirout and the great sea which washes their base, is the home of the Druses. In these heights of Lebanon, like the Savoyards and the Waldenses in the fastnesses of the Alps, dwell also the remains of a Christian people, called the Maronites. The Maronites accept the Bible as the source of their religious ideas, and are properly called Christians. The Druses are a peculiar people,—adopting Christian ideas and thoughts in part, but mingling and debasing them with a semi-paganism. In the heights of Lebanon are Christian missionaries from America, laboring diligently and successfully, and carrying back the blessings of Christianity to the lands from whence it came.

I stop my pen here, so far as the objects around me are concerned, in order that I may indulge in a few thoughts which naturally arise. It is from this place that I begin my return home. I hear the ocean's sound. I look out upon its vast waves,—so vast that they bind together distant continents,—and my heart sighs once more for my native land.

It is an hour of thought and solitary meditation. Every man has his history. I have mine. My feet are walking under the mighty shadow of Lebanon. My heart reposes in the mountains of America. It is a season of deep and joyful anticipation. It is a season also of gratitude. God has permitted me to see what I had desired, but which I had hardly hoped to see. I shut my eyes to the future, that I may indulge a moment in memory and fill my heart with thankfulness.

Once more I went back in memory to the sacred scenes which I was about to leave. I recalled my wanderings in the various parts of Palestine. I thought again, as one thinks of an absent friend, of the Sea of Galilee, of the Jordan, and the Mount of Olives. I called to mind the beautiful and varied scenery of Bethlehem, the valleys of Hebron, the hills of Nazareth, and the mountains "round about Jerusalem." I repeated, both in memory and in the deep consciousness of inward experience, those seasons of sweet and heavenly communion where I may be said to have walked and conversed with Him who bears the title of the "Son of man," on those hills and mountains which were now fading from my view. But the humble and believing Christian will understand what I mean when I say that I did not leave him behind. I found him there; but he does not and cannot cease to be present with the heart that receives him as the "Truth and the Life." In the deep conviction of his faithfulness I claimed and possessed, in thoughts and feelings which struggled for utterance, the consolations of his presence.

O Saviour! Thus I leave the land
Which thou hast loved and look'd upon,—
No more upon the hills to stand
Where thou hast stood in ages gone.
And yet the breeze, the sail that fills,
Is whispering to my pensive mind
That, thus in leaving Judah's hills,
I do not leave her King behind.

The faithful soul shall know it true
That every land and clime is thine;
That He who trod in Hermon's dew
Finds everywhere his Palestine.
I go,—but cannot go from Thee;
I tread once more the ocean's tide;
But He who walk'd on Judah's sea
Will not be absent from my side.

(LV.)

Departure from Beirout—City of Cæsarea—Stop at Jaffa—Reach Alexandria—Companions in quarantine—Sisters of Charity—Malta—Coast of Africa—Carthage—Straits of Gibraltar—Arrival at Liverpool—Departure in the Arctic for New York.

CITY OF NEW YORK, AUG. 1, 1853.

On Thursday, the 9th of June, I left Beirout on my return home. It was a long journey of six thousand miles; but faith and joyful anticipation had an influence in shortening the aspect of the distance. There were many vessels in the bay,—the larger ones at some distance from the shore. They were of different nations,—Austrian, English, French, and Sardinian. I saw no American flag. It is but recently that American vessels have traded here. Among the vessels was the French steamer the Tancrede. She floated proudly among the smaller ones around her. As she was to sail immediately for Alexandria, I took passage in her.

At Beirout I parted with the much-valued and beloved companions with whom I had travelled from England. Mr. Thompson went to Damascus, Mr. and Mrs. Walcott to Constantinople. I went to the Tancrede alone; and there was no one on board with whom I was acquainted. There were passengers from different nations; but there was no one from England or America with whom I could recall or establish some community of thought and feeling. As our captain gave the signal for departure, I looked once more upon the city. It rose gracefully from the shores,—its ranges of light-colored stone houses ascending one above another, interspersed beyond the walls with its flowering gardens and with its groves of orange-trees and mulberries. I saw the mountains of Lebanon for the last time.

The sun was setting when the steamer left the harbor. In the evening I walked the deck. The sails were set. The stars shone brightly. Around us was the great desert of the waters. With the stars and the wide heavens above, and the vast trackless ocean beneath, and with no one with whom I could converse, I felt much as in the deserts of Sinai. My heart was in solitude,—but in that great and glorious solitude which disrobes itself of false and earthly influences and leaves it with truth, with contemplation, and with God.

The next day we passed the site of the ancient city of Cæsarea,—the work of Herod the Great,—once so celebrated for its artificial harbor, and which has a connection with the events mentioned in the New Testament. This city was about fifty miles distant from Jerusalem, and thirty-five miles from

Joppa, in a north direction from the latter city. St. Paul was kept a prisoner in Cæsarea for the space of two years. It was in Cæsarea that the apostle made his eloquent plea before Felix, and also his speech before Festus and King Agrippa. Cornelius, the praying and alms-giving centurion who was converted to Christianity, resided here. This also was one of the remarkable scenes of the labors of the Apostle Peter.

Near the close of the day the steamer stopped at Jaffa,—the *Joppa* of the Scriptures,—of which I have given some account in a former letter. We anchored in the open ocean. Boats from the city soon came out. I took a boat and went on shore, —the boatmen, for the purpose of saving a little in the distance, carrying the boat through a narrow pass in the boiling and dangerous reef of rocks which encloses the old harbor. I saw once more the excellent American consul, who is a resident of this place, and is one of the reformed Armenians who are awakening thought and spreading truth in these regions. I was enabled also to make some further and very satisfactory inquiries in relation to the little company of Americans, to whom I have formerly referred, who are settled in the vicinity of Jaffa with a view to the instruction and benefit of the Jews. The labors of this small but devoted band, who pursue their work of benevolence on principles somewhat peculiar to themselves, are known to the Christian community.

In the course of a few hours we proceeded again on our voyage. This is the third French vessel in which I have sailed since I left America; and it is with pleasure that I bear a favorable testimony in each case to the good order and conduct of the crew, and the kindness which I personally experienced. In our voyage from Beirout to Alexandria, the weather was favorable, and nothing of special interest occurred. I had access to books, which were placed at my disposal by a French gentleman on board. The crew, with that vivacity and easiness to be amused which are characteristic of Frenchmen, contrived to occupy a portion of their time with the feats of a young bear which had been recently caught and taken on board from the Lebanon Mountains. The bear had made a rather intimate acquaintance with a cat; and once a day and sometimes oftener they were let loose upon deck, and by an amicable contest of attack and flight, of pursuit and vigilant retreat, in which the cat's activity had on the whole quite an advantage over the violent but clumsy movements of the bear, they beguiled many hours of the thoughtless sailors.

Our next stopping-place was the city of Alexandria, where we arrived early on the morning of the 12th of June. Slowly the vessel made its way through the narrow, winding entrance into the magnificent harbor. It was at Alexandria that we commenced our journey up the Nile and for the deserts of Sinai. I have said in a former letter what I had to say of that city. We had now, however, a new form of experience. Coming from Syria, we were obliged to pass a number of days in quarantine. A state of quarantine, though adverse to action, is generally not unfavorable to silence and reflection. But this is not always the case. In the room assigned me I had the company of a travelling merchant from South America, and a monk from Palestine of the Franciscan order. The merchant was from Colombia. He was a well-disposed man, a man of information, and made himself entirely agreeable. The monk was originally from France,—from some small town on the banks of the beautiful Rhone. He had been residing many years in Palestine, and was returning to the place of his residence in early life. He had with him a Bible in the Latin Vulgate translation, which he read almost constantly. It was pleasant to converse with him. He manifested no asperity or indifference towards those who differed from him in opinions. He was an old man, very gentle in his manners; had seen much of men and things; and I was favorably impressed with his appearance.

At Alexandria I left the French steamer, which returned in a few days to Beirout, on its way to Smyrna and Constantinople. Abandoning the plan which I had formed of again visiting France, I engaged a passage for Liverpool by the way of Malta, in an English screw-steamer,—the Glasgow. This vessel was delayed a few days after the expiration of our quarantine, which enabled me to revisit some of the objects and places in the city to which I have formerly referred. I found that even the lapse of a few months had made changes in its appearance. Additional buildings were in the rapid course of erection. The beautiful English church, which adorns the great European Square, was far advanced towards its completion; and I saw many signs of growth and prosperity, which led to the opinion that Alexandria might yet recover, by means of its great advantages of position, and under the influence of renovated rights and institutions, something of its ancient wealth and importance.

In the city of Alexandria are collected together many who have fled from the political convulsions and revolutions of Europe. In banishment, poverty, and sorrow, they often sink into the grave, leaving behind them orphan children, who need a degree of sympathy and care which could hardly be expected in a foreign country and under great differences of religion. But I found, on this renewed visit, that the "Sisters of Charity," an organized and permanent community of Catholics, who devote themselves to works of benevolence, had established themselves here, and had become the adoptive mothers of many of these orphans.

It was with pleasure that I visited their large Orphan-Asylum. No letters of introduction were necessary in order to gain admission. Giving a signal at the gate, which was at once opened, I entered one of the apartments, which was both parlor and library, and was soon introduced to one of the members of the establishment, a native of Ireland. She exhibited a calm propriety and dignity of manner, which indicated intellectual and social culture, as well as the quiet and self-controlling influences of religion. When I told her that I was from America, she showed an increased interest, the cause of which I did not at first understand. She showed me over the establishment, and very cheerfully gave much information in relation to it. At parting she informed me that she had two sisters in America, who, like herself, were members of the "Sisters of Charity," and although they resided at New Orleans, far distant from my place of residence, yet the sight of one from the same land gave her much satisfaction and seemed to bring them nearer to her. As a Protestant, but disposed to rejoice in everything which is good under whatever name, I mention these incidents with satisfaction and interest.

I sailed from Alexandria on Monday, the 20th of June, in the English steamer which I have mentioned. One of the last objects which I saw in leaving this "clime of the sun," and which still seems in its polished and lofty grandeur to stand before me, was Pompey's Pillar. The captain of the Glasgow was a Scotchman by birth, but had his residence in Liverpool. He had often been in America, and at one time had the charge of one of the Cunard steamers which touch at Boston. This led to some conversation and acquaintance, and made me feel quite at home. The arrangements of this steamer were admirable. There was a clergyman of the Church of England on board, and religious service was regularly held on the Sabbath, at which the crew attended.

We sailed for a time along the coast of Africa, and then directed our course towards Malta. We stopped a few hours at Malta, which we reached on Saturday, the 25th of June, but did not go on shore. A number of English ships-of-war were in the harbor; but the greater number had recently left for Constantinople, in anticipation of the outbreak of war between Russia and Turkey, which would necessarily involve England. I say necessarily; but, in using that expression, I do not refer to any necessity which God has created, or which a higher Christian principle and greater forbearance and love would not obviate, but to those pressing exigencies, those necessities of state, which arise out of the complications of diplomacy, and from the strength of human pride, interest, and passion. The idea of another general war in this age of Christian progress and civilization—a war without any assignable direction and without any termination which could be foreseen—was exceedingly painful to me. Malta is a great arsenal,—in the language of Scripture, a "munition of rocks." I had stopped here in going to Egypt, and gave some account of it in a former letter.

In going from Malta to Gibraltar, we were for some time in sight of the African coast on the southern side of the Mediterranean. One morning as we were sailing in the neighborhood of Cape Bon and along the Bay of Tunis, the site of ancient Carthage was pointed out to me. The very name excited no small emotion. Among my early recollections there is scarcely any place or any historical event which affected me more, or has left a deeper place in my memory, than Carthage and the events connected with it. The poets and historians of Rome, though not without biases unfavorable to strict truth, have eloquently commemorated the greatness and the terrible overthrow of her mighty rival. The Roman historians say that, when the young Hannibal appeared for the first time as a leader in the Carthaginian army, the old soldiers, now decrepit with years and living upon past memories, saw, in his form and countenance and military step, the restoration and the once more living presence of his father Hamilcar, under whom they had fought in their youth. It was thus that the mere sight of the spot upon which Carthage was built, now a sandy desolation, restored the city and the senate, and gave a momentary existence to the celebrated names which are associated in history with the arts of war or the wisdom of legislation. No assembled senate is there now. No ships of war or commerce cover the sea with their sails. No Hamilcar or Hannibal leads armies to battle. No Mago pleads his country's cause. On that sandy shore is the burial-place of a great nation. Her mighty image, as it exists in the dimness of history,—vast but faint in its outlines,—sits in sad but solitary grandeur on the place of her tomb.

Soon after leaving Cape Bon, our vessel changed its direction from the coast of Africa to that of Spain. We passed along the base of cliffs and mountains, with plains and valleys opening between them, but no longer resounding with the hum of a busy population, and destitute of their ancient fertility and beauty. This land too, though much changed both in its physical and moral attributes, is the birthplace—the ancient and celebrated home—of a great people. I could not fail to gaze with deep interest upon a country, whatever may be said of its present condition, which in past ages has had its varied epochs of bitter trial and successful conflict, and which has been illustrated by renowned literary names,—a country which the genius of Irving, Prescott, and Ticknor has made familiar, both in its history and literature, to American readers.

On reaching Gibraltar, Friday, the 1st day of July, our vessel went into harbor, and gave us an opportunity to wander for a few hours through the streets of the city, and to get some idea of its amazing strength as a military position. The beautiful bay of Gibraltar, formed by the isthmus and the lofty promontory called the Mountain of Gibraltar on one side, and by the mountains and coast of Spain on the other, is very capacious,—capable of holding a large fleet. The appearance of the rocky and insular height which bears the name of the mountain, and is the same with the MONS CALPE of the ancient Romans, is quite singular. With its northern termination lifting its rugged and frowning head above the southern, aided by the slight depression in the part of the summit which is between them, it easily suggests the idea of a lion *couchant*, reposing in strength, but ready to awake in terrible and irresistible action at any approach of danger. Numerous cannon, lining the shore or looking darkly from the sides of the mountain, are ready to pour forth destruction upon the invader. But Gibraltar is too well known to require a description.

In many respects the city of Gibraltar, with its magnificent bay, with the straits uniting two oceans, with the varied country around it, its position in relation to the countries on the Mediterranean, its immense fortifications, and its history, is one of the most remarkable of places. At this renowned spot was the termination of the most adventurous voyages of the ancient world. For many ages all that lay beyond it was a region unknown. But from that unknown expanse a new power has arisen. Strength is born of liberty. What was once a small barbarian island has become, by refusing the claims and domination of slavery, and by being true to itself, a mighty nation. Its presence and authority are felt in every part of the world. England, taking her position here by the right of conquest, though, it must be allowed, in violation of the rights of position and nature,—England, the mother of nations, and strong in thought and freedom as well as in physical power,—holds this great key and pathway of the East.

When, in coming through the Straits of Gibraltar, we passed from the Mediterranean to the Atlantic, my mind was the subject of a momentary experience, which was powerful but perhaps not unnatural. It seemed to me as if I were passing out of one world into another. The East, though my travels had been rapid, had taken a strong hold upon my imagination, and become a sort of home to me; but from the new scene upon which I was now entering it could be seen and known no more. The transition from one to the other was immense; so that I was reminded of that celebrated gate of Dante, standing at the boundaries of existence, which separated the world of the living from the world of the dead, where those entered who were not destined to return. In a moment, as it were, countries, climates, the appearances of nature, arts, history, were changed. The strong steamer dashed upon the waves. I stood upon the deck and looked back, like one that is loath to lose a beloved object, upon that Eastern world, from which the last ray of light was beaming. It was near the close of the day. On one side were the mountains of Spain. On the other were the mountains of Africa. The lofty heights which once bore the proud name of the Pillars of Hercules, and which the limited knowledge of antiquity had established as the boundary of things, stood face to face. The path of the narrow, foaming ocean was between them. In a few moments, as I stood gazing upon this memorable gateway, more majestic than the gates of Thebes, the clouds and darkness of heaven came down upon it and closed the portal of the Orient forever.

Farewell, bright vision of an hour!
  Fading away, like early dew,
All pass'd; and yet the soul hath power
  Its varied image to renew,—
Restored with tints as clear and true
As sunbeams in their morning hue.

The olive-grove, the mountain-height,
  The vale where many a flock is tended,
The shepherd's tent, the starry night,
  A vision past, but not yet ended,—
Vanish'd to sight, and left behind,
And yet eternal in the mind.

In memory shines that Eastern sky,
  By day and night as clear as ever;
In memory flowers that quickly die
  Resume the tint that fadeth never;
In memory frowns the sunless rock
Which shades the shepherd and his flock.

O strange, mysterious power, possest
  Of what is lost to outward sense!

To thee, the mirror of the breast,
I give this past inheritance,—
Knowing thou wilt not let it die,
But hold it for eternity.

With the aid of steam, and of the sails almost constantly set, we went rapidly on. Soon after leaving the Straits of Gibraltar, we passed the Cape of Trafalgar, which projects from the south-western coast of Spain,—going over the very place in the ocean which has been rendered celebrated by being the locality of Nelson's last great and bloody battle. Altering our direction at Cape St. Vincent, we approached near the coast of Portugal,—so near as to look into the spacious mouth of the Tagus and bring the environs of Lisbon full in sight. Altering our direction again at Cape Finisterre, we crossed the bay of Biscay, and, favored much by the weather, again came in sight of Ireland, and reached Liverpool the second time, July 16.

Here I found friends, who had just arrived from America, and gave me news of my family. I was once more welcomed by the valued Christian friend who had extended to me his hospitality when I reached England the first time. But I could not remain long. I made a rapid visit to London,—which seemed to me, after all I had seen, as entitled to be regarded, in comparison with other cities, as the great seat of commerce, of general intelligence, and of European liberty. I returned to Liverpool, took passage in the steamer Arctic, which sailed for America on the 20th of July, and, after a voyage which was not diversified by any special incidents, reached the city of New York on Saturday, the 30th of the same month.

In another and last letter I wish to say a few words on certain dispositions of mind which are favorable in distant travelling. But I will say a word more here. It is this. I am satisfied with the land and the home which God has given me. I will say a word more. I thought that I was an American; but I have found out that the world is my country. I am one of those who are willing to testify that man, in his central nature, is the same everywhere. In his joys, his griefs, his hopes, his affections, he is one. He may differ in his location, his history, his modes of thought, the form of government under which he lives, his language, his multiplied associations. But his heart, which embodies the secret of universal alliance, is one. He has learned the folly of separation. He sighs for unity.

This is the world's hope. And I will add, that it is this which points to the world's great duty. And that duty is to recognize more and more the idea of central unity, and to believe in and to aim at that unity continually, under the name and form of universal brotherhood, as the great object and the glorious result of Christian civilization.

The fact that I and my brother-man are born in different countries, that we speak different languages, that we live under different governments,—although these things are undoubtedly of the nature of dividing elements and tendencies,—cannot have the effect essentially to separate us while the chords of the heart are united together.

To this union—not so much of the intellect as of the affections—all things tend. War and all contention have become *obsolete ideas.* I do not say that they have become obsolete in *practice.* But I will venture to say that in the estimation of reflecting and enlightened minds, and considered as the means of effectual protection and of real and permanent good, they are rapidly becoming obsolete as ideas or truths. The world (and by the world I mean particularly the great masses of men, who have at last awakened to wider and clearer perceptions) is beginning to discover, that amid multiplied differences there is a common centre, that the differences among men are incidental and temporary, and that the central element is essential and eternal. The light of Christ in the soul has revealed it as a matter of speculative truth to them; and Christ's bleeding and mediating heart will make it good as a matter of practical and positive realization. Through the clouds and smoke of the world's long contest the harmonial sky is dawning. I have been at Trafalgar and have seen the ocean-wave that was reddened by the dying blood of Nelson; I saw the lifeless dust of Wellington carried to its grave; I have stood at the tomb of Napoleon. The day of warriors is over. And I hear once more from the heights of Bethlehem the voice, too long disregarded, (the voice uttered in numbers because it is the harmony of the universe, and uttered by angels because it is the announcement of angelic life,) which proclaims good-will to men, and heavenly peace on earth.

(LVI.)

At home—Home-feelings—My own room—Scenery around me—Reflections on travel—Divine companionship—Illustrations from the circumstances of my departure—Illustrations from the circumstances attending my arrival in England—God seen in his works—God seen in national providences—God seen in the arts—Oneness or unity of religious feeling—God in all places—God within us.

BRUNSWICK, MAINE, AUGUST 4, 1853.

I AM again at home. The date of this letter is the day subsequent to my arrival. I will say nothing of the joys I experience in being once more in the bosom of my family. If I could command adequate language on such a subject, still, I should hardly venture to trust my feelings. I will only say that my heart is grateful, not only for what I have experienced in the affections of my own family, but for every expression of kindness with which my other friends have received me.

I am seated again in the room in which I have spent the hours of a large portion of my life. I look out from my window. Below me is the beautiful village. Beyond the majestic river which encircles it—which flows in part from the mountains and lakes of my native State—are the hills of Topsham, crowned with trees and verdure. The clear, beaming sunlight comes down in silence on the tranquil forest. The scene fills both the eye and the thoughts. My heart rests.

But in again returning to other thoughts and cares, and in bringing these letters to a close, I will venture to say a few words on a subject which interests me much,—namely, the moral and religious aspects and influences of travel.

My general proposition on this subject is, that if a man wishes to travel into other countries pleasantly and profitably, he must take God with him for a companion,—starting with Him when he goes, in order that he may find Him and know Him and rejoice with Him on the way. He who travels thus will find God watching over and supplying his wants, establishing the harmonies between faith and providence, revealing the Infinite in the finite, and showing not only truth and beauty, but how all truth and beauty centre in Himself. What I have further to say will illustrate in some degree this general position. My statements, it is true, are the slight and imperfect records of personal experience; but I hope, without professing to exhaust the subject, that they will throw some light upon it.

I left my native country September 18, 1852. My leaving at that particular time was somewhat unexpected to myself, and under circumstances which precluded the ordinary preparation. I was unused to distant travel. My health, broken by long anxieties, was quite feeble. I knew not that I had friends, or should be likely to find friends, in foreign countries, and took no letters of introduction, except one to a person in London, which, however, failed of reaching its place of destination. In my physical weakness, which was one principal cause of my going abroad, and which naturally produced an unfavorable effect upon the mind's action, I could hardly be said to be able to take care of myself.

But still, the peculiar combination of circumstances which surrounded me constituted a voice of Providence, which seemed to me to require me to depart. Unwilling to go in my own will, I believed, nevertheless, that I was required to go in the decisions of a higher will. This conviction was a great consolation to me, because I had been led to adopt strongly the opinion that a man's safety and happiness depend very much upon his harmonizing with providential arrangements. Harmony with providence is of course harmony with the God of providence; and, as the providential adjustments which touched my case were such that I could not well do otherwise than I did, I did not doubt that I went not so much in self-choice and self-will, as because God required me to go. But where he was to send me, what I was to see, whether my health was to be restored, or whether I should be the subject of increased sufferings and perhaps of death itself in a foreign land, I did not know, nor had I any special anxiety to know. I stood upon the deck of the steamer Arctic, as she proudly made her way down the bay of New York, feeling that I held the only hand which could rightfully and truly guide me, and satisfied that I was led into this novel situation by a wisdom higher than my own. And this was sufficient for me.

The ocean was a new scene to me. I had never been upon it before,—at least, out of sight of land. Day after day brought nothing but the same expanse of wave added to wave. Space, multiplying itself by time, seemed to enlarge itself; and man, at least in his relation to material expansion, became a very little thing. And then came the accession of unknown forces. The winds and the waves beat upon us; and at one time, in St. George's Channel and near the coast of England, we encountered a very violent storm. Perhaps it was owing to my ignorance, but it seemed to me at this time as if our situation was a perilous one,—with a rocky coast near at hand, a raging sea, and in the darkness of the night. But I found the lessons of religious faith available at this trying juncture, and sustaining the soul without murmurs or fears. This is an illustration of what I have said in a general way of the relations of God to the incidents and exigencies which occur in journeying in foreign lands. The ocean was a revelation of God; the dangers of the ocean were a revelation of the littleness of man; and in the protection which shielded us in the hour of peril we found the truth of the Psalmist's saying, "Because thou hast made the Lord thy habitation, there shall no evil befall thee, neither shall any plague come nigh thy dwelling; for He shall give His angels charge over thee to keep thee in all thy ways."

I will illustrate the subject in other ways. We had scarcely entered the river Mersey and set foot upon the shores of England, when I formed an acquaintance with a gentleman of wealth and piety, never seen by me before, who offered me the hospitality of his house, and in various ways exhibited a strong and generous desire to render my stay in England profitable and pleasant. I have referred to him in one of my early letters. My personal obligations for the marked kindness of this excellent man* can never be forgotten; and it was the more pleasing, because I saw that his wealth, his position and influence in society and in the church of which he is a member, and his assiduous personal labors, were all devoted to the cause of truth, religion, and humanity. I thus found that Providence, in not furnishing at my departure the ordinary letters of introduction, had not left me without friends; and that full faith in the present and protecting care of God is a letter of introduction and credit, which the great Being on whom it is drawn would not allow to be dishonored.

Nor was this the only instance of providential interest and care. Other friends were raised up, other arrangements were made, almost without any care or effort on my own part, which gave a new distinctness and impressiveness to the great practical truth that God will take care of those who believingly put their trust in him.

In regard to the particular places and results of my journeyings, I have already said that I had no special anxiety. I knew that there was One who could plan for me better than I could plan for myself. I found, however, that the thought occurred to me from time to time, that it would be a consolation to me, in these last days of my life, if that Being in whom I trusted should enable me to travel in those lands and to see those places which have been rendered memorable by the events recorded in the

* Mr. George Pennell, of Liverpool.

Scriptures. I had no definite expectations; it seemed to be hardly within the range of possibility: but still it was natural that I should desire, if it should be God's will to grant it, to see the places where the Saviour was born, lived, and died. God was pleased, in a manner unexpected to myself, to raise up friends, by means of whose kindness this desire was fulfilled. The persons to whom I now allude were the valued American friends to whom I have already often referred. They cheerfully consented to admit me to the privilege of their society, took the most friendly interest in my comparatively helpless situation, relieved me from many duties and cares which would have been beyond my strength, and contributed in many ways to my happiness, as we travelled together in France, Savoy, Sardinia, Tuscany, Rome, Naples, Malta, Egypt, the peninsula of Sinai, and Palestine. It is hardly necessary to say that I could see nothing but the hand of God in this favorable and unexpected occurrence.

It was thus that, starting with God, or at least endeavoring to do so, I found God on the way. And I not only recognized and felt the divine presence in the arrangements which facilitated my travels, but also in other respects.

In the state of mind in which I was, and which led me to think much of things in their causes or original source, I could not travel without seeing God in the works of which he is the Author. With the exception of sin, the origin and relations of which are not easily understood, it is, I suppose, a just and commonly-received idea, that God has a real and positive relation to everything which exists or which takes place, both natural and moral. He is, therefore, not far from every one of us at all times. And there is a pure and believing state of mind, (of which the soul, as it advances in Christian experience, will not fail to be the subject,) in which all existences, and all events and providences also, will become of the nature of divine revelations. He, therefore, who has an opportunity of seeing most of nature, (I speak now particularly of physical or material nature,) may expect to see most of God, if he has within him that opened and purified eye by which the great fact of the divine presence and agency is perceptible. In other words, the world is *God's book*,—the embodied and finite representation, so far as it can be made, of that which is Infinite; and he who has an opportunity of turning over its pages and seeing most of it has an opportunity, other things being equal, of seeing and knowing most of God himself. In passing, therefore, from land to land, from ocean to ocean, along beautiful or mighty rivers, the Seine, the Arno, the Tiber, the Rhone, the Thames, the Nile, the Jordan, and over lofty mountains, the beautiful Tabor, the majestic Carmel, the snow-clad Alps, the wooded Apennines, the burning brow of Vesuvius, and the rugged granite peaks of Sinai, the conception of the Deity, aided by these vast objects of sight, greatly expanded and magnified itself. It seemed to me as if my heavenly Father, as he thus went with me from place to place, held me by the hand and opened in my presence on each new river's bank or mountain-height some new page or picture in that vast and wondrous volume of nature which is in part the record and monument of his unsearchable glory. The letters which formed the great name of Jehovah were made up, if I may so express it, of rivers and oceans, of vast plains and mountains; and I read and understood them on that account the more easily. I cannot tell how my heart rejoiced—how it exulted—in these new revelations.

I must say further, in giving an account of the religious suggestions to which an acquaintance with different and distant countries gives rise, that I was led to think much of God, and to appreciate more fully the excellence of his character, considered as the God of nations as well as of individuals.

There is a providence of individuals. There is also a providence of states and empires. And it is to the last I now particularly refer. It is not easy to tread among the ruins of buried or prostrate nations, without learning a moral lesson. And the more we know of the mighty power of right and wrong,—whether by the rewards or the sorrows which they bring,—the more we know of God, and the greater confidence we have in Him. I cannot be expected to go into particulars, but will make one or two allusions. If no nation of ancient times arose to greater power and influence than ancient Rome, extending her sway as she did over a great part of the world, it is also true, I think, that she reached that overshadowing position by a course characterized not unfrequently by deception, and almost always by pride and cruelty. In completing the measure of her glory—or rather what the world calls glory—she completed also the measure of her sin. And in travelling over Italy, we saw everywhere, in broken walls and scattered columns, the fragments of a prostrate nation, which had fallen at the touch of Providence, because it had been founded, not on justice and mercy, but on ambition and violence. Not only invading armies had trampled on her gates, but, making our way through the ashes and lava of Pompeii and Herculaneum, it was not easy to forget that burning mountains and tossing seas had also risen up in testimony against her.

At an earlier period Egypt had its grandeur. The Pharaohs were as proud and as cruel as the Cæsars; and the massive monuments of the Nile cannot justly be regarded as inferior in extent and grandeur to the magnificent ruins which are scattered on the banks of the Tiber. But the greatness of Egypt—a greatness which is sufficiently indicated and proved by the extent of its remaining desolations—could not support itself against that providential law which pronounces death upon everything that is not sustained by principles which meet the divine approbation. If I saw God, therefore, among the ruins of Rome, I saw Him also among the ruins of Egypt.

Nor was this all. Amid the tottering walls and the sea-beaten columns of the proud cities Tyre and Sidon, I had before me other evidences, perhaps not less striking than those to which I have referred, that God, in the light of his providential dealings with nations, is impressively revealed in his great attributes of power and justice. So true it is that morality, having its foundation in the unalterable constitution and relations of things, has its practical development and its commentary in historical events; and that desolation itself, when viewed in the light of a just philosophy, will "vindicate the ways of God to man." Palestine itself, the land of God's chosen people, found no exemption from this great truth. I looked down from the mountains of Judea on the Dead Sea, and remembered the fate of Sodom and Gomorrah, which sleep in silence beneath its dark waters. And as I stood on the Mount of Olives and beheld Jerusalem, I called to mind the sad prediction of the Saviour, which the sword of Titus and the gathering of the "Roman eagles" had accomplished.

My religious convictions were strengthened also in another way,—and so much so as to draw still more closely the bonds of communion and love. Providence so ordered my journey, as I have already been led to say, that I was enabled to travel over lands which have a connection with Biblical history; and everything which came under my notice tended to confirm that great record of God's intercourse with men. And thus I became more intimately acquainted not only with the God of nature and providence, but with the God of the Bible. I travelled that Appian Way—I passed the site of that Appii Forum and the Three Taverns—of which I had read, or to which I had found references, in the book of Acts. At Puccioli, where the Apostle Paul first landed in Italy, at the island of Malta, where he was shipwrecked, and at Rome, where he was a prisoner and where he was put to death for Jesus' name, I felt I was treading upon soil honored by eminent religious associations. On the Nile, at the Red Sea, in our long march through the wilderness of Sinai, at Hebron, at Bethlehem, at Samaria, at Esdraelon, at the Sea of Galilee, and in many other places, we found striking confirmations of the narratives and statements of the Bible.

I had never doubted the Bible. I ever had a deep-abiding conviction of its truth,—a conviction resulting not only from the external evidence which may be brought to bear upon it, but especially from the evidence which it carries in itself. And yet, in some way which perhaps it would not be easy for me to explain, the Bible seemed to me, when I had actually been amid the scenes of its wonderful narratives, to have more distinctness, more fulness of truth, more transcendent power. I shall not easily forget how, on Judah's hills and at the base of the mountains of Gilboa, the songs of David echoed through my spirit, as if they were flung for the first time from the master's lyre. On the hill of Bethlehem, in the valley of Nazareth, and on the Mount of Olives, the Saviour's life assumed a greater distinctness and reality, and I seemed to hear more audibly the divine words which proceeded from his lips.

I know not how it may have been with other travellers, but I am obliged to add, further, that the works of art which we saw from time to time in different countries not unfrequently inspired emotions which harmonized with and strengthened the highest religious sentiments. It is something to see the judgment-scenes of Michael Angelo, and to stand in the presence of the historical events of the Bible, as they are brought to light in the miraculous

Cartoons of Raphael. It would argue but poorly for a person's religious sensibility, who should not find it quickened and strengthened in some degree by Scripture scenes and events, as they are combined together, and revealed anew, as it were, in the paintings of Correggio and Murillo and of the other great masters whose works are so frequently found in the galleries of art and in the palaces of Europe.

And I think it may be said, further, that there is a sense in which the works of art may be regarded without impropriety as the works of God, and in which we may associate God with them, much in the same way in which we may associate Him with the works of nature. Who made the marble which the chisel has wrought into shape? Who fashioned the hand that holds the chisel or which guides the painter's pencil? From whom came that inspiring thought in accordance with which the marble is modelled, or which gives harmony and inspiration to color? Genius is not an accident; but everything which is true and good in it, everything which harmonizes with nature and gives strength to virtue, has a divine origin. To the eye of faith, which sees causes in effects and which traces the multiplied relations of things to their central element, God sits enthroned in the Roman Capitol, amid the countless works of art which he has inspired, no less than on the Alps and the Apennines.

These views might be presented in another and little different light. The traveller not only meets with flowers and trees, with rivers and mountains, which elevate his thoughts to God,—not only with works of art, which also have their moral and religious influences upon the mind, but the power of association, operating strongly in connection with memorable localities, restores, and places before him almost with the distinctness of real life, the powerful or illuminated men of other days who have imparted clearness to truth, or beauty to virtue,—men who have illustrated humanity by thought, or have honored it by suffering and action. I have referred to this, in part, in connection with what I have said of the associated influence of scenes in Palestine. But I would extend the view to all lands, to all periods of time, and to all truly great men. When I came to the places over which their memory and their spirits hovered, it is hardly an exaggeration to say that they appeared personally before me. The mind created them anew. Let it not be considered strange, then, if I say, in a sense which is susceptible of a just appreciation, that I met with Somers, Chatham, and Burke in the Parliament-House of England, with Wesley and Addison on the banks of the Isis and Cherwell, with Shakspeare in Windsor Forest and on Dover Cliffs, with Algernon Sidney on Tower Hill, with Fenelon at the Seminary of St. Sulpitius, with Dante at Florence, with Cicero in the Roman Capitol, with Moses in the wilderness, with Abraham, Isaac, and Jacob at Mamre and the cave of Machpelah, with David on the hill of Zion. The mind seized upon what remained, and restored what had departed. The inward senses were opened with a power greater than that which belongs to the outward. The eye of the mind saw them. The ear of the heart heard them.

Can atheism thus give life to the dead? Can infidelity, which has no confidence in virtue, thus restore the men of other ages, whose memory remains because their life was the teaching and the illustration of virtue? How can these things be, if there be no God? And how can they be, with that explanation which a belief in God alone can give of them, without a juster appreciation and a higher love of Him who, in being the Source of all things, is the Centre of all just thoughts, the Mind of all minds?

One of the pleasant things of a religious nature, which increases the interest and happiness of the Christian traveller in foreign countries, is the evidence which he often obtains of the essential unity or oneness of character which exists in religious experience. In Europe, Asia, Africa, America, the child of God is one. Under blazing suns and in polar snows, under all forms of government and diversities of education, as well as in all varieties of climate, the image of Christ is the same,—drawn in immortal lines by the same mighty Architect,—not always completed, but filling out, with each day's added lines and touches, into the likeness of that great and beautiful model which exhibited, in the person of Christ in his earthly incarnation, the soul of the Godhead in man's human heart. Names, sects, parties, have no power to hide it, any more than diversities of language, government, and color. This beautiful image I saw in my travels, in countries and places far remote from each other:—on the banks of the Po and the Tiber, in London, in Florence, in Alexandria, in Jerusalem, in the cottages of Waldensian mountains, as I had seen it before in the mountains of America,—differing, undoubtedly, in degrees of completeness, but always true to the great Master's hand. It needed no letter of introduction. I saw it with the eye of the heart. I embraced it with the arms of the affections. I cannot say how much I rejoiced in this multiplication of universal brotherhood. It was more pleasant to me than the beauties of nature, delightful as they are,—brighter than the light of the morning sun on the mountain-tops.

Among other developments of religious feeling, or perhaps I should say of those feelings which have a close connection with our religious nature, I am tempted to give the following illustration. It presents a form of experience related to, and yet in some respects very different from, that which I have just given.

One day, after reaching Alexandria, I occupied myself, in company with the friends who were with me, in making a short excursion along the banks of the Mahmoudie Canal. On the shore of the canal, engaged in various occupations, or strolling at leisure on its banks, were Turks and Arabs, and not unfrequently with a group of children around them. To me they were a new race of beings,—differing from what I had been accustomed to see in dress and in outward bearing and deportment, as well as in their history and language. But under these differences of dress and peculiarities of manner I recognized, in the "human face divine," the signatures of a common heart, a common nature. None of the outward differences to which I have referred, no diversities of descent and history, of language, or even of religion, were capable of limiting my affections. My eyes had no sooner looked upon them, than my heart gave them its sympathy and love as promptly and as strongly as if they had been, as in fact they were and are, "bone of my bone and flesh of my flesh." And I must confess that this unprompted unity of feeling made me very happy for a short time. I was rejoiced to find that in every part of the world I could meet a great multitude to whom I could apply, as representative of my feelings, the sacred names of brothers and sisters, of fathers and mothers.

This was my first experience. Only a very short time, however, had passed, when I had inward misgivings; and, indeed, the thought was strongly impressed upon my mind, as if by some unseen power, that I had done wrong in thus promptly giving my heart to those of a different religious faith. An inward suggestion seemed to upbraid me with placing confidence and affection in a race of men who rejected the Christian religion and had often shown hostility and contempt to that Saviour in whom alone I was entitled to place my dearest hopes. What was a Turk to me? Or what was I to a Turk? Had not the whole history of these Mohammedan races been adverse to Christianity? Had not the scimetar been bathed in the blood of Christians?

Whether these suggestions came from a good or

an evil source, from God or from Satan, I was at a loss to know. The embarrassment, however, and the sorrow, arising from this state of mind, were not small; and I was not relieved from them till I had made it a subject of inward reflection. I sought retirement. In simplicity and earnestness of spirit, I carried the matter to God, as the great Source of truth. I was soon relieved, and so convincingly and distinctly that I was not troubled afterwards. God said to me—if I may be allowed to employ the unusual language of the ancient Mystics, but which, I must confess, more accurately describes the intimations and experience of my inward consciousness than any other—that my business was *to love;* that God alone could know and appreciate the diversities of situations and creeds; that He alone could estimate the unpropitious tendencies of a birth and education in a heathen or Mohammedan land; that I could not be born into the image of Him who died for His enemies, while I repulsed from my bosom the man of any clime or any belief; and that, in all cases, he who wishes to convey the truth to any people, and to do them good, must carry before him, as its precursor, the open banner of a generous and disinterested affection.

One of the results of these long travels was a clearer and deeper impression than I had experienced ever before, that the presence and influence of God *are not limited by locality.*

Every man who has a truly religious heart has what may be called his sacred places. What I mean to say is, that every man, in looking back upon his past religious life, is able to recall places which are associated with religious incidents,—places which are allied in his recollections with resolutions of amendment, or with remarkable developments of religious truth, or which have been consecrated by the sorrows of penitence or by the joys of gratitude. This I suppose to be the general experience; and I am neither able, nor have I any desire, to plead an exemption from it. My mind has never ceased to recall such places; and often it has recalled them with profit and pleasure. I remember the Bible which my mother gave me; nor is the place forgotten in which she gave it. I remember the places where I read it alone. I remember the garden, the wood, the valley, the river's bank, where I spent many hours in pondering the problems of salvation, and in seeking the great Central Source of light. I remember the humble abodes, rude and solitary perhaps, but yet consecrated in the religious affections, where, in the evening of a long summer's day, I stole secretly apart, to listen to the prayers of gray-headed old men, or to learn from their lips the wondrous things of God in glory and of mankind redeemed.

The teachings of God, therefore, and the various religious influences of which he is the source, had become associated, in some degree, with places; and undoubtedly, forgetting the difference between the Finite and the Infinite, I had a secret feeling, hardly perceptible to myself, that such gracious influences were more likely to be repeated in some places than others. A wider experience dissipated this natural and common illusion. I found that God could travel as far and as fast as any of his poor children. And when I set my foot on the ocean, to visit, for the first time, climes remote and lands unknown, I left my country and friends, but did not and could not leave my God behind me. Wherever I went, I found him at my side. On the ocean and on the land, in the storm and in the sunshine, amid the matchless beauties of Richmond Hill and in the sterility of Arabian deserts, in mountain-tops and in lowly valleys, in the palaces of the Thames and the Seine and in the Bedouin's tent and the Fellah's cottage of clay, everywhere, and under all circumstances, I found Him present, to guide, to counsel and console. And it seemed to be an *actual*, and not merely a hypothetical and constructive, presence,—a presence which is recognized by the heart as well as by the intellectual conviction, and which harmonizes with the expressions of the Saviour, when he said, "THE KINGDOM OF GOD IS WITHIN YOU."

I have incidentally referred to this experience in some other letters. I made records of it from time to time. I have sometimes thought that it is the tendency of raised emotions, when they have harmony in themselves by being in harmony with God and the universe, to strive after an outward expression in numbers. Whatever is not in harmony—whatever is discordant with character, position, and all just relations—is, at least, not in the highest form of truth; and hence it was, perhaps, that these slight records of religious feeling, without making pretensions to poetical merit, often took the form of measure or verse.

I will give one or two illustrations. Our boat

was one day anchored on the banks of the Nile. I wandered away alone a considerable distance. I came to the vast silent sands of the Libyan desert, which limits the fertility and the cultivation of the Egyptian river. I sat down. Around me was vastness, desolation, unutterable silence. But this great solitude was peopled with the presence of God's company. If, in this vast but lonely place, my heart, as it seemed to me, was emptied of all earthly things, I seemed to be at least equally conscious that it was occupied and filled with the Infinite. I felt the pressure and the embrace of that mighty arm which holds the ocean and the land, the mountain and the desert.

'Tis thus in solitude I roam
  O'er many a land and tossing sea;
And yet, afar from friends and home,
  I find, O God! a home in Thee.

I pass from things of space and time;
  The finite meets or leaves my sight:
But God expands o'er every clime
  The clothing of the Infinite.

He left me not in that far land
  Which I have loved to call my own;
And, walking now on Egypt's sand,
  I feel that I am not alone.

He walks the earth, He rides the air;
  The lightning's speed He leaves behind;
His name is LOVE. And, tell me, Where
  Is sea or land He cannot find?

Oh, long I've known him. Could it be
  That, if He did not hold me dear,
He thus would travel land and sea
  And throw His arms around me here?

I could not leave Him if I would;
  I would not, if the power were given;

'Twould be to leave the True and Good,
The soul's Repose, the spirit's Heaven.

On other occasions also, and not unfrequently, I made slight records in verse of religious feelings, which would not be inserted here were it not they are to be read by those who will know in what way to understand them. In reflecting, for instance, upon the inward experience of which I had been the subject, I had a clearer view perhaps than ever before of that passage of Scripture to which I have just now referred,—"The kingdom of God is within you." Being in such a number of places and in such a variety of circumstances, I was enabled to understand more fully what I had already read in books of philosophy,—that external things take their character, in a great degree, from the mind; and that the kingdom of God in the soul, by the diffusion of its own beauty, can change any place, however rude and desolate in itself, into a heavenly mansion.

And, in accordance with this view, I found my heart allying itself with all objects, animate and inanimate, which came under my notice; and it found alliances and sympathies in return. The rock which symbolizes the hardness of a fallen nature was smitten and pierced within me; the fountain of the central deep was broken up; and love, which changes everything into its own beauty, flowed out in rivers. Not only varied and conflicting humanity, becoming harmonized at last into universal brotherhood, clasped me to its bosom, but also material and inanimate nature revealed itself as the clothing or outward expression of a divine principle and life within. There was a voice in the winds. There was a song in the ocean-waves. The desert struggled to scatter a few flowers at my feet. The very rocks smiled upon me.

With the kingdom of God in the heart, I found no difficulty in understanding the vision of the New Jerusalem and in beholding its descending brightness in everything around me. It is in the influence of such views and experiences that you will find, in part, the explanation of what follows, with which I now close this long letter:—

THE KINGDOM OF GOD IS WITHIN YOU.

How oft our thoughts and hopes arise
To thee, the City of the Skies!
How oft we sit in grief, and sigh,
Because thy brightness is not nigh,—
Forgetting that a Power is here
Which makes the high and distant near!

Oh, yes! To man the power is given
To bring to earth that distant heaven,—
The power of FAITH, which has the art
To build God's kingdom in the heart;
The power of LOVE, which has the skill
With God himself the soul to fill.

'Tis faith that conquers time and space,
And love makes heaven of form and place;
Their strength combined makes all things new;
It mars the false, it builds the true;
It plants on martyr'd heads the crown;
It brings the golden city down.

Oh, then, arise, poor child of tears!
Put on thy faith; put off thy fears;
And when the power which faith bestows
Hath met and crush'd thy spirit's foes,
Light in the heart love's shining gem,
And be thine own Jerusalem.

VALUABLE WORKS

PUBLISHED BY

HENRY LONGSTRETH,

915 Market Street, Philadelphia.

They will be sent to any address (post-paid) on receipt of the prices affixed.

I. LETTERS ÆSTHETIC, SOCIAL, AND MORAL.

Written from Europe, Egypt, and Palestine by Thomas C. Upham, Professor of Mental and Moral Philosophy in Bowdoin College. Whipple & Co. Second Edition, Henry Longstreth, Philadelphia. Price, $2.00.

THIS well-remembered title will awaken pleasant emotions in the breasts of those who were readers of the *Congregationalist* in the years 1852–53, during which they were published in our columns. By all such, and by all who know the peculiar charm of Professor Upham's style, and the genuine goodness, and genial piety of all which he does and utters, this volume will be sought for as the most delightful book of travels which has, for a long time, been issued from the press. Perhaps we do wrong, however, in using this phraseology, since the book has hardly been "issued from the press" at all; the extreme modesty of its author certifying to him that a few copies only would be wanted, and so a few only, for private friends, have been printed. Those who wish for one out of the little package in Mr. Whipple's hands will do well to be in season in their application, and we cannot help hoping that the demand may be such and so disinclined to take denial that the professor may soon come out in a second and public edition. It is a beautiful, thoughtful, and truthful record of the transatlantic experiences of no common man.—*The Congregationalist.*

We have frequently desired of late that our readers might share with us a gratification which we did not feel at liberty so much as to name,—the reading of Professor Upham's letters, written for the *Congregationalist* during his foreign tour, and now collected in a handsome volume. We received this volume as a gift of friendship from the author, and found upon its title-page the warning that it was a *private* edition, and so have felt bound in courtesy to keep to ourselves the enjoyment we have found in its pages. But, now that the *North American* has given a formal notice of the volume, we may feel absolved from all obligations of secrecy, and openly advise booksellers to make arrangements to have this "private edition" upon their shelves. As a book of travels it is somewhat peculiar. It deals little in what is styled the narrative or the descriptive, and follows no stereotyped method, but it has the rare merit of simplicity in narration and description, and it beautifully blends the subjective with the objective, so that the mental experiences and the moral inferences of the author are inseparably connected with what he sees. One will find in this volume a fine classic taste, a pure and sound judgment upon monuments and works of art, a nice historical criticism in regard to matters of antiquity, a deep vein of spiritual philosophy, a generous sympathy with freedom, and above all a philanthropy that knows no bounds of space or clime.

It was our privilege for many months to know somewhat intimately the workings of the mind that so artlessly reproduces itself in these pages; and the admirable blending of the Christian philosopher with the practical philanthropist, of the reasoner with the believer, of the teacher with the friend, of the earnest student with the childlike disciple,—this rare combination of high mental culture with high moral goodness, the whole chastened and moulded by the simplest faith,—led us to expect from the pen of Professor Upham just such a volume as we have now described. How with feeble health and impaired vision he had time and strength to prepare so many letters of such excellent quality, is to us a mystery. All who have known Professor Upham through his former writings will delight to be admitted to this familiar acquaintance, and to look upon his speaking portrait affixed to the volume. The invigorated tone of his countenance in this picture, as well as of his mind in the letters, causes us to despair of pronouncing his elegy, and therefore we make sure of this passing tribute.—*From the N. Y. Independent.*

After perusing the above-named book with exceeding interest, we laid it down with one deep and abiding regret, which further reflection greatly strengthens. That one regret is that it was issued in a private edition of four hundred volumes only, or that that was not immediately followed by one which might be accessible to all. With the author's previous religious volumes we are well acquainted, from the Mental Philosophy, which shed a flood of light upon a youthful, struggling mind; followed by the "Interior Life," which opened a new world to a feeble but sincere and aspiring spiritual nature, through the Life of Faith, aided by Catharine Adorna, as a practical illustration, and by Madame Guyon, as a beautiful exemplification of the power of these spiritual principles; closing with the "Divine Union," as the climax of all that may be grasped before "this mortal shall put on immortality." Then come the "Letters," the same, yet different; the same in principles, in sentiment, in style, bearing the Uphamic stamp in every chapter and on every page, yet different; for while the inner thought and feeling, the peculiar philosophy and religious views, of the author are impressed and interwoven with every line, yet here the outward world is grasped, analyzed, shadowed forth—nay, illuminated—by its connection with the inward, intellectual, spiritual life. The world of matter—this beautiful, unconscious earth, with its rolling ocean, its splendid cities, its teeming country, its wonders of art, its silent deserts, and its historic facts—is electrified or galvanized into vocal life, speaking everywhere of God, redemption, man's ruin and recovery, and of that glorious millennial future when, purified from its imperfections and defilements, perfected in arts and sciences, its Creator and Redeemer shall again pronounce it "very good."—*New York Christian Advocate and Journal.*

We count ourselves particularly fortunate to have been found within "the limited circle" beyond which Professor Upham, with too great, but characteristic, modesty, cannot persuade himself that these Letters "will possess any special interest." Books of travel have become proverbially trite and threadbare, rehearsing to us in regular succession the same routes of journey, the same marvels of nature and art, with the same barren and commonplace sentiments. Mere guide-books are they, in fact, to the tourist. To this unattractive class, however, Professor Upham's volume does not at all belong. Although he goes over much of the ground already described by his predecessors, yet he aims to give us rather the picture of his own mind as affected by the scenes and associations and charms of Europe and the Desert and the Holy Land, than a mere daguerreotype of their visible and tangible features. Such a transcript of an intellect enriched and disciplined by studious culture, of a sentiment liberalized and refined by a genial humanity, and especially of a heart purified and quickened by contemplative devotion, must have a value inestimably beyond the vapid sketches of professional sight-seers. Great historical learning and an absorbed study of Holy Scripture enabled Dr. Upham to find an ennobling and pathetic beauty and fascination in all the localities of the Old World; and he has thus described them to us as adorned by the reflected splendor of his own observation. It is new as well as profitable to us to be told how such a man was moved by the hallowed sight and memories of regions so often portrayed to us as objects for the eye rather than the heart to enjoy. The commonest experiences were to him invested with a significance and dignity which fail to strike meaner observers; and his volume is more precious to us as a record of intimate metaphysical and ethical development than of ordinary travel and enjoyment.

It is unnecessary to say that the style and diction are models of simple elegance and transparency. Professor Upham's works are too well known even to school-children to need any word of commendation from us. Several graceful poems, evidently prompted by actual emotion, not elaborated to eke out the pages, enrich the book. We give one, selected on the doubtful merit of its being the shortest we find, to exhibit the purity of the feeling and the melodious flow of the verse.

"O Saviour! thus I leave the land
Which thou hast loved and look'd upon;
No more upon the hills to stand
Where thou hast stood in ages gone.

And yet the breeze, the sail that fills,
Is whispering to my pensive mind,
That, thus in leaving Judah's hills,
I do not leave her king behind.

"The faithful soul shall know it true
That every land and clime is thine;
That He who trod in Hermon's dew
Finds everywhere his Palestine.
I go, but cannot go from thee;
I tread once more the ocean's tide;
But He who walk'd on Judah's sea
Will not be absent from my side."

Most earnestly do we call upon Professor Upham to give us an edition of these Letters which shall not bear the word *private* upon its title-page; meanwhile counselling our friends to intrude, if practicable, upon the "privacy" of the present issue. They shall then find themselves in communion with a large and wealthy mind and heart, and cannot but be benefited by the intercourse.—*From the N. H. Dover Enquirer.*

It is inestimably precious as a record of the author's inward life and spiritual experience, in communion with nature in her solitudes, her grandeur, and in her beauty, with humanity under various phases of civilization and religion, and with the memorials of supernatural events, sacred history, religious heroism, and Christian martyrdom. If his vision was sealed where other men's eyes are open,—if he closed his letters from Rome without so much as a reference to St. Peter's,—he more than compensates us by the promptness of his intuitions and the depth of his insight wherever the nobler faculties of mind and heart are concerned.

"Another feature (says the reviewer) of this charming volume is, the author's generous sympathy with every form and manifestation of the religious life, with sincerity and devotion under whatever name or rubric, and with whatever admixture of reputed error in speculative belief." "His genial sympathies are by no means confined to the Christian fold. . . . He seeks every opportunity of familiar intercourse with the poorest natives of the benighted regions through which his Oriental pilgrimage carries him, and announces the interchange of affectionate greetings and kind offices with some wretched family in a hut on a sand-waste, with the same serene satisfaction with which Dr. Sprague records a successful visit to a professor of world-wide celebrity."

"'Tis difficult to make selections where there is hardly a paragraph that is not remarkable either for descriptive power or for devotional sentiment; and still more difficult is it by detached passages to convey any idea of the quiet ecstasy of lofty contemplation, reverence, and love that pervades this portion of the volume, presenting the reflection of the soul whose emotional life is calm from its very depth and fulness, and which with every step upon the soil consecrated by the Redeemer's footprints drinks in his fresh benedictions." The article closes with the wish that this, "one of the choicest books of the day," may not be confined to the limited circle of friends for whose use and at whose solicitation it was printed.—*North American Review.*

May I be allowed to say with what pleasure I have read the "Letters Æsthetic, Social, and Moral," of Professor Upham, of Bowdoin College, written during his recent visit to Europe, Egypt, and Palestine, and fully expressive of those devout sentiments and all-comprehensive philanthropy which so eminently mark his many able works and are so beautifully illustrated in his personal character? The simplicity of a child is combined in him with great learning, a fine poetic taste, a profound philosophy, and affections which, like the light of the sun, encompass all forms of beauty and things of life. To know one such man is a great privilege. The college of which he is one of the chief ornaments, the State which enjoys the power of his example, may well be thankful for such a treasure. Let me add some value to what might otherwise be deemed of little worth, by copying a brief passage from the forty-third of these Letters, relating to the Wilderness of Sinai:—

"I am obliged to say, therefore, that a journey through the Wilderness of Sinai, which brings with it so many great thoughts as the product of its chaotic vastness, not only furnishes no apology for irreligion, no apology for atheistic unbelief, but, on the contrary, proclaims hostility against a light and irreverent spirit. God is there. His footprints are in the sand. His voice is heard in the winds. His name is written with sunbeams on the rocks. The very silence utters him.

"I wanted repose, and I found it in the desert. I wanted communion with God, and I found it there. I found it, in the day, in the vastness of its objects, and in its silence. I found it still more in the night, when magnitude enlarges itself, and silence becomes more silent. I found it in the earth beneath, and in the heavens above. Often I watched the stars. Beautiful as the heavenly mansions, they looked out from their blue abodes, clear and lovely, as if they were the eyes of that great Being who fills their urns with light. There was one, with its large angelic eye, that came with peculiar sweetness. It danced upon the mountain-tops. It had no audible utterance; but there was a divine language in its smile, which spoke of heavenly peace. It was in the desert of Sinai that I gave it a place in my memory. It was in the vast wilderness which had inspired the prophetic impulses and the songs of Moses that I watched the mild splendor of its beams, and endeavored to record the emotions excited by its mysterious but lovely presence.

"LINES WRITTEN IN THE WILDERNESS OF SINAI.

"I mark'd the bright, the silver star,
That nightly deck'd our desert way,
As, shining from its depths afar,
Its heavenly radiance seem'd to say,
'Oh, look! from mists and shadows clear,
My cheering light is always here.'

"I saw thee, and at once I knew,
Star of the desert, in my heart,
That thou didst shine, the emblem true
Of that bright Star whose beams impart,
From night to night, from day to day,
The solace of their inward way.

"There is a beam to light the mind,
There is a star the soul to cheer;
And they that heavenly light who find
Shall always see it burning clear,—
The same its bright celestial face
In every change of time and place.

"Star of my heart, that long hast shone
To cheer the inward spirit's sky,
Illumined from the heavenly throne,—
Thou hast a ray that cannot die.
'*Tis God that lights thee!* And with Him
No sky is dark, no star is dim."

N. Y. Journal of Commerce.

II.—Letters of Richard Reynolds, with a Memoir of his Life. By his granddaughter, Hannah Mary Rathbone, Author of "Diary of Lady Willoughby." Price, $1.

III.—Memorials of Rebecca Jones, compiled by William J. Allinson. Price, $1.

IV.—Select Memoirs of Port Royal: to which are appended Tour to Alet; Visit to Port Royal; Gift of an Abbess; Biographical Notices, &c., taken from original Documents by M. A. Schimmelpenninck, 2 vols. 8vo. Price, $4.

V.—Gleanings from Pious Authors: comprising the Wheat Sheaf, Fruits and Flowers, Garden and Shrubbery; compiled by Ann Alexander, of Ipswich, England, with a brief notice of the former publications of these volumes, by James Montgomery. Price, $1.

VI.—Life of William Allen, with selections from his Correspondence, 2 vols. 8vo. Price, $4.

VII.—Memoirs of Sir Thomas Fowell Buxton, Baronet, with selections from his Correspondence. Edited by his son, Charles Buxton, Esq. Price, $2.

VIII.—Life of Elizabeth Fry; compiled from her Journal, as edited by her daughters, and from various other sources, by Susanna Corder. Price, $2.

IX.—Memoir of Priscilla Gurney; compiled by Susanna Corder. Price, $1.

X.—A Selection from the Letters and Papers of the late John Barclay. Price, $1.

XI.—Memoirs of Maria Fox, late of Tottenham, England, consisting chiefly of extracts from her journal and correspondence. Price, $2.

XII.—Extracts from the Journal of the late Margaret Woods, from the year 1771 to 1821. Price, $1.

XIII.—Christian Instruction in the History, Types, and Prophecies of the Old Testament; illustrating those fundamental doctrines of the Gospel which are acknowledged by true Christians of every religious denomination. By Susanna Corder. Price, 50 cents.

XIV.—Thoughts on Habit and Discipline. By Joseph John Gurney. Price, 75 cents.

"It is one of those sterling books on self-government which no man can read without receiving both mental and moral benefit. Like all Mr. Gurney's writings, it is strictly orthodox in its views, catholic in its sentiments, apt in its illustrations, clear and forcible in its style."—*Bath Chronicle.*

"Its tone is decidedly religious; but its method is philosophical, while its style is popular."—*Athenæum.*

"The work is distinguished by that benevolent and parental mildness which so characterized the life and conversation of the author, and is calculated to win the heart while it convinces the understanding of the reader."—*Bath Herald.*

"This is one of the most useful works that could be put into the hands of young persons. We have never seen the subject more ably handled."—*Liverpool Courier.*

"We have few books extant containing, in so brief a space, so much sound practical instruction."—*Keene's Bath Journal.*

"Such *thoughts* are the great desideratum of the age, and, if carefully read and enforced in daily life, would contribute much to the well-being of society."—*Newcastle Guardian.*

"*Thoughts on Habit and Discipline* should be read by the young man anxious to make his way in the world in an honorable and creditable manner. There is a lovingness about the articles truly refreshing in these times of selfishness and recklessness."—*Lincoln Standard.*

"The younger portion of the community, and all who have influence with the young, whether as parents or as professional instructors, will find in these papers abundance to repay them for their perusal."—*Baptist Magazine.*

"Sound sense and devout feeling are distinguishing characteristics of this useful publication."—*Cheltenham Chronicle.*

"The proper study of such a book will go far to induce many others to tread in the steps of its lamented author, and to perpetuate the race of philanthropists of which he was, in the true sense of the word, an illustrious example."—*Rochester Gazette.*

XV.—Hints on the Portable Evidence of Christianity. By Joseph John Gurney. Price, 38 cents.

XVI.—A Visit to my Fatherland: being Notes of a Journey to Syria and Palestine in 1843. By Ridley H. Herschell, Author of a "Brief Sketch of the Jews," &c. Price, 38 cents.

This is a remarkably interesting little work written by a converted Jew.

XVII.—Hymns, selected from various Authors by Priscilla Gurney. Price, 38 cents.

XVIII.—Patience in Tribulation: A Short Memoir of E. E., an humble-minded Christian, who entered into rest August 13, 1825. Price 25 cents.

XIX.—Essays on the Evidences, Doctrines, and Practical Operation of Christianity. By Joseph John Gurney. Price, $2.

The Editor of his Life, Joseph Bevan Braithwaite, thus writes of this valuable work:—

"It was at the close of this year (1825) that he published the elaborate work in which, under the title of Essays on Christianity, he has embodied, in a condensed form, the result of the meditation and research of many years. With singular perspicuity of arrangement, he here unfolds the evidences and fundamental doctrines of the Christian religion; dwelling with peculiar force upon the great truths of redemption, more especially upon the glorious offices and divine character and perfections of the Redeemer, and the being, power, and work of the Holy Spirit. The tenth essay, in which the scriptural argument in proof of the Deity of Christ is carefully and powerfully stated, contains the substance of the more extended unpublished work upon the subject, which, as has been already noticed, he had commenced so early as the year 1815. The whole is enforced as well by a continued reference to the practical object and tendency of all Christian truth, as by a particular essay devoted to the important subjects of 'faith' and 'obedience,' in which the reasonableness and necessity of their combined and harmonious exercise are strikingly exhibited.

"Deeply sensible of the mysterious, and, to use his own expression in his Journal, 'unembraceable' character of many of the subjects treated of, it was his desire to keep strictly within the limits of that which has been revealed respecting them.

"The whole work breathes the spirit of one whose heart is warmed and animated by the love of Christ. Taught as he had been in the school of experience, and strengthened, in no small measure, to consecrate his faculties to the service of his Divine Master, he was enabled in this volume, and often with singular success, to employ his extensive acquaintance with the original languages of Scripture, as well as with Jewish and Rabbinical learning, and the remains of early Christian antiquity, in throwing a clear and steady light upon the momentous topics of which he treats. Indeed, it may be said, without disparagement to the many other valuable treatises extant upon these subjects, that it would be difficult to find a volume in which so much sound and important information is digested in so small a compass, and in so useful and practical a form, as in that now under consideration. Notwithstanding the sound scholarship apparent in almost every page, the style is clear, and adapted to the merely English reader; whilst the diligent student of the Hebrew and Greek Scriptures can hardly fail to derive instruction from the many incidental explanations scattered throughout the work, of obscure or difficult passages.

"The work, upon its publication, was very favorably received, and has since passed through numerous editions. In a few warm but expressive lines, the Bishop of Norwich assured Joseph John Gurney of 'the high opinion which he entertained' respecting it; and from his brother-in-law, Thomas Fowell Buxton, he learned the satisfaction which it had given to the Duke of Gloucester. 'I read it,' said the Duke, 'over, and over, and over again.' His old tutor John Rogers wrote with a warmth that may be excused towards a favorite pupil:—

"In the composition of these essays you have discovered an intimate acquaintance with the subject on which you treat; you have shown that your mind is impressed with a full sense of its importance, and that it has occupied your most serious thoughts;

you have displayed a great knowledge of the original languages in which the old and the new covenants were written, as well as of the Jewish and Christian antiquities; you have conducted your work in a regular and perspicuous method; and (what gives it the greatest value) you have evinced, in general, that excellent temper, and that Christian spirit, which ought always to characterize writings of this nature.

"FROM ROBERT SOUTHEY.

"Keswick, 4th January, 1826.

"I have gone through your volume with wonder as well as satisfaction, and I hope not without profiting by it. It would have been a surprising book from one who had been bred to the profession of divinity, and pursued the study with ardor during a long life. The evidence is full and complete, the deductions everywhere logical, the spirit truly Christian; and I cannot doubt but that it will be the means of bringing home many who have gone astray, and of preserving others from error.

"My heart went with you everywhere. There are two points only on which I hesitate in opinion. * * * * Do not think me presumptuous. From the changes through which my mind has passed I have learnt the useful lesson of distrusting myself; and for some twelve years I have been conscious of no other change than an increasing sense of weakness, and the necessity of a saving faith.

"FROM HANNAH MORE.

"Barley Wood, June 15th, 1826.

"It is a necessity to which I am too frequently driven, when I have been favored with a presentation-copy of a work from an author whose mediocrity I either knew or suspected, to return my thanks almost immediately, that I might not be compelled to the painful alternative of rudeness or flattery. You, my dear sir, are an author whose work, to borrow the language of one of the collects of our church, one may 'read, mark, learn, and inwardly digest' before one acknowledges the obligation conferred. There is much judgment in the arrangement, great perspicuity in the style, as well as depth and truth in the argument. I pray that it may please our gracious Heavenly Father, without whom nothing is strong, nothing is holy, to make this book an instrument of much good.

"FROM CHARLES SIMEON.

"K. C. Cambridge, January 25th, 1826.

"MY BELOVED FRIEND AND BROTHER:—

"I have proceeded half through your book *regularly* according to your direction, and have read it with great delight and edification. Your statements throughout are judicious and satisfactory, and the richness of your appeals to Scripture renders your book invaluable. * * * * I love your recapitulations exceedingly. The vast advantage of them to your readers is obvious; but they are not less useful to your own mind, in that they induce a habit of order, of terseness, of perspicuity. It is almost impossible for a man who recapitulates either to run riot or to talk nonsense. Bishop Pearson's perorations have always delighted me, and yours also will delight and edify many.

"I have just perused your most elaborate defence of the divinity of our blessed Lord. I think that the whole church will bless you for it; and in your dying hour it will be no grief to you to have taken so much pains in elucidating and confirming a point that is of such unspeakable importance to all who feel their need of a divine Saviour. Go on, my beloved brother, and may God long preserve you to be a blessing to the church and the world!

"After what has been said, it will not be necessary to do more than to insert extracts from a very few of the letters which he received, upon its publication, from the members of his own religious society.

"FROM WILLIAM FORSTER.

"Bradpole, [2d of 3d month,] 1826.

"Thou must allow me, in true brotherly love, to offer thee my warmest congratulations, that thou hast been enabled to bring out thy Essays. I entertain a most lively and cheering hope of the usefulness of thy work; that in this cloudy and dark day it will tend to the establishment of the wavering, to the fortifying of the feeble-minded, and put to silence the cavils of many a proud and self-sufficient gainsayer. To the anxious inquirer after the truth as it is in Jesus, I firmly believe it will be rendered peculiarly helpful and valuable. In short, I cannot but look upon it as one of those labors of love that will be made to abound 'by many thanksgivings unto God.' It would be strange if I did not feel more than a common and passing interest in the work; for, I think, I never found myself upon any occasion so much anticipated,—it gives utterance to my own views and feelings in such lucid and convincing language, and withal it solves some of my difficulties so thoroughly and satisfactorily.

"FROM JONATHAN HUTCHINSON.

"Gedney, 5th mo., 1st, 1826.

"I have lately finished a very deliberate reading of thy Essays, and, on the whole, with a satisfaction which enables me honestly to say that I am glad to have seen such a book before I die. I rejoice that a friend so dear to me should, consistently with his own avowed principle of human incapacity for any work that can be denominated good both in motive and act, have been *enabled* to write it. I hope this effort of labor and of love, for such I consider it, will prove of advantage to many, as I think it has been of edification to myself, by exciting me afresh, even under life's declining energies, 'to thank God and take courage,' and, under some renewal of faith and hope, reverently, I trust, to 'put on strength in the name of the Lord.'

"It was with peculiar satisfaction that he received the following from the well-known author of the English Grammar, then far advanced in years.

"Holdgate, near York, 2d mo., 1st, 1826.

"MY DEAR AND MUCH-ESTEEMED FRIEND:—

"I am obliged and gratified by thy kind remembrance of me in the distribution of thy volume.

"Being able to read but little myself, I have had the book read to me, and very much to my satisfaction. Proofs thou hast given abundantly of the positions contained in the volume being conformable to the Holy Scriptures. The work is happily calculated, both in its matter and manner, to comfort those who unite in the author's views and sentiments, to disperse the doubts of those who hesitate, and to produce conviction in the minds of gainsayers. Thou hast indeed by this pious labor very materially served the cause of truth and righteousness; and I trust thou wilt be blessed for it by Him whose blessing makes truly rich, and will accompany thee to the latest hour of life.

"Farewell, dear Joseph, in the best sense of the word!

"I remain thy very affectionate friend,

LINDLEY MURRAY."

XX.—A Popular Life of George Fox, the first of the Quakers. By Josiah Marsh. Price, $1.

Compiled from his Journal and other authentic sources, and interspersed with remarks on the imperfect Reformation of the Anglican Church, and the consequent spread of Dissent. The work abounds with remarkable incidents, which portray a vivid picture of the excited feelings that predominated during those eventful periods of English history, the Commonwealth and the Restoration.

XXI.—A Guide to True Peace; or, A Method of attaining to Inward and Spiritual Prayer. Compiled chiefly from the writings of Fénélon, Lady Guyon, and Michael Molinos. Price, 25 cents.

XXII.—The Plain Path to Christian Perfection; showing that we are to seek for reconciliation and union with God, solely by renouncing ourselves, denying the world, and following our blessed Saviour in the regeneration. Price, 25 cents.

XXIII.—Some Memoirs of the Life of John Roberts; written by his son, Daniel Roberts. Price, 25 cents.

This is a very remarkable Memoir of one of the early Friends. An eminent reviewer, speaking of John Roberts, says,—

"Roberts was by no means a gloomy fanatic: he had a great deal of shrewdness and humor, loved a quiet joke, and every gambling priest and swearing magistrate in the neighborhood stood in fear of his sharp wit."

XXIV.—A Journal of the Life and Gospel Labors of John Conran, of Moyallen, in Ireland, who died in the year 1827. Price, 50 cents.

www.ingramcontent.com/pod-product-compliance
Lightning Source LLC
LaVergne TN
LVHW021106110826
845150LV00001B/189